Welfare State
Programme

CONTEMPORARY SOCIAL RESEARCH SERIES
General Editor: MARTIN BULMER

12

Social Science and Social Policy

CONTEMPORARY SOCIAL RESEARCH SERIES

List of Figures and Tables

Tables

Acknowledgements

The publishers gratefully acknowledge permission to reproduce copyright material granted by the following:

To the Controller of Her Majesty's Stationery Office to reproduce Tables 4.3, 5.1, 5.2, 5.3, 5.4, 5.5, 5.6, 10.1, 11.4 and 11.5, and Figure 5.1, all of which are Crown Copyright.

To Gower Publishing Company Limited and Social and Community Planning Research for Tables 4.1 and 6.3.

To Cambridge University Press for Tables 4.2, 5.7 and 8.1.

To Penguin Books Ltd. and Professor D. V. Donnison for Figure 5.2, from D. V. Donnison, *The Government of Housing* (Harmondsworth, Pelican Books, 1967), p. 208. Copyright © D. V. Donnison 1967. Reproduced by permission of Penguin Books Ltd.

To W. H. Freeman and Company, New York, for Figure 8.3, adapted from p. 23 of D. N. Kershaw, 'A Negative Income Tax Experiment', *Scientific American*, October 1972. Copyright © 1972 by Scientific American Inc. All rights reserved.

To the British Sociological Association and Professor G. W. Brown for Figure 10.1.

Abbreviations

BMA	British Medical Association
CACE	Central Advisory Council for Education
CDP	Community Development Project
CIPFA	Chartered Institute of Public Finance and Accountancy
CPAG	Child Poverty Action Group
CPRS	Central Policy Review Staff
CPS	Current Population Survey
DES	Department of Education and Science
DHSS	Department of Health and Social Security
DoE	Department of the Environment
DRR	Disparity Reduction Rates
EIA	Environmental Impact Assessment
EPA	Educational Priority Area
ESRC	Economic and Social Research Council (formerly SSRC)
FES	Family Expenditure Survey
FIS	Family Income Supplement
GHS	General Household Survey
GREA	Grant Related Expenditure Assessment
ILO	International Labour Organization
IR	Inland Revenue
ISR	Institute of Social Research, University of Michigan
JASP	Joint Approach to Social Policy
LFS	Labour Force Survey
MSC	Manpower Services Commission
NFU	National Farmer's Union
NHS	National Health Service
NHSCP	National Household Survey Capability Programme
NIESR	National Institute of Economic and Social Research
NOP	National Opinion Polls
NORC	National Opinion Research Center, University of Chicago
NSF	National Science Foundation
ODC	Overseas Development Council
OECD	Organization for Economic Co-operation and Development
OEO	Office of Economic Opportunity
OPCS	Office of Population Censuses and Surveys
PAR	Programme Analysis and Review

PEP	Political and Economic Planning
PESC	Public Expenditure Survey Committee
PLP	Parliamentary Labour Party
PPBS	Planning Programme Budgeting Systems
PQLI	Physical Quality and Life Index
PRAG	Planning Research Applications Group
PSI	Policy Studies Institute
QOL	Quality of Life
RAWP	Resource Allocation Working Party
RPI	Retail Price Index
SBC	Supplementary Benefit Commission
SCPR	Social and Community Planning Research
SEAS	Social and Economic Accounts System
SEG	Socio-Economic Group
SIA	Social Impact Assessment
SIR	Scientific Information Retrieval (computer package)
SMR	Standardized Mortality Ratio
SPES	Social-Politisches Entscheidungs und Indikatoren System (W. Germany)
SPSS	Statistical Package for the Social Sciences (computer package)
SSDS	(UN) System of Social and Demographic Statistics
SSRC	Social Science Research Council (now ESRC)
UN	United Nations
UNSO	United Nations Statistical Organization

This book forms part of a project to try to understand the role which the social sciences can play in the formation and evaluation of public policy. It began ten years ago as a result of my own practical experience working as a statistician in British central government, in the Office of Population Censuses and Surveys. This was a most illuminating experience in many ways. It provided a perspective broader than that of academic sociology in universities, in which I had been engaged previously. It gave one a much fuller appreciation of both the advantages and the problems of working with large-scale quantitative data such as the results of the census, population registration and continuous and ad hoc social surveys. And it provided first-hand acquaintance within Whitehall with the problems of bringing social science expertise to bear upon current issues of public policy. In Britain the social sciences have not had an easy passage in the world of government policy-making, and it seemed worth trying to explain why this was so.

The first product of this interest of mine was an edited anthology on *Social Policy Research* (Bulmer, 1978), which largely reprinted (with one or two original chapters) a collection of papers on opinion polling, action research and social indicators, together with some perceptive general reflections by L. J. Sharpe, David Donnison and David Eversley. My introduction reviewed the general problem, though in retrospect perhaps it was unduly concerned with the rather marginal position of social scientists as British government officials, a structural problem which had led me to return to the academic world after a year as a civil servant. The collection was generally well received, and seemed to help provide an orientation to problems of utilization and institutionalization which British social scientists from several different disciplines were becoming more interested in.

Four years later, I published a monograph on *The Uses of Social Research* (1982) which developed these interests and provided a fuller treatment of certain aspects of the role of the social sciences in government. It had five main themes. After opening with a sketch of the history of applied social science in Britain, particularly survey research, the second and final chapters considered alternative models of the process of influence. In particular the so-called 'engineering' and 'enlightenment' models (see Janowitz, 1970) were examined, and an attempt made to elaborate some varieties of, or modifications to,

the latter. Two chapters then considered more strictly methodological problems of conceptualization, measurement and
explanation in applied policy research, using examples from the
study of deprivation, disadvantage, physical handicap, health and
illness. A case-study followed of the use of social research by
governmental commissions in Britain and America. The fifth theme,
treated in a separate chapter, was the institutional context of social
research in Britain, the main avenues of support, and the strengths
and weaknesses of the system. Quite fortuitously, the book was
published in 1982 in the midst of Lord Rothschild's review of the
future of the Social Science Research Council (Rothschild, 1982),
which had raised sharply a number of uncomfortable questions about
what use the social sciences could be. It therefore received more
attention than it perhaps deserved, though critics identified at least
two weaknesses, its failure to examine the actual processes of policy-
formation and influence within government, and the relative
unpersuasiveness of an approach to use in terms of 'enlightenment'
when faced with demands for justifications for social science in terms
of short-term utility.

The present book, which continues my interest, originally set out
to be something else, a second edition of the 1978 anthology on *Social
Policy Research*. It has turned into a quite different work, and is I
hope a better, fresher and more pertinent book as a result. There is in
fact no overlap in content between the two books, since the author of
the one chapter which I proposed to retain demurred at its
re-appearance. Nor is there significant overlap in content with the
second of my previous books. *Social Science and Social Policy* has
four main aims: to examine the policy process and consider the ways
in which social science can influence policy-making; to discuss and
exemplify the different methodologies which may be used in applied
social research; to demonstrate the importance of analysis and
inference in applied work; and to offer some general reflections upon
factors helping and hindering the more effective use of social science
in policy-making.

Its primary purpose lies in the second and third of these, which take
up nine of the thirteen chapters. This is right and proper for a book
which appears as part of the Contemporary Social Research series,
which I edit. The series is concerned with topics in the methodology
of social research, with the principles and practice whereby the
structure of the social sciences is kept standing. This structure
combines two separate elements, theory and empirical evidence.
That one without the other is barren and that both are necessary for

successful social understanding is one of the central themes of this book, as of the series as a whole.

The series is intended to provide concise introductions to significant methodological topics. Broadly conceived, research methodology deals with the general grounds for the validity of social scientific propositions. How do we know what we do know about the social world? More narrowly, it deals with the questions: how do we actually acquire new knowledge about the world in which we live? What are the strategies and techniques by means of which social science data are collected and analysed? The series seeks to answer such questions through the examination of specific areas of methodology. Titles in the series focus upon specific topics, procedures, methods of analysis and methodological problems to provide a readable introduction to its subject. The intended audience includes the advanced undergraduate, the graduate student, the working social researcher seeking to familiarize himself with new areas, and the non-specialist who wishes to enlarge his knowledge of social research. Research methodology need not be remote and inaccessible. The series is concerned above all to show the general importance and centrality of research methodology to social science.

There seems considerable value in demonstrating, in a relatively straightforward and accessible account, the varieties of research method used in policy research, if only to counter some of the stereotypes about such inquiries which exist among academics more interested in 'pure' research. One of the characteristics of applied social research in both Britain and America is that more of it is carried on outside universities than within them, in independent research institutes, commercial research firms and government departments. This is not fortuitous. Within the academic world, there is no doubt that applied research has a lower status than 'pure' disciplinary inquiry. For various reasons, universities are less receptive to highly organized, large-scale social research (Bulmer, 1983b) and less able to respond quickly to demands for rapid research. They do not in any case enjoy a monopoly in the conduct of empirical social inquiry. So there is some value in looking in detail at practice in other settings. Much of the applied research methodology discussed in Chapter 5–9 is in fact applied in non-academic rather than academic settings in Britain and the United States.

The first section of the book has a slightly different aim, to clarify what one means by 'use' by examining the ways in which policy is actually formed, and the various influences which are brought to bear in this process. Perhaps this excursion into the field of political science is rather presumptuous, which is why I have included in Part I two chapters by Carol Weiss and Keith Banting, much more expert students of these matters than I. Two other chapters, by Michael Carley and Stuart Blume, are also included in Parts II and III to make the special expertise of their authors more widely available. Those involved in knowledge production tend naturally to make assumptions about the rationality of the world and the advantages of having more knowledge rather than less. The burden of the first two chapters is to suggest that this is a wildly optimistic view of the process of social science influence, and that rational models of policy formation processes have a number of serious weaknesses.

The concluding chapter raises certain broader issues. Perhaps the most pertinent to emphasize here is the importance of the effective dissemination of the results of applied social science research. There are many channels by which the results of research can be spread, both publicly and more privately within organizations. One of the conclusions drawn from the analysis of policy formation is that this is a messy, pluralistic world of negotiation and pressures of all kinds, into which social science feeds as one input among many. This being so, the more widely the results of research can be disseminated the better. 'Grey literature', the mimeographed research report, is only the start of a process, which could include book, learned journal or magazine publication, press and radio and television coverage, direct approaches to relevant policy-makers by the researchers, and gaining the ear of influential politicians, civil servants and pressure-group activists. Many academic policy researchers are inhibited by academic norms which favour the learned journal article and the scholarly monograph as the approved vehicles of communicating knowledge. Those in non-academic settings, particularly within government, are sometimes constrained by bureaucratic obstacles to free publication of material other than the original report, and even that is not always published. More research is needed both upon the processes influencing policy outcomes, and upon how actors in the policy process learn about relevant social science work.

As a further contribution to exploring the field of social science research utilization, I have also edited for publication shortly after the appearance of this book a collection of original essays entitled *Social Science Research and Government: Comparative Essays on Britain and America* (Bulmer, 1987), in which a range of distinguished contributors reflect on the use made of social science by Westminster, Whitehall and Washington, and an attempt is made at some systematic comparison between the place of social science within the two systems of government. This encompasses both intellectual and institutional differences and similarities, and the extent to which particular methodologies have been employed in policy research. A concluding section examines the course of social science cutbacks instituted by the Thatcher and Reagan administrations.

Since a certain pessimism has afflicted British and American social science in the last five years, bearing a sense of being beleaguered by government, it is worth emphasizing in conclusion how strong and healthy applied social science is in 1985 compared to, say, 1960 or 1935. The scale and variety of activities is far greater, the range of methodologies used much richer, the place of such activities within government (despite all doubts about channels of influence) much firmer, and the influence of the social sciences upon general culture much more far reaching. Though fierce political battles have been fought (and no doubt will be in the future) to maintain spending programmes for social science, the landscape over which the battle is fought is altogether different from what it was twenty-five or fifty years ago. The applied social sciences are now established where once they scarcely existed. Though its history is much longer, large-scale applied social science is very much a child of the middle and later years of the twentieth century. As that century draws to a close, there is no reason to think that its scale, influence and importance will diminish much, and good reasons for an optimistic belief that despite some scepticism among political leaders, it may expand further.

It remains to acknowledge a number of debts incurred in the writing of this book. The main one is to others working in the same field. The rather personal tone of this introduction is intended to show how this book relates to the two others which I have written or edited in the same field over the last eight years. It should not convey, however unintentionally, any implication of an ego-centred view of this field of knowledge. My debts are in part acknowledged in the bibliography, but I would like to mention here specifically several books which have illuminated my own thinking in recent years, notably Weiss and Bucuvalas's *Social Science Research and Decision-Making* (1980), the collection edited by Kallen *et al.* (1982), Kogan and Henkel's monograph on *Government and Research* (1983), the collection on educational research by Husen and Kogan (1984) and Patricia Thomas's *The Aims and Outcomes of Social Policy Research* (1985). Many recent articles could also be mentioned but space does not permit. Among other conclusions, these studies suggest that the next step in pursuing this project must be more first-hand research into actual patterns of influence and use in particular cases.

An irony of institutional affiliation is that Keith Banting's book, from which Chapter 3 is an extract, is in part about the influence of my own department at the London School of Economics – Social Science and Administration – upon government social policy in the 1960s. Though its influence is today rather different, one of the benefits of working in such a department is that one is constantly reminded that there can be an end-product, in the form of changed policy outcomes, to the process of influence. Standing back to look at the process of influence in a more detached manner, one needs to be reminded from time to time of content as well as form. To congenial colleagues in the Department of Social Science and Administration, I am grateful for such a reminder. Indeed, being a member of staff of the School, one could hardly be in a better laboratory for observing some of the patterns of influence at first hand. Though when I meet former colleagues in government they remind me that it is ten years since I worked there, and much has changed, the year I spent as a civil servant was a formative influence and led indirectly to this book being written. More specifically, I would like to thank Karen Dunnell of OPCS Social Survey Division for commenting on and improving parts of Chapter 5. Valerie Campling has typed the manuscript with characteristic efficiency and accuracy, and a keen eye for stylistic inconsistency. Joan, Michael and Georgina bore with me while this book was being prepared, in the pursuit of my vocation as what my children call a 'writing doctor'.

MARTIN BULMER
London School of Economics
October 1985

I

Social Science and the Policy-Making Process

1

The Policy Process and the Place in it of Social Research

Social science today is part of the policy-making process in a way that it was not a generation ago. Governments of all political persuasions, on both sides of the Atlantic, rely upon social fact-gathering and analysis on an unprecedented scale. Consider the following brief examples. The Office of Population Censuses and Surveys in London conducts each year the General Household Survey (GHS), a national survey of a probability sample of 12,000 households. This provides data for government departments on demographic structure, employment, education, housing and health. It is the principal source of information about the proportion of one-parent families in the country, showing for example that in 1981–3, of families with one or more members below the age of 16, one in eight nationally and one in three in Greater London lived in single-parent families (Table 5.1 below). The Home Office has recently become interested in more sophisticated measures of crime, and has instituted the British Crime Survey (Hough and Mayhew, 1983, 1985). The first round, in 1982, involved interviews with a sample of 16,000 households to discover to what extent respondents had themselves been victims of crime personally or as a member of a household. The results showed that the 'dark figure' of unreported crime was sizeable. On the basis of the survey it was estimated that only half of burglaries and one in twelve of thefts from the person are recorded in official criminal statistics.

In the United States, considerable policy interest developed during the 1960s and has continued since in the idea of a 'negative income tax', the basic idea being that all adults in the population would fill in a tax return, but that the poorer members of the society, whose incomes fell below the tax threshold, rather than paying tax, would themselves receive a cash payment (the negative income tax). Policy-makers were concerned, however, that such a measure to help the needy would be a disincentive to the propensity to work. To test whether this was the case, the New Jersey negative income tax experiment was mounted at a cost of $8 million. This very large-scale piece of social research involved the selection of eight experimental and control groups in New Jersey and Pennsylvania. The members of the experimental groups received cash payments in addition to social security, subject to deduction for income earned. The different experimental groups varied according to the value of these additional payments (related to the poverty line) and the proportion of additional earnings which were taken account of in making deductions (the tax rate). This sophisticated study involved active social intervention ($2.4 million of the cost was transfer payments to participants).

In both Britain and the United States, epidemiologists and medical sociologists have taken a considerable interest in morbidity and mortality differences between different social groups. Age, sex and occupational differences have long received attention; more recently differences between social classes and status groups have been closely studied. In 1977 the British government commissioned an independent review of the field, published as *Inequalities in Health* in 1980 (Black Report, 1980). This not only presented a considerable volume of factual data on health inequalities (much of the data on morbidity from the GHS), but sought to analyse some of the social determinants of health status (an issue further examined in Chapter 12) and to make policy recommendations. One recommendation of some interest was to suggest that a more effective way of helping low-income families improve their health was not by providing extra resources for advisory services such as health education, health visitors or community nurses, but by additional cash payments to such families to increase the material resources available to them. This particular piece of policy research was at the same time factual, analytic and prescriptive.

These four examples will be discussed more fully in later chapters. They are introduced here to show the range of topics on which governments seek information; the variety of methods used to gather data; the different degrees to which the data are analysed; and the extent to which policy recommendations do or do not form part of the research. The different methods of data collection, analysis and dissemination used in policy research are a particular focus for discussion in the chapters which follow. Increasingly, the formulation of social policy is informed by the results of social science research, whether in the fields like family policy, crime, income maintenance or health cited in the four examples or in other fields such as housing, education, the personal social services, or equal opportunity. The policies which governments frame, and the ways in which those policies impinge upon the individual citizen, are affected by an important social science contribution.

To make this point, however, is very much the start of the analysis. In one sense, this book seeks to explicate the ways in which this contribution is made. In another, it seeks to point up the complexities both of the policy-making process and the ways in which social science feeds into it. There is no unitary account either of how policy evolves or how the knowledge-base contributes to its evolution which is wholly satisfactory. As so often, the real world defies easy compartmentalization.

To return for a moment to the four examples, one may pose the question: why would policy-makers want the kinds of descriptive data, analysis and recommendations which such studies produce? By policy-makers, one is referring primarily to politicians and senior civil servants in central government, to politicians and officials at the state and local levels in so far as they frame policies, and those who have some influence on the form which policies take at any level as activists in pressure groups or political parties, journalists and commentators, clients and members of the 'general public'. Answering the question why policy-makers seek, or at least accept, a social science contribution involves looking at the way in which policy is formulated in more general terms.

A common misapprehension of academic commentators on the policy-making process is that insights derived from social science have a particularly large contribution to make because they are based on factual knowledge which is rationally arrived at and applied to the problem. Indeed, rational models of the policy-making process have been quite influential in the literature. As Charles Lindblom observes, 'perhaps most people believe that the answer [to making policies more effective] lies in bringing more information, thought, and analysis into the policy-making process' (1980, p. 11).

Five elements may be identified in rational models, stages which are passed through in deciding upon a policy for action. These elements form an ideal type, an accentuation of reality to bring out its central distinguishing features in pure form.

(1) A problem which requires action is identified. The goals, values and objectives related to the problem are set out.
(2) All important possible ways of solving the problem or achieving the goals and objectives are listed. These are alternative strategies, courses of action or policies.
(3) The important consequences which would follow from each

alternative strategy are predicted and the probability of those consequences occurring is estimated.
(4)   The consequences of each strategy are then compared to the goals and objectives identified under (2).
(5)   Finally, a policy or strategy is selected in which consequences most closely match goals and objectives, or the problem is most nearly solved.

Social science knowledge may make a contribution at stages (2) and (3) in particular.

The importance of the rational model lies in its potential influence upon initiatives which governments take to improve the policy-making process:

> the concept of rationality has actively influenced a whole range of attempts, particularly in the USA and UK, to improve the quality of the policy-making system. Policy-makers have become aware of the weaknesses of the policy machinery and have therefore looked for ways of improving the processes and institutions of policy-making. (Richardson and Jordan, 1979, p. 19)

Thus approaches through Corporate Management, Planning Programme Budgeting (PPBS), the Public Expenditure Survey Committee (PESC) and Programme Analysis and Review (PAR) in both the USA and the UK became fashionable for a time, embodying rationalist assumptions. The model also has an intuitive appeal to social scientists who get involved in advising policy-makers, because it elevates reason and its knowledge-base to centre stage, a mode of thought congruent with and congenial to the way scholars work (Hogwood and Gunn, 1984, pp. 44–47).

It is therefore important to consider why the rational model does not provide an effective account of how policy is made, on the way to arriving at a more realistic model. The first objection concerns the word 'policy'. Policy-making is 'an extremely complex process without beginning or end, and whose boundaries remain most uncertain. Somehow a complex set of forces together produces effects called "policies" ' (Lindblom, 1980, p. 5). The rational model, however, assumes that the process of forming policy has a beginning, a middle and an end. Whether it can be separated analytically into discrete parts is debatable, on both logical and empirical grounds. For example, British policy on income support for young people aged 16–18 is divided between the Department of Health and Social

Security (Supplementary Benefit), the Department of Education and Science (guidelines for grants for maintenance of 16+ children still at school), and the Department of Employment and the Manpower Services Commission (work-creation schemes for the young unemployed). Attempts to integrate this provision and create a coherent scheme have foundered not only on departmental self-interest but also on the ramifications of policy-change for other areas of departmental responsibility – in the case of DHSS, for Supplementary Benefit rules more generally; in the case of the DES, for rules relating to student grants for the 18+ age group.

The rational model also ignores the extent to which one group's solution may become another group's problem. For example, income support for a particular minority, such as farmers or elderly widows, may create difficulties for other groups, such as consumers who consequently pay higher farm prices or employees whose state insurance contributions are raised. There is thus feedback between the first and last stages such that a sharp distinction between them cannot be satisfactorily sustained.

Further evidence about the appropriateness of a discrete concept of 'policy' is provided by empirical studies of knowledge-use by government officials. A particularly illuminating monograph on American federal, state and local-level bureaucrats in the mental health field showed that many of those interviewed denied that they made discrete 'decisions' or even policy choices, but rather saw themselves as doing their job. Carol Weiss and Michael Bucuvalas comment that knowledge-use then becomes tacit knowledge, part of the background of knowing one's field. The policy-makers studied

> see little opportunity for rational calculation and little need for it. They seldom engage in explicit formulation of problems, seldom undertake directed searches for information, seldom canvass the range of alternatives available, or calculate the relative merits of each alternative. They rely on what they already know to guide their pattern of workaday activities. (1980, p. 266)

The findings of this study mesh neither with rational models of organization theorists nor with more radical concepts of power put forward by some sociologists (see Lukes, 1974). The latter, for example, focus on different theories of who can mobilize resources and holds the influence to take decisions and, in an extension by political scientists Bachrach and Baratz (1962; 1963), non-decisions. A non-decision is a decision that results in suppressing or preventing a manifest or latent challenge to the interests or values of the decision-maker.

Weiss and Bucuvalas show that the officials studied had good reasons for not regarding themselves as taking either decisions or non-decisions.

> The acts of any one official are hemmed in not only by the history, traditions and standard operating procedures of the agency, but also by the acts of other staff members scattered across many bureaus, divisions and departments. In fields like mental health where authority is also dispersed across federal, state and local levels, even more staff have a say before a 'decision' is reached – not to mention the increasingly vocal (and increasingly institutionalized) participation of professional groups, client groups and citizens. And there is the potential for intervention by politically-appointed officials, legislatures and the courts ... Even on relatively small matters, staff in large bureaucracies have to take the viewpoints of many other people into account if they want to nudge policy in a given direction. (Weiss and Bucuvalas, 1980, p. 267)

This is not simply a point about bureaucratic inertia, though it helps in appreciating the energy which the innovator or reformer in modern complex bureaucracies like government departments needs to have to bring about change. The argument is that the system continues to tick over and function without those who operate it thinking that they individually have the capacity to frame policy. Where 'policy' originates is obscure, but certainly not with the individual official being interviewed. The capacity to formulate policy seemed to be so widely diffused that 'policy-makers' do not perceive themselves as having that capacity.

The finding may of course be put down to self-deception or lack of frankness, but this seems unlikely. The main focus of the study was the utilization of social science, and the finding about decisions was serendipitous. It is a finding with implications not only for rational models of policy, but for the impact of social science, since it suggests wider rather than narrower channels for diffusion and effect. To this point we will return.

An understanding of the policy-making process also requires an adequate model of the political process out of which policy emerges. The outlines of such a model will be presented here, although it is only a sketch and is more fully developed elsewhere. The role of groups in the political process was first analysed in depth by A. F. Bentley early in the twentieth century: 'All phenomena of government are phenomena of groups pressing one another, forming one another and pushing out new groups and group representatives (the organs and agencies of government) to mediate the adjustments' ([1908] 1967, p. 269). One of the principal characteristics of the policy-making process in industrial countries is that it is a process of adjustment between competing pressures exercised through the political process.

An example is provided by the conflict over increased child benefit in Britain in the mid-1970s. The Labour government was concerned about increasing the resources available to the lower paid, partly on the basis of research evidence about the incidence of poverty, but also at the prompting of the Child Poverty Action Group (CPAG). The government proposed in 1975 to remove tax allowances for children and replace them by increased cash benefits paid to the mother. The secretary of state claimed, in introducing the bill to give effect to the measure, that it was supported by everyone including the trade unions. In 1976, however, it became apparent that the removal of tax relief made it more difficult to hold down pay increases. Discussions took place between the prime minister and senior union leaders. As the Cabinet minutes recorded, 'on being informed of the reduction in take-home pay, which the child benefits scheme would involve, the TUC representatives had reacted immediately and violently against its implementation, irrespective of the level of benefits which would accompany the reduction in take-home pay' (*New Society*, 1976). The outcome was that the change was phased in more gradually. The case illustrates the point that a particular policy change was the outcome of conflicting pressures exerted through the political system, in this case involving the Treasury and the Inland Revenue as the two main government departments involved, but also the DHSS, the trade unions and the poverty lobby (CPAG).

The example also shows that 'group' does not necessarily mean an organized interest group like trade unions, employers' associations, the National Farmers' Union (NFU), or the British Medical Association (BMA). It covers 'issue' groups, like CPAG, but also more amorphous interests like the environmental lobby, or people suffering from disabilities, or a category of people like working wives. In some situations, separate government departments may be treated as interest groups with a degree of autonomy pursuing their own line (Richardson and Jordan, 1979, pp. 29–40). In the child benefit example, for instance, DHSS, the Treasury and the Inland Revenue each saw the issue in a rather different light and acted somewhat differently.

The competition of groups in the political process is not an equal or fair one. Groups attempt to manipulate the balance of advantage in their favour. Some groups are more powerful and effective than others. Moreover, particular groups have links with political parties, so that they try to capture or colonize the government when that party is in power. However, no group succeeds in gaining total control of a particular policy area, and even powerful interest groups like the BMA or the NFU have to accommodate to the aims and interests of ministers and officials. It is true that groups can use sanctions against the government. The 1974 miners' strike and the role of the BMA in negotiations on doctors' pay are evidence of this. But equally the government can exercise countervailing power, as in the various experiments with incomes policy, and the counter-example of the 1984 miners' strike, where in a head-on conflict the government subdued a trade union which defied it.

Group theory has been most fully developed by political scientists, but certain sociological theories are also congruent with it. Marxist social theory, for example, is a special case of group theory, identifying interests in terms of social class groups related to the ownership or non-ownership of the means of production. Ludwig Gumplowicz, writing at the end of the nineteenth century, held that the social process through history 'has consisted in the relations and reciprocal actions between heterogenous social groups' (Barnes, 1948, p. 192).

The relevance of group theory to the study of the relation between social science and policy lies in its pluralistic implications. If the policy-making process is one in which different interests are involved, social science research may feed into different parts of the system. The state has no monopoly of social inquiry. A feature of both British and American work on social policy, for example, has been the production of competing analyses of the same policy domain. This has been further developed in the United States, where there is a more competitive university system with strong alternative academic centres. In both countries 'think-tanks' have also developed not tied to the party system, with centres like Rand and Brookings in America and the Policy Studies Institute in London. Perhaps the clearest example in Britain is that of competing economic models developed in the Treasury, the National Institute of Economic and Social Research (NIESR), the London Business School, the University of Cambridge and the University of Liverpool.

Such diversity undermines the view that there is a single rational model in terms of which policy analysis can be conducted.

Group theory sets the stage for the making of policy, and hypothesizes that the outcome of any particular series of deliberations is likely to be the result of competing pressures, but it does not say much about the content of the negotiations between the parties in which policy actually gets made. The most fruitful conceptualization of this process seems to be that of Charles Lindblom, with his model of disjointed incrementalism coupled with partisan mutual adjustment. Policy-making is the science of 'muddling through'. In practice, compared to the rational model, policy-makers do not consider a wide range but a narrow range of alternatives. In comparing the limited number of alternatives open to them, those making policy do not waste time upon broader goals and values, but start with the problem and consider a manageable range of alternatives for dealing with it. There is a tendency, in general, for policy innovations to be small-scale extension of past efforts with an expectation that there will be a constant return to the subject for further modification. Successive limited comparisons are made. Such a succession of comparisons greatly reduces or eliminates reliance upon theory.

Policy-making involves achieving agreement between groups. There is more chance of agreement on a specific proposal than there is of agreeing on general objectives. Partisan mutual adjustment is the process by which an agreed policy is arrived at. The best policy is the one which achieves agreement between groups. Such a stress on the need to achieve accommodation between groups leads to decision-making taking the form of a comparison between pragmatic available alternatives. This process, moreover, is essentially a political one in which the main actors are partisan (not necessarily in a party-political sense) on behalf of the interests which they represent (which may, for example, be those of a pressure group or of a government department). The process of solving problems is interactive, in which interactions between political actors solve, resolve or ameliorate policies.

Action thus takes the place of analysis, which holds centre stage in the rational model. In saying that partisan adjustment rather than analysis determines policy, one is saying that policy is the outcome of the way in which people exert control, influence or power over one another. There are various means of substituting action for analysis. Instead of thinking through a problem to seek a solution, a solution can be reached by negotiation, or by delegation to someone who takes the decision, or by voting (Lindblom, 1980, pp. 26–8). In this situation, analysis plays a different role from the one it plays in the rational model. Analysis operates as an indispensable element, but less as the rational arbiter between alternative courses of action. It becomes a way of exerting control by means of which groups and individuals involved in the policy-making process use knowledge to influence others in the process of political interaction.

Incrementalism, too, is not without its critics. It has been attacked for presupposing that policy change proceeds by reaching consensus between the parties involved. This may not always be the case. In certain circumstances, existing policies may be quite inadequate, or a government is committed to drastic change, so that small-scale adjustments are either inappropriate or unrealistic (see Dror, 1964). And governments from time to time face large and fundamental decisions – for example, a declaration of war – to which the incremental model is of doubtful application (Etzioni, 1967, pp. 387–8). Lindblom himself has somewhat modified his position, allowing some role for analysis and denying that his model was a prescriptive view of the policy process (1979). Etzioni suggested a compromise in the middle ground between rationalist and incrementalist models, what he called 'mixed scanning', founded on a distinction between fundamental and more routine decisions. However, this view has not been widely adopted because of the difficulty of deciding what is and what is not a fundamental decision. A small minority of issues do lend themselves to more rational analysis, but even then, as the next example shows, there is many a slip 'twixt cup and lip. As a general model, one which emphasizes the pluralist, bargaining and incrementalist features of policy-making seems the most satisfactory starting point.

Two examples can briefly illustrate these points.. The London conurbation has a major airport at Heathrow west of London, and a smaller international airport at Gatwick 50 km to the south. Twenty years ago it became apparent that their capacity would be insufficient for traffic needs by the last decade of the century and that neither offered sufficient scope for expansion. A search for a third London airport was begun, which has been pursued ever since. The building of a second runway at Gatwick to expand capacity has been ruled out on environmental grounds. Expansion of terminal facilities at Heathrow has taken place, but needs will not be met unless a third airport is developed or a further major expansion occurs at Heathrow. In the late 1960s, the British government established the Roskill Commission to determine the optimum site for the third airport. The Commission as part of its work undertook a major cost-benefit study of alternative sites by an in-house research team (described by Flowerdew, 1980). The team produced a massive analysis which pointed to the choice of an inland site north of London, Cublington, eventually adopted by the Commission in its report.

Sir Colin Buchanan, however, in a note of dissent, recommended an alternative on the Maplin Sands in the Thames Estuary. When the report was published in 1971, the minister responsible (Peter Walker) chose Maplin as the site, apparently on the grounds that this would minimize environmental damage. Four years later, the next Labour government cancelled the planned expansion in a round of cuts and decided to put off a decision until the 1980s. In the 1960s the British Airports Authority had also proposed the expansion of Stansted airport (in Essex) which it owned. This was rejected by a planning inquiry. In the early 1980s, the government reverted to the plan to expand Stansted rapidly from 0.5 million to about 10 million passengers annually, and in 1985 (following a second planning inquiry) announced that this expansion would be implemented. In this span of two decades, policy took several different and contradictory turns, as different interests pressured ministers to act, including the British Airways Authority, users of air services, environmental groups (particularly those based near potential sites), and different government departments involved. Roskill produced an objective, rational study of the problem which was promptly rejected. The eventual outcome was to revert to a solution available in the 1960s but then judged unacceptable.

The second instance concerns the use of social science analysis by committee staffs in the United States Congress. Carol Weiss's study of this question (1987) shows that there are powerful pressures pushing staff to adopt a political rather than an analytic role. One of the principal ones is that staff are appointed either by the majority chair of the committee or by the minority (opposition) group, so bear allegiance to their political mentors. Though familiar through various channels with the results of social science analyses of issues these committees are dealing with, in their day-to-day work political considerations are pre-eminent. This reflects the fact that Congressional committees achieve their objectives (the preparation and passage of legislation) by partisan mutual adjustment between groups of members, taking into account representations from outside groups, and that in this process analysis is only one of the inputs to the proceedings.

Another important consideration also tends to undermine

rationalist models of policy-making. Such models incorporate assumptions to the effect that policy-making is improved if more information, thought and analysis are brought into the process. Yet they do not adequately explain how such expertise is to be reconciled with the democratic process. A society ruled by experts would be an unacceptable utopia in the present-day world (see Benveniste, 1973). How precisely does the policy analyst fit into the political process?

There is a related practical difficulty. How are those involved in the policy-making process able to cope with the information overload from which they suffer? Different actors face this in different ways. Politicians have the least time for reading and reflection. Notwithstanding a few exceptional British politicians such as Sir Edward Boyle and Anthony Crosland with considerable intellectual interests, most politicians have little time for extended reading. This extends even to verbal briefings. David Eversley (1978, p. 296) has graphically described how the social science adviser's mind is focused sharply by the request to summarize in five minutes the salient issues in a field for a busy politician. Members of the US House of Representatives spend on average eleven minutes a day reading, as opposed to meeting people, talking, telephoning, attending committees and sessions of the House (Weiss, 1987).

Other participants, particularly officials, are slightly freer of demands on their time, but they face the problems of sifting and interpreting the considerable volume of paper which passes across their desk. Even here, social science research suffers for several reasons. The penetrability of social science prose is not always very high, yet when communicating with policy-makers, clarity and simplicity of language are at a premium. Wordy and verbose reports using jargon and technical language are not calculated to put across findings in an effective way. Social science knowledge is fallible, and social scientists are aware of this. Hence their policy recommendations (if any) are likely to be couched in highly conditional form, hedged around with reservations. Such caution is not likely to commend itself to policy-makers who seek clear guidance and advice. The production of social science knowledge, moreover, as well as tending to verbosity, is slow and costly. This conflicts directly with the old adage that 'a week is a long time in politics'. To make research available effectively to policy-makers, faster and cheaper methods need to be used. There is also a premium on foresight in conducting research ahead of it being required by policy-makers, and having the ability to synthesize results and present them in lay language when they are needed.

A final limitation of the rational model lies in the fact that policy-making is ultimately a matter of judgement rather than a purely scientific process, though science may play some part in reaching those judgements. One implication of an incrementalist view of policy-making is that the selection of goals and the empirical analysis of action required, which are treated as distinct in the rational model, are not actually distinct but are closely intertwined. In choosing options to adopt in pursuit of a particular policy, one has reference to values among other considerations. And the choice of policy instrument is combined with the ranking of values. Values appear as an element in the policy process, and in the research inquiries accompanying it.

Max Weber long ago emphasized the role of values in problem-selection in social science, however objective and dispassionate the subsequent analysis.

> In the scientific criticism of legislative and other practical recommendations, the motives of the legislator and the ideals of the critic in all their scope often can not be clarified and analyzed in a tangible and intelligible form in any other way than through the confrontation of the standards of value underlying the ideas criticized with others, preferably the critic's own. Every meaningful value-judgment about someone else's aspirations must be a criticism from the standpoint of one's own *Weltanschauung*; it must be a struggle against another's ideals from the standpoint of one's own. (1949, pp. 59–60)

Values play a commanding role in the choice of policy problem to be studied and the subsequent definition of that problem. The very term, social 'problem', implies an evaluation of an activity, a statement that the activity is in some way rule-breaking, deviant or anti-social. Thus disruptive behaviour among working-class youth may be characterized as hooliganism, vandalism or juvenile delinquency, while similar behaviour among upper-middle-class college students is 'high spirits' or 'boys-will-be-boys'.

Values also enter into the policy conclusions and recommendations which may follow from a piece of research. Indeed, a besetting sin of a good deal of conventional research in British social administration has been a willingness to prescribe solutions to problems on the basis of inadequate analysis. As Robert Pinker has observed, '[in British] social policy and administration we begin with fact-finding and end in moral rhetoric, still lacking those explanatory theories which might show the process as a whole and reveal the relations of the separate problems to one another' (1971, p. 12).

What this points to is the need for more explicit incorporation of theory into the study of social policy, a case which has been argued elsewhere (Bulmer, 1982). Rational models tend to adopt an inadequate matter-of-fact, commonsense approach to social causation, as well as themselves constituting a normative statement about how policy is framed:

> The power and survival ability of the 'rational system' model is surprising given that its assumptions have been undermined by empirical studies of the policy process, and that its predictive record is uneven. The main explanation for its continued existence must lie in its status as a normative model and as a 'dignified' myth which is often shared by the policy-makers themselves. Acceptance of the rational model helps the researcher toward a comfortable life; it enables him or her to appear to engage in direct debate with the policy-makers on the basis that information provided by the researchers will be an aid to better policy-making. (Gordon, Lewis and Young, 1977, p. 29)

The contribution of social science research to policy-making is not then as straightforward as the rational model suggests. Nor, on the other hand, is it negligible. The social sciences do have a considerable impact upon policy, but it is necessary to look realistically at the ways in which that influence is exercised in a system where policy is a bargained outcome of conflicts between competing groups, proceeding generally in a disjointed incremental manner from one step to another. In Chapter 2, Carol Weiss provides a useful guide to the many meanings of research utilization, and the different models of the 'use' of social science which are available. She distinguishes between (1) the knowledge-driven model; (2) the problem-solving model; (3) the interactive model; (4) the political model; (5) the tactical model; and (6) the enlightenment model. None of these correspond exactly to the rational model discussed above, but strong elements of it are implied in the knowledge-driven and problem-solving models. Weiss is highly critical of these models. As she observes, 'Most studies appear to come and go without leaving any discernible mark on the direction or substance of policy' (p. 34), and the idea that research and analysis are used to arbitrate between competing policy alternatives is far from reality. But this does not mean that influence is negligible. There is supporting evidence for the other four models, and influence may take an indirect as well as a direct path.

The varying routes to influence will be examined by means of three examples which will be briefly discussed, the rediscovery of poverty in the 1960s, the activities of Royal Commissions in the 1960s and 1970s, and the Prime Minister's Central Policy Review Staff. The rediscovery of poverty in Britain in the 1960s is one of the themes of Keith Banting's study, the conclusions of which appear in Chapter 3. Banting shows how in the 1950s the dominant assumption was that poverty had been eliminated. Under the influence of Richard Titmuss, LSE Professor of Social Administration, Brian Abel-Smith and Peter Townsend set out to show that this was not so.

> They were convinced that myths about the generosity of the Welfare State had blinkered discussion of social policy, and in the late 1950's they set out to gather the evidence with which to challenge the comfortable assumptions of the day. Their research was explicitly political; they were setting out to reshape policy-makers' interpretation of their environment. (Banting, 1979, p. 70)

By adopting a new and higher poverty line, Abel-Smith and Townsend (1965) showed that 14 per cent of the British population, 7.5 million people, were living in poverty. They then became involved in both elite persuasion and a public campaign to bring about changes in income support. The Child Poverty Action Group was founded in December 1965 and began to work as an issue pressure group. But if these Fabian tactics made an immediate intellectual impact, their influence on policy was more gradual.

Research in this case was used as political ammunition at the outset, but the process of influence was not purely a political one. There was considerable political sensitivity to family policy in both Labour and Conservative parties, but the greater the distance from Westminster, the less support there was. Professional groups like social workers were weakly organized. Trade union support was weak. Business interests were opposed to higher public spending. Polls showed low levels of public support for new policy initiatives. The main impact of research was upon sections of the elite: intellectuals, sections of the Labour Party, the media, which were influential in bringing about change in policy.

The actual policy changes introduced were worked out behind closed doors by officials in the (then) Ministry of Social Security (now part of the DHSS). Treasury and Inland Revenue interests were also involved, and there was particular contention as to whether links could be established between the social security system and the tax system (which the IR opposed). The Fabian network was not involved in the actual policy options related to income transfer that were seriously considered. These were (1) a major increase in family allowances (now child benefit) as a universal benefit financed by the abolition of child tax allowances (this was the option eventually adopted a decade later); (2) a form of negative income tax (see p. 161 ff.), which would allocate benefits automatically to those with low incomes; (3) a means-tested benefit (such as Supplementary Benefit), paid only to those who applied and whose income fell below a stipulated level. (Abel-Smith and Townsend's new poverty line was itself defined in terms of the Supplementary Benefit level.) The final outcome was a universal increase in family allowances, subject to 'clawback', a device invented by Nicholas Kaldor, economist and adviser to the Chancellor of the Exchequer, which provided that tax allowances were decreased only enough to cancel the gain from the increased family allowance. This avoided the political unpopularity of reducing take-home pay by *abolition* of tax allowances, shifting resources from the average family to the less well-off. Even so, there was further extended in-fighting within Whitehall before a compromise solution was achieved. Here was disjointed incrementalism at work. Moreover, in the exchanges which occurred at that time were to be found the elements of subsequent policy: Family Income Supplement (FIS) introduced by the Conservative government in 1970, and replacement of tax allowances for children by child benefit in the mid-1970s. Policy usually does not shift by leaps and bounds but by relatively narrow and limited changes.

The family poverty case provides support for the interactive as well as the political ammunition model of research utilization. There was considerable interaction between academics, politicians and activists in CPAG, and then between ministers, officials and CPAG, whose views on the direction which policy should follow were taken seriously, though were not ultimately decisive. Some of the conclusions which Banting draws from his case studies are presented in Chapter 3, and the role of intellectuals will be discussed shortly. The point should be made here that the use of the family poverty research as political ammunition was unusually direct. There are other similar examples, for instance, the first survey of race relations in Britain (Daniel, 1968), clearly designed to influence the climate of opinion about race relations legislation, and said to have been aimed in particular at a group of wavering, right-wing Labour MPs. In these cases of family poverty and of race, research did have some direct influence. There are also negative counter-examples. The research staff of the Community Development Projects (CDPs) in the 1970s appear to have believed that their results would constitute political ammunition (see Loney, 1983, pp. 171–97). Their target, however, was unclear, and in terms of short-run policy impact the overall effect of what they published was not only negative but probably somewhat harmful to the cause of social science.

The world of politics and policy, however, is often unpredictable. The CDP teams might be criticized for political naivety in thinking that their work would gain a hearing. What is more difficult to deal with is the inbuilt uncertainty of not knowing how research results may be used. Social policy researchers operate in an uncertain environment, and one element in that uncertainty is not knowing who may pick on one's research findings to use in political argument. Indeed, if one follows Karl Popper's analysis (1972) of World 3, the world of objective knowledge contained in published research reports, once research enters that 'world' it is in principle available to anyone to use for whatever purposes they wish. A case of extreme sensitivity to problems of this type is provided by those who oppose further research on the subject of racial differences in IQ. They argue that the results of previous research are subject to considerable misinterpretation (citing the work of Arthur Jensen and H. J. Eysenck) and that the findings of new research could be used by those who believe in racial superiority or inherent racial differences to bolster up an untenable position. This is an extreme position, and a rare example. It does make the point, however, that the social scientist does not control the uses to which research is put.

When one turns to the use made of research by Royal Commissions, rather different models of research become appropriate. There is now a considerable literature on the use of research by Royal and Presidential Commissions (Chapman, 1973; Komarovsky, 1975; Bulmer, 1980; 1983a) which will not be summarized here. Rather two or three cases will be briefly considered and some general points extracted. Cynics often claim that the function of commissions is to bury an issue. A. P. Herbert, for example, maintained that

A Royal Commission is generally appointed, not so much for digging up the truth, as for digging it in; and a government department appointing a Royal Commission is like a dog burying a bone, except that the dog does eventually return to the bone. (1961, pp. 263–4)

In this view, to the extent that commissions undertake research, this is a tactical use of research. Research is used as an excuse for post-poning action. But such a cynical view is exaggerated, and the main importance of the use of research by commissions is in exemplifying the enlightenment model.

Commissions are set up to inquire into and make recommenda-tions about contentious issues of public policy which the government does not wish to deal with itself without receiving advice. The topics on which commissions deliberate are very various, but have included moral issues (obscenity and pornography is a favourite), questions of crime and criminal justice, the organization of professions (legal services), the organization of government activities such as the civil service itself (Fulton Report) or the personal social services (Seebohm Report), and so on. A new commission has to familiarize itself rapidly with its subject, which it typically does by taking written and oral evidence and by making visits. Increasingly in recent years it has also commissioned research, though what this has involved is variable: employment of consultants, of outside contract researchers, of a research director, or of its own research staff. Sometimes social scientist members of a commission have played an important role in guiding the research programme. Typically such research exercises place a high premium either on synthesizing available results or in commissioning rapid field studies which can be completed within the tight time-frame of the commission's work.

The British Robbins Committee on Higher Education in the 1960s was set up to examine the case for university expansion in a system (unlike the American) highly controlled by the government (through the intermediary University Grants Committee), the size of which is determined to a large extent by ministers. The Committee mounted an impressive body of statistical work, directed by Claus (later Sir Claus) Moser, to explore the social implications of university expansion, which showed that 'more did not mean worse'; in other words there existed a pool of ability in the 18+ age group which would benefit from a university education but which was not at the time receiving it. In one sense the role of research for the Committee was a problem-solving one. It demonstrated securely that the Committee could make a recommendation for major expansion of the system with the support of the research which it had undertaken. But it also performed an enlightenment function, for it helped to change the climate of opinion about educational opportunity, in this case for those age 18+. In the late 1950s and early 1960s, a body of research appeared, both from academic researchers and government committees which had commissioned social science research, showing that there were marked social class differences in educational opportunity, marked material and cultural hindrances to children from working-class backgrounds advancing through the educational system, and that many able children did not perform educationally up to their potential. Higher education up to that time was small in scale, provided places for only a very small proportion of each year-group, and was predominantly upper middle class in student intake. The Robbins Report (1963) helped to change the climate of opinion and usher in an era of expanded higher education in universities and polytechnics. If not as extensive as the mass higher education of North America, the expanded British system post-Robbins was qualitatively different from the one which preceded it and also involved the creation of a number of entirely new universities and polytechnics. In part that change may be attributed to the indirect influence of social science research.

A striking American instance of the enlightenment function of commission reports is provided by the National Commission on Civil Disorders (the Kerner Commission) which was appointed in 1967 and reported in 1968. Its staff was large, including social scientists and professional writers, its report hard-hitting. It held that 'Our nation is moving toward two societies, one black, one white – separate and unequal.' It pointed out that 'Race prejudice has shaped our history decisively in the past; it threatens to do so again' (Kerner Report, 1968, p. 203). Like many other riot commission reports, it pointed to the social conditions of the disrupters as the basic causes of the disorders. Like many other reports, its policy recommendations had little immediate impact and as a policy instrument it appears at first sight to approximate to the tactical model – setting up a commission as a means of appearing to do something about an issue. This would be a misleading conclusion. Its main impact was upon opinion more generally. 'Only as an educational document did the commission have any substantial success' (Lipsky and Olson, 1977, p. 226). The paperback edition of the report, which was exceptionally well-written, sold 1,600,000 copies within four months of its appearance, and four years later there were 2 million copies in print. Thus even though the commission's work had little immediate impact upon government, it exercised a considerable longer-term influence upon how white Americans saw issues of racial inequality and disadvantage. Critics suggested that by focusing on the underlying social causes, it implicitly denied that they resulted from purposive political action. Its statement that 'the need is not so much for the government to design new programs as it is for the nation to generate new will' (Kerner Report, 1968, p. 412) sidestepped the difficult political measures which policy change required. At the same time, it indicates the extent to which the commissioners were addressing a general audience going beyond the policy-making community.

Commission reports, then, tend primarily to serve an enlightenment function. Even if the government setting up the commission only wants to use that as a delaying tactic, an able commission can investigate its subject thoroughly and produce a notable report with long-term impact, even if in the short term it is ignored. Commission reports can only rarely be used as political ammunition because they tend not to be partisan documents. There are considerable pressures pointing towards reaching a consensus among the commissioners and producing a united report. In the process, some of the negotiating processes characteristic of group politics may begin to take place, though in a rather more detached and olympian way. Only in Sweden, where members of the legislature and government officials regularly sit upon commissions, are they used directly as a means of reconciling conflicting groups and producing policy proposals acceptable to the different interests involved (Premfors, 1983).

The third example of utilization is rather different, but again involves an attempt to bring analysis to bear upon the work of central government. The British Central Policy Review Staff (CPRS) was set up in 1970–1, to advise the prime minister and the Cabinet. Its brief was to work out the implications of ministers' basic strategy in terms of policies in specific areas, to establish relative priorities for different sections of the programme, to identify those areas of policy in which new choices could be exercised, and to ensure that the underlying implications of alternative courses of action were fully analysed (Plowden, 1981, p. 63). This rather general brief was all that was available. It was interpreted by the first head, Lord Rothschild, a distinguished natural scientist and science research manager, who recruited a small staff of not more than twenty to assist him.

In one sense CPRS provided an analytic facility for central government which was not social scientific, in that its members were expected to become expert upon a wide range of issues and spent relatively little time on any one topic. They became perforce generalists, applying policy analytic methods in a general way, rather than researchers or technical specialists. On the other hand, the social sciences were represented among its members most strongly by economists but also by political scientists, sociologists and demographers. Outside members came from universities but also from the business world, banking and consultancy.

These interests were reflected in some of the reports which it produced. These included the co-ordination of social policies, the long-term policy implications of demographic change, race relations policy (unpublished), relationships between central and local government, and the future of the motor industry. These reports were not its only work. It also made presentations on 'strategy' to the Cabinet, providing collective briefs as an aid to day-to-day ministerial discussion of specific issues, and played a part in the PAR system.

The backgrounds of the (changing) membership of CPRS were of some relevance to its work programme, for this was determined eclectically and to some extent opportunistically by the interests of the head and his staff, by the current preoccupations of the staff, and by chance. For example, during the 1974–9 Labour government, a lot of work was done on interdepartmental aspects of social policies, the so-called Joint Approach to Social Policy (JASP) (CPRS, 1975; Plowden, 1977). This was a preoccupation of ministers at the time but also reflected staff interests. The problem it tackled was the fact that policies and programmes of different 'social' departments, such as health, social security, housing or education, were planned and managed not only in isolation from each other but also from other activities not usually seen as 'social' at all, such as taxation. Their clients were often the same, but policies were not co-ordinated and their impact on individuals could be random and capricious.

The problem in practice was enormous, since it involved overcoming the high degree of autonomy and comparative inertia of individual departments in Whitehall. The programme adopted by CPRS involved regular meetings of ministers to consider strategy; 'forward looks' at future events in the social policy field; improvements in relevant social statistics; and several studies of specific topics such as policies for financial poverty, links between housing policy and other social policies, and the implications of long-term population change. This work had a considerable initial impact and aroused enthusiasm outside Whitehall. But by 1979 both CPRS involvement in JASP, and JASP itself, were at an end. The impetus was too difficult to sustain given the fall-off in ministerial interest and the complex problems of interdepartmental co-ordination. CPRS could not afford to be drawn into a managerial role, yet the existing system of Cabinet committees was inadequate to perform this task (Plowden, 1981, p. 86).

CPRS is an interesting case because it involved a small group of social scientists (and other professionals and civil servants) providing policy analysis, albeit of a generalist and perhaps rather superficial kind, at the highest levels of British government. The research element in its work was slight, but it drew at longer distance on the established findings of social science and sought improved social statistics from the Central Statistical Office to aid its task. In terms of models of the policy-making process, its contribution was of two types.

It clearly operated in an interactive way with the prime minister and ministers. It existed to serve them and to present analyses to them, often seeking to expose them to new ideas. Their role was often a persuasive one. The CPRS's controversial *Review of Overseas Representation* (CPRS, 1977) met with a hostile reception which 'painfully illustrated the British governing establishment at its reactive worst' (Plowden, 1981, p. 83). Immediately, the report had little impact, but in the longer term it helped to change the climate of opinion about Britain's representation abroad and how it should be judged. In this case, a good deal of the interaction was negative. CPRS challenged vested interests, and came to be seen as an interest group itself, agitating for change. Other reports that it produced initiated more positive forms of interaction.

The main contribution of CPRS in its brief existence of just over a decade (it was wound up by Margaret Thatcher in 1983) was to policy enlightenment. Its main achievement was

to change the climate of opinion among decision-makers – a process which at best will happen only gradually and in which the precise responsibility of everyone is likely to be blurred. The essential first stage of this process is simply putting issues 'on the agenda' of policy-makers. The policy analyst in government should not protest if his advice has no visible impact for several years; or if the impact takes the form of his ideas, sometimes disconcertingly modified, being claimed as their own by other people. This is the occupational deprivation of his trade. (Plowden, 1981, p. 88)

CPRS helped to sensitize ministers to new issues, or new perspectives upon old issues, but did not necessarily have an immediate impact. The influence is to be looked for in the longer term.

The discussion so far has exposed the rational model of decision-making to searching criticism, and considered alternative models of influence which are discussed more fully in the next chapter. In the remainder of this chapter social science as a mode of intellectual innovation, and its institutional location, will be briefly considered.

It is clear, particularly in a relatively tight-knit and centralized political system like the British, with the worlds of politicians, officials, journalists and leading academic consultants overlapping to some extent in London, that awareness of economic and social analyses is spread, even among those who are not very interested in applying their results. David Donnison (1972) has well described a number of overlapping and interlocking social groups, members of which know each other personally, who have made academic studies of social questions and who are social administrators, sociologists, statisticians or social historians, with a few geographers or political scientists thrown in. Most live or work in Greater London. Their favoured reading is probably *The Guardian, The Economist* or *New Society*. In addition to Brian Abel-Smith and Peter Townsend, they have included their mentor Richard Titmuss, Michael Young (see Bulmer, 1985), David Glass, A. H. Halsey and Jean Floud, and Donnison himself. Most are or have been members of the Fabian Society, though they are now also to be found in the SDP's Tawney Society.

Keith Banting in Chapter 3 offers some generalizations about the intellectual influence of this group during the 1960s. The individual who analyses problems in a new way, however insignificant they otherwise appear, takes the first indispensable step towards innovation. In his case-studies of housing, rent regulation, educational priority and family poverty, he finds 'the pervasive influence of intellectuals and professionals. The conceptual changes that are the preconditions of policy innovation regularly start with them' (page 46). Empirical social research becomes a weapon against political orthodoxy. Undoubtedly, the reformist Fabian tradition, particularly in social policy, has done a great deal to push governments in the direction of more radical extensions of state provision for social minorities, and by advocating government provision and regulation, for example in social security and in the labour market, to protect the interests of less well-off sections of the community. Banting is correct, too, in noting the international networks which are increasingly important; this was especially clear in the American influence on the form of the Educational Priority Area (EPA) project.

As Banting notes, however, knowledge is not power, and there is a wide gap between influence and implementation. Several questions may be raised about the general applicability of the propositions which he advances. Undoubtedly the 1960s were a particularly fertile time for social scientists advising British central government policy-makers. How far were they exceptional? The counter view to Banting's has been put in most extreme form by Charles Lindblom and David Cohen in *Usable Knowledge* (1979), where they point to the exaggerated weight which some observers place on professional social inquiry in policy-making. They emphasize in contrast the importance of 'ordinary knowledge', derived from common sense, casual empiricism, or thoughtful speculation and analysis. The stock of ordinary knowledge possessed by social scientists is not superior to that of many journalists, politicians, civil servants, businessmen or pressure-group leaders. The claim that social science offers knowledge that is superior to ordinary knowledge has some force – but only some. Much of the knowledge that social scientists produce is in fact ordinary knowledge.

This general critique is developed by Lindblom in *The Policy-Making Process* (1980), where he points out the limits to analysis as an alternative to politics. This has already been touched on, but the specific reasons for this bear on the present discussion. Social science knowledge is fallible, and those involved in the policy process believe it to be so. Its scientific and analytic techniques are insufficiently developed. Its predictive record, even (or especially) in economics, is patchy. Often the policy-maker steers an uneasy course between having too much and too little information. Often social science is too slow and costly.

This rather general criticism can be focused more sharply by looking at the effects of expanding educational research upon American educational policy. David Cohen and Michael Garet (1975) show that the enormous expansion in federally funded educational research after 1964 was expected to have a major impact upon policy, to inform decisions faced by policy-makers, and to provide authoritative and relevant evidence on the costs and consequences of social policies. Their conclusions are much more in line with an enlightenment model. When they looked at how individual studies affected individual decisions, the relationship was weak. But there was clearly a connection between traditions of inquiry on the one hand and climates of knowledge and belief on the other. The diffuse effects of knowledge were much clearer.

Nor was educational research authoritative. There was no clear connection between relevance, methodological sophistication and authoritativeness. Partly this was due to the multiple aims and faulty assumptions of social action programmes, which made evaluation difficult. But it was also due to competing conceptions of methodology among social scientists, and the fact that methodologically superior knowledge is more complex, arcane and hard to interpret. Discussing research on school effects (such as the Coleman Report on *Equality of Educational Opportunity* (1966)), they show that the knowledge produced improved by any scientific standard, but was no more authoritative by any political standard, and often more mystifying by any public standard. In other words, more research appeared to make the policy-making task more complex rather than simpler.

Cohen and Garet conclude that

a justification of applied research solely on the basis of instrumental rationality is illusory, because applied inquiry rarely seems to reduce intellectual conflict about policy issues . . . more and better applied research in education has not produced more clarity or any noticeable convergence in policy advice. Rather, it seems to have intensified or sharpened conflicting ideas about policy, research and research method. It has raised these conflicts to new levels of scientific sophistication and difficulty, and it frequently has transformed the issues en route. When research has affected public life, it has done so chiefly through its effect on global, diffuse and hard-to-control systems of knowledge and belief. (Cohen and Garet, 1975, pp. 38–9)

This contrasting example to Banting's of the impact of knowledge may of course be explained by differences between the academic and political cultures of Britain and the United States, both in the latter country being more pluralist and diverse. But this is an unlikely explanation. One feature of the British case described by Banting was the close affiliation of academic researchers with politicians in the Labour government, even in the case of Halsey and Abel-Smith acting as ministerial advisers within departments during the 1960s. One explanation for the pattern which Banting describes can be in terms of superior access to politicians and the ability at least to propound possible solutions to social policy problems. (Though, as Banting notes, 'social scientists could champion the interests of the poor, but they could not force the government to act'.) Philip Abrams (1968) earlier argued that one reason historically for the slow development of sociology in Britain was the permeability of the worlds of politics and policy-making to social scientists, which drew them from the purely contemplative role in the university. In the

1960s, leading Labour politicians had a strong interest in social science. Anthony Crosland, for example, had read quite widely in sociology and was a friend of Michael Young, the first chairman of the Social Science Research Council. Richard Titmuss was influential in the Fabian Society and as adviser to the Labour Party on superannuation. He was deputy chairman of the Supplementary Benefits Commission from 1969 to 1973; David Donnison succeeded him and was later SBC chairman from 1975 to 1980 (see Donnison, 1982).

The limitations of this mode of influence are apparent in periods like the 1980s when a government less sympathetic to social science is in office. Both in Britain and the United States governments came to office at the beginning of the decade which were not particularly predisposed to favour social science, and to some extent were hostile to it. This was reflected, for example, in cuts in the social science budget of the National Science Foundation in the United States (Miller, 1987) and in Lord Rothschild's review of the Social Science Research Council in 1982 (Flather, 1987), which for a time appeared to put its existence in jeopardy. When social scientists do not have the ear of politicians, their very existence may be threatened.

Applied social science research, however, is more enduring than a change of government. It is established in universities, independent research institutes, commercial research organizations and within local and central government. In Britain, it has expanded very substantially in the last quarter century. In the United States its history is longer. Applied social science has come to be of use to the various parties involved in the processes of group conflict which result in the evolution of policy, interpreting 'group' in its widest sense to include political parties, occupational groups within the civil service, and individual government departments. Banting's strictures on the relatively minor role played by groups in his case-studies in the 1960s refer to the role of outside, organized, pressure groups such as CPAG, and do not invalidate the generalizations offered earlier about the nature of the policy-making process. Indeed, the intellectuals whose influence was so important constitute a group exercising influence upon the policy-making process, in the approach argued here.

Banting, too, acknowledges the importance of institutional factors, and devotes considerable attention to discussing party politics and the administrative system. The institutional structure of social policy research in Britain has been discussed in earlier work (Bulmer, 1978, pp. 27–39; 1982, pp. 128–50) and is not a major focus of attention in the present book. But it is worth some mention here because it bears on the extent to which social science research is integrated into the policy process. Banting's contribution in Chapter 3 is relevant in discussing the role of officials and the civil service structure.

His discussion there provides powerful support for a view of the policy process as one in which competing groups marshal evidence to buttress the case they are making. In the 1960s civil service social research was weak. Even well-informed departments like the DES relied on external inquiries such as the CACE's, rather than on 'in-house' work by the Inspectorate. Private initiatives were common, including work done by individual academics in their own time, foundation-funded inquiries by academics and studies done for or by pressure groups. There has also been a very rapid growth since the 1960s in the independent research sector, where bodies like the Policy Studies Institute (PSI) and Social and Community Planning Research (SCPR) have the capability of mounting their own studies. Government research has expanded since the 1960s, but it still does not have a majority voice.

Officials play a key role in assembling advice and recommendations to ministers when legislation is likely, and thus act as filters to research findings. Banting brings out their key importance at this stage, as well as the fact that they are not passive middle-men. They actively frame the alternatives presented (often in a far from 'neutral' way, though not in a politically partisan manner) and maintain contacts with other groups, particularly interest groups, negotiating with them and lobbying them as well as listening to their submissions. One hindrance to the influence of social science has been the lack of familiarity of some civil servants with social science perspectives other than that of economics. The absence (except in rare cases in departments and the unique case centrally of CPRS) of social science advisers, who could perform a function analogous to that which is performed by economic advisers, means that research results, to the extent that they are taken on board, are interpreted at second or third hand. This is a further reason why anything approaching a rational model makes little sense in relation to policy-making in British central government.

Banting also provides strong evidence in support of the extent to which social policy may become compartmentalized between government departments, referred to earlier when discussing JASP. This is one way in which the impact of research can be reduced, to the extent that departmental interests focus upon their own specific responsibilities rather than those of a client group. For example, responsibility for children, for young people between 16 and 18, and for aspects of race relations are each split between several government departments. Specific pieces of research on each of these subjects is therefore likely to be interpreted by a single department, such as the DHSS or the Home Office, in terms of their own specific interests in that policy area, rather than taking an overall view. A specific example is income support for 16–18 year olds, mentioned earlier, which is handled by the DHSS, Department of Employment and DES. There are thus obstacles to research implementation which are inherent in the government structure.

Many social scientists remain dissatisfied with the impact which social science has upon policy. A good deal of the recent literature chronicles the obstacles which are encountered, and occasionally there is even a note of complaint that policy-makers are not more receptive. The argument of this chapter has been that to a considerable extent such obstacles are an inevitable outcome of the nature of the policy-making process in democratic industrial societies. It is not that there is not scope for making the contribution of social science more effective. There certainly is, particularly within central government in respect of use of social science advice, commissioning and dissemination of research, and maintaining an 'in-house' research facility. But even if the most desirable state of affairs conceivable so far for the production of social science knowledge were brought about, there would still remain intractable problems in bringing such knowledge to bear directly upon the policy-making process. For this reason, as a general characterization the rational model appears to be markedly inferior to the enlightenment model.

On the other hand, applied social science research is an extensive and productive activity at the present time. Later sections of this book consider different types of applied work, their qualities, impact and effectiveness. Just because the policy-making process is one of conflictual negotiation between groups does not mean that social science research cannot make a useful, more diffuse, general contribution. Even if the extent to which it is a determining factor in individual decisions (if, indeed, these can be identified) is uncertain, it undoubtedly plays an enlightening role for a number of the groups which participate in the policy arena.

2

The Many Meanings of Research Utilization*

CAROL H. WEISS**

This is a time when more and more social scientists are becoming concerned about making their research useful for public policy-makers, and policy-makers are displaying spurts of well-publicized concern about the usefulness of the social science research supported by government funds. There is mutual interest in whether social science research intended to influence policy is actually 'used', but before that important issue can profitably be addressed it is essential to understand what 'using research' actually means.

A review of the literature reveals that a diverse array of meanings is attached to the term. Much of the ambiguity in the discussion of 're-search utilization' – and conflicting interpretations of its prevalence and the routes by which it occurs – derives from conceptual confusion. If we are to gain a better understanding of the extent to which social science research has affected public policy in the past, and learn how to make its contribution more effective in the future, we need to clarify the concept.

Upon examination, the use of social science research in the sphere of public policy is an extraordinarily complex phenomenon. Authors who have addressed the subject have evoked diverse images of the processes and purposes of utilization. Here I will try to extract seven different meanings that have been associated with the concept.

The Knowledge-Driven Model

The first image of research utilization is probably the most venerable in the literature and derives from the natural sciences. It assumes the following sequence of events: basic research → applied research →

* Reprinted with permission from *Public Administration Review*, vol. 39, no. 5, Sept.–Oct. 1979, pp. 426–31. © 1979 by the American Society for Public Administration, 1120 G. Street NW, Washington DC. All rights reserved.

** Senior Fellow, Programs in Administration, Planning and Social Policy, Graduate School of Education, Harvard University.

development → application. The notion is that basic research discloses some opportunity that may have relevance for public policy; applied research is conducted to define and test the findings of basic research for practical action; if all goes well, appropriate technologies are developed to implement the findings; whereupon application occurs. (An example is Havelock, 1969, ch. 1.)

Examples of this model of research utilization generally come from the physical sciences: biochemical research makes available oral contraceptive pills, research in electronics enables television to multiply the number of broadcast channels. Because of the fruits of basic research, new applications are developed and new policies emerge (cf. Comroe and Dripps, 1976).

The assumption is that the sheer fact that knowledge exists presses it towards development and use. It is debatable how well or poorly this model describes events in the natural sciences. There is some evidence that even in areas of need in the natural sciences, basic research does not necessarily push towards application. For example, Project Hindsight indicated faster, and probably greater, use of basic science when it was *directed* toward filling a recognized need in weapons technology (Sherwin *et al.*, 1966; Sherwin and Isenson, 1967). In the social sciences few examples can be found. The reasons appear to be several. Social science knowledge is not apt to be so compelling or authoritative as to drive inevitably towards implementation. Social science knowledge does not readily lend itself to conversion into replicable technologies, either material or social. Perhaps most important, unless a social condition has been consensually defined as a pressing social problem, and unless the condition has become fully politicized and debated, and the parameters of potential action agreed upon, there is little likelihood that policy-making bodies will be receptive to the results of social science research.

I do not mean to imply that basic research in the social sciences is not useful for policy-making. Certainly many social policies and programmes of government are based, explicitly or implicitly, on basic psychological, sociological, economic, anthropological and political scientific understandings. When they surface to affect government decisions, however, it is not likely to be through the sequence of events posited in this model.

Problem-Solving Model

The most common concept of research utilization involves the direct application of the results of a specific social science study to a pending decision. The expectation is that research provides empirical evidence and conclusions that help to solve a policy problem. The model is again a linear one, but the steps are different from those in the knowledge-driven model. Here the decision drives the application of research. A problem exists and a decision has to be made; information or understanding is lacking either to generate a solution to the problem or to select among alternative solutions; research provides the missing knowledge. With the gap filled, a decision is reached.

Implicit in this model is a sense that there is a consensus on goals. It is assumed that policy-makers and researchers tend to agree on what the desired end state shall be. The main contribution of social science research is to help identify and select appropriate means to reach the goal.

The evidence that social science research provides for the decision-making process can be of several orders. It can be qualitative and descriptive, for example, rich observational accounts of social conditions or of programme processes. It can be quantitative data, either on relatively soft indicators, such as public attitudes, or on hard factual matters, such as number of hospital beds. It can be statistical relationships between variables, generalized conclusions about the associations among factors, even relatively abstract (middle-range) theories about cause and effect. Whatever the nature of the empirical evidence that social science research supplies, the expectation is that it clarifies the situation and reduces uncertainty, and therefore it influences the decisions of policy-makers.

In this formulation of research utilization, there are two general ways in which social science research can enter the policy-making arena. First, the research antedates the policy problem and is drawn in on need. Policy-makers faced with a decision may go out and search for information from existing research to delimit the scope of the question or identify a promising policy response. Or the information can be called to their attention by aides, staff analysts, colleagues, consultants or social science researchers. Or they may happen upon it in professional journals, agency newsletters, newspapers and magazines, or at conferences. There is an element of chance in this route from problem to research to decision. Available research may not directly fit the problem. The location of appropriate research, even with sophisticated and computerized information systems, may be difficult. Inside experts and outside consultants may fail to come up with relevant sources. The located information may appear to be out of date or not generalizable to the immediate context. Whether or not the best and most relevant research reaches the person with the problem depends on the efficiency of the communications links. Therefore, when this imagery of research utilization prevails, the usual prescription for improving the use of research is to improve the means of communication to policy-makers.

A second route to problem-solving use is the purposeful commissioning of social science research and analysis to fill the knowledge gap. The assumptions, as with the search route, are that decision-makers have a clear idea of their goals and a map of acceptable alternatives and that they have identified some specific informational needs to clarify their choice. This time they engage social scientists to provide the data, analytic generalizations and possibly the interpretations of these generalizations to the case in hand by way of recommendations. The process follows this sequence: definition of pending decision → identification of missing knowledge → acquisition of social science research → interpretation of the research for the decision context → policy choice.

The expectation is that research generated in this type of sequence, even more than research located through search procedures, will have direct and immediate applicability and will be used for decision-making. In fact, it is usually assumed that the specific study commissioned by the responsible government office will have an impact and that its recommendations will affect ensuing choices. Particularly the large-scale, government-contracted policy study, tailored to the specifications set by government staff, is expected to make a difference in plans, programmes and policies. If the research goes unused, the prescription to improve utilization that arises from this imagery is to increase government control over both the specification of requested research and its conduct in the field. If the research had actually met decision-makers' information needs, it is assumed, it would have been used.

Even a cursory review of the fate of social science research, including policy research on government-defined issues, suggests that these kinds of expectations are wildly optimistic. Occasional studies have a direct effect on decisions, but usually on relatively low-level, narrow-gauge decisions. Most studies appear to come and go without leaving any discernible mark on the direction or substance of policy. It probably takes an extraordinary concatenation of circumstances for research to influence policy decisions directly: a well-defined decision situation, a set of policy actors who have responsibility and jurisdiction for making the decision, an issue whose resolution depends at least to some extent on *information*, identification of the requisite informational need, research that provides the information in terms that match the circumstances within which choices will be made, research findings that are clear-cut, unambiguous, firmly supported and powerful, that reach decision-makers at the time they are wrestling with the issues, that are comprehensible and understood, and that do not run counter to strong political interests. Because chances are small that all these conditions will fall into line around any one issue, the problem-solving model of research use probably describes a relatively small number of cases.

However, the problem-solving model remains the prevailing imagery of research utilization. Its prevalence probably accounts for much of the disillusionment about the contribution of social science research to social policy. Because people expect research use to occur through the sequence of stages posited by this model, they become discouraged when events do not take the expected course. However, there are other ways in which social science research can be 'used' in policy-making.

Interactive Model

Another way that social science research can enter the decision arena is as part of an interactive search for knowledge. Those engaged in developing policy seek information not only from social scientists but from a variety of sources – administrators, practitioners, politicians, planners, journalists, clients, interest groups, aides, friends, and social scientists, too. The process is not one of linear order from research to decision but a disorderly set of inter-connections and back-and-forthness that defies neat diagrams.

All kinds of people involved in an issue area pool their talents, beliefs and understandings in an effort to make sense of a problem. Social scientists are one set of participants among many. Seldom do they have conclusions available that bear directly and explicitly on the issue at hand. More rarely still do they have a body of convergent evidence. Nevertheless, they can engage in mutual consultations that progressively move closer to potential policy responses.

Donnison describes this interactive model of research use in the development of two pieces of legislation in Great Britain. He notes that decisions could not wait upon completion of research but had to be made when political circumstances compelled.

Research workers could not present authoritative findings for others to apply; neither could others commission them to find the 'correct' solution to policy problems: they were not that kind of problem. Those in the four fields from which experience had to be brought to bear [politics, technology, practice, and research] contributed on equal terms. Each was expert in a few things, ignorant about most things, offered what he could, and generally learnt more than he could teach. (Donnison, 1972, p. 527)

In this model, the use of research is only one part of a complicated process that also uses experience, political insight, pressure, social technologies and judgement. It has applicability not only to face-to-face settings but also to the multiple ways in which intelligence is gathered through intermediaries and brought to bear. It describes a familiar process by which decision-makers inform themselves of the range of knowledge and opinion in a policy area.

Political Model

Often the constellation of interests around a policy issue predetermines the positions that decision-makers take. Or debate has gone on over a period of years and opinions have hardened. At this point, decision-makers are not likely to be receptive to new evidence from social science research. For reasons of interest, ideology, or intellect, they have taken a stand that research is not likely to shake.

In such cases, research can still be used. It becomes ammunition for the side that finds its conclusions congenial and supportive. Partisans flourish the evidence in an attempt to neutralize opponents, convince waverers and bolster supporters. Even if conclusions have to be ripped out of context (with suppression of qualifications and of evidence 'on the other hand'), research becomes grist to the mill.

Social scientists tend to look askance at the impressment of research results into service for a position that decision-makers have taken on other grounds. They generally see it as an illegitimate attempt to 'use' research (in the pejorative sense) for self-serving purposes of agency justification and personal aggrandizement. Using research to support a predetermined position is, however, research utilization, too, in a form which would seem to be neither an unimportant nor an improper use. Only distortion and misinterpretation of findings are illegitimate. To the extent that the research, accurately interpreted, supports the position of one group, it gives the advocates of that position confidence, reduces their uncertainties, and provides them an edge in the continuing debate. Since the research finds ready-made partisans who will fight for its implementation, it stands a better chance of making a difference in the outcome (Weiss, 1973).

One of the appropriate conditions for this model of research use is that all parties to the issue have access to the evidence. If, for example, bureaucrats monopolize research that would support the position of clients, then equity is not served, but when research is available to all participants in the policy process, research as political ammunition can be a worthy model of utilization.

Tactical Model

There are occasions when social science research is used for purposes that have little relation to the substance of the research. It is not the content of the findings that is invoked but the sheer fact that research is being done. For example, government agencies confronted with demands for action may respond by saying, 'Yes, we know that's an important need. We're doing research on it right now.' Research becomes proof of their responsiveness. Faced with unwelcome demands, they may use research as a tactic for delaying action ('We are waiting until the research is completed').

Sometimes government agencies use research to deflect criticism. By claiming that their actions were based on the implications and recommendations of social science research studies, they may try to avoid responsibility for unpopular policy outcomes. Or support for a research programme can become a tactic for enhancing the prestige of the agency by allying it with social scientists of high repute. Some agencies support substantial amounts of research and, in so doing, build a constituency of academic supporters who rally to their defence when appropriations are under Congressional review. These are illustrations of uses of research, irrespective of its conclusions, as a tactic in bureaucratic politics.

Enlightenment Model

Perhaps the way in which social science research most frequently enters the policy arena is through the process that has come to be called 'enlightenment' (Crawford and Biderman, 1969; Janowitz, 1972). Here it is not the findings of a single study nor even of a body of related studies that directly affect policy. Rather it is the concepts and theoretical perspectives that social science research has engendered that permeate the policy-making process.

There is no assumption in this model that decision-makers seek out social science research when faced with a policy issue or even that they are receptive to, or aware of, specific research conclusions. The imagery is that of social science generalizations and orientations percolating through informed publics and coming to shape the way in which people think about social issues. Social science research diffuses circuitously through manifold channels – professional journals, the mass media, conversations with colleagues – and over time the variables it deals with and the generalizations it offers provide decision-makers with ways of making sense out of a complex world.

Rarely will policy-makers be able to cite the findings of a specific study that influenced their decisions, but they have a sense that social science research has given them a backdrop of ideas and orientations that has had important consequences (see, for example, Caplan, Morrison and Stambaugh, 1975). Research sensitizes decision-makers to new issues and helps turn what were non-problems into policy problems. A recent example is child abuse (Weiss, 1976). Conversely, research may convert existing problems into non-problems, for example, marijuana use. Research can drastically revise the way that policy-makers define issues, such as acceptable rates of unemployment, the facets of the issue they view as susceptible to alteration, and the alternative measures they consider. It helps to change the parameters within which policy solutions are sought. In the long run, along with other influences, it often redefines the policy agenda.

Unlike the problem-solving model, this model of research use does not assume that, in order to be useful, research results must be compatible with decision-makers' values and goals. Research that challenges current verities may work its way into official consciousness (Aaron, 1978) and, with support from dissident undergrounds, overturn accustomed values and patterns of thought.

The notion of research utilization in the enlightenment mode has a comforting quality. It seems to promise that, without any special effort, truth will triumph; but the enlightenment process has its full share of deficiencies. When research diffuses to the policy sphere through indirect and unguided channels, it dispenses invalid as well as valid generalizations. Many of the social science understandings that gain currency are partial, oversimplified, inadequate or wrong. There are no procedures for screening out the shoddy and obsolete. Sometimes unexpected or sensational research results, however incomplete or inadequately supported by data, take the limelight. As an environmental researcher has noted, 'Bad science, being more newsworthy, will tend to be publicized and seized on by some to support their convictions' (Comar, 1978). The indirect diffusion process is vulnerable to oversimplification and distortion, and it may come to resemble 'endarkenment' as much as enlightenment.

Moreover, the enlightenment model is an inefficient means for reaching policy audiences. Many vital results of social science research never penetrate to decision-making centres. Some results take so long to come into currency that they are out of date by the time they arrive, their conclusions having been modified, or even contradicted, by later and more comprehensive analysis.

Finally, recent reviews of research on poverty, incomes, unemployment and education suggest that social science research has not led to convergent conclusions (Aaron, 1978; Cohen and Weiss, 1977); as more studies are done, they often elaborate rather than simplify. They generate complex, varied and even contradictory views of the social phenomena under study, rather than cumulating into sharper and more coherent explanation. The effect may be to widen and enrich our understanding of the multiple facets of reality, but the implications for policy are *less* simple and clear cut. When the diverse research conclusions enter the policy arena, the direction they provide for policy is confused. Advocates of almost any policy prescription are likely to find some research generalizations in circulation to support their points of view.

Research as Part of the Intellectual Enterprise of the Society

A final view of research utilization looks upon social science research as one of the intellectual pursuits of a society. It is not so much an independent variable whose effects on policy remain to be determined as it is another of the dependent variables, collateral with policy – and with philosophy, journalism, history, law and criticism. Like policy, social science research responds to the currents of thought, the fads and fancies, of the period. Social science and policy interact, influencing each other and being influenced by the larger fashions of social thought.

It is often emerging policy interest in a social issue that leads to the appropriation of funds for social science research in the first place, and only with the availability of funds are social scientists attracted to study of the issue. Early studies may accept the parameters set by the policy discussion, limiting investigation to those aspects of the issue that have engaged official attention. Later, as social science research widens its horizons, it may contribute to reconceptualization of the issue by policy-makers. Meanwhile, both the policy and research colloquies may respond, consciously or unconsciously, to concerns sweeping through intellectual and popular thought ('citizen participation', 'local control', spiralling inflation, individual privacy). In this view, research is one part of the interconnected intellectual enterprise.

These, then, are some of the meanings that 'the use of social science research' can carry. Probably all of them are applicable in some situations. Certainly none of them represents a fully satisfactory answer to the question of how a polity best mobilizes its research resources to inform public action.

An understanding of the diversity of perspectives on research utilization may serve many purposes. For one, it may help to overcome the disenchantment with the usefulness of social science research that has afflicted those who search for use only in problem-solving contexts. For another, it may enable us to engage in empirical study of the policy uses of research with better awareness of its diverse and often subtle manifestations; if immediate impact of a specific study on a specific decision is only one indicator of use, we will have to devise more complex but more appropriate modes of study.

Finally, we may need to think more deeply about the proper role of social science in public policy-making. There has been much glib rhetoric about the vast benefits that social science can offer if only policy-makers paid attention. Perhaps it is time for social scientists to pay attention to the imperatives of policy-making systems and to consider soberly what they can do, not necessarily to increase the use of research, but to improve the contribution that research makes to the wisdom of social policy.

3

The Social Policy Process *

KEITH G. BANTING**

The 1960s saw the British social policy debate transformed. The assumptions of the 1950s were swept aside, and poverty and inequality were reinstated as critical social issues. While the rediscovery of poverty did not come as a sudden blinding revelation, one dimension of hardship after another was thrust firmly into political consciousness, and the cumulative impact on the social policy agenda was very great. This change did not flow from any sudden shift in the structure of British life; perceptions of income trends changed dramatically while the actual distribution of income remained broadly stable. Nor was the change imposed on politicians by pressures from below; the poor remained unassertive themselves, and were undefended by well-organized allies. Rather, the rediscovery of poverty and the policy response to it were the products of the internal dynamics of the social policy process.

The new policies flowed through twin processes of intellectual and institutional adaptation. Policy-making is a conceptual activity. Individual policy-makers must perceive and define problems and devise responses to them. But policy-making also takes place within institutions. The structure of those institutions, and their relationship with the wider society, shape the choices of those in authority. The preceding chapters have revealed a persistent tension between the intellectual and institutional processes of policy change. This chapter draws together the patterns that have emerged into a more comprehensive picture of the social policy process.

* © 1979 Keith G. Banting. Reproduced with the permission of the publisher from K. G. Banting, *Poverty, Politics and Policy* (London: Macmillan, 1979), pp. 139–53.
** Associate Professor of Political Science, University of British Columbia.

Intellectual Innovation

When attention is focused on the individual policy-maker, the intellectual process stands out. From this perspective, policy change flows from shifts in the perceptions and attitudes of central decision-makers, and the policy process resembles a complex communications network within which information and ideas are exchanged. Policy innovations, in particular, highlight the intellectual process. The individual who analyses problems in a new way, or who recombines existing elements so as to introduce a novel pattern, takes the first indispensable step towards innovation (Barnett, 1953, p. 185). Those who contribute to such conceptual shifts are major agents of policy innovation, however insignificant they may otherwise appear in politics.

The number of people who contribute to this intellectual process is small. The ideas underlying the social policy innovations of the 1960s can be traced, in the first instance, to a few social scientists and professionals operating on the margins of politics. Crossman's key outside advisers numbered three or four; the group that documented poverty and drafted the Child Poverty Action Group's (CPAG's) policy proposals was only slightly larger; and the Educational Priority Area (EPA) idea was invented and sustained by another handful. Such individuals are, however, essentially middlemen between the intellectual and political worlds. They are most effective when they are drawing upon a broader stream of research, theory and opinion developing in their academic or professional communities. The innovative approach of the Rent Act reflected a growing professional disenchantment with the polarized nature of housing debates; the CPAG's proposals flowed from a decade of research and thinking by a new generation of academics based at the London School of Economics; and EPAs emerged from the general environmentalist consensus in educational research.

The influence of these social scientists and professionals is particularly marked in three phases of the policy process: awareness, definition and the specification of policy alternatives. The most obvious impact is on the awareness of problems. The 1960s offer compelling evidence of the role of empirical research in shaping the social policy agenda. More than any other group, the left-wing intellectual movement led by Richard Titmuss and his students revealed the persistence of poverty and inequality and documented the failures of the welfare state. Their surveys of housing, poverty and educational attainment filled major gaps in the information available to government, and slowly changed policy-makers' conception of British society. In effect, the social science community acted as a social seismograph, identifying and measuring problems hitherto ignored in political life.

But their influence does not stop there. Social scientists also shape the definition of the problems that they reveal. Social science theory and professional doctrine regularly penetrate the wider political world, and advisory committees in particular serve as mechanisms for absorbing such models of reality and legitimating them for political purposes. As a result, political argument often takes place within a wider consensus on the nature of the problem, which reduces the range of conflict substantially. Normally this process of diffusion takes time. The environmentalist consensus in education took over twenty years to develop and permeate political discourse; and the relative conception of poverty, first articulated by intellectuals in the early 1950s, was not widely accepted in politics until the mid-1960s. But occasionally the diffusion process is greatly speeded up. The evolution of professional opinion on housing was comparatively rapid, spanning as it did only eight short years between 1957 and 1965; and David Donnison and the other advisers exercised their greatest influence over the rent legislation in a matter of weeks, by shaping the new minister's conception of the private rented market and the stresses within it.

The policy options actively considered also owe much to intellectuals and professionals. The original inspiration for the innovative features of all the policies examined here sprang originally from the minds of such people. The most novel elements in the Rent Act were first suggested by Goodman, Donnison and Pilcher. The insistence that the tax and benefit systems were both instruments of redistribution, as well as the specific proposal that family allowances and child tax allowances be integrated, were injected into the poverty debate by politically active intellectuals; and the final clawback variation was invented by yet another academic 'irregular'. Similarly, EPAs were social science theory translated into concrete recommendations by social scientists.

In some of its phases, then, the social policy process is essentially a process of diffusion of information and ideas. The thin stratum of society composed of social scientists and professionals acts as an instrument of social analysis, a link between British society and its political institutions that is critical in the making of social policy. It alerts politicians to changes in their environment, interprets and reinterprets social problems for them, and generates a continuous flow of proposals around which political debate revolves. The images of reality that emerge are not necessarily correct, but they are politically potent.

This process of diffusion is the product, in part, of a wider international network, with social science research and professional conferences and publications forming the primary links between Britain and other countries. The absorption of foreign ideas is, of course, a highly selective process, and professional opinion in the host country must be sympathetic before an importation can be successful. But the modern exchange of policy intelligence between countries that do share common intellectual traditions can be rapid indeed. The EPAs were a classic case. The environmental consensus in Britain facilitated the exchange, but the American example was an essential catalyst. Indeed EPAs never escaped their transatlantic origins; subsequent American pessimism about such programmes was imported equally quickly, and Halsey and his friends were soon having to fight the pervasive assumption that negative evaluations of the American programme Head Start automatically applied to EPAs as well. Although in less obvious ways, the international exchange of ideas pervaded other fields as well. The Milner Holland Committee's examination of rent legislation in other countries was important in the Rent Act, and the idea of a negative income tax positively sped across national borders.

The impact of social science knowledge and professional ideas depends on several factors, the most important of which is uncertainty within government. The complexity of modern policy problems has increased the uncertainties of policy-makers generally and steadily expanded the role of professionals. But differences between issues remain. The professionals' influence is greatest when problems have been ignored, when they seem new and undefined, when existing approaches no longer seem adequate. Uncertainty was particularly marked in the rent case and, as a result, outside experts were invited into the heart of the process and exercised a decisive influence on the legislation. This is hardly the norm, however. The pattern discovered in the poverty and EPA cases is probably more common. Social scientists raised new issues and proposed innovative policies; but officials and ministers were more confident of their capacity to handle these problems, and the social scientists participated much less in internal deliberations.

While the degree of uncertainty is critical to the role of such experts, it is not the only factor involved. Confused policy-makers could still choose to muddle through on their own. Their willingness to listen to social scientists and professionals also depends on their attitude towards their particular expertise. Social science knowledge is intrinsically less verifiable than that in the natural sciences and accordingly exacts less deference. Although the status of the social sciences was certainly rising during the 1960s, the reaction of individual policy-makers varied enormously. Social scientists had far greater influence with the intellectual politicians in the Labour Cabinet, such as Richard Crossman, Anthony Crosland and Roy Jenkins, than with others such as James Callaghan; similarly their educational research carried much more weight with Boyle than with many of his Conservative colleagues. Officials' receptiveness also varied. Few officials, especially those older ones at senior levels, have had much social science training. Most studied classics or history at university, and some of them remain determinedly sceptical about the claims of social science: 'a lot of third-class words' was one assessment of sociology, 'just ideology' another. But other officials were sympathetic, and personnel changes could significantly shift departmental receptiveness, as the DES illustrates. In the early 1960s, official sympathy facilitated the appointment of David Donnison and Michael Young to the Plowden Council; in the late 1960s, the scepticism of a new set of senior officials dampened enthusiasm for their recommendations; by the early 1970s, yet another group were inviting Halsey into their deliberations on nursery education.

The extent of uncertainty and the status of the expertise in turn influence a third factor that is critical to its impact: the particular mix of communication channels through which ideas must pass. The diffusion of policy intelligence proceeds through a variety of channels. In addition to purely scholarly and professional publications, ideas flow back and forth in the public media. Britain is a relatively centralized society, and the institutions capable of disseminating policy intelligence are highly concentrated in London. The quality press, the weekly journals such as *New Society* and *The Economist*, the pamphlet series and publishing houses together constitute a national forum for policy discussion. Debates conducted in this forum rarely reach the bulk of the British public but they do engage informed opinion and policy-makers (see, for instance, the figures on the newspapers and journals read by senior civil servants in Rose, 1974). Outside experts can use this network to shift perceptions in Whitehall and Westminster, sometimes without even leaving their studies in Hampstead and elsewhere. These indirect exchanges are supplemented, however, by a series of more direct channels of communication between the professional and political worlds.

Informal consultations are a regular feature of the process, as Richard Crossman's group, the seminars in Tony Lynes' flat, the sessions in Anthony Crosland's home and Halsey's contacts with the DES all testify. Increasingly, contact is also formalized. Social scientists and professionals are regularly appointed to advisory bodies such as the Milner Holland and Plowden committees; and some become formal advisers to ministers, as did Nicholas Kaldor and later Brian Abel-Smith. In effect, social scientists and professionals have been partially integrated into Britain's policy elites. (At a later stage Richard Titmuss became vice-chairman of the Supplementary Benefits Commission and in 1975 Donnison became chairman (cf. Donnison, 1982 ed.).)

But the directness of communication in any particular instance depends on the degree of uncertainty and deference to expertise among policy-makers. When both are marked, as in the rent case, direct consultations are likely. Such contact is clearly the most efficient type, involving as it does less personal effort on the part of the outside adviser and less distortion of his message: Goodman, Donnison and Pilcher were able to get their ideas across clearly because of their direct participation in the drafting process. But when uncertainty and respect are reduced, social science and professional ideas have to pass through less direct channels, such as advisory committees and the public media. These channels remain important; they prepare wider political and informed opinion about new directions in professional thinking, preparing the way for government action, should it come. But reliance on indirect channels alone is a daunting task; greater effort is required, as the CPAG campaign indicates, and the messages are more vulnerable to reinterpretation, as the fate of the EPA proposal demonstrates. Thus the influence of social science and professional thinking on policy-makers varies considerably. The Rent Bill provided a unique combination of favourable factors: high levels of uncertainty, an intellectual minister and direct channels of communication. These factors were diminished in the other cases, and the professionals' impact was correspondingly less.

Despite such differences, however, our most striking finding is the pervasive influence of intellectuals and professionals. The conceptual changes that are the preconditions of policy innovation regularly start with them. In this sense, the social policy process has not changed dramatically since the nineteenth century. Empirical research has long been a powerful weapon against political orthodoxy. The way in which the assumptions about the Welfare

State were dissolved was simply a modern instance of the under-mining of the intellectual foundations of the Poor Law a century before. Leading activists may be more professional now, and the expansion of the universities, research institutes and professions may have provided a firmer institutional base for them. But the essential dialectic between knowledge and policy has not changed.

The interpretations of policy-making as a process of social learning advanced by Deutsch, Vickers, Heclo and others thus do illuminate a critical dimension of the social policy process. Such theories explain how problems are raised and defined, and how innovative policy ideas emerge. During the 1960s the problems of poverty and educational deprivation were not imposed on government by party conflict or group power. These issues flowed from new policy intelligence which shifted policy-makers' interpretation of their environment. Even in the case of the highly politicized rent issue, policy formulation was essentially a process of collective learning, in which party doctrine and electoral calculus gave way to expertise and social science data. Overturning established images of society and reshaping contentious areas of public policy are major accomplish-ments. The impact of knowledge cannot be denied.

Yet focusing on the intellectual process of policy innovation captures only part of the whole. Such a view overemphasizes the independence and potency of knowledge, as well as the openness of political systems to change. A problem defined is not a problem solved. Social scientists could champion the interests of the poor, but they could not force the government to act. Indeed they had remark-ably little impact on the salience attached to the issues that they raised; the CPAG campaign was their most elaborate effort and its success depended heavily on the sensitivity of policy elites. Similarly a policy proposed is not a policy adopted. A common pattern of the 1960s was for proposals from social scientists to find an echo in legislation, but in such a modified form that the original aspirations went unfulfilled. Expertise generates influence, and intellectual creativity can alter political thinking. But knowledge is not power. Ideas must be harnessed to more powerful forces to change the direction of social development. Analogies with learning fail to reveal the limits of knowledge because they underestimate the extent to which policy-making is an institutional as well as an intellectual phenomenon.

The Institutional Process

Politics in the field of social policy is largely a reactive process. The problems and proposals around which political discourse revolves usually originate elsewhere. But political parties, bureaucracies and interest groups constitute an institutional screen that filters the ideas seeking to penetrate the political world, and limits the extent to which the ideas that do slip through the screen are translated into public policy.

Party Politics
The beliefs and strategies of politicians are central to the screening process. Theories that highlight the potency of expertise often depict politicians as poor, uncertain creatures, constantly struggling to understand their environment and constantly unsure of what to do. But this is a very partial image. Complexity does not always breed indecision. Cognitive theorists emphasize that the human mind is essentially a mechanism for imposing order on ambiguous situations; individuals evolve structures of belief within which decisions can proceed smoothly even in complex circumstances (Steinbruner, 1974, ch. 4). So it is in politics. Politicians develop their own commonsense notions about social processes, derived largely from their personal experience, and their perceptual maps incorporate certainties as well as uncertainties. Some choices that appear complex to experts seem simple to politicians. Their images of reality may be incorrect, but they are held no less firmly for that.

Party doctrine and electoral survival are the most powerful sources of political certainty. Party doctrine is never comprehensive and seldom unambiguous; there are many gaps in which the role of expertise can expand, as the drafting of the Rent Bill illustrates. But when party perceptions do harden, the impact of expertise fades. In addition, politicians are continually anticipating the electoral consequences of their actions. Their judgements are largely intuitive and much political argument centres precisely on the shape of public enthusiasms and the elasticity of public tolerances. But the intuitive nature of such perceptions does not alter the certainty with which they are often held. Ministers regularly assert dogmatically that certain courses of action are simply not on. (Heclo, 1974, pp. 288–93, depreciates the importance of electoral competition in social policy on the grounds that advocacy and enactment of social insurance did not ensure electoral victory and that social programmes were often restricted rather than expanded in anticipation of voters' reactions.

However, the first objection seems too crude a measure, as the parties involved might have believed that their social policy initiatives would help them electorally. And the second objection in fact admits indirect electoral influences; surely an analysis of the growth of social policy should explain why it did not grow faster.)

Yet the impact of political judgements varies enormously between different phases of the policy process. Politicians do not usually raise the issues to which they respond, or define the terms in which they are debated. Only in the highly politicized issue of rents did parties take a lead in monitoring social change. In that case Labour strove mightily to focus attention on the developing pressures in the private rented sector and to shape the public conception of the problem. When parties do commit their energies in this way, their impact on the policy agenda is formidable: other dimensions of poverty remained hidden for years, but the problems of poor tenants were quickly recognized in political circles. Parties play such a role intermittently, however. Of all the problems crowding the social policy agenda of the 1960s, only a few emerged originally because of such intense partisan scrutiny. (In comparing British and Swedish housing policy, Headey (1977) argues that 'Labour have not sought to play an agenda-setting role and, by default, have allowed issues to be defined mainly by interests concerned to expand the . . . market.' While the evidence here generally points in the same direction, two qualifications are critical. First, while parties do not play a comprehensive agenda-setting role, they at least do so intermittently. Secondly, those who set the broader social policy agenda are not universally dedicated to expanding market relations.)

If social issues are only occasionally defined by politicians, their salience is always decided by them. Party ideology and electoral calculations were the twin forces at work in the policies considered here. If both party attitudes and electoral opinion pointed in the same direction, the result was decisive. Rent legislation was placed high on the agenda because Labour was emotionally committed to it and the issue provided electoral ammunition; EPAs were low on the agenda because they had little support from either the party or the electorate. On the other hand, when party ideology and electoral calculations pulled in opposite directions, as in the Conservatives' rent policy and Labour's poverty policy, politicians were torn. Deliberations were agonized and halting; the issues were repeatedly deferred; the final outcomes were inelegant compromises.

The impact of politics on the specifics of policy is much more intermittent. Specific party traditions, such as Labour's dislike of means-testing, may be critical. But parties do not always have such concrete preferences. The Minister of Housing turned to others for ideas, and there was no specific Labour approach to primary education. Similarly, electoral considerations had an uneven impact. Possible public opposition to income redistribution was crucial in limiting the response to family poverty, and clawback was evolved to neutralize the immediate danger posed by the standard rate taxpayer. Yet in the case of the more politicized Rent Bill, professional advice outweighed electoral caution; and the electorate's impact on the details of EPA policy was all but non-existent.

One way of illustrating the intermittent impact of party politics is to ask how government policy would have differed if the Conservatives had been in power in the late 1960s. The question cannot be answered conclusively, of course, and the premise may be incorrect; Labour's victory in 1964 unleashed great expectations of social reform and contributed to the willingness of professionals to raise issues in the first place. But some sense of the probable differences can be gleaned from Conservatives' statements at the time and from their actions when they were in office after 1970.

The Conservatives might have given lower priority to social spending during the economic traumas of the second half of the decade. The evidence is ambiguous, however. Labour had come to power stating explicitly that social policy reforms depended on an improved economic performance, and certainly the party did not envisage a massive departure from the past. Indeed, when Brian Abel-Smith compared the Labour government's intentions, as set out in its *National Plan* for 1964–70, with the last six years of Conservative rule, he concluded that, even though the government assumed a similar rate of economic growth, it planned for a slower rate of growth in social expenditures than had already been achieved under the Conservatives (Abel-Smith, 1966). When economic performance proved poorer than assumed, the painful scaling down of expectations began. Whether the Conservatives would have gone much further is difficult to decide. Certainly the process would have been less agonizing for Conservatives; some cuts might have come earlier; and the selectivist approach to spending would have received an added boost. But whether the total level of social spending would have been markedly lower in 1970 is unclear.

Probable differences in specific policies are only slightly clearer. The Conservatives would undoubtedly have opted for the means-test approach to family poverty. They demanded it at the time and enacted it in 1970. But the other cases are more doubtful. A

Conservative government would probably have responded more warmly to the Plowden Report as a whole, but the form of EPA policy adopted would have been similar. The Conservatives agreed with the rejection of a centralized programme in 1967 and maintained the decentralized approach after 1970. The rent case is the most intriguing. The Conservatives were pledged to provide protection for tenants if Milner Holland called for it, and certainly the civil service expected a Conservative government to reintroduce some controls. The scope of the controls might well have been less extensive, limited perhaps to the major conurbations. But the Conservatives' initial reaction to Crossman's machinery, and their adoption of it in their own legislation on private rented housing in 1972, suggest that they were not fundamentally opposed; their major departure was to implement Crossman's policy more quickly than his Labour successors as Minister of Housing had done. The final irony is that in 1965 a Conservative government might have been uneasy about introducing such a flexible system, designed as it was to raise rents, for fear of a massive attack from the Labour opposition. Certainly Crossman was privately convinced that this was the case.

Governments often see their most cherished programmes destroyed by outside pressures, and to some extent the story of the 1960s is one of party aspirations overwhelmed by economic crisis. But the intermittent nature of party influence also reflects the weakness of parties as planning instruments. Even in opposition, parties cannot always translate their preferences into concrete proposals. They may fail to agree internally on controversial issues such as rents and take refuge in ambiguity, leaving the tough decisions to a future minister. In addition, the research resources available to an opposition party are limited. Mistakes can be made, leaving the basic ideas vulnerable to political ridicule and administrative objections, and necessitating painful retreats later. (Punnett, 1973, pp. 205–15 argues that these problems make detailed planning an unwise strategy for opposition parties.) The party also faces an uncertain future, and may fail to anticipate correctly which issues will dominate over the next decade: Labour had no agreed position on family poverty or compensatory education when it entered office because neither was yet perceived as an issue.

The problems of developing distinct party policies are increased in office. The burden falls squarely on the relevant ministers, who are often isolated from each other and the wider party. Herbison and Crosland did reflect broad party beliefs and priorities in their responses to family poverty and EPAs, but Crossman felt completely free to turn to non-party sources of inspiration. Party checks on ministerial choices are hardly consistent. The prime minister was not deeply interested in the issues examined here, and extensive Cabinet deliberations occurred only in cases of interdepartmental conflict, such as family poverty. In comparison, the initial response to the EPA proposal was settled without reference to the Cabinet; and the only other ministers deeply involved in drafting the Rent Bill, the Law Officers, served more as guardians of the norms of the legal community than of the traditions of the Labour party. The impact of the Parliamentary Labour Party (PLP) and the annual conference was even weaker. Clearly on a major issue the prime minister, Cabinet, parliamentary party and conference can challenge a minister, and the fact that there was no such challenge to the policies examined here suggests that the party was not in fundamental disagreement. But it is equally clear that ministers are left with broad scope for manoeuvre. Governments with clear policies can be blown off course by powerful outside forces. But the unevenness of party planning also allows many ministers to drift off by themselves.

The Administrative System
The British civil service is seen as pre-eminently responsive to political authority. This image of neutrality, however, masks the reality of its influence. The historical record repeatedly testifies to the importance of the civil service in the evolution of British social policy, and the policy patterns of the 1960s do likewise. But, like other policy determinants, the impact of the civil service varies sharply from one phase of the process to another.

The norm of administrative neutrality takes its greatest toll on the shaping of the social policy agenda; officials have little impact on which issues are raised and how salient they are thought to be. Public bureaucracies can, if they wish, mobilize impressive resources to monitor and interpret society. In postwar Britain, however, officialdom did not do so in the social policy field. Departments produced endless statistical reports on programmes under way, but the data reflected prevailing conceptions of need and did not identify new social trends or problems; they did not measure the growing stresses in the private rented sector, the extent of family poverty or class differentials in educational attainment. At best the information generated by such programmes drew attention to the possible existence of these problems. In the early 1960s the monthly figures on homelessness and the wage stop acted as crude barometers of social stress; but because the figures did not measure the problem comprehensively, their meaning was open to dispute, and they posed little threat to the free play of political imagination.

The civil service did little to supplement such information with more elaborate monitoring mechanisms. Only the DES had equipped itself with a powerful intelligence system. The Central Advisory Councils for Education (CACEs) brought professionals and academics closer to the department, and drew officials, who helped to prepare the reports, into the continuing process of social interpretation. Other departments lacked such facilities. They were less able to anticipate lines of public attack and were left with fewer defences when they came. Administrators had no data with which to assess charges about Rachmanism or family poverty and had to mount special research efforts in the form of the Milner Holland Committee and the survey of family incomes. Such ad hoc efforts can legitimate pressing concerns with official data, but they provide only snapshot views of social processes and their reliability quickly fades. In general, civil service research in the 1960s reacted to events rather than shaping them.

The weakness of civil service research reflected its importance. Research can greatly complicate a government's life by multiplying the number of options and factors to be juggled. As Keynes observed, 'There is nothing a government hates more than to be well-informed; for it makes the process of arriving at decisions much more complicated and difficult' (quoted in Sharpe, 1975, p. 19). Research can also be embarrassing. It can reveal the inadequacies of policies to which politicians are committed, as in the 1957 Rent Act survey. It can extend public consciousness of problems, like poverty, that governments cannot readily solve. And it can challenge the government's own priorities, in the way that the Plowden Report did. In such circumstances, governments of all parties seek to suppress research findings, as in the Rent Act survey, or to dispose of over-powerful research systems, as with the demise of CACEs. For the politician who wishes to maximize his own control over the policy agenda, judicious limits on the monitoring of policy are very tempting.

But such a strategy merely shifts initiative in social interpretation from public to private expertise. Much of the influence of the social scientists during the 1960s was a reflection of the lacunae in the information available to the civil service. The initiative relinquished extended beyond the simple awareness of problems. Outsiders incorporated their own perspectives and standards in their research and thereby shaped to a greater extent the prevailing definition of problems as well. For instance, one of the most significant shifts in postwar social debate was the spread of the relative conception of poverty: 'need' was redefined for public purposes by private actors. Administrators found their Supplementary Benefits line turned into a general poverty line and poverty turned into a recurring problem. Officials grumbled about this development, but having surrendered the initiative in social interpretation they were left with only technical arguments about how high the line actually should be.

During the 1970s, the balance between independent and civil service research appeared to be shifting as departments improved their information systems. If the information balance shifts significantly, so will the policy process. The change may make officials more sensitive to outside efforts; but more probably the capacity to influence the policy agenda through independent research will decline as the civil service builds stronger data defences. Research initiatives will increasingly reflect governmental and administrative priorities, and the crucial definition of categories and standards through which social problems are interpreted will settle more firmly into official hands. Either outside experts will be drawn into internal processes or they will be increasingly reduced to being critics of official statistics. The first of these alternatives can be seen in Donnison's chairmanship of the Supplementary Benefits Commission (cf. Donnison, 1982, ed.). The second can be seen in an exchange between Peter Townsend (1972) and the rejoinder by DHSS Statisticians (1972) (see also Townsend's remarks reported in Hoinville and Smith, 1982, p. 197, ed.).

During the 1960s officials also had little influence on the salience of issues. EPA policy received qualified departmental support which in the absence of external pressures or sustained ministerial interest, was important simply in keeping the idea alive. But, by themselves, officials could not create the drive for major action; they did not mount campaigns either for or against rent controls or for or against action on family poverty. Indeed, civil servants generally believed that issues had to be perceived as such in the political arena before they could move. (For a similar example in the field of racial discrimination, see Deakin, 1970, p. 111.) Comparison with his nineteenth-century counterpart suggests that the modern official has a smaller role in setting the social policy agenda, and at least one older official sensed such a change over the last four decades. 'Before the war civil servants would have written a stiff memorandum, indicating that action was essential. But today there is a greater tendency to sit back; there has been a real falling off in forcing unpopular issues on ministers.'

Administrators come into their own, however, as soon as the actual drafting of policy begins. Officials' most sensitive function is the specification of the alternatives to be presented to ministers. Only in the drafting of the Rent Bill was this function shared. That sharing was due to the stubborn insistence of an aggressive minister; and the initial resistance he encountered revealed the strength of officials' assumptions that formulating advice was ultimately their job. Innovative policy ideas tend to develop outside. But officials are critical in adapting ideas to political realities, and much depends on their sympathy. Acceptance of the proposals of Crossman's outsiders was greatly facilitated because the department generally agreed with the attitudes towards the private market that underlay them; the CPAG was fortunate that some of the senior officials in the Ministry of Social Security also disliked the means-tested option; and the EPA advocates were unfortunate that few officials were prepared to battle for the specifics of their proposal.

Officials do not limit themselves to advising ministers. They also try – albeit with infinite discretion – to mobilize outside support for their policies. Major orchestrations of political support are usually carried out by the minister; Crossman managed the public campaign prior to the introduction of the Rent Bill and Herbison activated the TUC and backbenchers during the Cabinet split over poverty. But administrators were also involved. It was an official of the Ministry of Social Security who contacted the CPAG and convinced them to support the ministry's compromise. Similarly the DES cajoled the National Union of Teachers into accepting the salary supplement, and guided Halsey in his contacts with their minister, in hopes of pushing nursery education at least some distance along the discriminatory path that they too wished to tread.

The administrative structures within which officials labour also have profound policy consequences and can, on occasion, transform social policy ideas out of all recognition. Governmental structures, in effect, create a set of channels within which central policy-makers can operate with relative ease. Trying to change the channels, or operate outside them, however, is far more complicated, requiring changes in standard procedures and conventions in Whitehall, changes in relations with outside groups, and sometimes changes in the law. Avoiding such costs should not be confused with simple bureaucratic inertia. For the most part, existing structures serve the government well, and even the most active bureaucrat or politician will pause before overturning a vast array of existing institutions and understandings simply in order to achieve specific, limited ends. He may finally choose to confront existing structures, but doing so can only generate additional opposition inside and perhaps outside Whitehall. There is a strong incentive to achieve the ends, if possible, through existing channels.

The patterning of the administrative structure is clearly evident with regard to the social policies of the 1960s. In the first place, divisions of administrative responsibility compartmentalized social policy. A functional division of responsibility takes the situation of a single social group such as the poor and divides it up between a number of departments and agencies. Social security, wages and employment, education and housing are all dealt with by separate departments, and the assumption of responsibility for a problem by one department effectively determines the range of policy responses considered. The fact that the Ministry of Social Security took up the family poverty issue ensured an income-transfer approach: regulation of the wage structure through a minimum wage or a social service approach such as community action fell outside the department's jurisdiction and were not even considered.

No co-ordinated discussion of the best approach to poverty ever occurred, simply because the relevant administrative structures did not facilitate it. (Compare this with the range of approaches considered by the non-departmental task force that drafted the American War on Poverty. See Sundquist and Schelling, 1969.) Different departments responded to the poor in their own way. The battle over linking tax allowances and family allowances reveals the obstacles facing even a limited integration of programmes managed by different departments. Such administrative pluralism is often counter-productive. For example, the accumulation of tax policies and means-tested benefits provided by various departments has created an unintended 'poverty trap'; families receiving such benefits can find that an increase in their earnings actually reduces their standard of living. In the 1970s Whitehall launched efforts to co-ordinate social policies more effectively, but the evidence of the 1960s suggests that the obstacles are daunting (CPRS, 1975).

Standard operating procedures within each department also have policy consequences. Officials prefer to use established capabilities wherever possible, and in the three cases examined here their strongest stands came in defence of what they saw as procedural propriety. In the family poverty case, the family allowance approach was an administratively attractive option simply because the programme already existed; and the Inland Revenue's opposition to the use of the tax system for social purposes, together with the

Treasury's insistence on the prerogatives of the budget, generated great heat in the struggle. The EPA proposal was even more profoundly transformed to fit the administrative framework. DES sensitivity to the discretion of Local Education Authorities (LEAs) doomed the national programme; the building recommendation achieved a prominence never intended by its original authors while administratively more difficult parts of the package faded into the background; and at a later stage Halsey's hybrid nursery centres lost out to the existing schools structure.

Creating new administrative machinery provides greater flexibility, but it is a major task not lightly undertaken by officialdom. The Ministry of Housing did set up new machinery to regulate rents, but only when convinced that no alternative existed; and even then official nervousness about a possible administrative breakdown led to the system's almost surreptitious introduction. In addition, while new machinery does increase the room for manoeuvre, the escape from administrative norms is hardly complete. After a terrible row with his department, Crossman compromised on how rent officers would be appointed; and it was the views of the Lord Chancellor's department on the judicial nature of regulation that were written into the legislation.

Clearly the 'neutral' civil service is a myth in two senses. Officials do have policy preferences which they seek to advance. And even if officials avoid such commitments the structure of the administrative system within which they operate still leaves its imprint on the policies of the nation.

Interest Groups

By comparison with parties and the civil service, interest groups played a secondary role in the politics of social policy in the 1960s. The poor were not organized at all: they did not force their plight on to the political agenda, and policy did not change in response to their demands. Throughout the decade, the 'poor' remained a statistical category rather than a social group, with their numbers varying between two and seven million depending on the personal inclinations of the statistician. Similarly, the category of 'educationally deprived' took its meaning from the definitions of social scientists rather than the consciousness of the beneficiaries. As Robert Pinker has argued, it is possible that most of the people diagnosed as deprived are 'far less aware of their condition and far less ideologically motivated by it than those who undertake the diagnoses' (1971, p. 114). Certainly by comparison with the more affluent and politically aggressive sections of the community, the poor could be ignored with impunity. Those who stood to suffer from social policy were more vocal but not always more effective. Land-lords did have organizational representatives but their impact on the 1965 Rent Act was minimal. The financial costs of other policies such as income transfers and social services fell primarily on the taxpayer. The constraint from middle-income taxpayers was real, but they were imposed via politicians' electoral calculations rather than by means of organized groups.

Nor was social policy the product of a clash between the great peak organizations, the TUC and the CBI. British trade unions have long concentrated on economic issues and, while they are consulted on changes in income transfer programmes, the initiatives generally come from elsewhere. The only important TUC intervention in the cases examined here – the opposition to the means test – was orchestrated by the Minister of Social Security. Business and labour were, of course, deeply involved in the central issues of economic management, which had a powerful indirect impact on social policy. But a pattern of direct bargaining between the government and peak organizations over the specifics of social policy did not emerge in this period. In comparison with economic policy, governments are far less constrained by group action, and the enthusiasms and intolerances of party and public have freer rein.

The influence of professionals sometimes does flow through group action. The CPAG was essentially a social science group in its origins, leadership and information sources, and its success has stimulated similar groups dedicated to social policy reform. These groups, however, have few sanctions to impose on governments. Like individual social scientists, they can raise and define problems and options; but their final impact on policy depends on the receptiveness of others more powerfully placed. The professionals with the greatest independent power over social policy are those who staff the social services, such as doctors, teachers and, to a lesser extent, social workers. Their co-operation or at least compliance is important to government, and this fact gives them power. Certainly opposition from the National Union of Teachers was sufficient to reshape important parts of the EPA proposal.

But, overall, social policy was not the product of clashes between organized groups. In fact, as the family poverty case demonstrates, groups were as often adjuncts to the real contenders inside govern-ment as they were independent sources of policy direction. Obstacles to social policy reform did exist, and aspirations for social change were often blunted. But most often the opposition took the form of estimates in the minds of policy-makers rather than organized groups treading the corridors of power.

II

Types of Research Utilization

4

Types of Research Utilization: an Overview

The application of social science research to social policy inescapably involves considerations of social research methodology. Indeed, the principal claim to expertise of social policy researchers lies in their methodological competence, which is a necessary condition for carrying out effective and utilizable research. Without a sound methodological basis, such research can enjoy little credibility. Assessment of the methodological soundness of a piece of applied research is an essential first step on the road to utilization.

Consider three examples. Starting in 1983, the London social research organization Social and Community Planning Research has mounted an annual survey of *British Social Attitudes* (Jowell and Airey, 1984; Jowell and Witherspoon, 1985). A random sample of the population are questioned in depth, using reliable and tested survey instruments, about their views upon current social issues. The focus is upon attitudes and values rather than behaviour (which is extensively covered in the government's General Household Survey). Consider one finding from the survey's 1984 report, shown in Table 4.1. The outstanding priorities for additional public spending by government were health and education, with help for industry third and housing fourth. These findings are also consistent with other work, in the tradition of subjective social indicators (see ch. 7) which sought to establish whether there existed a clear order of priority preferences for different aspects of social well-being. These showed that in all cases health was ranked first (Hall, 1976; Knox, 1976a; 1978). The *British Social Attitudes* findings were at odds with the government's spending priorities at the time, which gave highest priority to defence and the police, which appear sixth and seventh in the list. In interpreting these survey results and judging their relevance and importance for policy debates, one must form some assessment of their reliability and validity. Such attitude statements are particularly likely to fluctuate according to the sponsorship of the survey, the way in which the question is asked and the circumstances under which the survey is carried out. The *British Social Attitudes* survey is carried out in a scrupulously scientific manner, but not all survey and polling data on social attitudes can be taken at face value. This is discussed further in Chapter 6.

Table 4.1   *First and Second Priorities for Extra Government Spending as Seen by the British Public in 1983*

Q.   Here are some items of government spending. Which of them, if any, would be your highest priority for extra spending, and which next? Please read through the whole list before deciding.

	First priority	*First and second priority*
	(%)	*(%)*
Health	37	63
Education	24	50
Help for industry	16	29
Housing	7	20
Social security benefits	6	12
Defence	4	8
Police and prisons	3	8
Roads	2	5
Public transport	1	3
Overseas aid	<1	1
(Sample size)	(1,761)	(1,761)

Source: Jowell and Airey (1984), pp. 77, 98–9.

In the example in Table 4.1 health came out as the highest priority. There is also considerable social science evidence that the incidence of disease and the provision of health care is unequally distributed (Townsend and Davidson, 1982). In the mid-1970s, the British government was concerned that resources within the National Health Service should be distributed more equitably between health regions to take account of differing patterns of health need in different parts of the country. It set up the Resource Allocation Working Party (RAWP), which reported in 1976. This recommended a formula for reallocating central government expenditure between regions, a major element in which was a measure of the need for health care. The working party was composed chiefly of technical specialists, who examined the available social indicators of health need. They distinguished between inputs to and outputs from the health services. The usual indicators of health provision used in previous work were in fact outputs, the results of the existing allocation of resources, such as doctors per patient, bed utilization rates in hospitals, availability of certain high-technology equipment, and so on. But these were not a measure of the state of health of the population prior to service provision, the 'input' to the service. To measure this they used as an indicator of need standardized mortality ratios for each health region in the country. These they considered the most satisfactory general health indicator, and one which reflected the existing regional differentials which their recommended formula was designed to modify. Few commentators upon RAWP have been able to fault this use of the indicator, but it is the king-pin upon which their analysis rests (taking account also of population size and the age and sex structure of the population). Problems of constructing and using social indicators are considered further in Chapter 7.

A quite different example of the importance of methodological assessment is provided by qualitative research upon socially deprived working-class families. Both in North America and Britain there is considerable policy interest in the social situation of such families and the need to frame effective policies to alleviate their problems is widely recognized. First, however, the nature of those problems must be understood. Two theoretical approaches have been widely held. In the United States, theories building upon the 'culture of poverty' have been popular, holding that poverty is a way of life, with distinct behavioural and attitudinal characteristics such as a fatalistic, present-oriented immediate gratification pattern, marital instability, a high proportion of one-parent families, and insecure low-paid employment. This theory has also been exposed to severe criticism (cf. Lewis, 1966; Leacock, 1971). In Britain the most important series of comparable studies have been concerned with the 'cycle of deprivation', the idea that poverty and disadvantage are passed on from one generation to another from inadequate parents, using inadequate child-rearing practices to bring up emotionally, socially and intellectually deprived children. These children fail at school, become unemployed or at best get unskilled jobs, establish unstable marriages and family lives, live in poor housing, and pass on these disadvantages to their children. This theory was put forward in 1972 by Sir Keith Joseph when Secretary of State for Social Services, and formed the basis of a large research programme by the (UK) Social Science Research Council (Brown and Madge, 1982).

Two qualitative studies which cast considerable doubt on these theories are Carol Stack's study of social support among black families (1974) and Frank Coffield *et al.*'s study of four English deprived families (Coffield, Robinson and Sarsby, 1980). Each is based upon a study in depth of a small number of cases, building up a detailed and theoretically informed picture of how they live, and showing that the difficulties they experience in their social circumstances are not explicable in the way that the theories postulate. What confidence can one have in such small-scale research? To what extent can these results be generalized? Would another social scientist who spent a similar amount of time with such families record similar information and produce similar findings (that is, are the results reliable)? These questions are considered further in Chapter 9, but they are another reminder that the methodology of research with potential policy applications has to be scrutinized carefully.

These examples point to the form taken by the second part of this book, an examination of the different types of methodology used in policy research. For it is only if these can be assessed effectively and critically that one can hope to take an informed approach to the social utility of social science. Six main approaches will be considered: (1) continuous social surveys providing behavioural data about the national population; (2) studies of social and political attitudes and their pitfalls, particularly opinion polls; (3) social indicators; (4) social impact assessment; (5) evaluation research and social experimentation; (6) qualitative policy research. This is not an exhaustive list, but it embraces the main types of method used in applied research. This way of distinguishing between styles of research places the main emphasis upon the methodology used.

An earlier classification (Bulmer, 1978, pp. 8–9), which remains useful, distinguished between intelligence and monitoring, basic, strategic and tactical research, and action research. The six approaches discussed in this section can be classified in this way, but it may be more useful to consider two main dimensions of difference. One is whether research is diagnostic or future-oriented. Does it seek to analyse what has gone before, or provide pointers to future action? Continuous surveys aim to do both, as do social indicators. Evaluative research is implicitly highly future-oriented, qualitative research primarily diagnostic. Different objectives are embodied in different types of inquiry. They are not all of a piece.

An even more useful distinction is between descriptive, explanatory and evaluative research. Descriptive research seeks to present a factual account relevant to the determination of policy. It can provide estimates of distributional characteristics of some policy-relevant phenomenon, and monitor changes in those characteristics over time. Both continuous surveys and social indicators may perform this task effectively. Explanatory research seeks to understand or account for the attitudes or behaviour observed, for example to explain why inequalities in health or poverty exist and persist. Evaluative research seeks to test the consequences of the adoption of particular courses of action, for example, to test which different type of penal treatment, or medical treatment, or educational programme, is most effective. Evaluative research, it must be made clear in relation to earlier discussion, does not mean research which is value-laden or prescriptive in intent. It means research designed and carried out in a scientific manner to assess the efficacy of particular policy measures in practice.

The distinction between the three is not an entirely hard and fast one. No piece of empirical research is ever an unvarnished account of 'the facts', and the idea of a 'theory-free' description is untenable. All social description involves conceptualization and measurement in which classification takes place in terms of more general categories, for example income, or disability or social class (Bulmer, 1982, pp. 51–8, 68–79). Explanatory research may sometimes be evaluative, if it focuses purely upon the variables susceptible to manipulation by policy-makers. In general, however, the threefold distinction is a tenable one.

Applied here to the six types of research methodology, continuous social surveys and studies of social attitudes are usually descriptive, though their results may be subjected to explanatory secondary analysis by others. Social indicators and social impact assessment are descriptive with evaluative implications, which may or may not be spelled out. Evaluative research and social experimentation, as their name implies, are evaluative in intent and effect. Qualitative research is usually descriptive and explanatory, with an emphasis on the latter. This section is thus weighted somewhat towards descriptive and evaluative research methodologies. To correct this imbalance, the book also contains other material emphasizing the explanatory aims of applied research and the pitfalls in its path. Part III of the book looks directly at the role of theory in policy research, with reference to explanatory research.

The ways in which social science research can impinge upon policy-making may now be considered in more detail in relation to a particular example, inequalities in health in the British National Health Service (NHS). The RAWP exercise discussed earlier was part of this process of inquiry, but the subject is a much broader one with a longer history. This case-study also demonstrates clearly the different dimensions to research upon any particular policy issue.

The NHS was established in 1948 to provide a unified and

co-ordinated health service for all citizens, available free of charge without distinction to those in need of health care. Yet the implications which the new system would have for health inequalities were not at the outset thought through. Though the service was based on the principal of equal access for equal need, this was reflected more in the form of the service than as a policy objective which was actively pursued: 'there seems to have been a naive belief that if there were no financial barriers to health care, then the neediest would make the most demands and receive the most services' (Maynard and Ludbrook, 1982, p. 109). In fact, if anything the reverse happened, if one accepts the formulation in Tudor Hart's inverse care law: 'the availability of good medical care tends to vary inversely with the need of the population served' (1971). Some effort was consistently made to achieve a more equitable geographical distribution of general practitioners (GPs), and by means of financial incentives and certain controls to achieve a greater equalization of patient list sizes. In relation to social class inequalities, less was done.

Even so, it came as a surprise to many policy-makers when in the 1970s it was pointed out that 'despite thirty years of "the welfare state", the differences in mortality rates between social classes are, if anything, getting wider rather than narrower' (Abel-Smith, 1978, p. 52). The findings on which such a statement was based are shown in Table 4.2. Both the RAWP exercise and the deliberations of the Working Group on Inequalities in Health chaired by Sir Douglas Black (Black Report, 1980; Townsend and Davidson, 1982) were undertaken to examine resource distribution and patterns of need, RAWP in relation to geographical inequality and the Black group in relation to social inequality. In recent years, health inequality has consequently acquired a political salience, not just in a party political sense but as a contentious issue of resource allocation both nationally between and regionally within the NHS regional budgets.

The starting point of the study of health inequalities is a clearer specification of what one means by 'health', by conceptual clarification. Does one mean the absence of disease, or does one have in mind a more positive conception involving well-being? The former is embodied in the familiar medical model of health as the treatment of disease, the latter in the definition of health adopted by the World Health Organization, 'a state of complete physical, mental and social well-being and not merely the absence of disease and infirmity'. Conceptions of health and illness vary among different groups within a single society, between societies, and within a single society over time. Witness changing and differing views of cigarette smoking and

Table 4.2   Social Class Variations in Mortality, 1930–2, 1949–53 and 1970–2

| Occupational class | Standardized mortality ratio (SMR): men, England and Wales | | | | Infant deaths per 1,000 legitimate live births | | |
| | Ages 20–64 | | Ages 16–64 | | | | |
	1930–2	1949–53	1970–2	1970–2*	1930–2	1949–53	1970–2
I Professional	90	86	77	75	32	19	12
II Managerial	94	92	81	—	46	22	14
III Skilled manual and non-manual	97	101	104	—	59	28	16
IV Partly skilled	102	104	114	—	63	35	20
V Unskilled	111	118	137	121	80	42	31
IV as a percentage of I	113	121	148	—	197	184	166
V as a percentage of I	123	137	178	161	250	221	258

* Occupations reclassified according to 1950 classification
Source: Maynard and Ludbrook, 1982, p. 108, drawing on Brotherston, 1976, Black Report, 1980 and Office of Population Censuses and Surveys, 1978.

its impact upon health. Hence 'illness behaviour' – the response to symptoms and the subjective definition of these as indicating the need to seek medical assistance – varies between cultural and social groups. Health has a subjective as well as an objective side. Economists are also keen to distinguish between health *care*, the provision and delivery of a medical service, and health *status*, the condition of an individual which is the outcome of many factors of which care is only one (Grossman, 1972).

The study of inequalities in health also raises philosophical issues, particularly what is meant by inequality. Is inequality good or bad? In what senses is one using the term? To what extent is it the function of health services to influence existing patterns of inequality? There is a large general literature on this subject (cf. Tawney, 1931; Williams, 1962; Joseph and Sumption, 1979; Letwin, 1983), as well as specific literatures on equality of opportunity in education, income and wealth inequality and so on. Some of the concern about health inequality in fact relates to equity of treatment rather than equality of status. Both ideas of 'territorial justice' – that there should not be arbitrary geographical variation in the provision of services (Davies, 1968) – and of equality of access to health care regardless of social background are arguments for equity and fairness in the provision of services. Trying to equalize health status is much more problematical and contentious. A parallel with income differences will make this clear. All parts of the political spectrum are agreed that the state must make some basic income provision for those members of society who do not have the means of minimum subsistence. There is no agreement, on the other hand, whether an objective of taxation of income is to achieve redistribution between those with higher and those with lower incomes, that is, to achieve greater equality of condition. So it is with health.

Underpinning these different philosophical views of health inequality are theories of their causation and models for the analysis of health outcomes. Economists and sociologists, for example, disagree about the role of human agency, exemplifying Duesenberry's aphorism (1960, p. 22) that 'economics is all about how people make choices. Sociology is all about why they don't have choices to make.' Economists analysing health inequalities emphasize the influence upon the outcome of individual choice. Le Grand (1985), for example, views health as a stock of capital, which depreciates over time because of ageing and, sometimes, unavoidable illness. However, individuals can offset depreciation by appropriate investment in health-promoting activities, such as receiving medical treatment or taking exercise. They may affect health negatively by engaging in health-consuming activities such as smoking or hazardous employment. Health status is a product of individual decisions concerning health-investment and consumption.

Sociological theories of health inequality, on the other hand, emphasize the social production of health outcomes through material and cultural influences (see Hart, 1985). A striking example of material factors is McKeown's argument (1976a) that nineteenth-century population increase was explained less by the influence of medicine than by falling mortality rates due to rising standards of nutrition. Improvements in the quantity, quality and distribution of food were due, in turn, to industrial growth and economic expansion. Similarly, Winter (1977) has shown that during the First World War the general level of health of the British working class improved somewhat, in his view because of a reduction of poverty by government controls of food prices and rents, allowances for families of men in the armed services, expanded employment opportunities in war production, and guaranteed minimum wages. Infant mortality rates fell markedly in areas like northern industrial cities, where they had previously been highest. There was no comparable change in more affluent areas in southern England. Inequalities in life chances, in other words, have an important influence upon inequalities of health status.

Cultural factors in health inequalities refer to the ways in which beliefs, ideas and activities of social groups act as risk factors in health outcomes. Patterns of behaviour are seen not as the outcome of rational calculation but of collective group ideologies and beliefs which override individual calculation of cost and benefit. Thus two findings of research, that mothers in lower social classes are less likely to seek antenatal care, and that men and women in lower social classes are less likely to have given up smoking, may be explained in terms of cultural factors rather than individual rational choice. Smoking patterns, for example, reflect the fact that smoking is culturally valued behaviour, that it has more value as a cultural symbol for working-class than for middle-class youth, and that the socialization of the middle classes makes them better equipped to respond to the idea that smoking is bad for health (Hart, 1985).

These issues of conceptualization and explanation are pursued further in Part III, and especially in Chapter 12 by Stuart Blume. They are raised here to show that even apparently straightforward descriptive research exercises mapping the extent of health inequality have theoretical implications which need to be considered carefully at the outset. Consideration of such issues, however, can only take one so far. At some stage, indicators of particular concepts have to be chosen, and empirical evidence relating to the phenomena with which one is concerned assembled and analysed. It is to this process that the following chapters in this section are addressed.

Empirical inquiry into health inequalities requires that one can first find empirical measures of both 'health' and 'inequality'. Health can conveniently be considered in terms of mortality and of morbidity (the incidence of ill health in a living population). Mortality may be measured by death as recorded on the death certificate, which includes in Britain information about the age, sex and occupation of the deceased and the medical causes of death. Morbidity may be measured in various objective and subjective ways: the extent of sickness absence from work, for example, or the number of patients presenting to GPs or hospital out-patient departments, or the occupancy of hospital beds, or self-reported illness. In general terms, the most widely used measure of the health status or state of health of a geographical or social group (such as a region or a social class) has been the objective measure of the standardized mortality ratio (which treats the mortality ratio of the total population as 100, and represents the varying mortality experience by sex, region or social class as ratios above or below 100). Thus the higher ratios of lower social class shown in Table 4.2 indicate a worse mortality experience and shorter expectation of life; the lower ratios for higher social classes indicate a better mortality experience, comparative to other classes, and a longer life expectation. The measurement of the need for health care is more problematic, since most of the objective measures concern outputs from the health services rather than inputs. Since very little data is collected by the NHS itself on the occupation or social class of patients, the main source on class differences in health care since 1971 has been the General Household Survey, which is now the main source on morbidity in the population. This provides data on GP consultation and hospital visits within a reference period, but also on self-reported sickness (whether or not a doctor was consulted). These data have been of particular value in examining social class inequalities in morbidity.

Some 'inequality' in health is geographical, and the definition of geographical areas to be compared is unproblematical. *Social* inequality is more complex, and has usually been defined in terms of social classes, 'segments of the population sharing broadly similar types and levels of resources, with broadly similar styles of living' (Townsend and Davidson, 1982, p. 47). Though other factors such as income, wealth, education, housing type or consumption pattern arguably play a part in determining a person's class position, the usual operational definition of a person's social class has been in terms of occupation (either their own or that of the head of their household). This is both because occupation summarizes several of the other characteristics, bearing quite a close relation to education and some relation to income, and is a conveniently available measure. Social classes are defined operationally by OPCS in its decennial *Classification of Occupations* (the latest is OPCS 1980), in which six social classes are distinguished, three non-manual and three manual. These are:

I   Professional (for example, doctor, lawyer).
II   Intermediate (including managers and administrators; for example, manager, middle-rank civil servant, nurse, school-teacher).
IIIN   Skilled (or junior) non-manual (for example, clerical worker, secretary, shop assistant).
IIIM   Skilled manual (for example, carpenter, electrician, butcher, bus driver, coal-face worker).
IV   Partly skilled manual (for example, agricultural worker, bus conductor, postman).
V   Unskilled manual (for example, cleaner, dock worker, labourer).

This is the social class breakdown used in Table 4.2. An alternative, slightly different OPCS classification is used in the General Household Survey, in terms of Socio-Economic Groups (SEG), but the six condensed SEG groups correspond very approximately to the Registrar-General's Social Classes, the older of the two OPCS classifications.

Empirical research designed to investigate health inequalities uses these operational definitions to investigate the health status of and health care received by the population. It is not feasible to cover here all the types of research dealt with in the following chapters, but three will be highlighted: continuous surveys, social indicators and qualitative studies. Among continuous surveys the General Household Survey is of pre-eminent importance for health policy. It yields data, for example, on smoking habits in the population which shows a consistent downward trend in smoking; for men from 52 per cent of respondents in 1972 to 36 per cent in 1984 and for women from 42 per cent in 1972 to 32 per cent in 1984. One of the most interesting findings has been the continued marked class difference in smoking habits, shown in Table 4.3. More than twice as many male unskilled manual workers smoke as professional workers; twice as many female unskilled manual workers smoke as female professional workers. The table also shows sex differences: more women have never or only occasionally smoked, and rather fewer women overall smoke than men. It does not show what is apparent from other data, that social class differences are widening. Smoking by men and women in professional classes declined by half between 1972 and 1984, whereas among unskilled manual workers it declined by only 15 per cent for men and 6 per cent for women (see Table 10.1 below).

Table 4.3   *Cigarette Smoking by Sex and Socio-Economic Group, Great Britain, 1984*

| | | Current non-smokers | | |
| | Current smokers | Ex-regular smokers | Never or only occasionally smoked | Base (= 100%) |
Socio-economic group	(%)	(%)	(%)	
MEN				
Professional	17	34	49	448
Employers and managers	29	37	34	1,413
Intermediate and junior non-manual	30	29	41	1,384
Skilled manual	40	31	29	3,063
Semi-skilled manual	45	27	28	1,350
Unskilled manual	49	21	30	478
All aged 16 and over	36	30	34	8,417
WOMEN				
Professional	15	21	64	384
Employers and managers	29	21	50	1,487
Intermediate and junior non-manual	28	17	55	2,436
Skilled manual	37	17	45	2,585
Semi-skilled manual	37	16	47	1,864
Unskilled manual	36	16	48	518
All aged 16 and over	32	17	51	9,788

Source: General Household Survey, Cigarette smoking: 1972 to 1984, *OPCS Monitor Series*, GHS 85/2 (OPCS, 1985).

The GHS thus provides objective evidence of health status which is relevant to the formulation of policies for the reduction of health inequality. It also permits comparisons to be made between health status and health care by comparing need with use, combining both subjective and objective data. The data from the GHS on self-reported illness is subjective in the sense that it records illness as perceived by the respondent themselves. Given the relative absence of social class data on morbidity other than the GHS (there is, for example, no regular source of class-related information on the use of British hospital services), it would be very difficult to provide evidence of the need for health care in different social classes if the GHS did not exist. The GHS also records information about GP consultations, so that use can be compared with need.

Table 4.4 shows the clear class gradient in self-reported illness. Table 4.5, which is slightly more complex, permits a comparison between these data and data on GP consultation rates. Focusing on the most disadvantaged groups, the semi- and unskilled manual working class, it shows the rates for these groups compared to that in the professional classes which is standardized as 100. So, for example, women in the semi-skilled manual group had 1.78 times the acute sickness of women in the professional class, and men 1.44 times the equivalent male rate. Two measures of acute sickness are provided, the second in terms of days per person per year, which shows a greater class differential than if the comparison is confined to a reference period of two weeks prior to the interview.

Table 4.4   *Reported Illness by Socio-Economic Group, Great Britain, 1976*

Socio-economic group	Percentage of group reporting acute illness, chronic illness or both	Base (= 100%)
Professionals	17.0	1,535
Employers and managers	18.7	4,536
Intermediate and junior non-manual	22.9	6,544
Skilled manual	21.9	11,448
Semi-skilled manual	25.5	6,053
Unskilled manual	32.1	1,717

Source: Le Grand, 1982, p. 38, using unpublished data from the General Household Survey 1976.

Table 4.5 then shows differentials in long-standing illness, which apart from semi-skilled females are somewhat greater than for acute sickness in the previous fourteen days, and limiting long-standing illness (which restricts the respondent's activities), where the class differential is higher, between 1.9 and 3.1 times the rate for the professional class. Given this higher rate of self-reported sickness, comparison may then be made with consultation rates for persons

Table 4.5   *Indicators of Ill Health: Rates for Partly Skilled and Unskilled Persons Expressed as a Percentage of Persons in the Professional Class (Professional Class Rates = 100 in All Cases), 1979*

Indicator	Semi-skilled manual		Unskilled manual	
	Females	Males	Females	Males
Acute sickness (restricted activity during previous fourteen days)	178	144	178	156
Acute sickness (days per person per year of restricted activity)	248	215	273	250
Long-standing illness	183	158	217	179
Limiting long-standing illness	244	190	311	230
GP consultations				
persons consulting	167	120	167	130
number of consultations	167	130	160	120

Source: Townsend and Davidson, 1982, p. 21, using data from *General Household Survey 1979* (GHS, 1981, pp. 117–23).

and by number of consultations. If the latter is taken, the differential in the rates for men is considerably below the differentials for all but acute sickness in the previous fourteen days, where it is slightly below, while for women the same pattern is evident except for long-standing illness among semi-skilled women, where the differentials are closer together. The differentials for unskilled women are particularly marked. In all cases, the consultation rate differential is below that for the incidence of sickness. The general conclusion to be drawn is that general practitioner consultation rates do not match the apparently greater need for health care of the semi- and unskilled manual working class. This conclusion is demonstrated by means of survey data from the GHS.

Table 4.5 refers to 'indicators' of ill health, and the term is used to denote empirical categories, by means of which a concept is measured. It has, however, broader connotations, as Michael Carley explains in Chapter 7. This chapter provides a useful introduction to a major field of endeavour, previously reviewed in Bulmer (1978, pp. 201–67) and in Carley (1981), as well as in a range of recent publications (for example, de Neufville, 1975; Land, 1983; MacRae, 1985). In a thoughtful earlier article, Hope (1978) has reflected upon some of the characteristics of indicators and their relationship to the social sciences. The prime interest here is in how indicators may be used in the policy-making process (see Rose, 1972) where again health provides an illuminating example (see also Culyer, 1983).

The search for global indicators of health is nicely exemplified by the RAWP exercise mentioned at the beginning of the chapter. The RAWP review sought a compressed, single, objective measure of regional differences in need for health which could be incorporated into a formula for resource allocation and would be put to practical use. It was therefore required to be robust, comprehensive in coverage, and not open to serious criticism on technical grounds. The use of GHS morbidity data was considered and rejected, partly because of problems of small sample size when broken down regionally, lack of fit with NHS boundaries, and a concern that differences in levels of self-reported sickness may be due in part to differences in the perception and reporting of sickness. (This effect may mean that the social class data quoted in Tables 4.4 and 4.5 actually *under*estimates class differences, if the propensity of those in lower social classes to describe themselves as ill is lower, which there is some reason to believe.)

The RAWP group also considered using statistics derived from the payment of sickness benefit which could be compiled for NHS regions. They rejected these because they did not apply to the whole population, but excluded the elderly, children and many married women, and because some of the regional difference could be attributed to differences in industrial structure. An alternative indicator which might have been used was regional in-patient and out-patient caseloads, but these were not sufficiently independent of the supply of health services. Nor do caseloads distinguish between degrees of need, or throw light on the extent to which need is unmet through lack of facilities. This indicator was too much dominated by supply of services, and was rejected.

The indicator finally adopted was regional standardized mortality ratios. Mortality statistics cover the whole population, are readily available, and of high reliability. The crude death rate shows marked regional variation. Mortality statistics were thus used as a proxy indicator of morbidity, on the argument that regional differences in morbidity explain the greater part of differences in mortality. The dead were thus used as a cross-section of the living to indicate regional differences in the need for care.

The final formula used in RAWP took account of the size of each regional population weighted by the age and sex structure and the standardized mortality ratios (SMRs). Since the demand for hospital services varies between conditions, specific SMRs were worked out for groups of conditions classified by underlying cause of death. The final factor taken into account was hospital bed utilization rates for each condition category, which vary considerably between conditions (for example, eye complaints compared to types of cancer). The resulting formula was robust enough to become a major tool for the redistribution at the margin of resources between, and later within, regions.

A very different style of research is represented by smaller-scale, more qualitative inquiries in policy research. These are discussed in Chapter 9. One example will be briefly mentioned here from the health field, bearing on the subject of health inequalities. It is an elegant study by Janet Askham entitled *Fertility and Deprivation* (1975). She interviewed ninety working-class families in Aberdeen to test certain theories about the connection between social circumstances and size of family. Her design involved a comparison between large families of four or more children in social class V (V4+) with small families of two children in social class III (III2), but in addition she looked at small families of two children in social class V (V2) and large families of four or more children in social class III (III4+). She could thus compare families of different size in the same social class and families of the same size in the upper and lower working class, as well as the polar groups III2 and V4+.

Although the study was survey based, the numbers involved were small: 30 in III2, 25 in III4+, 18 in V2 and 17 in V4+. The analysis of the data relies upon interpretation of case-studies and individual experiences as well as upon numerical distributions. The interest of the study lies less in the descriptive results, which are on a very small scale, than in the exploration of theories to explain deprivation. Why do some poor couples have large families which are greater than their resources can comfortably support? Askham tests several alternative theories, but two will be examined here: the cultural and the situational. The cultural is based on Oscar Lewis's 'culture of poverty' and posits a separate system of values and norms among the lower working class, whose characteristics include marginality, helplessness, inferiority, present-time orientation, inability to plan for the future, and so on. One reflection of this is larger families than the average. A situational explanation, on the other hand, suggests that groups are distinguished mainly by their lack of resources or social deprivation. Economic position – generalized command over goods and services in the long term – is important, as is lack of educational and occupational opportunity, lack of political power and lack of social status.

Askham concluded on the basis of her data that cultural factors could not explain differences in family building patterns. On the other hand, situational factors *did* seem to provide an explanation.

The two extreme groups, III2 and V4+, were markedly different in the extent of their experience of deprivation and insecurity. The critical factor seemed to be the type and level of stability of occupation held, with antecedent experiences of deprivation predisposing to particular types of occupation. When deprivation is low, orientations developed which emphasize thought for the future, planning one's life and concern for material achievement. When deprivation is extensive, orientations developed which were present-oriented, more passively accepting, and less attuned to striving for material achievement. Hence this type of inequality of health outcome seemed to owe more to material circumstances and social experience than to cultural attitudes and values held. This example is of the more explanatory use of research in probing health inequalities, a theme returned to in Part III.

The aim of this chapter has been to preview the chapters which follow and to give an overview of types of research utilization. Much of this has been by means of a specific example: social and geographical inequalities in health status and health service use. The intention is to give the reader a sense of a real policy problem which matters, socially and politically, and to which research is capable of contributing important and in some cases decisive data. The focus in the ensuing chapters is necessarily somewhat more methodological, but the procedures which are discussed are in all cases capable of relevant and direct application to policy arenas, even if in doing so the social scientist must retain a keen critical judgement.

5

Continuous Social Surveys: Monitoring Social Change and Analysing Interrelationships

Governments have traditionally relied upon three main sources of statistics. These are population censuses, civil registration of births, marriages and deaths, and statistics produced as a by-product of administrative processes. The census, for example, goes back to 1790 in the United States and 1801 in Britain. Civil registration began in 1837 in Britain. Each of these sources has its strengths and limitations. Civil registration is complete and highly reliable, since it is virtually impossible to conceal a birth or death, but the data are of limited interest and primarily used by demographers. Censuses provide 100 per cent coverage of the population (with a slight margin of error), giving a snapshot picture of the demographic and selected social characteristics of the population once every ten years. Their main limitations are that the topic coverage is severely limited (in the British census, major variables such as income or ethnic group have never been included) and that results rapidly become out of date. The problems of administrative data are greatest: lack of fit between the categories used and those of the social scientist; uncertain reliability due to their collection by junior officials; lack of consistency of definition; coverage determined primarily by administrative arrangements; and 'missing data' for those who do not fall within the official orbit (cf. Morgenstern, 1960; Bulmer, 1980b).

Since the Second World War, policy-makers have increasingly come to rely upon social surveys as an additional source of data. The Government Social Survey in Britain (now part of OPCS) and the Bureau of the Census in the United States have developed considerable capacities, and in addition much research is nowadays commissioned for policy purposes by government from academic survey research centres, such as the Institute of Social Research at the University of Michigan and the National Opinion Research Center at the University of Chicago in the United States and Social and

Community Planning Research (SCPR) in the United Kingdom (cf. McKennell, Bynner and Bulmer, 1987). Examples of the sort of ad hoc survey conducted are very various. In two recent years in Britain OPCS Social Survey Division published studies for other government departments on smoking attitudes and behaviour, smokers among secondary school children, recently moving households, women and employment, registration with GPs in inner London, visiting museums, and the heights and weights of adults. Such data form part of the monitoring and intelligence function of social research, by which it contributes to policy formulation.

A more recent development has been the growth of continuous social surveys, also called annual or multi-purpose surveys, which are the subject of this chapter. The first such general-purpose survey appears to have been the Indian National Sample Survey, set up in 1950 at the instigation of the statistician P. C. Mahalanobis with the active support of Prime Minister Nehru (Murthy and Roy, 1983, p. 109). The oldest British continuous survey is the National Food Survey, which began in 1940, but better known to social scientists is the Family Expenditure Survey (FES), which began as the Household Expenditure Inquiry in 1953–4, and has been in continuous operation as the FES since 1957. As the name implies, it is a very detailed inquiry into patterns of household income and expenditure, the results of which were and are designed to improve the weighting pattern used in the General Index of Retail Prices. In addition the survey indicates how expenditure patterns of different types of household vary. It also throws light on the relationship between household income and circumstances of households, and the extent to which various members of a household contribute to its income. The survey can also provide estimates of the earnings of broad groups of individual members of households.

The most important multi-purpose continuous survey in Britain is the General Household Survey, carried out annually since 1971. This was explicitly designed as a multi-purpose inquiry for government departments, focusing on six main areas: population, family structure, housing, health, employment and education, with subsidiary topics included from time to time such as smoking, drinking, leisure, bus travel, or incidence of burglaries. Its aim was to provide a regular, updated picture of social conditions across a wide range of subject areas to assist in the formulation and examination of social policies. It aims to maintain a balance between continuity in the provision of trend data and responsiveness to new topical policy needs. Unlike the ad hoc surveys carried out by OPCS, the GHS is not problem-oriented but aims to provide a general statistical capability. Because it is continuous, it can measure changes over time, as in the example of cigarette smoking in the last chapter. For small sub-groups, data can be aggregated for more than one year to examine trends. It includes a wide variety of topics for individuals, families and households, so that different levels of aggregation can be used in analysis of its results. One of its most important characteristics is that data can be linked, to examine the relationship between different conditions and factors, for example, health, housing and social class position. This is something which individual government depart-ments (e.g. DHSS, DoE) are unable to do either because they lack comprehensive data or because of confidentiality constraints upon linkage with data held by other departments. Thus in the GHS, different subject areas can be interlinked, and social conditions examined in relation to face-sheet characteristics, as in the example of social class and health in the previous chapter. Although the bulk of questions remains unchanged from year to year, because the survey is an annual one demands on it can change from year to year and it can provide a flexible response by including questions which its customer departments request.

A typical ad hoc social survey for a policy purpose may have a sample size between two and four thousand. These are averages; occasionally surveys are larger or smaller. The continuous surveys are larger. The FES for some years had a sample size of 11,000 and the GHS a set sample of 15,000 households, recently reduced to 12,000, with a response rate between 81 and 84 per cent. This size of sample is necessary in order to obtain usable cell sizes when variables are cross-tabulated. Even then, representation of some social minorities such as one-parent families or ethnic groups may be so small that data has to be aggregated for two or three years to produce satisfactory results. This is done, for example, for the data in Table 5.1 below.

One other continuous survey, which has a much larger sample size, should be mentioned. This is the Labour Force Survey (LFS) which began in 1973 as part of the UK's participation in the statistical programme of the European Economic Community. It is somewhat analogous to the American Current Population Survey (CPS), which dates back to 1947 and is used, among other things, to provide monthly estimates of the proportion of the American labour force which is unemployed. For some years the LFS was biennial, carried out at one point in time (rather than on a continuous basis) to obtain comprehensive information on key sectors of the labour force. In 1981 a set sample size of 105,000 households (approximately half of 1 per cent of all households) yielded 85,000 responding households. From 1984, the design has changed (White, 1983). The LFS has become an annual survey, with two elements, aimed to produce both good 'point in time' estimates of labour-force characteristics and to measure changes in these characteristics as they occur. This aim is met by an annual survey in the spring of each year yielding about 45,000 responding households, and a continuous survey throughout the year with some 15,000 responding households per quarter, 60,000 for the full year. In the continuous survey, each responding household will be included for five quarters, so there will only be 3,000 new households per quarter. For the recalls to the other 12,000, approximately 70 per cent will be made by telephone from the OPCS office at Titchfield in Hampshire.

This is a considerable innovation for government surveys, though the use of telephone interviewing is growing, particularly in the United States (see Dillman, 1978; Groves and Kahn, 1979; Frey, 1983). It is possible because the LFS schedule is much shorter and less complex than that for the GHS or LFS. The primary purpose of the LFS is to provide internationally comparable statistics on the size and structure of the labour force. It also permits accurate comparisons to be made in unemployment levels between Britain and other countries, since statistics of registered unemployed persons are not comparable with those in other countries (Hakim, 1982, pp. 115–16). Because of the large sample size, topics and variables such as unemployment and ethnic origin can be analysed more adequately than in FES or GHS data. Like the GHS, though in a more limited way because of the shorter schedule, information on the social characteristics of households and people can be related to their behaviour in the labour market.

The importance and authority of the data obtained in these continuous surveys derive not only from their comprehensiveness, the relatively large sample sizes, or the high standards of their field-work conducted by OPCS Social Survey Division, but from the fact that they are nationally representative. Their sample designs are such that they give a nationally representative picture of social, economic and labour conditions in Britain, so that their results can be generalized (making allowance for a margin of sampling error) to the population as a whole. Thus when the GHS shows that over the 1970s there was virtually no change in the incidence of burglaries and thefts from private households or in the proportion of these offences reported to the police, the Home Office would be justified in extrapolating these results to the population nationally.

Between 1975 and 1983, the sample design of the General Household Survey was a two-stage design in which probability sampling methods were used to select electoral wards at the first stage, and addresses within wards at the second. At the outset of the sampling procedure, wards were stratified by seventeen regions (Wales, Scotland, London and south-east England being subdivided) and a distinction made between metropolitan and non-metropolitan counties (Glasgow being treated as a metropolitan county). Within region and area type, wards were then ranked by a socio-economic indicator, the proportion of heads of households in SEGs 1, 2, 3, 4, 5 and 13 (largely professional and managerial workers). Then the wards were divided into 168 strata of equal size. Within each of these 168 strata, wards were further ordered by the percentage of heads of households who were owner-occupiers. Four factors were thus used to stratify the sample: region, area type, a socio-economic indicator of social status, and housing type. The aim of such stratification is to take into account in the sample design of factors known to contribute to variation among the sample drawn, and thus to ensure that in respect of those characteristics the sample is more likely to be nationally representative than if a simple random sample of wards was taken.

When the 168 strata of wards had been formed and the wards ranked by housing type, four wards were selected from each strata in any given year, making 672 selections in all. Each ward was allocated to a quarter, and then to a month within that quarter, for fieldwork. Every year, one-third of the wards in the sample are replaced, so that in a given year one-third of wards were selected in that year, one-third in the previous year and one-third in the year before last.

At the second stage, twenty or twenty-five addresses were selected using probability methods from each ward (depending on whether the ward is part of a four- or five-week fieldwork cycle). A check was made to ensure that no address was selected more than once while the ward formed part of the first-stage sample. The addresses were then converted to households at the interview stage. Not all addresses are those of private households. In the 1980 GHS, for example, 14,563 addresses were selected of which 610 were demolished or derelict, empty or used solely for business purposes, and another 115 were institutions (such as hospitals, residential homes or boarding schools) which are excluded from the sample. There were thus 13,838 addresses containing domestic households. At most addresses there will be only one household, but for those where there are more, interviewers are given sampling rules to determine how many households to interview (GHS, 1982, p. 4). Thus in 1980 the total effective sample of households was 13,943, 105 above the eligible sample of addresses.

Since 1984, a new sample design has been introduced using the Postcode Address File, a computerized listing of all Post Office delivery points in the country broken down by postcode areas and subdivisions. A two-stage procedure was again used, using postal sectors (roughly similar in size to electoral wards) as the first stage units and delivery points (in effect, addresses) as the second stage units. In the 1984 survey, postal sectors were stratified in England and Wales according to the characteristics of the *districts* in which they lay. The stratification variables used were region and area type, socio-economic group of head of household, percentage of households renting from a local authority and percentage renting privately. For Scotland, sectors were classified according to *sector* characteristics, because an analysis of census variables by sector was available for Scotland (*OPCS Monitor*, GHS 85/1, July 1985, pp. 12–13).

The GHS sample is thus selected according to stringent probability methods. How good a response is achieved? Interviewers, when they have identified households, are instructed to interview all persons in the household over the age of 16. However, if one or more persons are difficult to contact, proxy interviews may be carried out about them with another responsible adult present in the household. The overall response rate to the GHS can be calculated on various bases. Including all households where an interview has been completed for all members of the household (but excluding households where at least one member could not be contacted or refused to allow even a proxy interview), the response rate has been steady at between 81 and 84 per cent in the period 1971 to 1984. For example, it was 82 per cent in 1980. Of the 18 per cent non-response in 1980, 13 per cent was due to refusal when contacted. A study in 1971 showed that refusals were disproportionately concentrated among the elderly and among the self-employed and unmarried men living on their own. There are also some regional variations in response rates, varying from 86 per cent in East Anglia and 85 per cent in Yorkshire and Humberside to 81 per cent in the West Midlands and 75 per cent in Greater London. Only the latter, however, is markedly out of line with other regions. Such estimates as OPCS have made do not suggest that the pattern of non-response seriously biases results from the GHS (Barnes and Birch, 1975).

The response rate of 82 per cent thus refers to personal interviews completed by an OPCS interviewer in the home of the household selected, with a small minority of proxy interviews where a member was absent. The interview involves completion of a twenty-page Household Schedule, and in 1984 a sixty-five page Individual Schedule, though the Household Schedule is completed at the outset and not all questions are asked of all individuals. The average length of interview is about ten minutes for the household schedule and thirty minutes for each individual interview. The GHS is an elaborate and thorough inquiry, though arguably not as arduous for those participating as the FES, where respondents are asked to produce during the interview payslips, bank books and so on to verify income, and afterwards are asked to keep a two-week diary of expenditure, for which a nominal payment is made. In the 1980 GHS survey, for example, there were a total of twenty-one pages of questions on health (GHS, 1982, pp. 248–58), although ten of these were directed specifically at persons 65 and over. This was a block of new questions included at the request of the DHSS to assess the extent to which a national sample of the elderly had difficulty in getting about and looking after themselves, had social contacts, and made use of health and welfare services (for some results see GHS, 1982, pp. 168–214). As an example of the type of questions asked, two pages of the interview schedule dealing with health are reproduced in Figure 5.1.

Interviewing is conducted by professional OPCS interviewers who are carefully selected from a large pool of applicants, screened for suitability as interviewers, intensively trained including practice interviews, given a briefing prior to going out in the field, and given a day's refresher at periodic intervals. OPCS Social Survey Division has high standards of survey fieldwork, and also produces the standard British guide to interviews in large-scale structured surveys (McCrossan, 1984). The questions which the interviewers asked respondents in the GHS are mainly, apart from a few questions on job satisfaction, questions about present or past behaviour by the respondent or their ability or propensity to behave in certain ways. It thus deals primarily with objective characteristics, and does not aim to provide data on social attitudes, discussed in the next chapter.

Output from the General Household Survey comes in several forms. The survey is conducted annually, and after coding the relatively small number of open-ended questions and editing for completeness and consistency, the data are processed by computer and output in the form both of data tapes enabling customers to do their own analyses and a very large number of tabulations (about 1,500 per year) produced to the specifications of OPCS's customer departments, such as the DHSS, the Department of Employment, the

Home Office, the Department of Environment and the Scottish Office. The tapes and tables ordered are supplied direct to departments within six months to a year after the end of the annual survey cycle, and OPCS then publishes a selection of results within six to eight months in its *Monitor* series. The General Household Survey annual volume usually appears eighteen months after the end of a year's fieldwork. Unpublished tables not included may be available to researchers on request from OPCS Social Survey Division.

Increasingly, however, social science researchers both within and outside government also analyse GHS data in another form. Tabulations of aggregate data, however comprehensive, never allow one to make all the cross-tabulations and multi-variate analyses one would wish. As mentioned, OPCS therefore also produce data tapes for computer analysis of individualized GHS data, so that the researcher has available the answers to each question of all those (or because of its size, of some of those) in the sample. These data are rendered anonymous geographically, so that only region is shown, to prevent any possibility of identifying the actual individuals interviewed. Thus if the sample contains a doctor with three cars and two children at private schools, but all you know is that he lives in the south-west region, there is no possibility of deductive disclosure (Boruch and Cecil, 1979).

In this individualized form, GHS data are suitable for secondary analysis (a subject treated in Hakim, 1982). Several of the health studies using GHS data quoted previously are of this type. When the GHS was first made available in this form, the hierarchical nature of the data set, encompassing households, families and individuals, posed some formidable problems for unsophisticated users, but these have increasingly been overcome by the preparation of Statistical Package for the Social Sciences (SPSS) – compatible files by a sociological research group at the University of Surrey, available through the Economic and Social Research Council (ESRC) Data Archive. Recently the Surrey group have published smaller extracts of GHS data on stratification, gender and poverty in Britain (Gilbert *et al.*, 1985). These problems are expected to diminish as GHS data for the years from 1983 onwards is to be produced by OPCS in Scientific Information Retrieval (SIR) format, a package which facilitates the analysis of complex hierarchical data of this type.

This characterization of the care with which the GHS is conducted and made available is a testimony to its rigour and scientific character, essential qualities if ministers and officials are to be satisfied that data derived from it can be used as a basis for sound

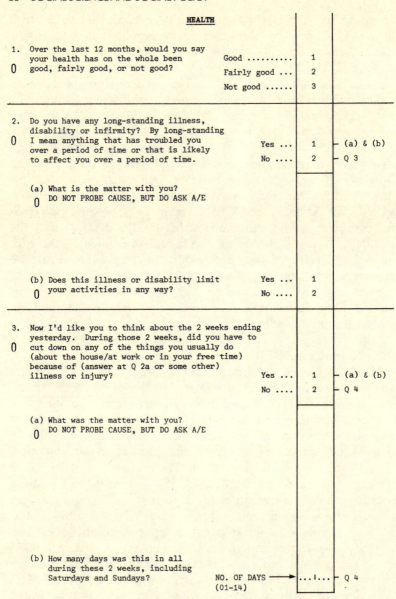

Figure 5.1   *An extract of two pages from the General Household Survey interview
schedule for individuals, 1983.*

4. During the 2 weeks ending yesterday, apart from any
visits to a hospital, did you talk to a doctor
for any reason at all, either in person or
by telephone?

EXCLUDE CONSULTATIONS MADE ON BEHALF   Yes ..   1   — (a)-(h)
OF CHILDREN UNDER 16 AND PERSONS   No ...   2   — Q 7
OUTSIDE OF HOUSEHOLD

(a) How many times did you talk
to him in these 2 weeks? ⟶ ...1...

	1st CONSULT	2nd CONSULT	3rd CONSULT	4th CONSULT
(b) On whose behalf was this consultation made?				
Informant	1	1	1	1
Other member of household 16 or over	2	2	2	2
GIVE PERSON NO. ⟶	...1...	...1...	...1...	...1...
(c) Was this consultation				
under the National Health Service	1	1	1	1
or paid for privately?	2	2	2	2
(d) Was the doctor				
a GP (ie a family doctor)	1	1	1	1
RUNNING PROMPT or was he a specialist	2	2	2	2
or was he some other kind of doctor? (SPECIFY)	3	3	3	3
CONSULT NO.				
(e) Did you talk to him				
by telephone	1	1	1	1
RUNNING at your home	2	2	2	2
PROMPT in his surgery	3	3	3	3
at a health centre	5	5	5	5
or elsewhere?	4	4	4	4
(f) Did the doctor give (send) you a prescription? Yes ..	1	1	1	1
No ...	2	2	2	2
(g) Did he give (send) you a National Insurance Medical Certificate? Yes ..	1	1	1	1
No ...	2	2	2	2
(h) Did he refer you to a hospital for tests, investigation, or treatment? Yes ..	1	1	1	1
No ...	2	2	2	2

SEE Q 5

Source: General Household Survey, 1983; Series GHS no. 13 (HMSO, 1985), p. 258.
(Reproduced with the permission of the Controller of Her Majesty's Stationery Office)

policy-making. But what kinds of use are actually made of GHS or FES data, and in what ways do their results feed into the policy-making process?

The GHS is firstly a source of descriptive data not otherwise available, or readily available, from other sources. The information on self-reported illness is one example. Information on family composition is another. There has been increasing interest in recent years in the social situation of one-parent families, particularly since the relaxation of the divorce laws. The Finer Committee (1974) reviewed the problem, but was handicapped by the absence of firm statistical data on the number of one-parent families and the proportion they comprise of all families in the population. The matter is of considerable importance in relation, for example, to poverty. One estimate suggests that as many as six out of ten one-parent families are living below the poverty line (compared to only one in seven of couples with children) and that this proportion rises to seven out of eight where the single parent is not working (Layard, Piachaud and Stewart, 1978, p. 29). To know how family composition is changing is therefore of importance to government.

The GHS provides information about one-parent families, as shown in Table 5.1. Because of the small number of one-parent families in the sample in any one year, data relating to such families have been aggregated over three years. It is also important to note that the data refer to families containing one or more dependent children (under 16, or age 16–18 in education), not to all families. The table shows that in 1981–3 13 per cent, or just over one in eight, of families with dependent children were headed by a lone parent. (In metropolitan urban areas of the country, the proportion is higher, and in inner London it rises to approximately one in three.) Over time, the proportion of families headed by a lone parent increased from 8.3 per cent in 1971–3, or one in twelve, to 13 per cent in 1981–3. Most of this increase is accounted for by an increase in divorced mothers from 1.9 to 4.9 per cent – in 1981–3 one in twenty of families with dependent children were headed by a lone divorced mother – and of single mothers from 1.2 to 2.5 per cent. The proportions of widowed and separated lone mothers, and the very small group of lone fathers, remained stable.

The category of single-parent families is not homogeneous. Further analysis shows that single lone mothers had (in 1980) a median age of 24 and of all lone parents were the most likely to be living in households containing other people as well as their children. Widowed lone mothers, on the other hand, had a median age of 50

Table 5.1 Changing Family Structure in Great Britain for Families with At Least One Dependent Child,* 1971–1983 (percentages)

Family type	1971–73	1973–75	1975–77	1977–79	1979–81	1981–83
Married couple†	91.8	90.7	89.8	88.9	88.1	87.0
Lone mother	7.1	8.0	8.8	9.7	10.4	11.6
Single	1.2	1.3	1.5	1.7	2.2	2.5
Widowed	1.8	1.9	2.0	1.9	1.7	1.7
Divorced	1.9	2.5	3.2	3.8	4.1	4.9
Separated	2.1	2.2	2.1	2.3	2.5	2.4
Lone father	1.2	1.3	1.3	1.3	1.5	1.4
All lone parents	8.2	9.3	10.2	11.1	11.9	13.0
Base = 100%	14,105	13,655	13,972	13,178	12,984	11,540

* Dependent children are persons aged under 16, or aged 16–18 and in full-time education.
† Including married women whose husbands were not defined as resident in the household.
Source: General Household Survey, Preliminary results for 1983, OPCS Monitor Series, GHS 84/1 (OPCS, 1984), p. 3.

and were most likely to be living with their children only. Separated mothers had a median age of 33, divorced mothers one of 36, and four out of five lived with their children only. Lone fathers had a median age of 45, but the small numbers in the sample do not allow useful analysis by marital status.

The GHS also permits analyses to be made of the occupational, educational, health and housing circumstances of single-parent families, though aggregation of more than one year's data may be required to yield large enough cell sizes. For example, one-parent families were twice as likely as married-couple families to be living in property rented from a local authority or a new town. Nearly two-thirds of lone-parent families lived in this type of accommodation, compared to one in three of other families with dependent children. One-parent families were also less likely than other families to live in a detached or semi-detached house and more likely to live in a terraced house, a flat, or rooms (GHS, 1982, pp. 10–11, 24).

There is also considerable interest in several government departments more generally about changes over time in the structure of households and families, for example for purposes of demographic forecasting, for supply of services like care for the elderly, for payment of state benefits or for intervention in the housing market. In the housing market, the rate at which existing households dissolve and new households are founded is critical to what is happening. This is shown diagrammatically in Figure 5.2. The rectangles represent three tenure groups: owner-occupiers, council tenants, and other types of tenancy. The arrows represent household movements, their areas being proportional to the numbers of households involved in each type of movement. New households are formed outside the circle and enter each type of tenure group. Movement between tenure groups is shown by arrows between the rectangles and within each tenure group (for example, from one owner-occupied house to another) within each rectangle. The arrows into the centre of the circle show the dissolution and amalgamation of households.

Nationally, a declining number of households – now only one-third – consists of parents with dependent children. A steadily rising proportion – currently about one in six – consist of one person over retirement age. One-person households of younger people are growing in numbers, as are lone parents with dependent children, now amounting to 4 per cent of all households. One-person households of all types have grown from 11 per cent of households in 1961 to 22 per cent in 1978 (Donnison and Ungerson, 1982, pp. 177–83). An analysis of the relationship between household structure, type of

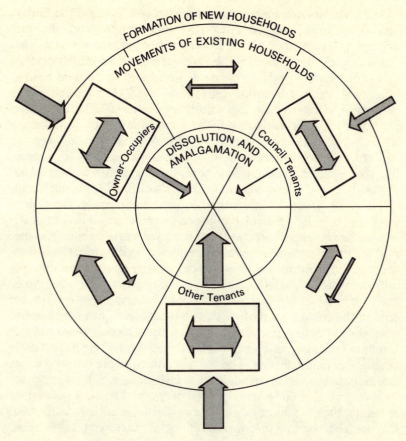

Figure 5.2   *The movement of households in England.*

Note: The size of the arrows is proportional to the numbers of households.
Source: Donnison, 1967, p. 208.

tenure and income using data from the Family Expenditure Survey shows that there are marked differences between incomes of households with the same type of tenure, particularly between the economically active and economically inactive. Moreover, the biggest differences in the incomes of households are now due not to the head of household's earnings but to the balance between earners and dependants in the household (Donnison and Ungerson, 1982, pp. 185–7). Data from the FES and GHS can thus readily be used to follow the changes in household composition which have such important implications for the demand for housing of different types.

The GHS has also been used in research conducted at the Policy Studies Institute, to provide alternative projections of future number of households in Britain for the Department of the Environment. The standard projections used by the DoE were based on headship rates (the proportions of people in any demographic group who head a household) derived from the 1961, 1966 and 1971 censuses extrapolated into the future and combined with OPCS population projections to give estimates of the future number of households. Basically this relied on extrapolation of past trends, and did not take account of factors influencing those trends, particularly for groups like young people over 18 whose headship rates were well below 100 per cent. The model developed (Ermich *et al.*, 1982; Ermich and Overton, 1984) showed that other variables than demographic ones played a role in predicting household formation. For example, income had an important effect, and previous marriage enhances the probability of forming a separate household, holding other variables constant. 'Loneship' rates were calculated, the probability of different sorts of individual adult forming a separate household broken down by age, sex, marital status and income, which could be used in the construction of an alternative model. The authors were thus able to refine considerably the simple model of household formation used by policy-makers to take account of the importance of socio-economic factors. The point of this example is to show the benefit derived from the availability of GHS data, which are superior to the census from several points of view. They are available annually, they can be constructed into desired economic units, and they include essential information on social characteristics which is absent from the census.

Access to GHS data also permits finer analyses of family structure than census and registration data allow (Murphy, 1984b). These do not permit analysis of relationships between co-resident and non-resident family members, of wider kinship ties, of longitudinal aspects of the family over time or *de facto* rather than *de jure* status. The GHS does; for example, women of child-bearing age are asked to provide full marital and birth histories which permit both retrospective and prospective analyses of the determinants and correlates of family change. In 1980 elderly persons were asked about visits to and visits from relatives, the frequency of visits, and whether one took place during the month before interview. Thus GHS data have been used by Brown and Kiernan (1981) to analyse patterns of co-habitation in Britain. Murphy has examined several aspects of family structure using GHS data. He has used the data to assess the extent to which pre-marital births, post-marital births or marital breakdown are leading to the conventional life cycle of the single adult living alone, followed by marriage, followed by the birth of children who then grow up in a stable family becoming less common (1983). He has also examined the question of whether childless marriages are more likely to break down than marriages with children. The results showed that having children very early in the marriage (and before it) led to an above average rate of breakdown, but with marriages that lasted five years or more, it was childless couples whose marriages were most likely to collapse. Couples with two children were by far the least likely to separate. Further analysis confirmed that couples who started having children early had a greater risk of marriage breakdown, and showed that this risk increased if there were four or more children (Murphy, 1984a). He and Sullivan (1983) have also examined the relationship between events such as marriage and births, and current housing tenure of women under 50. 'No other single source comes close to providing such a comprehensive picture of the contemporary family and the factors which might be thought to influence it' (Murphy, 1984b, p. 18).

In this example, as in the modelling of households, GHS data are used analytically as well as descriptively. Staying for the moment with descriptive uses, this is exemplified by GHS data on smoking and drinking, some of which (on smoking) was presented in the last chapter. Questions about smoking were asked each year from 1972 to 1976 and in alternate years since. Questions about drinking have been included in alternate years since 1978. The questions seek to classify respondents according to the frequency with which they drink alcohol and how much they usually drink on any one occasion, rather than to provide accurate estimates of individual's alcohol consumption. More precise data about the type and quantity of cigarettes smoked are obtained.

Table 4.3 showed smokers by sex and socio-economic group when discussing social class inequalities in health. Table 5.2 shows descriptive data on smoking habits over time. Table 10.1 shows a widening class differential between 1972 and 1984. The most striking pattern is the decline in smoking over time for both men and women, by one-quarter for men from 1972 to 1982 and by women by one-fifth. The downward trend has been more consistent for men than for women. Women do not smoke as much as men, but over time the differential has narrowed. Other data show that the sex difference in smoking is largely confined to those over the age of 60. Since 1980, there has been no difference at all between the sexes in the 16 to 24 age group.

Table 5.2   Trends in Cigarette Smoking for Men and Women Aged 16 and Over in Great Britain, 1972–1982

	1972	1974	1976	1978	1980	1982	1984
MEN							
Current smokers	52	51	46	45	42	38	36
Ex-regular smokers	23	23	27	27	28	30	30
Never or only occasionally smoked	25	25	27	29	30	32	34
Base = 100%	10,351	9,852	10,888	10,480	10,454	9,199	8,417
WOMEN							
Current smokers	41	41	38	37	37	33	32
Ex-regular smokers	10	11	12	14	14	16	17
Never or only occasionally smoked	49	49	50	49	49	51	51
Base = 100%	12,143	11,480	12,554	12,156	12,100	10,641	9,788

Source: General Household Survey, Cigarette smoking: 1972 to 1984, *OPCS Monitor Series*, GHS 85/2 (OPCS, 1985), p. 4.

Such descriptive data is of interest to social analysts such as journalists and academics. But it also has practical uses, for instance in enabling public utilities such as British Rail or London Transport to judge the likely impact of further extension of non-smoking areas on stations, trains and buses. It is used by government departments such as DHSS and the Treasury in judging the effectiveness of curbs on smoking through direct exhortation or by fiscal measures. Yet to revert for a moment to the discussion in Chapter 1, it will be apparent that such data are but one input among many into the process by which policy evolves. Backed by medical opinion, government action against smoking is less infirm than it was, but it could go further in the interests of preserving the nation's health. Whether more restrictions should be placed on advertising or sports sponsorship by cigarette manufacturers, or whether the already considerable duty on tobacco should be increased sharply with the aim of reducing consumption, are policy issues in which many interests and considerations are involved. Descriptive data on smoking patterns can inform those debates, but are unlikely to determine their outcome.

Drinking patterns, similarly, provide interesting data, though the health implications at least of light drinking are less clear. The medical profession is now more explicitly opposed to advertising and sports sponsorship by brewers and distillers, and the government has legislated to control the sale of alcohol at football grounds. Recalling the RAWP material in the previous chapter, Table 5.3 shows regional differences in drinking for men in 1980. The measure of type of drinker takes account both of frequency of drinking and the number of units consumed on a particular occasion (GHS, 1982, pp. 149–50). Some qualifications have to be attached to the results due to sampling errors, but the general pattern is consistent with that in other years. The more northerly regions contain the largest proportions of heavy and moderate drinkers, though Scotland does not stand out from the Great Britain figure as it did in the 1978 GHS. Family Expenditure Survey data show that expenditure on alcoholic drinks is higher in Scotland than in the UK as a whole, but that expenditure in the more northerly English regions is even higher. It is interesting to speculate about the relationship between alcohol consumption and regional mortality levels. Though it is possible that there is some direct influence, it is more likely that drinking is related to the class composition and industrial structure of different regions, and so reflects underlying social and economic differences. There are marked class differences in drinking patterns, particularly between non-manual and manual workers, which partly account for regional differentials.

Table 5.3 *Regional Differences in Drinking for Men Aged 18 and Over, Standardized for Age, 1980*

| Region | Type of drinker | | | |
	Abstainer or occasional (%)	Light (%)	Moderate or heavy (%)	Base (= 100%)
North	13	36	50	598
Yorkshire and Humberside	15	41	44	897
North West	13	39	48	1,160
East Midlands	15	49	36	701
West Midlands	14	46	39	981
East Anglia	14	57	29	390
South East	14	56	29	3,050
South West	18	56	26	702
Wales	16	38	46	490
Scotland	16	47	36	990
Great Britain	14	49	37	9,959

Source: General Household Survey, 1980; Series GHS no. 10 (HMSO, 1982), p. 161. (Reproduced with the permission of the Controller of Her Majesty's Stationery Office).

The discussion so far has concerned descriptive data of considerable, even direct, interest to policy-makers but where the fit between data and policy has been fairly loose. The use of data from the FES in the construction of the General Index of Retail Prices provides an instance where the relationship is much tighter, feeding social research data directly into one of the single most important economic indicators in the country. The Retail Price Index (RPI) is a measure of the changes in the level of retail prices in the UK month by month, which is commonly used as a general measure of the rate of inflation. Given the key political and policy significance of the inflation rate for national economic management, the level of pay settlements, the competitiveness of industry and for popular judgements about the 'success' of the government of the day, how it is constructed must be seen to be objective, reliable and open to public scrutiny. What role does the FES play in its construction?

The RPI has its origins in the official 'cost of living index' which started in 1914 'to show the average percentage increase in the cost of maintaining unchanged the standard of living prevailing in working-class families prior to August 1914' (Department of Employment, 1975, p. 971). This covered basic goods only, and became increasingly inappropriate as living standards rose. It was replaced after the Second World War by the present RPI which aims to provide a broad measure of changes in the general level of retail prices. The index is a measure of changes in prices, not in the cost of living. It does not measure changes in the kinds and amounts of goods and services people buy or in the total amount spent in order to live.

There are two elements in the construction of the index. One is the regular pricing of a range of goods and services on a week-to-week and month-to-month basis, in order to measure price changes. The other is to develop some method to determine which prices to collect and a formula to convert the large number of individual prices collected into a single index. The method of collecting prices is well described in official publications (Ministry of Labour, 1964; Department of Employment, 1975) and is carried out for some items by local office staff in Department of Employment unemployment benefit offices and for other items centrally. The important role played by the FES lies in the second field, in determining what prices to collect and how to weight them. For any measure of relative aggregated price changes depends crucially on the weights given to different items. These vary between different income levels, age groups, and parts of the country. They also vary over time. Long-term comparisons of working-class expenditure patterns, for instance, show a steep decline in the proportion of income spent on food, from 60 per cent in 1914 to closer to one-third fifty years later.

Since 1957 the FES has provided the information used to construct the weighting in the RPI. Before that period the index reflected working-class expenditure patterns, but it now includes all salaried and wage earners except the 3 or 4 per cent of very highly paid households, and pensioner households for whom a separate index is constructed. The total basket of goods and services priced in the survey of price changes is divided into ninety-five sections (such as milk, butter, gas, newspapers, floor coverings) and these are combined into eleven broader groupings shown in Table 5.4. The weights given to each grouping are derived from the FES. Up to 1975, a three-year moving average from the latest available data was used. Now up-to-date figures for the last twelve-month period from July to June are employed (Kemsley, Redpath and Holmes, 1980, p. 2).

Table 5.4   *Weights Used in the Construction of the Retail Price Index, 1968, 1975 and 1985*

	1968	1975	1985
Food	263	232	190
Alcoholic drink	63	82	75
Tobacco	66	46	37
Housing	121	108	153
Fuel and light	62	53	65
Durable household goods	59	70	65
Clothing and footwear	89	89	75
Transport and vehicles	120	149	156
Miscellaneous goods	60	71	77
Services	56	52	62
Meals bought and consumed outside the home	41	48	45
All items	1,000	1,000	1,000

Source: Department of Employment, 1975, pp. 972–3; 1985, pp. 104–5.

The FES gives, for the households coming within the scope of the index, the average amount spent on the groups of goods and services making up the basket. Thus the weights used in 1975 were derived from data for the period July 1973 to June 1974. The FES data on spending patterns is thus fed directly into the formula for constructing the index, and is regularly updated. The effects of this updating may be seen in Table 5.4. Spending patterns change, particularly with rising levels of prosperity, and the proportionate weight of different items changes. Food continued its downward slide as a proportion of household expenditure, to reach just below one-fifth in 1985. Clothing declined somewhat, and in the light of Table 5.2 the fall in the share of tobacco is not surprising. The marked increase in the share of expenditure on durable household goods and on transport and vehicles reflects rising prosperity and the expanding market for consumer goods. In constructing the index, the FES is the means by which government keeps track of shifts in expenditure. From one year to another they are not large, but over a longer period can be considerable.

The FES is not above criticism. It is known that respondents regularly understate their expenditure on alcohol and tobacco, and so in constructing the weights in the RPI other national statistics on consumption of these commodities are used to adjust the FES-derived weights. The survey has achieved a response rate of about 70 per cent over the years, which is respectable for a thorough inquiry of this type. There are, however, some biases resulting from the response rate which may affect the data. Response declines with age, and is less for smaller households than for larger. There is a lower response rate from households without children, and from the self-employed, particularly those with employees (Kemsley, Redpath and Holmes, 1980, pp. 30–1). Nevertheless, the FES remains an impressive survey and one which effectively contributes directly to the construction of a major national policy indicator.

The analytical use of continuous surveys has already been referred to and exemplified in the discussion in the previous chapter on health inequalities, and hinted at in the earlier example of the use of GHS data to study the social situation of families, including one-parent families. In these cases social researchers are using the logic of survey analysis (cf. Rosenberg, 1968; Hirschi and Selvin, 1973) to disentangle some of the social determinants of human behaviour. The study of poverty provides another striking example of the use of continuous surveys as an analytic data source. The rediscovery of poverty in the 1960s, discussed in Chapter 1 and Chapter 3, hinged on Abel-Smith and Townsend's study *The Poor and the Poorest* (1965), which was a re-analysis of FES data for 1953–4 and 1960. More recently Fieghan, Lansley and Smith (1977) returned to the FES for a study of changes in the level and incidence of poverty in the period 1953 to 1973.

A notable analytic use of the GHS is provided by Layard, Piachaud and Stewart's (1978) re-analysis of individualized 1975 data to explore the causes of poverty for the Royal Commission on the Distribution of Income and Wealth. The focus here is on only one aspect of their study, one-parent families. As already noted, a high proportion of one-parent families fall below the poverty line, and they include two-fifths of all children living at or below Supplementary Benefit level. The causes of income poverty in these families are relatively straightforward. All but 15 per cent of single parents are women. If they do not go out to work, they are mainly reliant on social security benefits, and on allowances from the absent father which only half of them get. There is little financial incentive to take a job unless it is full-time at a reasonable hourly rate, but most manual jobs available to women are at poor rates of pay.

In Layard et al.'s study, poverty is measured with reference to the Supplementary Benefit (SB) level and is defined as 140 per cent of SB level. Table 5.5 shows the family income relative to SB level for different types of parent. Nearly two-thirds of one-parent families, compared to less than one-fifth of two-parent families, have incomes below the poverty line, and the disproportion (38 per cent compared to 4 per cent) is much greater below the 100 per cent SB level. Where the parent was a man the difference is not marked, because most lone fathers in the sample worked. Where the lone parent is a woman, the incidence of poverty is high. Widows are slightly better off because of widow's benefit, which is not reduced if the widow earns a little herself. There was little difference in the proportion of single, separated or divorced women living in poverty, though single women had the lowest incomes.

Table 5.5   *Family Income Relative to Supplementary Benefit Level for Different Types of Parent, 1975*

Type of parent	Family income as a percentage of SB					
	Under 100	100–139	140–200	Over 200	All	N
Single woman	58	14	21	7	100	43
Widow	18	38	18	28	100	51
Separated woman	43	26	22	10	100	88
Divorced woman	51	28	13	8	100	67
Lone man	12	9	33	45	100	42
All one-parent families	38	24	21	17	100	291
All two-parent families	4	15	38	43	100	2,984

Source: Layard, Piachaud and Stewart, 1978, p. 98.

This was apparent when average income of each type of single-parent family was analysed, as shown in Table 5.6. Separated and divorced women averaged £5.10 and £5.40 respectively in allowances from their husbands, ex-husbands and fathers of their children, amounting to about one-quarter of original income. Only widows had any substantial income from occupational pensions or investments, and they received the highest net state transfers.

Whether or not a lone mother worked, and the extent of her earnings, were a crucial determinant in whether the family was in poverty. Of those earning between £1 and £10 per week, 88 per cent were below 140 per cent of SB level, of those earning between £20 and £29 per week, only 42 per cent were. There is a linear relationship between level of income and likelihood of being in poverty. It falls off as income increases. As Layard and his colleagues show, the important structural features related to this are the very high marginal rates of taxation for lone mothers receiving Supplementary Benefit or with low earnings. Only if they could work for at least thirty hours a week would lone mothers be likely to escape the 'poverty trap'.

Table 5.6   *Average Income from Each Source for Different Types of One-Parent Family in 1975*

| Source | Type of parent | | | | |
	Single woman	Widow	Separated woman	Divorced woman	Lone man
Earnings	£14.30	12.00	16.60	12.70	45.40
Self-employment	0.10	2.20	1.20	1.30	2.10
Occupational pension	—	1.20	—	—	0.20
Regular allowances	1.20	—	5.10	5.40	—
Unearned income	0.10	2.80	0.10	1.10	0.80
Original income	15.70	18.10	23.00	20.50	48.50
Net transfers (benefits less taxes)	8.30	16.50	5.70	4.80	–5.90
Income (after benefits and taxes)	£24.00	34.60	28.70	25.30	42.60
N	43	51	88	67	42

Source: Layard, Piachaud and Stewart, 1978, p. 101.

This brief example shows the potential of GHS data for exploring relationships between social policy variables. The final example, also drawing on the GHS, shows its use in the evaluation of need for services and policy outcomes, a type of research more fully treated in

Chapter 8. Bebbington and Davies at the Personal Social Services Research Unit, University of Kent, undertook a study of equity in the distribution of home help services (1983). Their concern was first with distributive justice, the equity of service provision between people in different areas, a social policy principle also underlying the RAWP exercise discussed earlier (see Davies, 1968). Secondly they were concerned with the target efficiency of service provision, that is the extent to which a service reaches those judged to be its most appropriate beneficiaries.

Their study of the home help service used 1980 GHS individualized data and looked first at the 'need' for services among the elderly, about whom additional information was collected in 1980. 'Need' was measured in terms of three different definitions, one of which was 'Persons who are either unable to manage certain domestic tasks for which adequate help is not available in the household, or who are disabled and have only limited outside support' (Bebbington, 1984, p. 26). This was measured by scaling responses to questions about disability and self-help in the survey. Data on hours of help received from home helps were similarly scaled. The results are shown in Table 5.7. This indicates that while services are relatively generously provided in metropolitan areas, they are less good in rural areas.

Table 5.7   Target Efficiency for the Home Help Service in Different Types of Area, Calculated from the 1980 General Household Survey

Measures derived from GHS	Inner London	Outer London	Metropolitan boroughs	Urban shires	Rural shires	All
'Need' service (N)	39	49	162	268	143	661
Receive service (R)	22	26	108	123	55	334
Ratio: R/N (%)	56	53	67	46	39	51
Number in sample	183	349	900	1,701	874	

Source: Bebbington and Davies, 1983, p. 315 and Bebbington, 1984, p. 26.

Bebbington and Davies also looked at sex differences in target efficiency, and showed that among elderly people not living on their own, the service was far more frequently provided when the wife only was disabled (in 27 per cent of cases) than where the husband only was disabled (11 per cent). Receipt of home help service is more likely in a household in which a husband cares for a disabled wife, than for a wife caring for a disabled husband. This example of a relatively simple type of evaluation research shows that the potential of the

GHS in such research is considerable. Indeed, Bebbington and Davies describe the GHS as 'the most important empirical source for British equity studies in the fields of health and welfare' (1983, p. 310).

6

Public Opinion Polls

Continuous surveys like the General Household Survey collect data about reported behaviour or attributes which is objective and can often, at least in principle, be checked against other sorts of data. If you ask, for example, about visits to the GP or to hospital, it is possible (on a sample basis) to check this information against medical records. With public opinion polls and surveys of attitudes about social questions, one moves into a different realm. Here the focus is upon values, attitudes, opinions held by members of the public about political and social issues of the day, and by implication upon social policy. How are such views elicited, how reliable are they, and what status do they have in framing policy?

In many respects polls and attitude surveys, in their political form, are the most visible type of social research. The results of political opinion polls appear regularly in the press, and the changing fortunes of political parties are followed in the crystal balls of the pollster. Political parties themselves take polls very seriously, and often commission their own private polls to chart their changing fortunes. Polls have their origins in journalism, though they link up with less sensational forms of survey research. Ever since George Gallup successfully predicted the result of the 1936 US Presidential election using sampling methods when the massive *Literary Digest* poll using non-sampling methods failed to do so (Teer and Spence, 1973, pp. 13–15), political polls have been fostered by the press as a complement to the more haphazard soundings of public opinion taken by journalists. The major polls are financed and sponsored by news media. 'The polls, as creatures of the press, came into being, and continue in being, to provide news stories for newspaper readers' (Teer and Spence, 1973, p. 21). The polls are used to play back public opinion to the public as part of the news. 'They are published by newspapers for the same sort of reasons as the columns of racing tipsters. Their function is to amuse or inform newspaper readers, and editors commission them for no other purpose' (Teer and Spence, 1973, p. 55).

Thus it is not uncommon to see a set of data such as Table 6.1 in one's morning newspaper. This example is taken from *The Guardian*. Those in the popular press are presented even more simply and sensationally but the basic idea is the same: to show how a sample of the population would vote if a general election were held at the time of the poll. Polls, moreover, are a rare type of survey research whose predictive validity can be tested. At the time of elections, polls are published right up until the day of voting, and so the actual result from the ballot box may be compared with the outcome predicted in the polls. Their record, within a margin of error of a few percentage points, is a good one, though sometimes the difference of a point or two is sufficient to switch victory from one side to the other. There have been exceptions, such as the British general election of 1970, when virtually all the polls predicted a Labour victory of between 2 and 9 per cent, whereas the actual result was a Conservative win by 2.4 per cent. A detailed investigation after the election suggested that the explanation lay largely in an eleventh hour swing back to the Conservatives which was not picked up in time by most of the polls.

Table 6.1   *Support for Major Political Parties among British Voters as Shown in Marplan Polls, 1983–1986*

Party supported	General Election 1983 (%)	1985			1986		
		July (%)	Sept. (%)	Dec. (%)	Jan. (%)	Feb. (%)	March (%)
Conservative	44	31	31	35	29	27	32
Labour	28	34	32	33	36	36	35
Alliance	26	33	36	30	33	35	31
Other	2	2	1	2	2	3	2

Source: The Guardian, 26 September 1985 and 13 March 1986, reporting results of polls conducted by Marplan. The data in the last column are derived from face-to-face interviews with 1,404 adults aged 18 and over, in a 'tightly-controlled quota sample' drawn in 103 randomly selected constituencies. Fieldwork was between 6 and 10 March, 1986.

The methods used by polls are those of the social survey. Answers are obtained to a series of questions from a representative sample of the population, usually by a personal interview between the respondent and the survey research interviewer, in the respondent's own home. Thus there is little difference in principle between the polls and the continuous surveys discussed in the last chapter. Both survey agencies like OPCS and SCPR which conduct social surveys for social policy, and the market research firms which carry out polls, use broadly the same procedures. There are, however, certain differences. The types of questions asked in polls, trying to tap people's attitudes and intentions, are somewhat different from factual questions about past or present behaviour. To this we will return. Polls also often differ in the sampling methods, making more extensive use of quota sampling.

The General Household Survey sampling design is a probability sample (see pp. 83–5) in which identifiable dwellings are selected at the second stage to which interviewers are sent with instructions to interview all persons over 16 in households at that address (and no other; no substitution is allowed). This procedure is a demanding one in that the interviewer must call and recall at that address until the members of the sample are contacted and agree or refuse to be interviewed. The virtue of the approach is that if probability methods of sample selection are used, then confident inferences may be made from characteristics of the sample to characteristics in the population, with calculable margins of sampling error attached to each estimate. In quota sampling, widely used in polling, the method of selection is different and because of this there is no basis in statistical theory for estimating population characteristics from the sample. The sample is selected as follows. At the first stage, selection of areas proceeds on similar lines to that outlined for a survey like the GHS. However, at the second stage the interviewer is not given numbered addresses or named individuals to visit. Instead, the inter-viewer is instructed to interview so many people of a certain type, for the sample is stratified by a few characteristics thought likely to influence the result. Common stratifying factors are sex, age and social class. Thus the interviewer will be instructed to contact so many men age 18 to 44, in non-manual occupations, so many women age 45 and over in manual occupations, and so on. Thus the target for the interviewer is set in terms of so many people of a particular type, rather than chosen addresses or individuals. The interviewer chooses the people to interview, commonly by knocking on doors in order to interview people at home. Statistically, the results from quota samples, which are very widely used in polling and market research (mainly because they are cheaper than probability selection methods) can not confidently be generalized to larger populations. The commercial proponents of quota sampling claim that they produce estimates of voting intentions just as reliable as those produced by probability methods. This is an area of dispute with no resolution in sight. Statisticians remain sceptical about the merits of quota sampling (see Moser and Kalton, 1971, pp. 127–37) while polling practitioners maintain that they produce satisfactory population estimates generally validated by the polls' record in predicting election results.

The polls differ from continuous surveys in appealing to an entity called 'public opinion' which it is their task to measure. What is meant by public opinion? Until the advent of polls, 'public opinion' meant the expressed opinion of elected representatives, people in leadership positions and pressure groups who claimed to know what 'the public' wanted. When opinion polls arrived on the scene in the 1930s and 1940s, they made new claims to be able to present the views of a wide cross-section of 'the public' on matters of concern to them. But the debate about them is of older origin. Jean Jacques Rousseau, for example, said: 'Opinion, queen of the world, is not subject to the power of kings; they are themselves her first slaves' (quoted in Noelle-Neumann, 1984, p. 133).

Older ideas such as Rousseau's 'general will' or the *volonté de tous* rub shoulders with modern conceptions of public opinion as the aggregated response of individual citizens in mass society. At the beginning of the century, A. V. Dicey published *Law and Public Opinion in England* (1905), and drew forth the criticism from A. F. Bentley, theorist of interest groups, that 'there is no public opinion . . . [which is] not actively reflecting or representing the activity of a group or set of groups' (quoted in Palmer, 1936, p. 252). There is clearly a relationship between public opinion and interest groups. A representative recent definition sees public opinion as 'the aggregate of views held by the public on matters of interest, both public and private, upon which they may be expected to act in some way when the matter requires' (Nieburg, 1984, p. 8). Ties of ethnicity, race, language, religion or region influence attitudes and opinions. Such demographic or social categories may be seen as incohate or latent interest groups, capable of being mobilized by active organization and self-consciousness. So making an interest group effective may involve mobilizing public opinion. The Child Poverty Action Group discussed in Chapter 1 tried to mobilize middle-class public opinion in the mid-1960s to press the case for government measures to alleviate child poverty.

In the light of the earlier discussion, it is clear that 'public opinion' as measured by polls is not necessarily the same as the views of interest groups. There is, moreover, a definite difference between 'matters of interest, both public and private', 'the public interest' and 'public opinion'. The three are not the same and need to be clearly distinguished. 'Public opinion' is another factor to be taken into account among the competing pressures bearing on the formulation of policy, alongside the activities of pressure groups and other interest groups. Bentley, writing before the days of social surveys, could not conceive of public opinion as separate from group activity. Yet it clearly is. As the example of polls on trade union issues discussed shortly shows, 'public opinion' as reflected in the polls is not necessarily the same thing as the activities of trade unions or pressure groups, whose leaders have been elected by internal democratic processes. Indeed, there has been a continuing tension between the views of elected representatives, who believe that it is their job to reflect and interpret the views of their constituents, and scientifically conducted polls which purport to give a picture of majority opinion. Polls did not exist in Edmund Burke's day, but his famous speech to the Bristol electors in which he argued for representative democracy as opposed to popular control stated one powerful objection to polls, that they usurp the role of those whose business it is to make judgements to frame policy in favour of the shallow aggregate of crowd belief (Marsh, 1982, p. 136).

A different objection to the pollsters' definition of public opinion is that polls indeed measure or tap a set of views which are in the air at any one time, a climate of opinion. Understanding the dynamics of public opinion formation, however, involves understanding the effects of social pressures, such as the 'bandwagon effect' of publishing polls affecting how other people subsequently vote. Noelle-Neumann has advanced a persuasive theory of what she calls the 'spiral of silence': that these social pressures also encourage people to speak or to stay silent when faced with a polling interviewer. She hypothesizes that once a view is perceived as a minority point of view, particularly if it is declining in popularity, then its advocates will remain silent, thus reinforcing the impression of a majority consensus. She defines public opinion as 'an understanding on the part of the people in an ongoing community concerning some affect- or value-laden question which individuals and governments have to respect at least by compromise in their overt behaviour under the threat of being excluded or losing one's standing in society' (Noelle-Neumann, 1984, p. 179). Pushed further, it can be argued that polls themselves generate information about issues of public concern and can create the impression of particular ways of framing these issues. They thus may help to set political agendas, and can become tools of subtle political manipulation as well as objective recording of what 'the public' thinks on a political issue.

It will be apparent that even a definition of 'public opinion' is problematical. In the 1960s, a review of the term produced about fifty different definitions (Childs, 1965). The entry in the *International Encyclopaedia of the Social Sciences* states that there is no generally accepted definition (Davison, 1968, p. 188). Nor will an operational definition of public opinion as that which public opinion polls measure suffice, since polls are criticized precisely for methodological weaknesses stemming from their methods of measurement. Polls do not question voters deeply on their political attitudes, but rely on single-item measures. More thorough research by political scientists indicates that public understanding on many issues is quite rudimentary and that opinions can be very unstable. Yet this does not unduly worry those who conduct polls, for 'A poll is an item of transient news. Its sponsors are not concerned with reaching an understanding of electoral behaviour or opinions. They are concerned solely with that behaviour and those opinions for their own sake, or in so far as the latter coincide with their own policy stances' (Teer and Spence, 1973, p. 21).

These methodological criticisms nevertheless need to be taken seriously. They boil down to three aspects of the opinion of the respondent which is elicited in the poll. First, how much information is available to the respondent? People find it hard to admit to ignorance of the workings of the political system, yet there is extensive evidence of lack of political knowledge beyond the most basic issues like party identification. A large proportion of voters, for example, do not know the names of leading ministers other than the prime minister. Stanley Payne (1951) found in the 1940s that 70 per cent of a sample of respondents gave a verdict upon an entirely fictitious Metallic Metals Act. In opinion questions where a 'no-opinion' category is provided, the proportion of 'don't knows' is always so much higher than when it is not included that one may suspect that people are answering on the basis of inadequate knowledge.

A second issue is how salient opinions are for a respondent. Schuman and Presser (1978) have shown that there is a consistent 15–20 per cent of people who would not be prepared to allow speeches against democracy in their locality, but who would not forbid it. The explanation may lie in the salience of opinions. In this case, the respondent focuses upon the words 'allow' or 'forbid' rather than the issue on which their opinion is sought.

Thirdly, how intensely do respondents feel about a subject? This criticism is frequently put forward by those who argue that public opinion cannot be treated as the unweighted sum or average of individual opinions. In the United States, for example, public opinion is strongly in favour of gun control whereas legislation is permissive. A study of the intensity with which respondents held views for or against gun control showed that those favouring control held their views more strongly, but that those opposed were more likely to judge a political candidate and alter their voting intentions because of his or her views on control. Gun control policy, in other words, is a function of the pressures exerted by different lobbying interests as well as the result of what 'public opinion' thinks about the matter.

Critics of polls are scathing about their methodological weaknesses.

Polls produce unsatisfactory and inconsistent evidence on key topics, due to over-reliance on single-item attitude measurement ... These single-item questions are cheaper, make better headlines and their marginals are more easily pushed around to support a specific point of view. These volatile answers to weak and unvalidated questions are then treated as *vox populi* and a place is claimed for them in the political process which ignores all the conceptual and technical difficulties in their production and use. (Marsh, 1982, p. 135)

Against this has to be set the reasonably consistent record of polls in predicting the outcome of elections. At least in relation to electoral behaviour, their record is not too bad. The problems arise when they venture into eliciting opinions on wider social and political issues, with the implication that these findings are relevant to policy.

The ways in which polling and attitude data may be fed into social policy need, therefore, to be considered more fully, in judging whether the effect of the polls is to enhance or diminish the social science contribution. The following discussion covers both polls and attitude surveys of a rather more penetrating kind. In a useful paper, Platt (1972) has pointed out that there are two dimensions to the use of survey data in policy-making, the type of data which are presented and the time-scale to which they relate. This is shown in Table 6.2. Survey data may be used to present facts, to test theories, and to inform the value judgements which are an integral part of policy-making, each with reference to the existing state of affairs, the mechanisms of change, and the desired state of affairs in the outcome.

Platt's argument is that the complexity of using survey and polling data is often overlooked when considering their relevance to policy. Not only are there two dimensions to be taken account of, so that

Table 6.2   *How Polls Can Contribute to the Illumination of Policy Issues*

	Existing state of affairs	*Mechanisms of change*	*Desired state of affairs*
Facts	A	B	C
Theories	D	E	F
Value judgements	G	H	J

Source: Platt, 1972, p. 80.

evidence may be relevant to any one of nine boxes, but within any one box the interpretation of the evidence needs care. Take box A, facts about the existing state of affairs, about which polls and surveys are regularly used to provide data. Even here matters are not straight-forward. She gives the example of a survey of consumers, people involved in the situation of interest, without any specialized knowledge. They might include, for example, council-house tenants in a housing survey, or members of a social minority, such as the elderly if the study was concerned with provision for old age. This has the advantage in circumventing the need for general population surveys of opinion, by focusing upon those whose opinions and characteristics are most directly of interest. Such studies, however, frequently lack controls, in the sense that the sample's responses may be related to circumstances of concern (for example, being elderly) or may be related to other characteristics which, by a process of self-selection, have led them into these circumstances. What could one infer, for example, from the findings of a poll of spectators attending football matches about facilities in stadia? Certainly as important data would be the views of those who might in some circumstances attend matches, but do not because conditions at grounds put them off. Yet they would by definition be excluded by the method of sample selection.

In a review of research on consumer opinion in social work, Shaw (1976) points out the need to ensure that opinions of the group are properly sampled. He observes that studies by Triseliotis (1973) of adult adoptees applying for the information in their original birth entries, and by Mayer and Timms (1970) of clients of the Family Welfare Association, are not a representative cross-section of all people in that category. This sampling problem is particularly acute when dealing with members of social minorities, since the sampling frames available may be limited or biased in certain ways. For example, if studying consumer satisfaction with a particular service which is confined to those identified as eligible to receive that service, one would be missing those left out of service provision or who chose to exclude themselves for some reason. The general point is that while it is often desirable to narrow down studies of consumer opinion to people directly involved in the situation or condition of interest, particular care must be taken in sampling to include *all* those potentially relevant, and also to build into the research design a meaningful comparison with other groups so that the results for the particular consumer group can be interpreted in a wider context. These points apply with even more force to boxes B and C in Table 6.2.

There are a number of implications of polling and survey data for the formation of policy-relevant theories (boxes D, E and F) which are discussed by Platt (1972, pp. 81–2). One particular issue will be considered here, the relationship between attitudes and behaviour. An expressed attitude does not necessarily predict the behaviour which might appear to follow from it, which can be affected by social pressures and the existence of other attitudes. There is now a large social-psychological literature upon the disjunction between expressed opinions and actions (see Deutscher, 1973). Thus attitude data has to be treated cautiously if it is to be used to build theories which will 'inform' policy decisions. For example, investigators of people's willingness under certain circumstances to move their jobs, or their homes, or both, cannot rely simply on responses to attitude questions. In the specific circumstances of redundancy or urban renewal when moving is an option or a necessity, many factors will come into operation including past experience, perception of alternative opportunities, incentives and the financial implications of particular courses of action.

The use of polling and attitude data to frame recommendations (boxes G, H and J) may take one of three forms: the survey elicits respondents' opinions, and the researcher bases his recommendations for action upon them; data on attitudes and behaviour are collected, and the researcher then suggests policies compatible with the attitudes and to facilitate the behaviour; or data on attitudes, opinions and behaviour are collected but the researcher frames his own independent conclusions on policy. Polling data are particularly likely to be misinterpreted and abused if the first of these courses of action are followed. At its crudest, this argument is of the type: polls show that a majority of the population favour the reintroduction of capital punishment for certain offences, therefore the government should legislate to reintroduce capital punishment.

If policy is to rest on respondents' opinions alone, certain conditions must be satisfied. There should be no other significant groups, besides those represented in the sample, whose opinions differ. If there are, their views may conflict and the policy conclusions to be drawn may not be unambiguous. This is not infrequently the case when commercial and environmental interests clash over the merits of particular planning applications. Then it is essential that if opinions are expressed, they should be firm, general and long-run views and be relatively permanent. As noted earlier, polling methods often do not provide a sound guarantee of this. Respondents' opinions should also reflect a well-informed consideration of the causes of current problems, the possible alternative ways of dealing with them, and the likely costs and further consequences of adopting each of the different alternatives. There is a particular tendency for opinions of services to be derived from what is currently available, and so to have an inbuilt conservatism. Finally, it should be feasible administratively and politically to act upon the respondents' opinions. In practice these conditions can rarely be satisfied, and so the idea of basing policy directly upon respondents' opinions is one fraught with difficulty. Even so, polling data are sometimes presented in the popular press as if this will be the case.

A more fruitful use of opinion data is for the social scientist to make use of such data in framing policy recommendations but to arrive at those recommendations on the basis of his or her own analysis, ensuring that the conclusions are compatible with the survey data. A good example is provided by Michael Bayley's study of the mentally handicapped, *Mental Handicap and Community Care* (1973). Bayley shows the crucial importance of the mother in caring for mentally handicapped children at home, and describes their experiences in detail. He shows that the mother's attitude is critical in helping families to manage the 'daily grind' of looking after their children by creating a 'structure for coping'. He shows that parents' dismissal of the value of occasional visits from social workers to provide emotional support makes sense when what is needed is 'structural' help that is regular, reliable and punctual, and geared into the daily slog of caring for the handicapped child. Bayley thus built the families' perceptions of what they needed into his analysis, without allowing this to determine the conclusion. His recommendations were consistent with those attitudes but were arrived at independently on the basis of a fuller analysis.

This example also makes the point that there are limits to the extent to which policy-making can be directly informed by polling-type data. Claims to 'democratic' legitimation of policy action by polling-type data must be judged by rigorous criteria which will usually show that such claims are spurious. While acting on respondents' opinions will rarely be possible, taking them into account frequently will be in the context of a fuller analysis. What this discussion also underlines is the extent to which policy is inevitably the outcome of a variety of inputs. To make special claims for the authority of one source, in this case polling data and attitude measures, is both unwarranted on the merits of the argument and unrealistic in relation to how policy gets formulated.

The mention of 'democratic legitimation' raises a more general critique of polls as a source of guidance for policy-making. This holds that polls are not merely an amusing adjunct to journalism but an influential means of setting agendas rather than producing discrete media 'effects'.

If public opinion is crucially related to which issues receive a public airing, then polling activities require much closer scrutiny than they have received in the past. Bandwagon effects have been something of an Aunt Sally. The role of polls in putting issues on the public agenda by making it appear that they are things about which people are currently concerned is more important if much less frequently discussed . . . The people who frame, commission and report opinion polls have a great deal of influence in this agenda-setting sense. (Marsh, 1982, pp. 139–40)

Public opinion polling is often concerned with issues that divide societies and produce debate and dissensus – political partisanship, moral issues of public policy like crime and punishment, the merits of wage claims, the power of particular trade unions, and so on. How issues are presented can be subtly influenced by the vocabulary used in asking questions. Does one refer to 'defence expenditure' or 'arms expenditure', 'terrorists' or 'freedom fighters', 'reduction in public expenditure' or 'cuts in social services'. Those who commission and conduct polls can decide when to hold a poll, what to ask questions about, how to frame the questions, which ones to report and whether to report them.

Marsh agrees that there is increasing evidence that the mass media influence politics and political discourse. For

as the manual/non-manual divide declines as a basic cleavage in Western politics, and as 'issue politics', nurtured by the mass media, grows, the evidence for media effects is also growing.

[Moreover] the persuasion paradigm of early media research missed the point that the major effect of these media is to set the very terms of the debate. The more successfully they do this, the more completely they have their influence. (1982, p. 138)

Consider a few examples of different kinds. In May 1968 National Opinion Polls (NOP) found that 67 per cent of respondents said they approved of Enoch Powell's policies on race. However, a follow-up by SCPR showed that less than half of respondents could say what Enoch Powell's policies were. The knowledge of the respondent is thus highly relevant to interpreting poll results, but this is frequently not done. In New Zealand in 1973, the question was asked: 'Do you believe that the 1973 Springbok team should be allowed to come to New Zealand?'; 68 per cent were in favour and 30 per cent against. When the question was modified to: 'Should an all-white Springbok team come to New Zealand?', 36 per cent were in favour and 59 per cent against. The effects of question-wording and social desirability can materially affect the outcome of a survey.

Special attention needs to be paid to the way in which polls on all matters are reported, but particularly where sensitive questions are asked which purport to represent the views of the public. The need to report the actual question asked in polls of voting intentions, sampling details, the response rate and the proportion of 'don't knows' or 'no answer' is a criticism often levied by academics against newspaper reports of polls. Where the question concerns a more diffuse political or social issue, the need for care is even greater.

The following example makes the point. In 1976 Gallup undertook a survey for the BBC-television programme *Man Alive*. One of the questions asked was: 'Which of these do you think has the most power and influence in the country today: Mrs Thatcher (leader of the Opposition); Mr John Methven (Head of the Confederation of British Industries); Mr James Callaghan (the Prime Minister); Mr Jack Jones (General Secretary of the Transport & General Workers' Union).' Of 1,028 individuals interviewed in a quota sample, 53 per cent opted for Mr Jones, 25 per cent for Mr Callaghan, 5 per cent for Mrs Thatcher, 3 per cent for Mr Methven and 15 per cent said that they did not know or could not answer (Marsh, 1979, pp. 276–7). Yet reports in the press referring to the poll did not give details to enable the reader to see the comparison being made. The *Daily Mail*, for example, referred in passing shortly afterwards to 'Mr Jones – named the most powerful man in Britain in an opinion poll'. Had an open-ended question been asked, without specific reference to these four figures, a quite different pattern of response would have been likely to result. The results of polls may be slanted and distorted by the way in which they are reported.

Sponsorship of polls is also a vexed question. Those who carry out opinion polls do so in close collaboration with their clients, usually the media but sometimes pressure groups or interest groups who seek to illuminate opinion on contentious matters in which they are involved. Marsh argued that 'The sponsors take all the important decisions. They can choose what to have a poll about, how to word it, when to have it, whom to ask the questions of; and newspaper owners can control how and when and whether it is reported . . . each of these decisions can markedly affect the appearance of this public opinion' (1979, p. 283). There are various examples of this effect. In the 1975 Referendum on whether Britain should or should not join the Common Market, different wording could produce different results, according to an NOP poll before the referendum which tested different questions (Butler and Kitzinger, 1976, p. 60). In industrial relations polling, questions may be posed in different ways to produce different answers. Some of this difference may be attributed to technical differences among pollsters, who are often after all survey professionals, about the best way to proceed. But the involvement of the sponsor, and the extent to which this influences the behaviour of pollsters, is a grey area. 'The fact of the matter is that different sponsors do pay for rather different questions to be asked . . . The borderlines between the broad topic, the selection of issues within a topic, the presentation of those issues and the fine detail of question-wording are very indeterminate' (Marsh, 1982, pp. 143–4). Hence the need for great caution in taking all polling results on social and political issues at face value.

What is the impact of polls on the policy-making arena? Political parties take their results very seriously and commission their own private polls. But one can point to counter-examples, for instance, the extent to which legislators ignore polls which show that a majority of the public favour the return of capital punishment. Four different views of the polls' influence will be briefly considered. The first is that the public and policy-makers are generally sceptical of the findings of polls (including political polls) and keeps their own counsel. American data from election polls in the 1960s suggested that polls were pretty fragile as predictors, as opposed to something interesting to look back on after the event (Jowell and Hoinville, 1969). Public scepticism is sufficient for poll results to be ignored if they do not accord with people's beliefs. This is certainly so among policy-makers. Politicians, though dependent upon polls of electoral support, tend to distrust polls in general because they can appear to usurp the role of the elected representative. Senior civil servants who have a detailed knowledge of their policy area are even less likely to be swayed by polling evidence. The best defence against the polls, in this view, is that by and large people are sophisticated enough not to take them very seriously.

The contrary view, which has already been briefly discussed, views the polls in a more sinister light. They are seen to perform an agenda-setting function. 'Public opinion polls play a powerful part in social control, reminding individuals of what everybody else thinks about various issues. This is not to argue that they are infinitely manipulable, or that they are worthless or that they should be banned' (Marsh, 1979, p. 284). This view of the polls, when stated carefully, does not suggest that polls are tools in the hands of sponsors – they are, after all, carried out by dedicated professional survey researchers – but that their influence is not negligible. They do frame issues and inform public debate in certain ways, and in certain areas, such as industrial relations, with a consistent slant. Marsh charges that polls are used to set against the views of trade union leaders on wage claims, wage restraint, trade union rights and various aspects of welfare provision (1982, pp. 140–1).

This criticism is important, but there is a need to disentangle the argument that polls are used to change people's attitudes from the claim that they are used to reveal what 'the public' thinks and wants. A third view places more weight on the former. It argues that polls have effects on respondents' opinions, but only in certain circum-stances and in certain ways. Noelle-Neumann's 'spiral of silence', for example, hypothesizes that where opinions become polarized, those in the minority will be progressively less willing to reveal their opinions publicly to pollsters, while retaining their views privately. Thus public opinion may *appear* to change over time, whereas it in fact reflects a pattern of behaviour on the part of the minority. Research upon 'bandwagon' effects in political science have shown that the publication of polls does have some effect upon voting intentions. In a recent experimental study of attitudes to abortion, Marsh (1984) has shown that varying the information given to respondents in experimental and control groups about *trends* in public opinion on abortion had a marked effect upon those whose opinions on the issue were least formed, and little or no effect upon those whose opinions on the subject were strongly for or against. People told that the trend was in a permissive direction were much more likely to endorse permissive views. In this view, polls do have effects but they are not uniform and operate only upon a part of the public.

The fourth view, that the polls are a key element in democratic opinion formation, can be held positively or negatively. In either case, the polls' close relation to journalism is of their essence. On a favourable view, their publication in the press tells the public and policy-makers what people think about particular issues, and thus informs the decision processes of a democracy more fully than if they were not available. Such a tendency to rely on the polls is particularly evident in the United States, where news stories in the press about political decisions are spattered with references to relevant poll findings. On an unfavourable view, such a use of polling data tends to undermine formal democratic channels and lead to a kind of media-led populism, where evidence of 'what the public thinks' is used to sway what policy-makers decide. Overall, neither positive nor negative view is particularly convincing in Britain. The British distaste for the use of the referendum as a test of political opinion is evidence of a preference for more indirect forms of political representation and opinion forming. There is no compelling evidence that poll data have been used to influence discrete political decisions in a particular way. The debate about the influence upon policy of the media (of which the polls are only a rather minor part) is inconclusive, though there is evidence that on certain emotive issues, such as black immigration (Hartmann and Husband, 1974) or welfare claimants (Golding and Middleton, 1982) the media may have an amplifying effect on intensifying public prejudice.

Consonant with the view stated earlier of public policy-making being the outcome of competing forces, the media may legitimately be regarded as one of these forces, and the polls as one adjunct to the media's operation. This is to put their operation into perspective in relation to the overall policy-making process. They are thus not a key or even a major determinant of public issues, but one factor among a number which can influence policy outcomes. To be sure, in certain cases like industrial relations questions and moral issues, they may be appealed to as having particular authority, but in many situations their findings are of no greater or less significance than the views of pressure groups, officials or politicians. The polls' primary function is to serve an entertainment function for newspapers and television.

To the critical reader of polls, including social scientists, certain questions have to be asked of any poll findings (Marsh, 1979):

(a)   how important is the issue to the people interviewed?
(b)   how were the questions worded?
(c)   how was the sample drawn?
(d)   how carefully have the results been reported?
(e)   who sponsored the poll and why?

The importance of each of these questions will be apparent from the previous discussion. The basic problem with taking polls too seriously is the issue of what constitutes 'opinion' about a particular issue, discussed above. Depending upon the knowledge of respondents, saliency of issues, and the way in which questions are worded, it is perfectly possible using single-item instruments to elicit crystallized opinion statements which do not reflect the underlying reality. This is the paradox with which pollsters struggle. The results of general elections usually appear to validate their predictions, yet on many issues there are good grounds for believing that the answers to single-item questions are unstable and liable to rapid change.

This chapter will conclude by looking at two examples of academic research into subjective attitudes relating to social policy, the British Social Attitudes Survey (Jowell and Airey, 1984), results from which appeared at the beginning of Chapter 4, and P. Taylor-Gooby's study of attitudes towards welfare (1982; 1985). These both use survey methods and questions to elicit respondents' attitudes, but arguably do so in a more thorough manner than the typical opinion poll. Thus, the SCPR Social Attitudes Survey is funded by private foundations and Taylor-Gooby was supported by ESRC. Commercial interests are not involved, and SCPR was particularly insistent on separating support for the survey from any involvement in the design of the survey (Jowell and Airey, 1984, p. 4). Both studies are fully reported in the literature, and answers to particular questions can be scrutinized to see the questions asked and the relationship to other items in the questionnaire. The sample design is also clear. The Social Attitudes Survey, unlike most market research studies, used probability sampling (as does the GHS); Taylor-Gooby's study used a quota sample (1982, p. 328). The directors of both surveys were well aware of the importance of question-wording and the salience of issues to those questioned. Indeed, quite unlike the typical opinion poll, both accounts begin with careful qualifications about the value of research into subjective attitudes.

Jowell observes that

The existence of replies is by no means an assurance of validity . . .

Attitudinal questions are particularly liable to variations in wording or content ... no amount of effort can ensure unbiased question wording ... Both in the selection of topics for inclusion and in the choice of questions to be asked, the researcher is required to make numerous value judgements. Impartiality remains an essential but imperfectly attainable goal of research. (Jowell and Airey, 1984, pp. 5–6)

Taylor-Gooby acknowledges the role of government and other agencies in seeking to influence opinion; the special circumstances of the survey interview which may affect opinions expressed; the instability of attitude structures over time; and the fact that attitudes cannot be equated with actions (1985, p. 22). So the authors of neither study enter it unaware of the imperfections of the survey as a method of trying to investigate their problem.

The Social Attitudes Survey used a structured questionnaire, Taylor-Gooby's study used a questionnaire administered by a post-doctoral social anthropologist with considerable experience in unstructured interviewing (1982, p. 328). SCPR emphasize the need for scepticism when faced with the data from questions of the type they are using. They did not want to push people into expressing attitudes that they did not hold, and so encouraged their interviewers to accept 'don't know', neutral or other answers to questions. Some questions elicited a fairly high proportion of non-commital answers. Moreover, they recognize the multi-level structure of values, beliefs, attitudes and opinions (cf. Oppenheim, 1966, p. 110) and the fact that individuals may not be consistent in the attitudes they hold. The Social Attitudes Survey is designed to form part of an annual series, and many of the items will only reveal their usefulness when the data for two or three years are available, so that changes in attitudes and the directions of change can be followed. Marked fluctuations in answers to a particular item over a three- or four-year period would be *prima facie* evidence that it was not consistently measuring a stable attitude. Jowell is even critical of the term 'public opinion'. 'Our data demonstrate that on nearly all social issues there are actually several publics and many opinions' (Jowell and Airey, 1984, p. 8).

This is not the place to attempt to summarize either study, to which the reader is referred, but some flavour may be given of the findings. In the Social Attitudes Survey a series of questions were asked about the National Health Service. The Survey confirmed that in general there was a high level of support, but dissatisfaction was shown with some aspects of the service. Only 29 per cent responded positively to a question suggesting, in effect, a two-tier health service, 64 per cent were opposed, and 7 per cent didn't know (ibid., p. 84). Half the sample saw the NHS benefiting low-income families, and around one-quarter as benefiting high-income families, but the better-off thought it did more for the poor, and the latter thought it benefited the better-off more.

Levels of satisfaction with the NHS were mixed. Just over half were very satisfied (11 per cent) or quite satisfied (44 per cent); one-quarter were quite dissatisfied (18 per cent) or very dissatisfied (7 per cent) and one-fifth neither. There were higher than average levels of dissatisfaction in London and the south-east, and more satisfaction in Scotland. There was also considerable variation in satisfaction with different parts of the NHS. Whereas one-quarter of respondents expressed general dissatisfaction, the percentages expressing dis- satisfaction with particular services were generally much lower. These ranged from dissatisfaction with attending hospital as an out- patient (21 per cent) through dissatisfaction with local doctors or GPs (13 per cent) and NHS dentists (10 per cent) to being in hospital as an in-patient (7 per cent), with health visitors (6 per cent) and with district nurses (2 per cent). With most services men were more likely to express dissatisfaction than women, and young people than old people.

On the question of private medicine, no clear class, age or even income divisions emerged. The differences appeared to be much more ideological ones related to party support. The results of one question on this subject are shown in Table 6.3. Respondents were permitted to choose more than one option on the card shown, and a number did so (totals thus add up to more than 100 per cent). From these responses it appears that there is a middle bloc of about two- fifths of responses with the view that present arrangements are about right. Outside of this, a clear majority of Conservative identifiers favoured expansion of private treatment, while a majority of Labour identifiers favoured contraction or abolition. Even so, this was not a clear-cut relationship, in that 36 per cent of Conservatives were critical of private expansion and 25 per cent of Labour supporters favoured it.

Data of this type illustrate well the problems of making direct use of attitude surveys in policy-making. What does one make of it? It could be argued on the basis of these data that there is substantial support for the status quo between the NHS and private medicine. Or that a significant minority of the population favour the expansion of

Table 6.3   *Views of a National Sample about Private Medicine in Britain, 1983*

Q. Which of the views on this card do you support? You may choose more than one, or none.

Statements on card	Total (%)	Political identification		
		Conservative (%)	Alliance (%)	Labour (%)
Private medical treatment in Britain should be abolished	10	3	9	19
Private treatment in NHS hospitals should be abolished	26	16	30	36
The present arrangements for private medical treatment and the NHS are about right	41	44	39	39
Private treatment outside NHS hospitals should be encouraged to expand	26	37	26	15
Private treatment generally should be encouraged to expand	20	31	18	10
None of these	4	3	4	3

Source: Jowell and Airey, 1984, p. 88.

private medicine. Or that a significant minority favour the contraction of private medicine. Or that attitudes to private medicine, rather than reflecting social characteristics, are primarily determined by political allegiance, and that attitude data are not independent but determined by political partisanship. Whether the last of these views is plausible cannot be decided from Table 6.3 alone, but would require further data and considerably more complex forms of analysis to resolve. The example nicely illustrates the point that one cannot step straight from data to policy inference.

In Taylor-Gooby's study with a sample of 240 respondents in the Medway towns in Kent, he examined particularly support for private market provision. He distinguished opinions which respondents held about the principle of private provision from their personal preferences about the state and the market. In relation to the first, about three-quarters of respondents approved the principle of tolerance of the right to contract out of state welfare for health care, education and pension provision. In relation to personal preference, respondents were asked at the end of the questions on private provision, in respect of health care and education, the question: 'If it cost the same to use state as private provision, which would you choose?' About two-thirds chose private provision for health care, with slightly lower proportions for low-income and manual groups, and Labour supporters.

A follow-up question asked for reasons for the choice. Two-thirds had had previous favourable experience of treatment, one-third thought state services needed support. Those who chose private provision did so mainly on the grounds that standards were better (51 per cent) or service was quicker (38 per cent). Dissatisfaction with the NHS was only mentioned by 9 per cent, and belief in the free market was insignificant as a reason (2 per cent). 'It seems likely that it is a calculus of self-interest based on life-experience and belief rather than values about the role of the state and market that is important in this area' (Taylor-Gooby, 1985, p. 41). A free-market advocate might argue that a free-market system would be more responsive to patient demand, and therefore standards would be higher and service quicker. There is thus an indirect relationship even if a direct one was not apparent in responses. But this sort of relationship illustrates the difficulty of making inferences from attitude statements, even about levels of satisfaction with service provision, directly to policy conclusions.

This brief overview of the findings from two studies supports the argument that public opinion is complex. Attitudes and opinions, moreover, may not be held in a way which coincides with the policy options being pursued by policy-makers. Taylor-Gooby, for example, shows that there is a balance of support for public and private sectors of welfare. 'The welfare state seems to attract homogeneous support among all social groups, even those party supporters and class and tenure groups who also have a tendency to favour the private sector' (1985, p. 52). The ambivalence of such findings reflects an ambiguity in people's attitudes, combining elements of an ideology of self-interest with a belief in collective provision:

neither the critics nor the defenders of the welfare state should seek to treat evidence of popular opinion that conflicts with their standpoint as spurious on the grounds that such attitudes are manufactured by conspiracies of the media or bureaucrats. There are bases within existing opinion both for a felt need for universal services and for the ideology of the market. By the same token the expression of public opinion may be vulnerable to swift changes, depending on the salience of either aspect. (Taylor-Gooby, 1985, p. 345)

The further one goes into these issues of public attitude and opinion, the more complex they become and the more problematical it is to derive either clear factual or prescriptive statements from them about the direction which policy should take.

7

Tools for Policy-Making: Indicators and Impact Assessment *

MICHAEL CARLEY**

Introduction

In the mid-1960s a growing dissatisfaction with the amount and quality of social information available to government decision-makers spawned what came to be known as the 'social indicators movement'. Initially this was a reaction against an over-emphasis on measures of economic performance as indicative of social well-being. These economic indicators had obvious limitations in evaluating wider social welfare considerations, such as qualitative aspects of life, equity and the side effects of externalities of economic prosperity, such as environmental pollution. Since that time the use of social indicators has become integrated into the policy process, both to indicate the need for policy intervention and to help evaluate the results of intervention. The following are some of the more specific criticisms of an over-reliance on solely economic criteria for policy-making:

(1) Gross economic measures often obscure critical aspects of income distribution within societies.
(2) The market valuations of goods and services are not necessarily related to their welfare content.
(3) Such measures cannot be related to the meeting of basic human needs, human rights, psychological satisfaction, or life fulfilment (Encel, Marstrand and Page, 1975; de Neufville, 1981).
(4) Economic development is only one part of the social or human development equation (Miles, 1985).

* ©Michael Carley 1986.
** Research Fellow, Policy Studies Institute, 100 Park Village East, London NW1 3SR.

Although the phrase 'social indicators', as opposed to economic indicators, was not coined until the 1960s, there is general agreement that the historical basis for this activity goes back to the work of the British economist A. C. Pigou (1924), who argued in *The Economics of Welfare* that the neo-classical economics could no longer ignore the concept of social costs that might cause public welfare to differ from private welfare. This difference reflected an imperfect working of the market economy and a role for intervention in the workings of that economy.

Pigou went on to point out that overall public welfare could be lessened by those social costs, or disservices, that exceed the private costs of production. He gave examples: the lessening of the amenity of residential neighbourhoods by factory construction, or the cost of police services related to liquor sales; neither of which would be the concern of factory owners or distillers in their corporate balance sheets. He argued that these types of social costs had to be quantified to determine their effect on the net social product. Today we sometimes call these social costs 'impacts'.

Pigou's arguments on social cost had little effect until the 1950s, when the concept was incorporated into welfare economics, and especially cost-benefit analysis, as what the economists now call externalities. The social cost concept explicitly argued that a consideration of externalities was essential to good decision-making, and this suggested a whole variety of social factors that needed to be measured. This concept of social cost, and also social benefit, is an important dimension not only of social indicators research, but also of related fields of policy analysis, such as cost-benefit analysis and social impact assessment (Carley, 1980). Also, in development planning, a similar concern arose over what was seen as an excessive and misguided reliance on macro-economic growth, and the notion of a 'trickle-down' of benefits from rich to poor, as measures of national development. In all cases, the reaction was towards the derivation of more accurate indicators of social development, of which economic performance is one part.

The rest of this chapter looks at the use of social indicators in the policy process, first in Western industrialized countries, and then for development planning for the Third World. More specific applications of social indicators are examined in terms of the evaluation of service delivery and for social impact assessment. The concluding section reviews some of the political, bureaucratic and methodological difficulties associated with the use of social indicators in policy-making.

Social Indicators: What Are They?

It is perhaps worthwhile to begin in the simplest terms. In everyday life we use certain kinds of symptoms or tokens as indications of less visible yet important states of being or situation. For example, the colour of a man's face or the temperature of his forehead tells us something about his health, based on our experience. Colour or temperature, therefore, may be crude indicators of health. In the field of socio-economic policy we can assume that action of government (usually) exists to maintain or improve the well-being of individuals or society as a whole. If we accept this, then for either policy development or programme evaluation the government needs some way to ascertain that maintenance of or improvement in well-being is taking place. That is, measurements are needed, unless intuitive assessments are to be relied on. Unfortunately, we are unable to measure well-being directly, since neither individuals nor countries carry convenient gauges of well-being. So surrogates for more direct measures of well-being are required. These surrogates may be termed social indicators, which are measures of an observable trait of a social phenomenon that establish the value of a different unobservable trait of the phenomenon.

This points up two important characteristics of social indicators: they are 'surrogates' and they are 'measures'. As surrogates, social indicators translate abstract or unmeasurable social concepts (such as 'safe streets') into operational terms (such as incidence of reported crime) that allow consideration and analysis of the concept. A social indicator must always be related back to the unmeasurable concept for which it is a proxy. As 'measures', social indicators are concerned with information that is conceptually quantifiable, and must avoid dealing with information that cannot be expressed on some ordered scale.

A Definition of Social Indicators

There are numerous definitions of social indicators, many not very rigorous. A good definition, however, is Carlisle's (1972, p. 25), in which a social indicator is described as 'the operational definition of any one of the concepts central to the generation of an information system descriptive of the social system'. The two most important elements in this definition are, first, that social indicators are the result of 'operationalizing' abstract concepts, such as health, by translating them into measurable terms in the form of proxies such as 'number of days without sickness'. Secondly, social indicators are part of an 'information system' that is used by policy-makers in understanding and evaluating those parts of the social system over which they exert some power. This information system must satisfy, therefore, not only analytic requirements for making resource-maximizing decisions, but equally important political and bureaucratic needs.

Input, Throughput and Output Measures

Social indicators may be measures of input, throughput or output. Input measures are the resources available to some process affecting well-being in the social environment, for example, number of doctors per unit of population. Secondly, 'throughput' indicators are usually based on workload or caseload measures – number of doctor visits for work-related injuries, for example. Thirdly, there are intermediate output indicators, which are measures of the results of specific activities performed, for example, extension of life expectancy, or reduction in morbidity and infant mortality. These constitute some of the most policy-useful social indicators. However, they represent quantity, not quality, of life and so there are final output measures of such concepts as a 'healthy' population or a 'better' environment. Final output measures are often measured by subjective social indicators, and most objective social indicators are of the input, throughput or intermediate output variety.

Social Indicators – a Spectrum of Policy-Related Activity

Just as there are multifold definitions of social indicators, so there is an enormous diversity of activity being carried out, in and out of government, under the banner of 'social indicators'. It is worth looking at the range of these activities to begin to grasp, if only unsystematically, the breadth of the field.

One of the most recognized forms of social indicator effort involves the assembly or collection of social measures. The best-known of these collections are the national social reports now issued by no fewer than thirty countries. These social reports, like *Social Trends* for the UK, are usually large compendia of tables, charts and textual material designed to tell, in a broad way, what is happening to social conditions and trends in a country at the national level. There are also important international social reports, for example, the World Bank's annual *World Development Report* and UNICEF's annual *State of the World's Children*. Such social reports provide background data on social change, and for many people are the most visible manifestation of social indicator activity. Some people argue, however, that they only contain social statistics rather than indicators because the information they provide does not directly represent cause-and-effect social relationships. Whatever stance one accepts, however, social reporting is too important to ignore in any consideration of social indicators.

A second important social indicator activity involves those indicators being developed, refined and in use directly to assist or guide government decision-making. These can be roughly divided into macro- or national-level indicators and micro-, local- or programme-level indicators, with regional indicators somewhere in between. An example of a macro indicator is the unemployment rate which, as we know, figures heavily in government decision-making and in political debate in many countries. This rate is considered important as an indicator of national well-being and potential socio-economic problems, and numerous social and economic policies are considered in the light of it. Similarly, the Retail Price Index is an important and time-honoured macro indicator of the level of inflation in the UK. There was considerable furore when Mrs Thatcher's government attempted to replace it with a new standard-of-living index, calculated on a different basis.

An example of a macro indicator used in the USA is the FBI's 'uniform crime index' which is often cited in arguments for allocating resources to various police forces to 'fight crime'. Many authors have argued that the uniform crime index is open to manipulation and distortion, for example, by increased reporting of crime which often results in apparent rises in the crime rate, and vice versa.

At the regional level there is considerable usage of sets of social indicators by government as 'territorial indicators of need', which Bebbington and Davies (1980) suggest represent one of the mainstream applications of social indicators in the UK. For example, the EEC uses a series of indicators to determine the eligibility of regions within Europe for industrial financial assistance. Similarly a complex formula is used in the UK to allocate health service resources among competing regions. Developed by the Resource Allocation Working Party (RAWP, 1976), this quantitative approach makes use of a series of indicators of 'need' or demand on the health services, such as numbers of elderly, and indices of mortality in different regions. Like the uniform crime index, the RAWP formula always proves contentious when used as a means of determining government expenditure. Such contentiousness is generally the case for all social indicators used to allocate resources, and perhaps none more so than the Grant Related Expenditure Assessment (GREA). This is a complex set of equations of social and economic indicators by which the UK's central government determines the amount of grant it will give to each local authority in the country. The GREA is intended to reflect a hypothetical level of expenditure related to relevant economic, social and demographic criteria, which gives an indication about how much money would, on average, be spent on service delivery by reference to a national norm (Jackson, 1984).

At the micro level, social indicators are also used to delineate territorial need or to evaluate the quality of government programmes designed to meet need. In the UK there has been considerable development of indicators useful for identifying geographical areas or population sub-groups towards which policy might be directed. Some claim to be neutral, that is, they do not take a stance on what constitutes need; rather, they simply identify like neighbourhoods across a range of social indicators. An example of this is the complex system of the Planning Research Applications Group (PRAG) which has the capacity to classify residential neighbourhoods across Britain. Other sets of social indicators are intended to identify areas of special need, or deprivation, towards which governmental programmes are directed. An example of such a programme in the UK is the Housing Action Areas which offers residential improvement grants and special local government powers to improve the physical environment. A similar use of indicators is the 'under-privileged area index' developed by Jarman (1983; 1984) to identify local areas with the greatest need for general practitioner medical services and attention to primary health care.

A third type of social indicator activity involves attempts to move away from the more ad hoc collections of indicators towards systems of indicators with an integral structure and rationale. Such systems attempt to offer a multiple or comprehensive, and systematic, perspective on social phenomena by the use of many social indicators covering a wide variety of important human activities. Some of these systems are international in scope, for example, the UN's System of Social and Demographic Statistics (SSDS) or the Organization of Economic Co-operation and Development's (OECD) elaborate scheme. Others are national, like the German SPES system (Social-politisches Entscheidungs und Indikatorensystem).

Criteria for Policy-Related Social Indicators
From the above range of social indicator applications as tools of the policy-making process, it is easy to see why there is little agreement over exactly what constitutes a social indicator (Carley, 1981). Such agreement may not be necessary as long as there is a continuing

critical re-examination of the essential concepts in the field. It was partly this process of critical examination which led many people to revise downwards their initial optimism about social indicators to a more practical perspective. The overly high expectations stemmed not so much from delusions of grandeur on the part of advocates (as some critics suggested) as from pressing information needs in and out of government. And while the social indicator field may not yet have met those needs, it will hardly do to dismiss it for its partial failure. The need is still there, and if the problem is that the policy task is more difficult, and the methodological tools need more refining than was originally conceived, this does not mean that the task should be abandoned.

This suggests that all good social indicator research must be concerned with two things. First, it must consist of methodologically appropriate techniques, that is, techniques which do not ignore the important criteria by which discipline research is evaluated. Such criteria include attention to the problems of quantification, prediction, causality, aggregation and value judgements internal to the analysis. This can be described succinctly as the internal logic of social indicators.

The second aspect of good social indicator research involves an understanding of the process of policy formation with its essential, and sometimes paramount, emphasis on such factors as political value judgements, value manipulation and bureaucratic maintenance. This dimension reflects an iterative cycle in which the policy-formation process may be informed by various social indicator studies (each with its own particular methodology or technique). In turn, the contingencies of the policy-making process must serve to establish some of the parameters which define the individual social indicator efforts. This consideration of the policy formulation process can be described as the logic of policy decision. The need to consider this logic is sometimes used to distinguish policy analysis from academic research.

Good social indicator research reflects some combination of the above two points, the mix according to policy needs and the intent of the researchers. Either aspect is ignored at great peril. Early efforts over-emphasized the immediacy of policy information needs at the expense of attention to methodology, and the result was reports based on implied causation, which were later rightly dismissed when it became apparent that the social causes and effects implied simply were not true. If some of the high hopes of the movement were dashed by this lack of attention to methodology, so be it. But it will not do to throw the policy information needs baby out with the methodologically muddy bathwater. Good social indicator research is simply about two things: it aids decision-making and policy formation, and it attempts to contribute to improved social knowledge, which indirectly aids decision-making.

Subjective Social Indicators and the Quality of Life
All of the above examples of social indicator applications make use of what are known as objective indicators. Objective indicators are operationalized by counting the occurrences of a given phenomenon, such as environmental stimuli and behavioural responses, which are measurable on an interval or ratio scale, and amenable to the usual methods of data analysis. Another important area of social indicator and survey research makes use of subjective social indicators, which are based on reports from individuals on the 'meaning' aspects of their reality and as such represent psychological variables which are usually presented on an ordinal scale. Questionnaires, interviews and opinion polls elicit this subjective information. For an example, time-series arrest statistics, or money-income levels, are objective social indicators, while feelings and perceptions of individuals about street safety, or relative deprivation, are subjective social indicators. An excellent example of the interweaving of subjective and objective indicators is Social and Community Planning Research's *British Social Attitudes: The 1985 Report* (Jowell and Witherspoon, 1985), which sets out to explore, not a unitary public opinion, but 'several publics and many opinions'.

Aside from the straightforward questions in an opinion poll, subjective indicators are usually based on questionnaires composed of a series of rating scales that ask respondents to codify their satisfactions with, or evaluations of, a large variety of the aspects and circumstances of their lives (Cullen, 1978). This is often done by using a five- or seven-point Likert scale which involves statements such as 'My housing meets all my family's housing needs' presented in conjunction with a scale listing possible responses, such as (1) agree strongly, (2) agree, (3) indifferent, (4) disagree, and (5) strongly disagree. These Likert scales give a relative intensity of respondent feelings if not interval values. A complete set of such statements with attendant scales are used to elicit feelings as a basis for developing social indicators. Techniques of more sophistication that yield interval data are also used. These force the respondent to consider positive and negative aspects of particular feelings simultaneously. Such techniques include, for example, Clark's (1974) 'budget pies' for assessing citizen feelings about urban expenditure, or the use of priority evaluation games for evaluating preferences in environmental and transport planning (Hoinville and Courtenay, 1979). The latter technique was used by researchers to assess public preferences related to the current rejuvenation of some of London's underground stations.

Activity in the subjective indicator field has its roots in the work of both Hadley Cantril and Abraham Maslow in the 1950s and early 1960s. Cantril and his associates interviewed a cross-section of people from various countries to determine what aspects of life they found important from positive and negative points of view, and where they scaled their personal standing in the present and future. This was done by presenting the respondents with a 'ladder of life' device, or the Cantril Self-Anchoring Striving Scale (Cantril, 1965, p. 22), on which a person expressed perceived variations between his or her ideal condition. These variations were assessed on a scale ranging from 0 for the worst to 10 for the best possible situation in any one of a number of life areas. This work is reported in *The Pattern of Human Concerns* (Cantril, 1965).

Similar to Cantril's work, and frequently cited, is the work of Maslow (1970), who proposed a hierarchial classification of five levels of human needs. On the lowest level are the physiological needs, for food, water, sleep, shelter, sex and so on. On the second level is the need for security and safety for self and family. The third level is made up of various facets of the needs for 'belongingness' and love, and the fourth level includes the needs for independence and freedom. On the highest level in this hierarchy are the needs for aesthetic beauty and knowledge as ends in themselves.

There are two important points to this hierarchy. First, Maslow argues that needs must be met in some semblance of ascending order, that is, physiological needs must be met before any higher-order needs can be met. Secondly, Maslow argues that man is 'self-actualizing', that is, 'what he can be, he must be'. Humankind's self-actualization process (quality of life) can be helped or hindered by the nature of society. This concept of self-actualization implies a strong relationship between the more general nature of society and the environment, as often measured by objective indicators. Further, the concept of hierarchical human need implies that relationships among areas of life satisfaction are as important as expressions of satisfaction with any one area. This means that careful attention must be paid to both the structuring and the interpretation of surveys from which social indicators are developed. For example, the inherent value of proximity to recreational facilities may be quite different for people whose housing situations vary from adequate to inadequate.

Beyond these early research efforts, interest in subjective indicators was renewed in the 1970s, at least in part by a lack of confidence in the correlation between objective indicators and life quality. For example, Schneider (1974, p. 508) warned: 'The use of objective measures alone as quality of life indicators is . . . highly suspect.' His research into over thirty objective indicators used in US urban areas showed poor correlation between these common indicators and individuals' satisfaction with various aspects of their lives. Other research into work satisfaction shows strong socio-economic strata differences in the correlations between socio-economic indicators and life satisfaction.

Research in Canada points to similar conclusions. Kuz (1978) undertook a study in Manitoba based on twenty-five objective indicators and thirteen subjective measures. He concluded that quality of life research using only objective variables is suspect in that it examines only one aspect of a multi-dimensional problem and that the subjective realities are equally important to overall quality of life. Kennedy, Northcott and Kensel (1978, p. 464), in a study of social indicators for Edmonton, Alberta, found similar results and suggested that 'the reasons for this low or lacking relationship between objective states and subjective perceptions lie in the fact that different individuals can be satisfied or dissatisfied by the same objective conditions'.

In other words, two important social processes are at work in human society. First is the fact that one objective condition (such as poor accessibility to public open space) can quite easily elicit very different subjective responses from different individuals (for example, strong dissatisfaction versus complete indifference). Secondly, and to compound the situation, similar subjective responses can result from widely differing objective situations. For example, people may experience as complete a satisfaction with life in a caravan home as with life on a large country estate. Given that both these processes will be simultaneously existing in society, and will vary according to population sub-groups and even from individual to individual, it is not surprising that researchers find a poor correlation between objective indicators and subjective responses. Attention to subjective social indicators is seen as a means of increasing this correlation between indicator sets and the reality of well-being.

The broadest study in the quality of life (QOL) field, and one very much in the spirit of Cantril, if not in the methodology, is that of Andrews and Withey (1976) on Americans' perceptions of the quality of life. Their research involved interviews with over 5,000 respondents and addressed the following issues:

- the significant general concerns of Americans;
- the relative strengths of each concern vis-à-vis well-being;
- the relationship of the concerns to one another in terms of co-variation and distinction;
- the relationship of the perception of general well-being to particular concerns;
- the stability of evaluations of concerns;
- comparability between population sub-groups.

The benefits of this type of research are that it provides a data base against which subsequent measures can be compared and that it gives information on the distribution of perceptions across society and on the structure and interdependence of these perceptions. Further, it helps in understanding how people evaluate and feel about such areas of life as family, job, housing and neighbourhood and how they combine various feelings into an overall evaluation of the value of life. The basic concepts in the Andrews and Withey model concern well-being at several levels of specificity. The most general are global indicators, which refer to life as a whole. The next level is of 'concerns', which are aspects of life about which people have feelings. These are divided into 'domains' and 'criteria'. Domains are subject areas (house, marriage and so on) that can be evaluated in terms of the criteria (privacy, comfort, security and so on).

Similar research is that of Knox (1976a; 1978), who attempted to gauge whether there exists a clear order of priority preferences for different aspects (domains) of social well-being, and whether this varies by social class, age, region or neighbourhood. Knox used an eleven-point self-anchoring scale to establish priority rankings. He found that overall (for Britain) the rankings are health (most important), then family life, social stability, housing, job satisfaction, neighbourhood, financial situation, educational opportunity and recreation. The ranking of health first corroborates similar findings of an earlier study (Hall and Perry, 1975). Beyond an overall consensus on the importance of health, however, Knox found considerable variations in preferences expressed by social, economic, demographic and geographic population sub-groups. Especially noteworthy are the strong regional variations for the domains of educational attainment, leisure and social status. This type of research could be of considerable value to social researchers who are attempting to determine the significance of social or economic impacts. Knox's research demonstrates that regional variations must be taken into account.

Measuring Improvements in Public Service Delivery

Both the dramatic growth of public expenditure over the past few decades and the need to get 'value for money' in that expenditure have given rise to attempts to use objective and subjective indicators to measure tangible improvements and cost effectiveness in public service delivery. Sometimes termed 'productivity measurement' or 'performance auditing', at the extreme these various terms define anything from detailed time-budgeting studies of the activities of individuals or small groups to overall measures of the effectiveness of public policy. In many ways these efforts can be termed 'programme impact assessment', and in practice performance measurement most often makes use of objective indicators of efficiency in terms of the conversion of organizational inputs and outputs. Effectiveness measures (as opposed to efficiency) are usually citizen assessments, using subjective indicators, of the perceived quality of service delivery.

Areas subject to study include recreational services, library services, police and fire services, public transport, and educational and other social services. Proponents of performance measurement studies argue that at any governmental level such studies can (1) help determine progress towards targets or goals set by public administrators; (2) identify problem areas and help set priorities for efforts at improving productivity; and (3) help implement worker incentive schemes. Comparison between local governments or operational units may also help set priorities for allocating resources. Such performance measurements are very similar to measures that have been used in some impact mitigation agreements in the USA between industry and local government, and have direct applicability to many formal impact management, mitigation and compensation schemes.

The Urban Institute suggests the following criteria for selection of performance indicators:

(1) Appropriateness and validity: indicators must be quantifiable, in line with goals and objectives for that service, and oriented

towards the meeting of citizen needs and minimizing detrimental effects.

(2) Uniqueness, accuracy, and reliability: indicators need not overlap, double counting should be avoided, but some redundancy may be useful for testing measures themselves.

(3) Completeness and comprehensibility: any list of indicators should cover the desired objectives and should be understandable.

(4) Controllability: the conditions measured must be at least partially under government control.

(5) Cost: staff and data collection costs must be reasonable.

(6) Feedback time: information should become available within the time frame necessary for decision-making. (Hatry *et al.*, 1977)

Measures of performance take a number of forms. A common indicator is the ratio of input and output, with the amount or level of service delivery as the output measure, and the employee hours or unit cost of service provision as the input measure. Examples of such measures in the crime control and recreation fields are speed and apprehension of criminals after crime per employee hour, percentage of crime cleared after X days, number of hours of recreational facility operation per monetary unit, and number of hours of citizen recreational participation per employee hour. The assumption in each of these types of measure is that the quality of the output is held constant or improves as more efficient ratios are achieved. The output measures most easy to develop are those that cover services with the most tangible outputs. For example, refuse collection measures are much easier to obtain than measures of policy efficiency or social service effectiveness. In the police case a measure such as 'number of arrests per employee hour' may encourage such perverse effects as inadequate investigation. This type of problem, however, may reflect not so much an inadequacy in the approach as the primitive methodology for measuring some service outputs.

Another common supplement to these measures are citizen evaluations of the quality of service provision. This generally takes the form of interviews of actual or past clients to ascertain the number satisfied with a service per monetary unit or employee hour expended. Such measures thus combine the traditional and somewhat suspect number of clients served with satisfaction levels. The Urban Institute suggests that this form of measure will be particularly important to those who believe that citizen, or client, satisfaction with services is a major product of government services.

Social Indicators and Development Planning*

In the developing countries, the initial support for the idea of building up social indicator systems was due to the well-known insufficiency of the traditional economic indicators to characterize the different dimensions of the development process. However, with time, a set of problems similar to those faced by developed countries came about with regard to social indicator development. Among them are first, the lack of an agreement upon a conceptual model for the development process obstructed the design of social indicator systems (Cornia, 1982), and the failure of different models of planning developed during the 1950s and 1960s has had a negative impact on the attempts to measure social aspects of development (Seers, 1977). In the second place, often when social indicator systems were developed, they were highly complicated and required a great volume of information. The technical background of possible users of such systems is often limited in developing countries, and information overload is a common difficulty. Thirdly, many proposals for social indicators ignored difficulties regarding data collection and analysis in developing countries. For example, while in developed countries data collection for a census takes no more than twenty-four hours, it could take a full year in developing countries, requiring a very complex logistical operation. Publication of information related to a census may have a time lag of five years or more.

Reliability of information is another problem. While in developed countries there is a tradition in data collection and social reporting (there are well-trained interviewers; the population is culturally predisposed to answer and co-operate with interviewers, and so on), this situation is almost non-existent in developing countries. Another reliability problem can be illustrated by the following example.

Numerous indicators exist to describe the state of health, but due to the nature of health statistics, none of them are without problems in interpretation. The magnitude of the usual indicator, Coefficient of Infant Mortality, does not always correspond to reality in the developing world because of the lack of registration of vital statistics, especially births. For this reason this indicator of infant mortality can show great changes from one year to the next. It is most likely that these differences do not represent any real changes in the state of health of the population, but rather reflect changes in the quality of

* Some portions of this section draws on an earlier work, jointly authored by Carley and Bustelo (1984).

data collection or in the motivation for people to report births. If this is suspected it is often necessary to use a supplementary indicator, Proportional Infant Mortality, which represents percentage of total infant deaths under one year of age. The logic is that infant deaths are less under-reported than infant births, but such a notion must be based on first-hand knowledge of the population under consideration. In any case, accurate infant mortality statistics are difficult to come by when the baseline data of infant birth is underrepresented.

Towards New Indicators of Development
One useful direction of international statistical work is the National Household Survey Capability Programme (NHSCP), launched in 1979 in response to resolutions of the UN Economic and Social Council and sponsored by UNICEF, the World Bank and other agencies. One of the main objectives of NHSCP is to help countries build up simplified and low-cost data systems. To achieve this, the NHSCP concentrates its efforts on building and upgrading the capacity of countries to conduct national surveys of social and economic conditions. Survey methodology has been chosen for its simplicity and for the possibility of integrated data collection.

Among the specialized agencies of the UN, the United Nations Educational, Scientific and Cultural Organization (UNESCO) has been one of the most active organizations in the field of social indicators. Pioneering work was done to identify and select indicators of human resources and to aggregate them into a general index. From the area of human resources, the organization later moved into the wider area of indicators within the context of development and social change (UNESCO, 1976a). Other works on indicators by UNESCO (1976b) explore the area of environmental quality and quality of life. UNESCO (1978) discusses problems of indicators of quality of working life, proposes definitions and methodologies for measuring environmental quality, and presents some quality of life models. UNESCO (1981a) suggests a series of socio-economic indicators for development planning and UNESCO (1981b) looks at the changing roles of women in development.

The International Labour Organization (ILO) has developed indicators of labour force participation, employment, income distribution and so on that are incorporated into the regular work of the United Nations Statistical Organization (UNSO). All agencies of the UN, particularly UNESCO, the World Health Organization, and the Food and Agriculture Organization, co-operate with UNSO on the development of social statistics.

Several developing countries have attempted to implement social indicator systems. In Brazil, the Brazilian Institute of Geography and Statistics (IBGE) has published two volumes (1979a, b) of selected indicators based mainly on National Household Surveys. A discussion of the different uses of social indicators is presented in the introduction of the first volume. The main indicators presented are related to population, families, health, education, family expenditures, employment, income distribution, housing and so on. Disaggregation is by regions and rural/urban breakdowns are presented. The work by IBGE is a pioneer effort in Latin America. However, this work has not had as great an impact on policy as IBGE would like, so the project has been reoriented to more focused problem areas, such as that of children and women (IBGE/UNICEF, 1981a, b).

Indicators of Poverty and the Assessment of Basic Needs
Within the definition of social indicator work adopted here, evaluations of poverty and standards of living are very important. They are particularly relevant to planning and especially in identifying which development projects have a greater social impact in the sense of speeding up the process of basic needs satisfaction and/or reduction of social disparities. Many of these social indicator efforts are part of a wider interest in studying the relationships between economic growth, income distribution (in cash and kind) and quality of life; and between basic needs indicators and human welfare. This basic needs approach is based on the recognition that GNP or GDP per capita is a very poor measure of social development. Concern is therefore refocused on the need to eradicate absolute poverty by concentration on human needs such as nutrition, education, health, clothing and shelter. Strategies for so doing include combinations of growth, redistribution of assets and income, and restructuring of production. The assessment of such strategies requires a set of indicators for measuring and judging changes in rates of deprivation.

A consideration of these issues has given rise to the 'human development' approach in which the necessary links between the social indicator field and the concept of human development are made systematically and extensively (Miles, 1985). Aspects of applied social indicator work (social accounting and social reporting) are located within the critical debate over the nature of social development. In particular the approach takes a negative orientation to macro-economic indicators as sole measures of human well-being and to the reliance on modernization or 'trickle-down' theories as measures of successful national development. Here the reaction is towards the development of more holistic and/or accurate indicators of *social* development, of which national economic performance is one part. The development of these measures of either quality of life or human (or social) development recognize explicitly or implicitly a hierarchy of human needs as put forward by Maslow, Galtung and others; of which basic needs are the first level of human needs, the fulfilment of which is a presupposition for advancement to the satisfaction of other, higher levels of needs, and thus social progress.

One practical attempt at a composite basic needs measuring system is the Physical Quality of Life Index (PQLI) proposed by researchers at the Overseas Development Council. The PQLI proposes three equally weighted indicators as an adequate measure of minimum human needs: life expectancy at age 1, infant mortality, and the literacy rate (Morris, 1979). The attention of these measures to output of process or programmes, rather than to inputs, is seen as an advantage in analysing a wide range of intervention policies.

In order to measure the speed with which differences between two PQLI's are reduced, the concept of Disparity Reduction Rates (DRR) has been introduced. This rate measures the degree to which a country is reaching its target level of development (Grant, 1978). A related attempt to aggregate indicators is the 'satisfaction of basic needs composite index' which defines national performance in satisfaction of needs in the areas of nutrition, medical services, housing and employment (Richardson and Forgette, 1979). The PQLI effort comes in for methodological criticism by Larson and Wilford (1979) who argue that, in this composite measure, each of the three indicators are closely correlated and therefore redundant, and that there is little difference between GNP per capita and the PQLI as a measure of human welfare. Both, it is suggested, suffer from similar deficiencies.

The PQLI is a very simple social indicator system, and the criticism may be justified. More telling perhaps is the debate which rages around notions of development, like basic needs, and social indicators as measures of development. At the risk of over-simplification this can be described as the 'culture of poverty' argument versus the structuralist argument, that is, poverty as an individualistic phenomena or as a societal phenomena. The implications of the answer are dramatic. For example, the structuralist argues: 'What is wrong with "Basic Needs"? It is a diversion and a cold-blooded stratagem. It carves people into layers of poverty – relative and absolute, sets up arbitrary statistical criteria of judging levels of growth and, in the end, aims at amelioration rather than the eradication of poverty' (Gauhar, 1982). On the other hand, one only has to examine some of the excellent work being done within the framework of the basic needs approach (for example, Ghai *et al.*, 1979; ILO, 1977, 1981; IBGE/UNICEF, 1981a, b) to see that such criticisms may be doctrinaire and pedantic. As with many social problems, solutions are seldom easy, and an over-emphasis on the structuralist argument (which may be clear as a mode of analysis) often ignores the complex political and social reality of the development situation and the necessity and benefit of community and regional development work. These arguments of course are directly paralleled by arguments in developed countries over the use of social indicators to analyse regional disparities and allocate resources in, for example, the provision of health services. This is true as well about arguments over whether regional equity considerations are to be allowed to play a role in the pursuit of national economic well-being.

Consideration of these arguments is topical because such recent approaches as basic needs or human development are already under threat by the combined factors of a recent orientation in national economic planning towards monetarism, and also the worldwide economic recession. These factors have resulted in the diversion of funds by central governments away from social development and back towards economic development initiatives. The same trends may also result in the elevation of a national-level structural orientation to planning and a diminishment or even eclipse of concern for regional disparities which may be a critical dimension of the problems of poverty and underdevelopment. One lesson here is that it is almost always impossible to separate the use of social indicators for policy-making and resource allocation from questions of distributional equity and questions of centre–periphery relations. These questions are of equal issue in first, second and third world countries.

In any event, there is not the space here to delve further into the complex argument about what constitutes social development. Nevertheless, it is one that every person interested in social policy and the use of social indicators should be conversant with. A good review of all sides of the debate can be found in Stohr and Taylor (1981) and in Miles (1985). Arguments for and against the basic needs approach can be found in Dell (1979), Leipsiger and Lewis (1980), Selowsky (1981), Streeten *et al.* (1981), and Cole and Lucas (1981).

Social Impact Assessment

During the past decade there has been growing interest in attempting to anticipate the socio-environmental effects of large public and private sector investments. This interest stems from the rise of the environmental movement, which like the related social indicators movement is based on the assumption that a limited economic perspective on technological change and development may ignore social and environmental factors and unintended consequences of action, all of which have marked effects on the quality of life.

More specifically, interest in assessing socio-environmental factors associated with particular projects arose as a reaction against the deficiencies of traditional assessment techniques. These, it was felt, over-emphasized economic criteria in judging project worthiness. For example, cost-benefit analysis seemed unable to deal with the question of the distribution of costs and benefits (or impacts) across various sectors of society, and with 'intangible' or unquantifiable effects. And yet these factors could have obviously dramatic impacts on quality of life.

This dissatisfaction with traditional methods of economic analysis was related to a number of trends which have been collectively associated with the environmental movement. One was reflected in an increasing concern over the depletion of non-renewable resources. This was embodied in the growth–no growth debate highlighted by the famous Club of Rome report *The Limits to Growth*, developed at the Massachusetts Institute of Technology (Meadows *et al.*, 1972). This was a global model with variables of population growth, food supply, resources depletion, capital investment and population. The model was criticized for its simplistic assumptions (Poquet, 1980) but it did serve to heighten the growth–no growth debate and focus attention on conservation, not only of resources, but of the environment. Related to this was an increasing concern over air, water and land pollution, and attention to the interdependence of a variety of aspects of human life.

One result of the trend towards an environmental movement was legislation in the USA in favour of an environmental impact assessment (EIA) process, which ensured political awareness of contentious environmental issues. Also, the procedures laid down for EIAs generally require alternative and environmental consequences to be considered before project approval decisions are made. It is this public awareness which is perhaps the main achievement of the environmental movement.

An EIA process is now required for major projects in many countries. In 1985 the EEC issued a directive on environmental assessment which will introduce common principles for the assessment of environmental effects stemming from major public and private projects. Member states have until 1988 to provide advice and establish mechanisms for the implementation of the directive. Similar procedures are already in place in Canada, Australia and New Zealand. For developing countries, the United Nations Environment Programme has published 'Assessment Guidelines for the Siting of Industry'.

No particular methodologies were specified for early efforts at EIA and the results were perfunctory. In an attempt to provide a comprehensive perspective the emphasis on the biophysical aspects of development was expanded to include the socio-economic aspects as well. However, the resultant environmental impact statements, while becoming increasingly sophisticated in biophysical analysis, were unable to demonstrate the successful incorporation of social knowledge into the EIA process. This gave rise in turn to social impact assessment (SIA) in which the focus is on the demographic, social and economic aspects, as distinct from the biophysical, so as to give them proper attention.

Although there has been some cross-fertilization between the social indicators field and the social impact assessment (SIA) field, it has not been extensive. While this may seem surprising at first, it is probably due to two factors. First, there is a lack of interdisciplinary integration in the social sciences generally. Secondly, although social indicators and SIA both involve the practical application of social measurement to decision-making, they have tended to focus on different things. SIA has concentrated on predicting the impacts of particular developments, and has been project-specific and of a limited pre-project duration. Social indicators research, on the other hand, has concentrated on attempts to develop measures of the quality of life, on indicator systems for monitoring an existing situation in society at a particular administrative or geographic level, and on the development of performance measures of public service delivery.

To date, most SIA is directed at resource development or large-scale construction projects. Around various facets of the development of the UK's North Sea oil and gas reserves, for example, social impacts have been examined in many geographical areas and related to such diverse aspects of development as secondary industry, small businesses, health patterns, migrating workers and leisure. In North

America social impact studies have addressed diverse topics such as urban development, power generation, transmission line corridors, coal mining and new communities. Less attention has been paid to SIA for human service planning and programmes, but such studies are beginning to occur on a more regular basis. In whatever field is addressed, impact assessments have generally been fashioned in an ad hoc but fairly comprehensive manner, based on the demands of the project and the general creativity of the investigator as opposed, for example, to a cost-benefit analysis which is most usually conducted to a similar format in many differing projects.

Social Impact Assessment: What Impacts?

Social impact assessment attempts to complement the study of natural, or biophysical, environmental impacts with information on the social and socio-economic impacts which may be associated with a new project, policy or programme. These impacts, or alterations in living conditions, include changes in psychological and physiological factors, community processes, and changes in the production, distribution and consumption of goods and services. Sometimes such considerations are included in an EIA but often they are glossed over. In addition to the question of 'which impacts?' SIA is also concerned with 'who gains' and 'who loses?', that is, which groups in society gain benefit or suffer disbenefits. SIA also considers the issue of mitigation – the easing or transferring of the burden of disbenefits. Both environmental and socio-economic assessment techniques are often required for an analysis of the same proposed project and impacts may well be closely related. In the study of a possible new road, for example, increased noise and pollution (environmental impact) may lead to psychological stress and relocation decisions (social impact) and reduced property values (economic impact). At some point in the decision process the results of various types of studies must be integrated as trade-offs are made among project benefits and social and environmental costs.

The process of environmental and social assessment are similar and usually involve these steps:

(1) Establish a data base which describes the existing situation.
(2) Develop means of describing change related to the proposed project.
(3) Forecast change in the base situation with and without the given project, including qualitative and quantitative aspects.

Most SIA's consist of an objective data base and projections related to socio-economic and demographic impacts and possibly subjective data gathered by interviews with the public, experts and politicians. Most SIA's deal at least with the following types of impact:

(1)   demographic impacts including labour force and population shift, employment multiplier effects, displacement and relocation problems, and changes in population make-up;
(2)   socio-economic impacts, especially changes in income and income multiplier effects, employment rates and patterns, and taxation and rates;
(3)   institutional impacts including demands on local financial and administrative services, for example, in the fields of housing, water, sewers, schools, police, criminal justice, health and welfare, recreational facilities and others and especially changes in capital and operating budgets;
(4)   psychological and community impacts, especially changes in intangible aspects of life, for example, social integration, community and friendship networks, sense of place and community cohesion.

There are dimensions of impact which are common to most analyses. First, there are direct and indirect impacts. Direct, or primary, impacts are immediately related to the proposed project or programme. Indirect, or secondary or tertiary, impacts are induced by, or associated with, proposed change and are the 'second-order' effects of direct impacts. For example, a direct impact of a decision to build a refinery at a particular location may be the migration of a large construction crew to that location. Indirect impacts will stem from the multiplier effects associated with the fact of that crew's taking up residence – economic impacts such as increased local spending on goods and services, environmental impacts such as pressure for housing or construction on agricultural land, and social impacts such as increased demand for health and social services. In most cases the indirect impacts will far outweigh the direct impacts in magnitude. The main point, however, is not any rigid distinction between direct and indirect impacts. Rather it is the importance of the interrelationships among impacts, and the need to specify cut-off points for the consideration of multiplier effects. These will be of decreasing relevance to the impact assessment as they become more direct.

Secondly, impacts may be socially concentrated or dispersed. Concentrated impacts are those associated with a particular locale or affecting a particular segment of the population, while dispersed impacts are spread thinly over a wider range. The more concentrated the impacts the more likely that opposition or pressure groups will play an important role in the reaching of the development decision. Thirdly, impacts have duration in that they occur over time and may cease to occur at some point. For example, noise and heavy traffic associated with the construction of a power station may cease when construction is complete. Finally, impacts have geographical scale which range from on-site, through local, regional and national up to global. Here the specification of cut-off points for consideration of impacts related to scale is essential. For example, the construction of an industrial plant on a green field site may be favoured locally by those who stand to benefit from increased trade and employment prospects, disfavoured regionally by those who are concerned about a loss of open space, and yet favoured again nationally by those considering the investment implications of the project.

Social Impact Assessment in a Policy Context

There has been a lot of debate in the SIA field in the recent past over its supposed role in the decision-making process. One school of thought perceives it as a social research exercise aimed at anticipating the effects of change by applying the skills of various academic disciplines like sociology, anthropology, political science and so on; in other words, supplying needed information to enlighten decisions. Other people, however, see the most important task in SIA as mobilizing public involvement in the decision process – a participatory role. In fact, valid and valuable SIA can ill afford to ignore either role. The opinions and reactions of residents in the study area, and other individuals concerned with a project, are essential to an understanding of the objective data generated by social research. Such opinions and reactions are gathered, not as a public relations exercise, but rather to ensure concentrated public participation in the assessment process, which means an essential two-way flow of information and interaction between the public and the developer or government agency. The public response and the attitudinal information generated by such a process are important for bringing SIA closer to an elusive social reality which can only very partially be mirrored by analytic techniques. Public participation also helps all the actors in the decision process put some measures of priority, positive or negative direction, and sensitivity to the various factors in the assessment problem. Most importantly it promotes the intensive public debate which leads to healthy political decisions. A useful perspective attempts to combine the social research and participatory roles of SIA.

The context of impact assessment is summarized by Hyman (1983) as consisting of:

(1) alternatives in policies and projects;
(2) conflicting, multiple objectives of society as expressed by sets of actors with diverse values, skills and resources;
(3) uncertain information on the non-deterministic causal links between human actions and physical and biological effects; and
(4) limited amounts of time, money, and expertise for analysis.

The essentially political function of assessment is increasingly recognized as predominant over any limited technical orientation (Meidinger and Schnaiberg, 1981). This is an important emerging theme in the literature of SIA. The impetus for it is the obviously paramount role of value judgements and value conflict in development decisions, irrespective of the methodological or predictive elegance of any impact assessments. This paramountcy of values is too apparent to be ignored, nor is it. Tester (1981), for example, argues that objectivist, structural/functional approaches to impact assessment often do not work where there are diverging value systems. De'Ath (1982) and Bustelo (1983) make the same point with regard to developing countries vis-à-vis the developed ones. The result of this attention has been an increasing recognition of the relationship of impact assessment to planning and political decision-making. Boothroyd and Rees (1984), for example, trace the evolution of impact assessment from 1975 to 1983 as 'from pseudo-science to planning process'.

Most responses to this perspective on SIA fall within the pluralist-reformist camp of social research. A few are more extreme in arguing that such approaches as impact assessment reinforce the power of capital while preserving the myth of pluralist democracy (for example, Sandbach, 1980).

A realistic discussion of social assessment and the pluralistic decision process can be found in Torgerson (1980), where it is argued that the predominant tendency in many current efforts at SIA can be characterized as *elitist* in that they have a technocratic orientation, with the analyst assuming the role of an expert engaged in detached scientific inquiry. Such elitist impact assessors emphasize objective data, ignore social conflict, and give only a token nod to public involvement in the process. This elitist stance arises out of a functionalist orientation in sociology, that is, one based on the assumption that communities have monolithic, discernible social goals, the degree of attainment of which can be measured. This orientation is rejected in that social systems may well be defined by the systematic promotion of certain value stances at the expense of others, that is, they are about pluralistic rather than monolithic social processes.

An alternative approach is to foster the participatory mode of SIA which recognizes the value orientation of the social researcher, and the necessarily ambiguous, or subjective, nature of studies of social phenomena. This ambiguity means intuitive judgements will always be present in an SIA. In the participatory mode active public participation is viewed as essential to the SIA process and the *right* of affected parties. Such participatory impact assessment is in itself an educative social process which may help change society. The final assessment arises, not from some formula-derived numerical calculation, but from inter-group conflict and co-operation over development proposals.

Monitoring Systems: Tying Indicators to Impact Assessment

It is becoming increasingly obvious that static impact assessment processes developed to date are insufficient in concept and practice to deal with the reality of a dynamic social and policy context. This has given rise to a recent emphasis on socio-economic and environmental monitoring as a logical timely extension of the assessment process. To distinguish, impact assessment anticipates future impacts based on extrapolation of data and experience in similar situations, while monitoring observes or reports on actual events as they occur, by measurement and analysis. Monitoring is a continuous assessment for the purposes of project and/or impact management, programme or project evaluation, and policy development. Monitoring is undertaken to enable governmental agencies to keep policies, decisions and programmes responsive to unforeseen changes in the decision environment, unintended impacts, demographic changes, and changes in the institutional framework. In short, monitoring is feedback, and feedback is essential for the working of systems. Two monitoring systems are discussed below.

Social Economic Accounts System

An extensive system of indicators, developed in the United States by Fitzsimmons and Lavey (1976; 1977), is the Social Economic Accounts System (SEAS), which presents 477 community-level indicators organized into fifteen programmatic categories. SEAS is designed to enable public officials, developers and social scientists to monitor the effects of various types of public investment upon a variety of indicators. These indicators are taken to reflect the quality of life of individuals in various domains, and the relative social position of groups of people in the community.

The indicators within each of the programmatic areas or sectors (education, health, welfare and so on) are organized into state variables, which describe people's lives at one point in time; system variables, which describe the institutional arrangements affecting people's lives; and relevant condition variables, which are state and system variables from other sectors affecting the sector under consideration. Within the state and system variables, some are subjective social indicators obtained by resident survey. For example, there are forty-four health sector variables in the SEAS system. Within the health sector, for example, a state variable is 'number of deaths per 1,000 live births', a system variable is 'number of full-time physicians per 1,000 population', a relevant condition variable is 'mean age of population', and within the state variables an attitudinal variable is 'personal satisfaction of residents with health services'. Notice that the state variables tend to be output measures, while the system variables are measures of input and throughput.

The authors of SEAS have also developed a paradigm for the analysis of communities that conceptualize community as a systematic, interactive, and dynamic entity. The purpose of this paradigm is to provide the researcher with a common framework for using the community, with its subsystems, as a unit of analysis. An operational definition is proposed in which linkages are established among the fifteen programmatic indicator categories, five 'concept' categories (interaction, changes and so on), and eight potential research objectives (for example, to identify types of interaction). In this manner it is suggested that a common framework is provided whereby various research activities relating to a specific community, or the concept of community, can be integrated to improve the practical understanding of communities. Given this necessary attention to causal relationships in communities, SEAS could be adapted to the requirements of the SIA analyst who needs to monitor community-based social change.

CIPFA Community Indicators

Another indicator system is the Community Indicators Programme of the United Kingdom's Chartered Institute of Public Finance and Accountancy (CIPFA). Similar to SEAS, with an emphasis on community as a unit of analysis, it is less comprehensive, but it actually publishes social indicator data for UK communities and attempts to aid decision-making by local governments. The system relies on existing data sources. Wherever possible, indicators of individual 'need' are used in preference to input or throughput measures. The criteria for structuring the indicators are that they be readily comprehensible, disaggregated to the local government level, and as up to date as possible. The need indicators are further classified into normative need, that is, target standards laid down by various levels of government, and perceived need, which is felt by individuals or expressed institutionally, for example, in the form of a waiting list for public housing.

An interesting aspect of the CIPFA system not generally found in other social indicator systems is the identification of principal client groups for the range of services that the local government might offer. This makes the indicators themselves more relevant. Client groups are of three types: those directly identifiable (such as school pupils), who impose a mandatory obligation for service; those indirectly identifiable (such as the elderly), whose needs may or may not be met by local agencies; and the population generally, for such services as public transport. For example, a service need for the population group 'under 5' is 'pre-school education', and indicators of service provision include 'places per 1,000 population' and 'pupils per pre-school assistant'. For the client group 'total population', one service is libraries and an indicator of service provision is 'book stock per 1,000 population'.

The community indicator system is useful for two reasons. First, it is designed to facilitate the setting of priorities for resource allocation among various services in a local area, both for policy and budget planning. Secondly, it assists in performance measurement – the study of efficiency or the ratio of input to outputs, and the study of effectiveness, which is the extent to which goals or objectives are met by service provision. CIPFA is especially noteworthy for its efforts to be relevant to community-level decisions and for disaggregating data for various client groups. Such community service indicators would be useful measures of service impact in SIA monitoring programmes, as would many of the indicators developed for measuring changes in public service delivery.

Conclusion

Aside from difficulties associated with the relatively primitive state of social theorizing, there are a number of problems with using social indicators and assessment techniques in the policy process. They are no more than part of the analytic component of a wider policy process which has an essential, and often paramount, emphasis on such factors as value judgements, value manipulation and bureaucratic maintenance. Also social indicators are never value neutral but always contain value judgements, either implicit in problem definition and indicator selection, or explicit in formal value-weighting schemes. Social indicator researchers must be aware of the dangers of 'cultural imperialism' where their own value sets and assumptions tacitly guide the research.

There is also the sheer difficulty of establishing the significance of responses and findings. The meaning and values represented by responses may vary greatly. Beyond that, a number of researchers have noted a tendency for people to respond in an overly positive manner at a general or global level (Campbell, Converse and Rogers, 1976; Allardt, 1977). At the same time at specific domain levels, people are quite willing to be critical of their life situation and express considerable dissatisfaction about specific matters. This casts doubt on the efficacy of attempting to develop global measures of life quality, and it may be that domain-specific research (housing, health, recreation and so on) has the best chance of capturing the rather elusive reality of well-being and is the most practical application in impact assessment.

For community monitoring programmes, one difficulty can be the sheer volume of the statistics produced, and such reports may contain pages of data irrelevant to community problems. Researchers seldom wish to camouflage critical issues but sometimes do just that by refusing judiciously to select and highlight data critical to the issues and putting out reports that are too broad and vague and have not concentrated on policy-manipulable variables. Such unaggregated quantitative data strain the very limited time resources in the policy process.

Misguided attempts at comprehensiveness that result in 'information overload' must be dealt with by attention to synthesis and communication. Overaggregated data, on the other hand, will be accused of hiding information vital to the decision process and of offering vague generalities. This is a classic dilemma of analysis, to which the only solution is the judicious presentation of information geared to the particular problem at hand. It would be helpful if selected social indicators were accompanied by a written 'measurement rationale' justifying why a statistic should be regarded as a measure of the social variable under consideration. Such a rationale makes explicit researchers' logic that substantiates the selection of one indicator over another, and reduces the dangers of cultural imperialism in the assessment process.

8

Evaluation Research and Social Experimentation

Applied social science research takes several forms. In Chapter 4 a basic distinction was made between descriptive and evaluative studies. In the intervening chapters, four types of descriptive study have been outlined, and in this chapter, attention shifts to evaluative research. Whereas descriptive research may be pursued for basic, disciplinary purposes or with applied intent (and applied examples have been discussed in earlier chapters), evaluative research is part and parcel of policy. Its aim, broadly stated, is to discover whether a particular policy is actively accomplishing what it set out to accomplish. 'The purpose of evaluation research is to measure the effects of a program against the goals it set out to accomplish as a means of contributing to subsequent decision-making about the program and improving future programming' (Weiss, 1972, p. 4).

Evaluation research involves systematic assessment of policy outcomes. 'Measuring the effects' entails the use of a rigorous research methodology, while focus on 'the effects' denotes a concern with outcomes of policy, rather than efficiency, honesty, equity or some other criterion. The comparison of actual effects with stated goals implies the use of explicit criteria for judging how effective a policy is. The feedback of evaluation into future decision-making makes clear that evaluation has a social rather than a purely technical purpose. Obviously policies and programmes will differ in their scope, size, duration and complexity and as a type of research, evaluation may be applied in many widely differing contexts. Nevertheless, there are certain basic features which differentiate it from more familiar types of descriptive and analytical work (Weiss, 1972, pp. 6–8).

Evaluation research is intended to be used by decision-makers, and seeks answers to questions posed by decision-makers, rather than by academics. Though given a good deal of freedom in the design of the study, the basic questions to be answered are set by policy-makers and administrators. A most important element in evaluation, which distinguishes it from other types of research, is whether the programme meets certain criteria (in other words, is it effective?). A statement of policy goals is therefore a necessary element in the research. Evaluation research is a type of action research, and this may pose problems for its conduct, since professional staff involved in service delivery are part of the research setting and may not co-operate fully with the researchers' aims. Established procedures in the organization may on occasion clash with research objectives. Unlike basic social science research, the publication of evaluation studies is not a foregone conclusion, and the evaluation researcher bears allegiance to the organization which funds the study and to the future improvement of policy as well as to the advancement of knowledge itself.

Evaluation studies are conducted to aid decision-makers in reaching conclusions about continuing a policy; or improving a policy; or adding or withdrawing specific features of a policy; or introducing similar policies elsewhere; or allocating resources between competing alternatives; or accepting or rejecting the theoretical basis on which a policy rests. A useful distinction to make sense of some of these different purposes is between formative and summative evaluation (Scriven, 1967). Formative evaluation produces information that is fed back during the implementation of a policy in order to help improve it. Summative evaluation is done when a policy has been implemented, to assess the overall effectiveness of the policy at the end of the implementation process.

In practice, there are considerable problems in making evaluative research designs work. Perhaps the major difficulty is lack of explicitness about what policy-makers expect the policies they instigate to do. The aims of a policy may either not be stated at all, or stated in such general rhetorical terms (for example, 'the eradication of poverty and want') as to be valueless for a scientific evaluation. Policy-makers (especially politicians as opposed to civil servants), are particularly likely to resist explicitly formulating the aims of a policy, because it gives too many hostages to fortune. So long as the aims of the policy are unstated or implicit, a gloss may be put on the actual outcome to explain why it came about. An explicit statement of purpose permits a careful comparison with the outcome with possibly unflattering or embarrassing results for the initiators of the policy. When undertaking a piece of evaluation research, considerable effort may be needed to get those responsible for the policy to state goals in a clear, specific and measurable form (Weiss, 1972, pp. 26–30).

Other problems facing the evaluation researchers include the gap which may exist between the aims of those promulgating a policy and its actual implementation in the field. A number of studies of public bureaucracies have suggested that the lower levels of such organizations are to some extent worlds in themselves. How 'street-level bureaucrats' in schoolteaching, social work, the police and similar organizations interpret policy objectives set at a high level may be different, and constitute a further complication in the design of the study (cf. Lipsky, 1980; Prottas, 1979).

Though policies are conceived by their implementers to achieve certain objectives, the real world is more complex. Many different factors affect particular outcomes, so that policies designed to influence the unemployment rate or the fertility rate, for example, may become confounded with other social pressures and social changes, making the impact of the policy very difficult to disentangle. Moreover, many social policies are designed to reach poorer and less well-off sections of society, who are usually difficult to study, in that they may be hard to find, difficult to follow over time, and in some cases lack the verbal skills upon which sophisticated measurement methods depend. As a final obstacle, those policy-makers who design and implement policy changes usually have no regard for any possible evaluation to be carried out. This often has the effect of limiting the design of the study, particularly ruling out the most powerful type of design, the randomized controlled experiment.

Despite these practical difficulties, evaluation studies can feasibly be carried out, and the model of experimental design holds powerful sway at the design stage of such studies – indeed, it is the ideal. In this respect evaluation research resembles basic social science research, in which the logic of experimental design exercises powerful influence as a guide to sound methodological procedure (cf. Stouffer, 1950), whether or not it is attainable in practice.

> The same model of causality that underlies non-evaluative social research also applies to evaluative research. A chain of interrelated events which for research purposes has only an arbitrary beginning and ending [is] joined by a similarly arbitrary number of intervening steps. All social events have multiple causes and multiple effects and the antecedent–consequent segment chosen to be understood (non-evaluative) or to be changed (evaluative) is dependent upon the research worker's definition of the problem. Thus, no single factor is a necessary and sufficient cause of any other factor and social change can be brought about through many different channels. (Suchman, 1967b, pp. 330–1)

The relationship between independent and dependent variables is thus stated in terms of probabilities, not certainties. The major empirical task is to test for the existence of a significant relationship between independent and dependent variables and then look for intervening or control variables which may influence that relationship. The logic of this procedure is the same for evaluation research as for basic social science research, except that the independent variables are those influenced by the policy whose effects are being investigated, and which are susceptible to manipulation by the policy-maker.

The problem in non-experimental research is to control or randomize the effects of other variables, so the experimental design is preferred. The design is summarized in Figure 8.1. Two groups, an experimental and control group, are selected in such a way that individuals are randomly assigned to each. Measurements are then taken of both groups before the policy change is introduced for the experimental group. At an interval after this change, measurements are taken for both groups again, and the difference between the 'after' and 'before' measurement for each group calculated. If the difference for the experimental group is significantly greater than the before/after difference for the control group, then the policy change may be said to have had a measurable effect.

	Before	Exposure to policy change	After	
Experimental group	a	Yes	b	If the difference between b and a is greater than the
Control group	c	No	d	difference between d and c, the policy change has had a measurable impact.

Figure 8.1   *The logic of experimental design in evaluation research.*

A different way of representing the experimental design of evaluative research is shown in Figure 8.2, which elaborates on the practical treatment of the experimental and control groups and the conditions under which the experiment is conducted. The references to a 'placebo' and to the 'double blind' procedure is a reminder of the prevalence of this type of research in the evaluation of different types of (drug-based) treatments in medicine. The clinical randomized controlled trial is a well-established form of evaluation. It does not always rely on random allocation to experimental or control groups, but if it does not do so it is not then a true randomized experiment. Examples of social policy experiments will be discussed shortly; they represent the ideal in social evaluation studies assessing the overall impact of studies, and the apogee of methodological rigour. In the United States, in particular, many studies of this type have been conducted, on subjects such as negative income tax, housing allowances for the poor, subsidized health insurance, counselling services in prison, police patrol practices, learning in primary schools, and so on. (For a comprehensive bibliography, see Boruch, McSweeny and Soderstrom, 1978, and Boruch, 1987.) Though less common in examining large-scale social policy issues in Britain, experimental designs have been used on a more limited scale in studies in education and criminology.

The essential requirement of true experiments is the randomized assignment of people to experimental and control groups. For various reasons to do with the administration of programmes, this may not be possible: the design of the programme, professional judgement in the selection of clients to benefit from particular treatments, ethical obstacles, and so on (cf. Rivlin and Timpane, 1975). Where random assignment is not possible – as is so in a majority of cases – quasi-experimental designs may be adopted (cf. Cook and Campbell, 1979). These have all the features of the true experiment except random assignment. Various ways are found of controlling most (though not all) of the possible threats to internal validity and enable inferences to be made about the effects of a policy. One way to do this is by time-series before and after measurements, spanning the period in which the policy change was introduced, if possible incorporating comparison with a similar series for another group where the change was not introduced. This is what Donald Campbell in his classic paper 'Reforms as experiments' (1969) terms the interrupted time-series design. The example he discusses there is the state of Connecticut in the USA, whose governor ordered a crackdown on speeding, and whether the effects of this policy were as dramatic as its political proponents claimed. The study involved examining trends over time and comparing those trends to other similar states without a crackdown policy.

Another influential quasi-experimental design is the non-equivalent control group. This strategy is often adopted in drug trials where the experimental group is a pre-selected group of patients, for

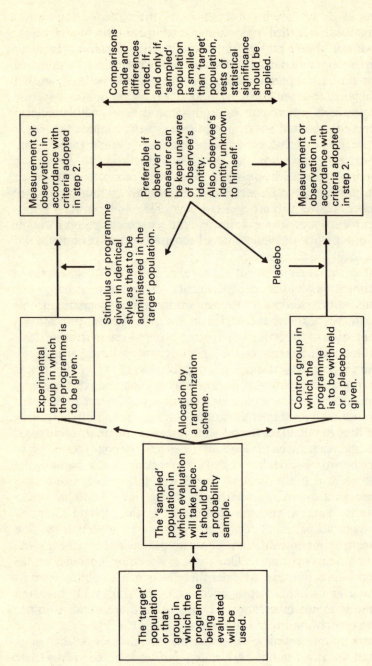

Figure 8.2 A flow chart to illustrate optimum principles and sequence to be followed in conducting a valid experimental design to evaluate a health programme.

Source: Suchman, 1967b, p. 335.

example, those with a particular medical condition. The control group is selected from a similar patient population by matching individuals in each group on a limited number of relevant characteristics (for example, sex, age, social class, medical state). The aim is to make the control group as similar to the experimental group as possible but this is not done by randomization. As one cannot know surely which characteristics to match, it is possible that any differences observed between experimental and control groups are due to extraneous characteristics rather than true effects of the policy. For example, in studying those in receipt of a policy benefit, comparing them with a control group not in receipt of that benefit, there may be motivational differences which distinguish the members of the two groups. On what basis did members of the experimental group join, were they self-selected, or volunteers, and how did they compare with the controls? Quasi-experimental and other non-experimental evaluative research designs will be considered shortly, but first an example of a major randomized experiment will be discussed.

This is the American New Jersey–Pennsylvanian negative income tax experiment (Kershaw, 1972; Watts and Rees, 1976–7; Heclo and Rein, 1980). Though elements of the idea may be traced further back, the idea of negative income tax was first propounded in 1943 in Britain by Lady Juliet Rhys-Williams and about the same time by George Stigler and Milton Friedman at the University of Minnesota (cf. Stigler, 1946). These early suggestions aroused little interest, and it was not until Friedman mentioned the idea in his book *Capitalism and Freedom* (1962) that the attention of a wider circle of economists was attracted. It fell on fertile ground because America (like Britain at about the same period) had re-discovered poverty and was looking for ways of dealing with the twin problems of low incomes and rising welfare dependency.

The Economic Opportunity Act of 1964 created the Office of Economic Opportunity (OEO) and ushered in what has become known as the American 'War on Poverty'. There was support in OEO for introducing negative income tax as national policy implemented by legislation, but this was thought to be politically unacceptable, because the criterion for eligibility was not inability to work but income level. However, there was sufficient support for the idea to lead to the monitoring of a test of a possible national policy, carried out as a true experiment with random assignment of members to different income conditions. The experiment, which began in 1968, was 'the most sophisticated and carefully conducted large-scale social experiment ever carried out in the United States' (Heclo and Rein, 1980, p. 42).

The concept of negative income tax involves a downward extension of the tax system that would pay out cash (negative taxes) to those below a predetermined poverty line. Changes in family income would be monitored, so that as income rose from earnings, the negative tax would be reduced. However, the rate of reduction would be less than the extra earnings, up to a certain point, so that the family was always better off the higher its own earnings. The two essential elements of the idea were that there was a minimum income guarantee level, determined by the number of people in the family, and a marginal tax rate which would reduce the benefit (or negative tax) by less than 100 per cent of each dollar of private income. In putting forward the idea, Friedman argued that it would strengthen individual initiative by enabling poor people to make their own decisions on spending and saving and would cut back on the growing government welfare apparatus. The idea had a particular appeal to economists who were influential in OEO and led to the decision to fund a large-scale trial.

A key question about such a scheme was whether it would reduce participants' incentive to work. The actual title of the experiment was the New Jersey Graduated Work Incentive Experiment. What would be the effects of providing a guaranteed minimum income to all, and what would be the effects on work incentive of different marginal tax rates as a family's earned income brought them above the minimum? Would recipients choose not to work because of the cushion provided by negative income tax? These problems were close to the heart of problems of political implementation on a large scale, and were the focus for the experiment as it was conducted. Given a guaranteed annual income, how much, if any, would recipients reduce their work effort?

The New Jersey negative income tax experiment was conducted jointly by the Institute of Research on Poverty at the University of Wisconsin and Mathematica Inc. of Princeton, New Jersey, a private research firm. It ran from 1968 to 1972 and cost $8 million, $2.4 million of which was paid to those who participated in the experimental groups. It was conducted in New Jersey because it was a densely populated area of the north-east near to Washington and with a high proportion of poor people. The cities selected for sample selection were Trenton (the state capital), Jersey City, Passaic and Patterson. Scranton in Pennsylvania was added to restore the ethnic balance and include some poor white families in a sample otherwise preponderantly black or Puerto Rican.

The experimental design was to test the effects of minimum income support upon work incentives, and involved contrasting treatments of members of the experimental and control groups. The control group received no cash payment, though they were interviewed at intervals throughout the duration of the experiment. The experimental groups were all treated as if a negative income tax existed. Their income was assessed on a regular basis, and they were paid a cash supplement to bring the family income up to the minimum level. Since the purpose of the experiment was to examine the effects of different minimum support levels and marginal tax rates, eight experimental groups were included in the study (plus one control), as shown in Figure 8.3

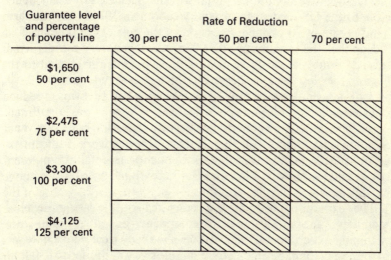

Figure 8.3 *The eight experimental groups in the New Jersey–Pennsylvania negative income tax experiment.*

Note: Shaded areas represent the eight groups.
Source: Kershaw, 1972, p. 23. ©1972 Scientific American Inc. See p. xi.

The two variables in the design were the guarantee level and marginal tax rate (or rate of reduction). Different levels of minimum income guarantee were chosen to test variations in labour market behaviour. The poverty line was set at $3,300 (in 1967), and the four groups chosen had incomes of $3,300 per annum (100 per cent of the poverty line), 50 per cent ($1,650 per annum), 75 per cent ($2,475 per annum) and 125 per cent ($4,125 per annum). The other choice to be made concerned the rate of reduction to be applied. The effects of varying this can be illustrated by numerical examples. If a family's income guarantee is, say, $3,000 per annum, and the rate of reduction is 50 per cent, for every $1,000 the family earns above the minimum, it will keep $500. Thus, if it earned $1,000 above the minimum, the family's negative tax is reduced by $500, and it receives $2,500 negative tax plus $1,000 dollars earnings, or $3,500 in all. If its earnings are $2,000 dollars, it receives $2,000 negative tax and $2,000 earnings, $4,000 in all. When earnings reach $6,000, the family receives no negative tax, since half that income is the amount of the negative tax.

Different assumptions may be made about the appropriate rate of reduction. If the rate were 30 per cent a family would continue to receive negative tax until its total income reached $10,000 a year, close to the US median for a family of four in 1967. On the other hand, a rate of 70 per cent keeps down the cost of the scheme, but means that the maximum of $4,285 is reached very rapidly, and severely limits the incentive to work, since the marginal tax rate is so high. In the New Jersey experiment, three rates of reduction of 30, 50 and 70 per cent were chosen. 'The reasoning was that this group of rates covered the relevant policy range, in as much as a national programme would never be designed with a reduction rate lower than 30% (on cost grounds) or higher than 70% (on work-disincentive grounds)' (Kershaw, 1972, p. 23). Eight experimental groups were constructed as shown in Figure 8.3, four extreme possibilities being excluded as unlikely policy options.

The experimental treatment consisted of the assignment of members of the sample drawn to experimental or control groups, and within the experimental group to one of the eight treatments. Because of the cost of the experiment, total sample size was limited to between 1,000 and 1,500 households. The process of selecting the sample was long and arduous. It was done using probability sampling methods to select blocks in the five cities with low average incomes at the time of the 1960 census. Within these blocks, 48,600 housing units were listed and 27,350 preliminary screening interviews conducted, as a basis for enrolling subjects in the study. This yielded a final total of 1,357 families, 632 in the control group and a total of 725 in the eight different treatment groups. About one in five families dropped out during the study, more in the control than in the treatment groups. Drop out declined with the generosity of the guarantee level and the reduction in the tax rate.

The study was conducted and administered from the Princeton office of Mathematica (Ferber and Hirsch, 1982, pp. 54–8). To be eligible, families had to be intact, with the main wage earner between 21 and 58, and an income less than 150 per cent of the poverty level. When eligibility was established, a long enrolment interview collected data on labour force participation of each member, job changes, attitude to work, financial situation, educational and medical histories, family structure and political and social attitudes. This was repeated every three months for the duration of the study. Families in the experimental group reported their incomes and family composition every four weeks and, on the basis of this information, received a cash payment to bring their income up to the specified minimum. (For those in receipt of state welfare benefits, this was a sum which, added to the benefits, brought their income up to that level.) Sample members were paid for filing income returns, and control group members for each interview and for monthly reporting of current address. Families were free to do whatever they wanted with the negative tax payments received, and continued to be paid (for the duration of the experiment) even if they moved elsewhere during the study.

What results did the study produce? In relation to labour market behaviour, none of the guarantee levels or marginal tax rates had a statistically significant effect on labour force withdrawal. Moreover, some of the findings for families were in the opposite direction. Black, but not white or Puerto Rican, families worked harder and earned more as a result of the guaranteed income. There was some effect on the behaviour of wives, who in white (but not black or Puerto Rican) families reduced their hours worked and labour force participation by one-quarter. No significant effects of the experiment on health, fertility, marital dissolution or school attendance were shown. The lack of effects in general can be interpreted in two ways. It may be taken to show that negative income tax schemes do not have the effect on labour market behaviour which some of their political critics allege, namely to reduce participants' propensity to work. Alternatively, critics have pointed to biases in selection, attrition and welfare programmes to explain the lack of effects between different groups.

It is some interest, therefore, to look at certain other studies of a similar kind subsequently carried out. These are summarized in Table 8.1. As in the first experiment, the key variables were the guarantee level and the treatment rate. Details of the studies may be consulted elsewhere (Feber and Hirsch, 1982, pp. 79–91). In general, the findings support those of New Jersey about labour market behaviour. The effect on the behaviour of the main wage earner is

Table 8.1 Background Information on Income-Maintenance Experiments

Item	NJ–Penn.	Rural NC–Iowa	Denver	Seattle	Gary
Eligibility					
Race	All	Black, white	All	All	Black
Age of head	18–58	18–58	18–58	18–58	18–58
Sex of head	Male	Both	Both	Both	Both
Type of family	Intact	Any	Two or more	Two or more	One dependent
Consumer unit	Household	Family	Family	Family	Household
Income relative to poverty line	Under 150%	Under 150%			
Site(s)	Trenton, Patterson–Passaic, Jersey City, NJ, Scranton, Pa.	Two rural areas, one in N. Carolina, one in Iowa	City of Denver	City of Seattle	City of Gary
Treatment variables					
Support levels (ratio to poverty level)	0.5, 0.75, 1.00, 1.25	0.5, 0.75, 1.00	1.00, 1.26, 1.48[a]		0.75, 1.00[a]
Tax rates	0.3, 0.5, 0.7	0.3, 0.5, 0.7	0.5, 0.7, $0.7-0.0254y$, $0.8-0.025y$		0.4, 0.6
Counselling (c) and training (t) subsidies	None	None	$c, c+0.5t, c+t$		None
Day care subsidies	None	None	None	None	35%, 60%, 80%, 100%
Time horizon (years)	3	3	3, 5, 20	3, 5	3
Experimental combinations	8	5	84	84	4[b]
Sample size					
Initial	1,216	809	2,758	2,042	1,799
Final	983	729			
Period of study	1967–74	1968–76	1971–91	1970–91	1971–7
Period of fieldwork	1968–72	1970–2	1971–91	1970–6	1971–4
Sponsor(s)	OEO, HEW	Ford Fdn, OEO, HEW	HEW	HEW	HEW, Indiana
Principal contractor(s)	IRP, Mathematica	IRP	IRP	SRI	MPR

[a] Rough approximations of ratios of dollar support levels.
[b] Excludes four experimental child care subsidy rates applied to selected families.

slight, but is more substantial on secondary earners, particularly the spouse. Differences by ethnic group were not the same as in New Jersey, reduction in hours worked being appreciably greater in black and hispanic families as a result of participation. Various effects were shown in relation to health costs (reducing medical debt), housing (moving out of subsidized housing) and expenditure (increase in purchase of consumer goods by experimental group families). In the Seattle–Denver experiment, there was a significantly higher rate of marital dissolution among experimental families, particularly for those in receipt of less generous income guarantees.

A further set of findings, which have received rather less attention, concern the way in which such schemes are administered. The running of the experiments proved to be more complex than was at first anticipated. Effort had to be devoted to working out rules to be applied and to explaining the basis on which participants should report income (confusion of gross and net pay was common) and the principles by which transfer payments were made. This is a matter of considerable importance, affecting as it may do subjects' under-standing of the consequences of labour market behaviour. Those administering the experiments had to develop complex rules for entitlement and the experiments' most important contribution 'may be, not what it tells about people's work behaviour, but about supposedly technical questions of administration' (Heclo and Rein, 1980, p. 43). Indeed, the idea of a negative income tax in Britain was introduced for discussion and then abandoned in the 1970s precisely because of what were seen as intractable practical obstacles to its effective administration.

Criticism of income-maintenance experiments has concentrated on several features of the schemes. One is that the effects of recruit-ment, mortality and attrition will be apparent in the outcome variable, and therefore the results will not be unbiased. For example, to the extent that self-selection operates, participants may see the experiment as an opportunity to increase their future earning power, rather than act as a 'cushion' on which to relax for a while. The length of experiments is also relevant. The five-year Seattle–Denver study found more marked labour market changes in the fourth and fifth years. Secondly, critics maintain that an experiment is often an idealized version of a policy, which it may be difficult to maintain under the same conditions as a national policy. Thirdly, parameters relevant to the policy effects may change significantly when an experimental policy becomes a national one. Participants' under-standings of what is happening, for example, are likely to be significantly higher when policy is a national one (Nicholson and Wright, 1977). This in turn may influence in one direction or another the outcome of the experiment. Finally, the cost of such exercises is considerable. The Seattle–Denver experiment cost three times the New Jersey–Pennsylvania project, and other American experiments in employment and housing even more. Cynics also point out that the significance of the results of large-scale experiments are far from proportionate to the expenditure on them.

In fact, the more interesting question, reverting to theme, is to ask how these experiments have fed into the policy-making process. Heclo and Rein summarize (1980, pp. 34–41) the outcome in policy terms the following way. OEO was the prime mover in the experiments, despite its rejection of the principle of transfers, because of its brief for 'opportunity' and the influence of economists within it. The early findings of the New Jersey experiment were intended to be used to get political and public support for a new Family Assistance Plan, which had been worked out in advance of the experiment. However, the preliminary results produced not support for welfare reform but more controversy. Meanwhile, basic notions of negative income taxation diffused into other legislation before evidence about incentive effects could be discerned. Action did not wait for tested knowledge.

> Finally, when knowledge from the experiment did become available, it proved to be far from decisive. Instead, it was surrounded by uncertainties and raised more questions than it settled. Moreover ... there were no immediate users of the experimentally-derived information inasmuch as the ferment for reform had passed. When the weakness of the final experimental results surfaced, experimentation had already won wide acceptance in the social science community as an important aid in policy development. (Heclo and Rein, 1980, p. 36)

This is not an unfamiliar story, and one to the implications of which the reader will return in the final chapter. For the moment let it be noted, and let us consider further the place of social experiments in evaluation.

Social experiments remain the Rolls Royces or Cadillacs of evaluative research design both because of their superior inferential power and because of their glamour. Yet they are not without their critics. One criticism centres on the effects of randomized social experiments. Typically the results are inconclusive or the amount of variance explained small. While this is true of most types of social research, correlation data from *ex post facto* non-experimental comparisons may provide as conclusive evidence (cf. Sinclair and Clarke, 1981, pp. 109–10). Another criticism centres on the feasibility of isolating discrete variables for study under experimental circumstances. A desire to maximize internal validity leads to purging independent variables (through randomization) of other variables to which they are inevitably linked. The New Jersey experiment, for example, was imposed upon an existing welfare structure and a wide range of ethnic, geographic and class variations, yet these were ignored in the design which concentrated on the work behaviour of isolated households assumed to be relatively independent of each other (Berk and Rossi, 1976, pp. 340–1). Thus elegance of experimental design, it is argued, is achieved at the expense of building oversimplified models of the real world.

Proponents of field experiments argue justifiably that the feasibility of such studies is often underestimated and the obstacles exaggerated. Nevertheless, the ethical problems in large-scale experiments are considerable, ranging from criteria for the assignment of subjects to experimental and control group, through the extent of information which subjects are given, to questions of confidentiality of identities of those participating and of the resulting data. Experiments are a form of social intervention which, as the rise of marital dissolution in the Seattle–Denver experiment shows, may have unpredictable consequences.

Two different criticisms pursue a similar theme. One is that though social experiments may show effects, these are usually not repeatable in the future in subsequent experiments or in practice. This is a variation on the theme of the lack of replication in social science, with the added implication that certain effects may be apparent in the circumstances of one experiment which do not appear subsequently. The other criticism is that even if experiments do show strong effects, these rarely have a major impact on policy unless they satisfy other criteria such as being a tightly designed study addressed to specific hypotheses, the results of which challenge received wisdom on a particular subject (cf. Acland, 1979). Finally, the political assumptions which underlie some experimental research have been attacked. Evaluation research may validate a particular view of social problems by emphasizing certain outcomes as opposed to others. The issue of work incentives in the income-tax experiments, for example, was one which preoccupied conservative members of Congress. Other objectives, such as improved health or enrichment of leisure time, were avoided or played down in the design of the study (Berk and Rossi, 1976, p. 339).

Taken together these criticisms are not an overwhelming attack on the use of large-scale social experiments, but do suggest caution in approaching them. They are not, it appears, the panacea that, for example, randomized clinical trials are sometimes held out to be by medical researchers. They have real strengths, but also limitations by comparison to other types of evaluation research. They tend to be treated as the ideal, but in practice other types of design may be effective for some kinds of evaluation. Most people after all do not drive around in Rolls Royces or Cadillacs, even if they represent some peak of automobile engineering perfection.

Quasi-experimental designs have already been briefly considered, but more needs to be said about non-experimental designs in evaluation research. Though lacking the rigour of experimental designs, they have distinct uses particularly for formative evaluation. They are somewhat less satisfactory for summative evaluation. The most extensively used design is the after-only comparison, comparing the effects of different kinds of policy in different settings after the event. A good example would be different types of regime in penal institutions.

An elegant defence of what they term cross-institutional designs of this type is offered by Sinclair and Clarke (1981). The method proceeds by comparing a large number of institutions of a particular type within a single research design. Measures of various aspects of treatment are correlated with measures of outcomes. A considerable number of institutions need to be included, but if this is done, then the design is potentially suitable for evaluating institutions as various as prisons or courts, looking at police behaviour or examining vandalism on housing estates. Barbara Tizard (1975) used the method to study residential nurseries, and Michael Rutter et al. (1979) to study ordinary secondary schools. Since the policies which are being evaluated are commonly provided through various institutional settings, this is a particularly appropriate design to use.

An example of such a study was that by Sinclair of probation hostels to which young offenders were sent by the courts as a milder alternative to borstal or approved school. The proportion of boys who absconded or further offended varied from 14 to 78 per cent in England and Wales between hostels. This variation could not be accounted for in terms of the intake of each hostel nor by size, age range, location or sentencing policy. Differences in success rates were as great between wardens who succeeded each other in the same hostel as it was between hostels. The study showed that a considerable proportion of the variation could be accounted for by the way in which the warden and his wife ran the hostel. Wardens with the lowest rate of premature leaving were those who maintained strict discipline but expressed warmth towards the boys and were in agreement with their wives about how to run the hostels. Other combinations were associated with lower success rates. The study shows also the importance of the 'intermediate environment' in penal policy implementation, though it exercises effects in combination with a history of prior delinquent behaviour.

As a type of design, Sinclair and Clarke (1981) argue, the cross-institutional design is capable of picking up 'effects' which randomized experiments (for example, comparing a 'traditional' with a 'therapeutic' regime in a pair of institutions) may not be able to do. This is in part because in studying a range of institutions, attention may be concentrated on the most or least successful ones in the field. Research covering a number of units which can order these on a range of different regime variables has a better chance of disentangling the precise effect of particular factors on outcome. Though correlation analysis does not prove causation, it may in certain cases, as the example of lung cancer shows. In certain cross-institutional designs, such as the example cited, very large treatment effects may be demonstrated, and if these can be shown to be unrelated to background factors but related to type of treatment received (e.g. type of regime) then the relationship between intervention and outcome may be usefully evaluated.

In a discussion of American evaluation research, Rossi and Berk draw attention to the potential for after-only comparisons where random assignment is impractical or impossible, using multivariate statistical techniques coupled with extensive data collection efforts to obtain measures of some of the confounding factors. Though statistical perfection can never be achieved, 'quite often, useful and reasonably accurate measures of programme effects can be obtained despite modest violations of the required statistical assumptions' (Rossi and Berk, 1983, p. 200).

Another non-experimental design is the before-and-after study of a single action project, taking a series of measures of participants as they move through a programme, to see how well the hypothesized changes aimed at are achieved. These types of data can be supplemented by intensive qualitative analysis of events and processes. An example is provided by the Kent Community Care Project, undertaken by Bleddyn Davies and David Challis. Its aim was to evaluate more effective care in their own homes of the frail elderly population, on the margins of need for residential care. This action project aimed to provide more cost-effective, flexible services suited to individual's needs, and the reduction or postponement of the need for residential care. The study is described in detail elsewhere (Challis and Davies, 1980; Davies, 1981), but it included giving social service departments' area management teams much greater financial control in managing their own budget, and made particularly extensive use of paid and unpaid helpers.

The design of the evaluation involved an analytic history of policy and practice, data collection on a wide range of outcomes, and detailed attention to the structure of costs and inputs (with a view to applying opportunity-cost principles). The motivations of paid and unpaid carers were probed in intensive interviews when they were first recruited and again a year later (cf. Qureshi, 1985). Comparison was made with 'conventional' provision of social services for the elderly, but not using a randomized design. Given the small number of clients in the scheme,

> randomisation would be unlikely to do much to ensure comparable groups ... With small numbers and subjects hetero-geneous with respect to circumstances affecting outcomes, randomisation would be unlikely to ensure much more comparability than a quasi-experimental design. Moreover, randomisation may be a sacred cow that actually contaminates the field without yielding much milk; it may add little to the potential of the project for making inferences. (Davies and Challis, 1981, p. 182)

The project being evaluated was a small-scale one, which it was not feasible to launch in several areas simultaneously. It was concentrated in the Isle of Thanet in Kent. The evaluation therefore focused on differences between project areas. The design of the evaluation focused on the variance between clients with different characteristics in different circumstances within the small project area, and the impact upon them of innovation in service provision and delivery. The researchers argued that a mix of hard evaluation data and softer analyses of different kinds provided the optimum research strategy in this particular case.

A third type of non-experimental evaluative design is the 'after-only' study in a single setting. Such an *ex post facto* design suffers from various problems. Measurements are made of the effects of intro-ducing a new policy after the event, attempting to infer what have been the results of the policy change. The problem is that evidence is lacking both for a control group which has not been exposed to policy change, and for the prior state of the group being studied. Data may be collected in the form of retrospective reports by participants of their prior status, but reliance on such recall data, particularly about attitudes and feelings, is problematical (Moss and Goldstein, 1979). Such designs, moreover, are vulnerable to many confounding effects, such as changes over time in those affected by the policy, selective drop-out and so on (Weiss, 1972, p. 76). It is often difficult to disentangle the supposed effect of policy innovation from such artefacts.

An 'after-only' study may, however, have more limited usefulness in throwing light on the delivery of services to those for whom they are intended, and particularly on whether recipients are getting what they are supposed to be receiving. This is related to the phenomena of lower-level workers in an agency – so-called 'street-level bureaucrats' (Lipsky, 1980) – subtly transforming the aims of policies and programmes when putting them into operation with clients. The problem is very often that study of such situations is difficult, either because of sampling problems or because of interference effects in trying to introduce an observer into face-to-face interaction between bureaucrat and client. An ingenious systematic study of such an interaction was Reiss's (1971) study of encounters between police and citizens. Research assistants rode with police patrols to record systematically each encounter between the officers and members of the public. A considerable number of observers were used so that comparable independent measures were made; there was not reliance upon one or a few social scientists (Reiss, 1968). The results of the study portray how such encounters were generated, how the behaviour of citizens influenced the police response, and what was the outcome of this behaviour.

Such studies have a particular role to play in evaluation, with implications for administrative control or future legislation.

> Programs that depend heavily on personnel for delivery, or that involve complicated programs calling for individualised treatments of beneficiaries, are especially good candidates for careful and sensitive fine-tuning research because such programs increase the difficulties of implementation. (Rossi and Berk, 1983, p. 195)

'After-only' evaluation studies can provide real insights into how such difficulties might be tackled.

Two other types of non-experimental evaluation research should be mentioned, though they are less distinctive and overlap with general styles of social research. Identifying and mapping the existence of a social problem does not automatically lead to policies to tackle the problem. Greater understanding is needed of the genesis of the problem. To this task, policy-oriented general social science research is relevant, providing evidence and understandings grounded in middle-range social science theory. Two examples will illustrate the point. To frame policies to alleviate unemployment and underemployment among urban blacks, the nature of the problems they face in finding employment needs to be understood. Studies such as Eliot Liebow's ethnographic study of *Tally's Corner* (1967) aid in this, though not directly oriented to policy. Liebow shows how, in a group of apparently 'workshy' young black men, all have sound rational reasons for rejecting offers of low-paid construction work which they could have taken (see extract on pages 181–2). He illuminates their job-searching behaviour in a way that is relevant to policy-making or more rigorous evaluations of policy.

Treatment of juvenile delinquents is another area in which much formal evaluation research has been carried out. This too requires an understanding of the underlying and precipitating factors in the causation of delinquency, to which middle-range criminological research is relevant. Knowledge about the phenomenon is important to estimate how proposed changes might work. Policy-oriented researchers are interested primarily in the variance in behaviour which is susceptible to influence by policy measures. This may in fact be quite small but it is important to be able to identify policy-mutable variables and estimate the effects on them of planned intervention.

The other type of non-experimental research is monitoring, a continuing process of systematic research surveillance. This overlaps with the area of social indicators, but is not identical with it. Monitoring seeks to trace trends in key variables which are important to policy-makers. Thus the British Crime Surveys of 1982 and 1984 (Hough and Mayhew, 1983, 1985), carried out by the Home Office, were aimed at estimating the amount of crime reported by victims, the so-called 'dark figure' as opposed to crime statistics based on incidents reported to and known by the police which are affected by differential propensities to report and record different types of offence.

Such studies do not only cover the incidence of conditions, but may involve assessment of need. National disability studies in Britain in 1969 and 1985 have served this purpose. The well-known study by

Coleman and others of equality of educational opportunity (Coleman Report, 1966) was intended by Congress to provide an assessment of how educational services and facilities were distributed by race and socio-economic status. 'Although needs assessment research is ordinarily undertaken primarily to develop accurate estimates of the amounts and distribution of a given problem, and hence is intended to be descriptive, often enough such research can also yield some understanding of the processes involved in generating the problem in question' (Rossi and Berk, 1983, pp. 187–8). This was so in the Coleman study.

Another form of monitoring concerns whether services are reaching those for whom they are intended. Case-registers, for example, are used in a number of areas in Britain to monitor the mental health of the local population, and are described by Wing (1981, pp. 262–9). Some registers attempt to collect more detailed information in order to monitor progress. In Salford, for example, chronic schizophrenic patients who need regular supervision from community psychiatric nurses are placed on an 'active list', so that contact and treatment can be regularly checked. This is an example of a system designed both for practice and research. Sometimes monitoring of service coverage is carried out purely as a research exercise.

The discussion in this chapter so far has been concerned with different methodological strategies for evaluation research and social experimentation. It has emphasized the need for rigorous and high methodological standards in designing such research, which is greater than in the case of basic research because findings may immediately be fed to and influence the decisions of policy-makers. It would be quite misleading to give the impression, however, that evaluation research is conducted in a vacuum. It is not. It is conducted to assist in the analysis of problems and policies which are highly political both in their definition and in their determination.

Berk and Rossi, for example, have argued that evaluation research has become part of the process of defining social problems. Most evaluations are of specific or new government programmes, and many (though not all) studies show insignificant or trivial effects of such interventions, which contributes to a growing sense of the intractability of social problems. This may merely reflect the timidity of policy-makers. Social policy innovations rarely exceed the limits of the dominant political ideology, and the weak effects of programmes are likely to be a consequence of this. There are other effects.

Perhaps most important, the astructural, ahistorical biases of evaluation methodology reinforce the idea that the rationale for social change can rest on impartial and objective assessments of societal performance. Evaluation findings are put forward as judgements above politics, based on scientific data, not organised interests. (Berk and Rossi, 1976, pp. 341–2)

Clearly evaluation, however rigorously conducted, is not above politics, and becomes part of the complex process of policy formulation discussed in Chapter 1. But precisely how it can come to terms with this political dimension is the subject of disagreement. For some, applied research is so tainted, so sullied with the compromises of practical politics, that it is outside the pale. For others, involvement in evaluative research leads to the adoption of a radical analytic stance. The case of the Community Development Projects (CDPs), reviewed in an earlier collection (Bulmer, 1978, pp. 110–200), is an example. The projects were established in twelve localities in Britain from 1970 as action-research attempts to increase understanding of social needs, try to improve co-ordination of central and local services, and encourage local participation. Action teams of community development workers had alongside them university- and polytechnic-based research teams to carry out evaluation. Within a short time, the research teams began to reject the original 'social pathology' model and propose a 'structural' alternative which emphasized the contribution of industrial loss to inner city decline.

This, at least, was the myth propounded by CDP activists themselves, though it is open to doubt (Loney, 1983). The significant point here, however, is not the merits or demerits of the politicization of CDP which occurred, but its consequences for systematic evaluation research. Generally this was catastrophic. The ambiguous role of the research teams was resolved either by merging with action teams and abandoning evaluation, or attempting to maintain an academic stance and arousing the hostility of the committed action researchers (Marshal et al., 1978, p. 46). Because of the shift towards analysis in terms of the national economic determinants of local disadvantage, little in the way of systematic evaluation was carried out, while general analyses of the problems of the inner city took their place. Much of the output of CDP teams was a research-based general social critique, not an examination of the implementation and consequences of specific social interventions. As an action-research project, CDP was methodologically unsophisticated and in its ultimate outcome set back systematic large-scale evaluation studies in Britain by some years.

An alternative view of the role of evaluation research has been put forward by a group of government researchers (Marshall *et al.*, 1978). They criticize the 'social engineering' assumptions which underpin conventional evaluations treating the researcher as a technical specialist at the service of the policy-making apparatus, and argue for evaluation as 'illumination' (Parlett and Hamilton, 1976) serving more general democratic goals. Research-based evaluation of social policy should not simply be the last stage in the process, a measure of effectiveness when everything else is settled, but a continuous process throughout the definition of problems and formulation of policy.

> Research can contribute to the knowledge of the resources and services required by different groups, how they are likely to be used, and the wider problems which may ensue, such as obstructions by other interests, implications for other social policies, ethical matters, and the influence of public perceptions or misperceptions. (Marshall *et al.*, 1978, p. 59)

Research should be available publicly to inform debate, to change people's attitudes, and alter the conditions for the implementation of policy.

In this view, research would focus more on means (acceptability) rather than ends (effectiveness) and would carry out studies from many viewpoints, distributing findings to all parties for information and open criticism. There would be no forced attempt – such as wrecked the CDP programme – to reconcile opposed values; their existence would be recognized and acknowledged. 'Policy-making in practice is more concerned with means than ends, and especially with political competition for scarce resources' (ibid., p. 41). There is much that is commendable in this view, linked as it is to a commitment to government by agreement and openness in deliberations about policy-making.

It may be asked, however, how well it accords with the reality of government decision-making in industrial societies. Is it really feasible to envisage policy-making taking place in much more openness than at present, given the entrenched position of ministers, civil servants and back-bench MPs, not to mention pressure groups, the media and other outside interests? A more realistic strategy directed towards the same objective may be to foster alternative centres of evaluation research which can challenge analyses put forward from more conventional standpoints. Parliamentary select committees and trade unions are both institutions which might fruitfully initiate evaluation studies. Indeed, this is precisely the direction in which the US Congress has moved. The General Accounting Office (equivalent to the British Comptroller and Auditor-General) now has an evaluation research division staffed by a large group of professional social scientists, which carries out evaluations of programmes which are mandated in federal legislation. This is to provide Congress with its own independent evidence to rival that available to the executive branch (Rist, 1987). Marshall *et al.* (1978) are right in arguing for evaluations of broader scope and from different points of view, but in the type of interest-group based political system which operates in Britain and the United States, this is likely to be achieved less by some rather nebulous appeal to openness and free exchange of information. Rather, one should seek to establish alternative centres of analysis from which different scientific evaluation studies can be carried out on different assumptions, and their results compared.

A third approach to evaluation research in a politically charged environment is to acknowledge that evaluation research may rest on significant moral and political value judgements, but to maintain that nevertheless 'evaluation research has some of the same liberating potential as other social science activities. Good social science is at least a demystifying activity' (Berk and Rossi, 1976, p. 342). If common assumptions are tested with data, scepticism is reinforced by increased understanding. Knowledge may itself be a good, even though it is not the only or even a significant determinant of the outcome of policy debates. Analysis which is objectively arrived at has an important contribution to make to policy determination, particularly in the medium to long term.

> Of course, demystification merely strips away the crust of conventional wisdom. The same set of startling findings can be interpreted in either a conservative or more radical direction . . . While evaluation research is political, it is no substitute for politics. Social science can demystify, but it remains the task of politics to interpret the meaning of demystification for direction of political policy. (Berk and Rossi, 1976, pp. 343–4)

The claims of social science to be taken seriously rest not only upon methodological rigour but on theoretical insight. Chen and Rossi (1980) have argued that the apparent lack of effects shown by evaluation studies is attributable to their failure to match research designs to programme designs. There is a need in designing evaluations to blend the potential effects as defined by the programme with possible effects derived from social science knowledge and theory concerning the subject in question. Such a multigoal, theory-driven approach to evaluation is likely to be more fruitful than one which simply takes the administrator's goals at face value. The negative income tax experiment had a strong theoretical input from economics, but arguably this theory was too narrow and the range of possible outcomes envisaged (mainly labour market behaviour) too restricted. Social scientists have to offer as evaluators not just methodological know-how but also theoretical understanding.

This will not resolve the question of the place of values in evaluation research, but it makes clearer the claim of social science to independent knowledge. Analysis and action remain in the final outcome distinct. The best safeguards against evaluation research becoming a tool of those holding the reins of power are to maintain its demystifying role, to encourage the development of alternative, competing, centres which produce evaluations based on alternative assumptions and theories, while insisting upon the rigorous scientific standards which it has been the aim of this chapter to explicate.

9

The Value of Qualitative Methods

The methods considered in the last chapter tend to the 'hard' end of the methodological continuum, following strict canons of research design and producing quantitative results. This is not true of all evaluation research, but it is the predominant style. The question may be posed, however, whether there is not room in policy research for more qualitative research methods and styles. The dominant impression is that policy research conducted in and for government is overwhelmingly quantitative, and that the use of qualitative methods is a luxury enjoyed by some academics who are prepared to relax their standards of methodological rigour. Yet when one looks at what in practice is being done, the impression is somewhat misleading. There are also logical objections to regarding quantitative methods as uniquely rigorous.

To quote the evocative title of one article, 'Are randomized experiments the Cadillacs of design?' (Acland, 1979). 'If you are a policy-maker and you have a choice between a survey that asked the wrong questions very explicitly, or an ethnography that asked the right questions but you cannot tell how they were asked and of whom, which one would you pick to base policy on?' (Agar, 1980, p. 10). Do the results of research have to be in the form of numbers to be taken seriously by policy-makers? There is legitimate argument among social scientists both about the optimum type of design for particular purposes and the ways in which data should be collected and presented. The aim of this chapter is to examine some of those methods which are qualitative rather than quantitative, 'soft' rather than 'hard'.

Various examples of qualitative research have been mentioned in earlier chapters. One can serve as an example. Eliot Liebow's *Tally's Corner: A Study of Street Corner Men* (1967) is an ethnographic study carried out in a black area of Washington DC. It addresses, in part, similar issues about unemployment, income maintenance and work incentives affecting the poor and disadvantaged to those in the negative income tax experiments, but in a very different way. Liebow got to know a group of young black men who hung around a take-away food shop on one street corner in the ghetto (hence the title), by dint of living in the area and spending a period of months getting to know the men he was studying, hanging around with them and taking part in various of their activities. It was an in-depth study. Liebow gathered rich data about various aspects of their lives, but studied in all no more than fifteen men. He got to know them well (while making clear that he was a social scientist) and presented his interpretation of their social situation and world-view, with frequent verbatim quotation. *Tally's Corner* provides an analysis of the lot of the young black unemployed which is highly relevant for policy, yet is cast in a very different form to that of most evaluation research.

The following passage describes observations of labour market behaviour:

A pickup truck drives slowly down the street. The truck stops as it comes abreast of a man sitting on a cast-iron porch and the white driver calls out, asking if the man wants a day's work. The man shakes his head and the truck moves on up the block, stopping again whenever idling men come within calling distance of the driver. At the Carry-out corner, five men debate the question briefly and shake their heads no to the truck . . .

What is it we have witnessed here? A labor scavenger rebuffed by his would-be prey? Lazy, irresponsible men turning down an honest day's pay for an honest day's work? Or a more complex phenomenon marking the intersection of economic forces, social values and individual states of mind and body? Let us look again at the driver of the truck. He has been able to recruit only two or three men from each twenty or fifty he contacts. To him, it is clear that the others simply do not choose to work.

Quite apart from the question of whether or not this is true of some of the men he sees on the street, it is clearly not true of all of them. If it were, he would not have come here in the first place; or having come, he would have left with an empty truck. It is not even true of most of them, for most of the men he sees on the street this weekday morning do, in fact, have jobs. But since, at the moment, they are neither working nor sleeping, and since they hate the depressing room or apartment they live in, or because there is nothing to do there, or because they want to get away from their wives or anyone else living there, they are out on the street, indistinguishable from those who do not have jobs or do not want them. Some, like Boley, a member of a trash-collection crew in a suburban housing development, work Saturdays and are off on this weekday . . . Some men work for retail businesses such as liquor stores which do not begin the day until ten o'clock. Some laborers, like Tally, have already come back from the job because the ground was too wet for pick and shovel or because the weather was too cold for pouring concrete . . .

Also on the street, unwitting contributors to the impression taken away by the truck driver, are the halt and the lame. The man on the cast-iron steps strokes one gnarled arthritic hand with the other and says he doesn't know whether or not he'll live long enough to be eligible for Social Security. He pauses, then adds matter-of-factly, 'Most times, I don't care whether I do or don't.' Stoopy's left leg was polio-withered in childhood. Raymond, who looks as if he could tear out a fire hydrant, coughs up blood if he bends or moves suddenly . . .

Others, having had jobs and been paid off, are drawing unemployment compensation (up to $44 per week) and have nothing to gain by accepting work which pays little more than this and frequently less. Still others, like Bumboodle the numbers man, are working hard at illegal ways of making money, hustlers who are on the street to turn a dollar any way they can. (Liebow, 1967, pp. 29–33)

Tally's Corner is written in fine prose. At one level it can be enjoyed as a vivid description of a life rather far removed from that of the typical middle-class reader. Critics of qualitative research of this type charge that such studies are usually largely descriptive, that the line dividing them from journalism is a fine one, and that the results cannot be generalized to a larger population. What the critics overlook is that the description conceals a rather subtle analysis of a social problem, and that far from being journalism, such studies are carried out within a body of theory and following clear methodological guides. Liebow, for example, explicitly criticizes theories of the subculture of the poor and attempts to explain their behaviour more in situational terms.

It is useful to consider some of the differences between quantitative and qualitative research more generally. Table 9.1 contrasts two paradigms of applied social research, the quantitative and the qualitative. These are ideal types, accentuated one-sided views of reality to bring out the essential differences, without implying that they are all present in particular cases. The characteristics of the quantitative paradigm are exemplified by the field experiment with random assignment discussed in the preceding chapter. Those of the qualitative paradigm are exemplified in Liebow's study. His research seeks to interpret behaviour from the actor's frame of reference, although the social scientist adds his own interpretation and analysis. The research was conducted in a naturalistic setting, without controls on the observations which Liebow made. The study is subjective in the sense that it is one social scientist's interpretation, based on his own participation, without checks from others and without replication. Liebow was an 'insider' in so far as a white research worker can be in a black ghetto. His research produced rich data with claims to validity despite the limited range of its ability to generalize. It sought to understand the process of becoming and being unemployed and black in the inner city, offering theoretical generalizations about this process, even though they did not rest upon data about many cases. Liebow's research was exploratory rather than hypothesis-testing, in the sense that he sought to construct an explanation from the results of his field studies, rather than starting out with an initial preformed idea.

Table 9.1   *Contrasting Quantitative and Qualitative Paradigms in Policy Research*

Quantitative paradigm	*Qualitative paradigm*
Advocates use of quantitative methods	Advocates use of qualitative methods
Positivist in orientation: seeks objective facts about and causes of social phenomena with little or no reference to subjective states of individuals	Phenomenological or *verstehen* in orientation, seeking to understand human behaviour from the social actor's own frame of reference
Obtrusive and controlled measurement	Naturalistic and uncontrolled observation
Objective	Subjective
Removed from the data: the 'outsider' perspective	Close to the data: the 'insider' perspective
Verification-oriented, inferential, confirmatory and hypothesis-testing	Discovery-oriented, descriptive, exploratory and inductive
Outcome-oriented	Process-oriented
Reliable; 'hard' and replicable data	Valid; 'real', 'rich' and 'deep' data
Generalizable; multiple case-studies	Ungeneralizable; single case-studies
Particularistic	Holistic
Assumes a stable reality	Assumes a dynamic reality

Source: Reichardt and Cook, 1979, p. 10.

Different types of quantitative research have been discussed in Chapters 5–8. What do qualitative methods used in policy research look like? They may be classified in various ways. Ethnographic research in the manner of *Tally's Corner* is but one style. The following different modes of qualitative research may be distinguished:

(1) The historical study of policy development. Keith Banting's work in Chapter 3 is an excellent example of the genre, combining documentary research with interviews with former participants in the policy process within an historical framework. As one goes back in time, reliance on documentary sources becomes total. For example, Paul Starr's study of *The Social Transformation of American Medicine* (1982) uses a range of varied sources, published and unpublished, to trace the evolution of the American medical profession.

(2) Contemporary documentary research. It is possible to base the study of a policy-related issue entirely upon available contemporary documents. These could include published documents such as parliamentary reports, government publications or newspapers, and unpublished documents, particularly of organizations involved in the policy-making process. Studies based on content analysis are often of this kind (e.g. Hartmann and Husband, 1974), though not always exclusively using documentary sources.

(3) Intensive, informal interviewing is another characteristic method in qualitative policy research. Respondents whose social situation or behaviour is the object of study are selected, and they are then questioned at length. Instead of using the structured, pre-coded type of interview schedule discussed in Chapter 5, however, such interviews use many more open-ended questions and may be more discursive in character. Dennis Marsden's study *Mothers Alone* (1973), discussed below, tried to make the interview as much like a conversation as possible, while in Frank Coffield *et al.*'s case study of four deprived families (Coffield, Robinson and Sarsby, 1980) the research began with unstructured interviews and developed into one akin to friendship, though with the research purpose explicit throughout. Some of the four families were visited as many as thirty times. This is unusual even for intensive interviewing, but completely different from the conventional large-scale survey interview involving one visit to ask largely pre-structured questions.

(4) Non-participant observation is a possible though rarely used method. Indeed, one of the oldest examples of applied research

in Britain, Mass Observation, which began in the 1930s, used methods of direct observation (without communication) taken from ornithology (Stanley, 1981; Calder, 1985). The reason the method is used relatively rarely is the limits upon the inferences about people's behaviour which can be made from observing without speaking to them and eliciting their own interpretations.

(5) Participant observation, also called 'field research', 'intensive fieldwork' or 'ethnography', is therefore a much more commonly used method. This was the method used in *Tally's Corner*. If access can be negotiated, this can provide most illuminating insights into the ways of life of people to whom policies are directed, the workings of organizations which deliver services to clients, and the processes by which policies are arrived at in high-level policy-making. *Tally's Corner* provides one example of the first type. Another is James Patrick's covert participant observation study, *A Glasgow Gang Observed* (1973), which provides rich material for the understanding of gang dynamics and its relationship to delinquency. Ethnographic studies of the second type include Peter Blau's *The Dynamics of Bureaucracy* (1963), which examines a state employment agency and a law enforcement agency to show the way in which formal structures are modified in informal practice by 'street-level bureaucrats' (see Lipsky, 1980). Jonathan Rubinstein's study *City Police* (1973), by a researcher who trained as a policeman and travelled around in patrol cars in a north American city, provides a bird's eye view of how police on patrol duty deal with the day-to-day contingencies which face them. High-level policy-making is the subject of Heclo and Wildavsky's *The Private Government of Public Money* (1974), which deals with Treasury control of public expenditure in Britain. The researchers were given access under limiting conditions principally relating to policy content to the deliberations of senior civil servants and ministers in various government departments, and relied on a mixture of attendance at meetings, informal interviewing and reading documents. The study is discussed further below, but it is a reminder that the term 'participant observation' is misleading. The method usually involves several different types of data collection, within the framework of continuing interaction between researcher and subjects over a period of weeks or months.

(6) Personal documents are also used on occasion as a source in

policy research. Chicago criminologist Clifford Shaw, whose ecological research is discussed in Chapter 11, also made strenuous efforts to collect life histories of delinquent boys, and to analyse them systematically. After careful checking, he published the story of one of them, Stanley, in *The Jack Roller* (Shaw, 1966), which provides a vivid picture of a career of juvenile delinquency and crime (see also Plummer, 1983).

(7) A rather different type of qualitative input to policy-making, to which we will return, is that provided by the social scientist as adviser or consultant to the policy-maker. This is a different role to that of the more dispassionate and detached researcher discussed so far, but very frequently involves feeding in qualitative research results and insights. It also provides a reminder that the ultimate goal of applied research is to influence policy.

This classification is not completely exhaustive, and many studies in fact combine more than one type, for example using both documentary and observational data, or historical records and informal interviewing in the same study. The number of possible permutations is considerable and 'triangulating' different data sources is a means of strengthening the validity of conclusions reached.

There is a danger in propounding the two paradigms, the quantitative and the qualitative, that they will be perceived as denoting real rather than ideal-typical differences and will become sharpened into hard-and-fast and mutually exclusive alternatives. To be sure, there are social scientists who treat them like that. If one contrasts experimental psychologists with symbolic interactionist sociologists of deviance, then one may have a real difference quite close to the ideal-typical difference. On the other hand, if one contrasts evaluation researchers and social anthropologists, one finds surprisingly that there is considerable interest in qualitative methods among the former (see Weiss and Rein, 1972; Cook and Reichardt, 1979) and a good deal of use of quantitative methods among the latter (see Pelto and Pelto, 1978; Agar, 1980, pp. 119–36). The paradigms stand for competing meta-methodological views of social science, and are set out here to highlight differences between quantitative and qualitative research. In the practice of policy research, however, the distinction is an artificial one, and as will be seen there are many examples of the combination of different methods. Making the distinction too sharp rests on two errors. One is to posit a necessary connection between the general paradigm and the use of particular methods. This is invalid; there is no necessary connection (see Reichardt and Cook, 1979, pp. 10–16; Bryman, 1984). The other error is to regard the quantitative/qualitative divide as a rigid and unbridgeable chasm. There is now a considerable methodological literature showing that such a sharp distinction is unsatisfactory (Trow, 1957; Reiss, 1968; Sieber, 1973; Burgess, 1982, pp. 163–88; Bulmer and Warwick, 1983, pp. 275–312; Bryman, 1984). Criticisms are being directed incorrectly at methods when they are really directed at the paradigmatic world-view. What is much more fruitful is to consider the merits of different methods for the study of particular types of problem, and the possibilities of combining different methods in the study of the same problem.

Different research methods are not inherently better or worse than any other on the basis of intrinsic qualities, but superior or inferior for particular purposes. An illuminating example, linking this and the previous chapter, is the critique by Weiss and Rein (1972) of the difficulties of using rigorous evaluation designs to study the effects and outcomes of broad-aim social programmes. Broad-aim programmes like the US Model Cities planning programme defy effective experimental evaluation because the situation being studied is essentially uncontrolled, the treatments are not standardized (for example, between different cities) and the design is often limited in the information it can produce. The lack of positive effects found in large-scale evaluations was discussed in the previous chapter. But

> the task of research cannot be merely to document that the programme failed to work, but rather to identify the processes by which the programme was defeated. In this way, the experience of the programme may become a basis for the design of programmes more likely to be effective. (Weiss and Rein, 1972, p. 240)

(A critique of one such programme appears in Marris and Rein, 1972, pp. 242–61.) As a result, Weiss and Rein argue for a case-study method, using process-oriented qualitative research. The aim is to build up a near-to-complete description of the community or institution before intervention, the nature of the intervention, and the new system which develops after the intervention. Thus an in-depth analysis of resistances to change, the part played by administrative and political considerations, and the interpersonal dynamics of programme implementation can be provided, in a way that the more rigorous but more distant approach of the randomized experiment cannot.

The possibilities of combining different methods in policy research also needs to be taken more seriously than it usually is. Even the structure of a book such as this is not helpful in that respect, since it tends to imply that different methods are alternatives. Of course in any particular study, different methods may be combined. In studying health policy, for example, one might combine the use of social indicators with data from the General Household Survey (a continuous survey) and the results of a qualitative study of the impact of disadvantage, or of service use, or of the interaction between health and other social conditions. Howard Becker has used the image of a mosaic to characterize how social scientists build up a picture of social phenomena which interest them. Different pieces are fitted together, different methods providing different pieces of the picture (types of data and angles on the problem), until the whole picture is assembled. The way in which this can be done in qualitative studies will be addressed shortly.

The mosaic image extends to the combination of qualitative with quantitative methods. One use of qualitative methods is at the pilot stage of preparing a larger-scale quantitative study. But its uses are considerably wider. Qualitative data can act as a validity check on statistical data, providing insight into actual conditions on the ground and avoiding misinterpretations which may arise from excessive reliance upon figures processed through several hands.

> Qualitative data can give the policy-maker a 'feel' for the setting, the program, and the participants that reams of statistical printouts can never match. Computer printouts are difficult mechanisms by which to convey the nuances of a setting or a program, the enthusiasms of the participants or the problems that have led the program to the brink of disintegration. (Rist, 1984, p. 165)

The value of 'triangulating' methods – looking at the researcher's problem from at least two methodological perspectives – helps to correct biases which are inevitably present in each method. Qualitative and quantitative methods can work well together because they are relatively disparate:

> the fact that many of the likely biases in quantitative methods have been so openly acknowledged has been partly responsible for the growing dissatisfaction with these methods and the increasing

advocacy of qualitative methods in some quarters. Certainly the quantitative tradition in evaluation could learn much from the accumulated expertise of bias elimination that has been developed in the qualitative tradition. (Reichardt and Cook, 1979, p. 24)

However, there are also considerable obstacles to the use of quantitative and qualitative methods together; not only money and time, but the training of social scientists in particular disciplines which emphasizes one or the other, and the powerful sway which the competing quantitative and qualitative paradigms hold over different groups of policy researchers. The point being made, however, is that there is nothing sacrosanct about the division. Indeed, when scrutinized critically neither the logical nor the methodological line between qualitative and quantitative methods is a hard-and-fast one.

Qualitative methods are not just different ways of collecting data for policy research. They often, though not invariably, imply a different type of research design. Three of these will be briefly considered, to bring out the distinctiveness of this style of approach to policy studies. Historical studies of policy often adopt a genetic design. The explanation of outcome is to be sought in the genesis of policy and its impact. This is then studied by following through historically the way in which the policy and its impact developed. There are examples from penal and health policy which illustrate this type of approach very well (cf. Lewis, 1980; McConville, 1981). Two particular problems have to be faced. The 'whig' interpretation of the history of social policy is particularly easy to fall into, viewing past developments from the standpoint of the present, and seeing the route from past to present as being broadly one of evolutionary improvement (see Butterfield, 1931). Such a teleological view is unsatisfactory, because it fails to explain *why* policies took the form that they did, and diverts attention from a critical assessment of their outcome. The other difficulty concerns the theoretical framework to be adopted. Policies in a particular area may be viewed in different ways. Penal policy and the role of prisons in the eighteenth and nineteenth centuries, for example, may be viewed as the extension of altruism and the replacement of relatively barbaric physical punishments by the relatively human 'penitentiary', or (along with other 'asylums') as weapons of class conflict or instruments of social control (Ignatieff, 1981).

A contrasting type of design is the single-case experimental design. The approach is relatively unusual in many areas of policy, but has had particular applications in mental health and assessing work of the helping professions such as psychiatry, counselling and social work where the focus is on helping an individual or family. To some extent clinical research has adapted to the situation, and many of the designs developed have special relevance to clinical work. They include ABAB designs (a variation of the one-group pre-test post-test design), multiple baseline, and multiple treatment designs. They depend upon developing standardized methods of assessment and rigorous inter-observer reliability scores. In general, these methods have been confined to applied psychology, and have been relatively little used in policy and evaluation research. There is a full discussion in Kazdin (1982).

Apart from genetic designs, the most characteristic design used in qualitative research is the case-study. Here the focus is upon the in-depth analysis of events and processes within a single milieu, without explicit attempts being made to compare the situation in that milieu with other situations. Usually, however, there *is* an explicit attempt to generalize and theorize on the basis of the case-study materials. Conventional methodologists working within the quantitative paradigm disparage case-studies. Samuel Stouffer's comment on single-case designs is representative: 'When this happens, we do not know much of anything' (Stouffer, 1950, p. 357). Donald Campbell and Julian Stanley opine that 'such studies have such a total absence of control as to be of almost no scientific value' (1963, p. 6). Such views are still widely held, but there is growing appreciation of the value of qualitative methods and a perception that case-studies may complement the more extensive quantitative inquiries. In the field of evaluation, Weiss and Rein defend case-studies from their detractors, arguing for the study of a single case or set of cases as a basis for generalization to a larger class (1972). Donald Campbell, indeed, has gone so far as to retract his earlier severe strictures upon case-studies (1979). Unconvinced by Weiss and Rein's advocacy of 'qualitative knowing', he advocates comparative case-studies as a means of feeding 'qualitative common-sense knowing' into evaluation research. He also admits that in case-studies, theory can be developed by generating other predictions or expectations about the milieu being studied and in a limited sense be rigorously tested.

This controversy over case-study designs versus alternatives is of limited value pursued in the abstract. It is more helpful to consider the positive merits of the case-study and how it can be used in practice to yield insights in policy research. Its first merit is that the researcher, once involved in a setting for a time and accepted as part of the scene, is recording ordinary behaviour, not special responses which may be a result of experimental intervention or being the subject of a research interview on one occasion. For example, a vivid vignette of how nurses label mental patients is provided by Rosenhan's report of covert observers who were admitted to mental institutions by feigning hearing voices. Once admitted, they announced that the symptoms had disappeared, and openly studied the wards to which they were admitted, including taking notes of what was going on. Several nurses had written in case notes observations such as: 'engages in compulsive writing behaviour' (Rosenhan, 1982, pp. 29–36). Such a finding would not have come from an interview.

Secondly, and related, the observer is working in proximity to those being studied, not at arm's length as in the field experiment or social survey. Van Maanen observes that using quantitative methods 'it is quite possible to get a Ph.D. in any of the fields concerned with organizational study without even observing organizational life in any detail, up close, for any length of time' (1983, p. 265). Field research methods do give the researcher that first-hand knowledge ('acquaintance with' rather than just 'knowledge about', in William James's terms) which is an aid to understanding the events and processes which are the object of study. To be sure there are problems generated by proximity, of possibly 'going native' or of 'over-rapport', as well as the underlying problems of external validity. But the value of getting a 'feel' for life on the 'inside' should not be gainsayed. An impressive range of participant observation studies of organizations, from Gouldner's *Patterns of Industrial Bureaucracy* (1954) through Dalton's *Men Who Manage* (1959) and Goffman's *Asylums* (1961) to Kanter's *Men and Women of the Corporation* (1977) and William Muir's study of the police (1977) testify to the value of getting close to the phenomena.

Case-studies are typically longitudinal studies in the sense that they are following people and processes through time. One of the main costs of field research is the commitment of time – often months – which it requires. But there is a pay-off. In contrast to the cross-sectional nature of most survey research, it enables the researcher to follow events as they occur, trace sequences of events and gather data on the behaviour, attitudes and values of the participants in the setting (Rist, 1984, p. 163). Thus in *Patterns of Industrial Bureaucracy* (Gouldner, 1954), the research team was able to observe and interpret the effects of the introduction of a new style of management upon the workforce when a new manager came to the plant.

The change could be tied to the innovation in management style in a way which a single cross-sectional study would not have permitted.

Case studies also permit the analysis of change in a sensitive fashion. This is a distinct point to that about their longitudinal nature, because case-studies frequently incorporate a historical dimension. This may be grounded in documentary research, or in the oral recollection of participants, but there is a commitment to looking at sequences over time, rather than the interconnections of variables at one point in time. The analytical framework often has an orientation to change and process, as in the concept of the 'natural history' of a delinquent career. Understanding such processes is frequently of key importance in planning policy interventions. For example, in framing policies concerned with the transition from school to work, or with prevention of drug use, unless the processes of transition are adequately understood, policy intervention may be ineffective or have unintended consequences. 'Perhaps the greatest area of promise in case studies concerns their ability to "move" with the reality of dynamic factors' (Heclo, 1973, p. 93).

Indeed, Heclo suggests that the case-study is capable of grasping subtle movements in policy, using an auditory rather than a visual-spatial metaphor.

> A musical phrase is a successive, differentiated, though non-addictive whole; the quality of a new tone – a policy – becomes tinged by the whole preceding musical context, which itself acquires retroactive meanings as new tones unfold. Thus the policy case study might concentrate . . . upon the successive differentials in a moving but forever incomplete process of 'becoming' . . . relating events to antecedent contexts. (ibid., p. 94)

This discussion of case-study design has identified the case-study preponderantly with participant observation research in the field. In fact, as indicated earlier, case-study research is broader than this, encompassing the use of historical sources, contemporary documents, personal documents and on occasion more structured interviews. Several of the notable organizational studies mentioned on page 185 display this richness and flexibility of analysis. At their best, case-studies can provide rounded accounts of a setting which integrate a variety of different data sources. This underlines the ultimate futility of juxtaposing qualitative and quantitative methods of policy research. Case-studies that use a variety of sources blur the lines of distinction and emphasize the complementarity of different methods.

Case-studies are also more than detailed description, though that is often one of their characteristics. They are not purely idiographic but have considerable theoretical potential. Indeed, 'case studies of policy should be distinguished by their theoretical perspective, for without such a perspective the study is at best an interesting contribution to historical scholarship and at worst an uninteresting, episodic, narrative' (Heclo, 1973, p. 93). Two aspects of this are most relevant to their strengths as a type of research design. Case-studies tend to generalize inductively, but often by a particular form, analytic induction (see Bulmer, 1979; Hammersley and Atkinson, 1983, pp. 201–4). 'Generalizations are to be built from the ground up and offered tentatively on the basis of their ability to contain fully the data in hand. In the ideal, no variance remains unexplained' (Van Maanen, 1983, p. 255). This capacity to frame provisional theories is one of their contributions to policy-making at a theoretical level.

The other lies in their contribution to comparative analysis. Systematically conducted case-studies may provide the basis for comparisons within a single study (e.g. Reiss, 1971) or between more than one study in a similar area. The point is emphasized by several advocates of case-studies relevant to policy (Weiss and Rein, 1972; Heclo, 1973; Campbell, 1979). Comparative analysis involved looking at variables which vary in contexts which themselves vary. It is only by systematically looking at varying contexts that one can disentangle the truly unique from the generic phenomena. 'Particular merit resides in any mode of analysis, such as case studies, with the "requisite variety" to specify realistically these likenesses and differences' (Heclo, 1973, p. 95). Comparisons may be made across space, across time or across subject areas. An example of a comparison across space is provided by Hugh Heclo's studies of Treasury control in British central government (Heclo and Wildavsky, 1974), and of the Federal civil service in Washington (Heclo, 1977). Within a much smaller compass, one city, William Muir (1977) compared the policing styles of twenty-eight police officers and used this to generalize about the dilemmas facing the contemporary American policeman. Examples of comparative studies across time are *Patterns of Industrial Bureaucracy* (Gouldner, 1954) and William Plowden's study of the evolution of British policy towards the motor car (1971). Comparative case-studies across subject areas are rarer, but Blau's study of two contrasting public bureaucracies is an instructive example (1963). All of these studies seek to derive generalizations from the insights provided by setting one case against another case.

Donald Campbell (1979) argues that the comparison is most rigorous if undertaken by someone from one culture studying another culture, whose results are then checked by an investigator from the culture being studied, while a parallel investigation is carried out in the culture of the first investigator by someone from the culture which the first investigator is looking at. Such cross-national designs with built in cross-checks on validity are very rare. Dore's studies of British and Japanese factories (1973) to some extent fit the specification, but they were hardly case-studies and relied upon more extensive methods of research. They are a reminder that useful though case-studies are as a type of design for policy, they are capable of much improvement. The scope for comparative study is great, its potential as yet only partially realized.

If these are some of the features of case-study design which give it a distinctive and positive role in policy studies, what insights can case-studies offer into the nature of problems facing the policy-maker? This issue will be briefly addressed using certain examples from British policy research to exemplify points. The studies cited include Marsden's study of lone mothers (1973), Coffield, Robinson and Sarsby's study of social deprivation (1980), studies of homeworkers carried out by the Department of Employment (Cragg and Dawson, 1981), and Heclo and Wildavsky's study of Treasury control of public expenditure vis-à-vis spending departments (1974).

Case-studies can first of all give some sort of sense of the distribution and nature of a phenomena in the society. They are not the best means of discovering frequencies, but they can draw the attention of policy-makers to factors which influence behaviour and constitute problems for those affected. Homeworkers or outworkers are people who work in or from their homes for an employer who supplies the work to be done and (in the case of manufactured goods) is responsible for marketing and selling the result. There are estimated to be between 200,000 and 400,000 homeworkers in Britain. In a small-scale qualitative study of fifty homeworkers, Cragg and Dawson (1981) probed the reasons which led married women to undertake this type of work. Money and a broader sense of fulfilment were the two main ones given, with money predominant. All the separated or divorced women and the wives of low-earning husbands regarded their earnings as essential to the family budget. About a third of respondents were in this category. But a substantial minority undertook the work out of a desire for a worthwhile activity. Money was not the only motive in doing what is often regarded as hard and unrewarding paid work at home.

Respondents in the study often had no clear idea of their rates of pay or of their income over an extended period. They tended to focus only on the amount received in a given week or for a given batch of work. Many respondents, especially the lower paid, had never calculated their hourly earnings, and were surprised and depressed when this was done during the interview. All respondents were paid on a piecework basis and payment was tailored to the fastest workers. Despite some publicity about homeworkers' pay, the majority of respondents were unconcerned or unhopeful about how their position might be improved. There was no awareness of wage councils, and trade unions were regarded as uninterested if not actually undesirable. Overall, a majority were apathetic or defeatist about attempts to help them. These findings from the small-scale qualitative study (Cragg and Dawson, 1981) could be set alongside other quantitative evidence about the same problem produced by the same research group (Hakim, 1980; Hakim and Dennis, 1982).

Dennis Marsden's study, *Mothers Alone* (1973), examined poverty in the fatherless family on the basis of 116 interviews with lone mothers with children, a 56 per cent response rate from a sample approached via the Supplementary Benefits Commission (then called the National Assistance Board). Though not strictly speaking a case-study, it is based on intensive interviewing and more akin to a case-study than to a larger-sample, non-experimental comparison design. To highlight here two series of findings, the study found that the average total income of these families was 123 per cent of the SB scale rates. One in twelve of the families had cash incomes below 90 per cent of the scale rates. Widows were least poor, while unmarried mothers were the poorest of all (see Table 5.6 above). A major cause of dependence was lack of support from the children's fathers. Where court orders had been made, these were well below the permitted maxima. Turning to feelings about poverty, Marsden reports that the mothers' feelings of deprivation were entwined with feelings for the child.

Young children were a tie, but they were often thought a compensation for all hardships, including the absence of the father. An unmarried mother said of her baby son: 'He's my riches. I'd rather have him than all the money in the world' . . . It was evident that ultimately having children could soften the harshness of comparisons of living standards with childless couples who were manifestly much better off financially. But although children were sometimes seen as a compensation for hardships, over a third of mothers said they were most sharply pierced by feelings of deprivation *through* their children: the comparison group was the children's friends. (Marsden, 1973, pp. 68–9)

In Coffield *et al.*'s study in depth of four deprived families, similar insights are provided about the circumstances of low-income families, the interconnectedness of various social problems, and how families cope. One of the families studied, the Martins, were long-term unemployed. The researcher's summing of the situation indicates the burdens under which this particular family laboured, and the way in which they were stigmatized in the community.

The picture of the Martin family is one of a family with few, if any resources, struggling to cope . . . Their income support was adequate to keep them alive, but allowed nothing for leisure, for travel, or for breaking the monotony of their everyday routine. Their existence was and continues to be a subsistence existence. The family did not experience either . . . violence . . . or isolation . . . They were, however, seen as a 'dirty' family . . . The dirt was a symbol of their lack of status in the community. Their house was kept clean and seemed more orderly than the houses of [other families studied]; the label 'dirty' indicated that the Martins were not acceptable within the community in which they lived. (Coffield, Robinson and Sarsby, 1980, pp. 120–1)

These brief examples give some flavour of the insights which case-studies can provide into the circumstances of social minorities whose living circumstances and life styles are remote from those of the average policy-maker. They also illustrate clearly the value of proximity to those studied in case-study design, referred to earlier.

Case-study research can also provide evidence about the impact of policy upon those for whom it is intended. Marsden, for example, provides an analysis of the lone mother's experiences of Supplementary Benefit of direct interest to policy-makers. The service was still stigmatized and very inadequately publicized. Mothers felt humiliated by pressures put on them by officers to work, and the intention if not the letter of official rules seemed to be distorted or ignored. The application of the cohabitation rule was also a source of stress in relationships with officials. 'Thus, in spite of the official claim that the rules are morally neutral, in the operation of the means-test and cohabitation rules, the NAB officers were in effect acting as agencies of social control in supporting conventional sexual morality and the institution of marriage' (Marsden, 1973, p. 275).

Moving to a more general level, Coffield *et al.* draw attention to the need for more overt, explicit and co-ordinated *family* policies. Policies tend to be child-centred, but deprived children live in deprived families which bear deprivations as a family. Several services could be more effectively directed to the needs of low-income families. Health services could be more respectful and encouraging to parents. Family income support needed to be better co-ordinated to reach the mother in a simpler, more identifiable and regular flow of cash. These points were being made by academic commentators on social policy, but Coffield *et al.*'s argument has that much more force by being backed up by an in-depth analysis of the way in which the lack of a family policy impinged upon the four families studied.

Case-studies can also be a means of weighing up the outcomes of policies. Marsden, for example, is concerned to show how 'an under-budgeted, discretionary service must remain permeable by community stereotypes of the low status and deserts of certain groups in the population' (1973, p. 291). Groups whose behaviour was in some way different from the rest of society were treated differently by those administering policy. Street-level bureaucrats at the point of contact between a government department and the public applied criteria common among their own social stratum to the assessment of cases, when applying discretionary elements in assessing entitlement to supplementary benefit. The officer's own values influenced their behaviour because of the high discretionary element and because supervision could not be complete. This analysis can then be related to an account of the procedures whereby large government departments process people, and the way in which the aims set out in legislation or by senior policy-makers may in practice be modified by those lower down in the organization (see Hill, 1976; Prottas, 1979; Lipsky, 1980; Littrell, Sjoberg and Zurcher, 1983).

These are a few examples of the use of case-studies to study the nature of social problems, the impact of policies on clients, and the outcomes of policy. Case-studies may be used, in addition, to study the policy process itself and the nature of decision-making. Heclo and Wildavsky's study of Treasury control of British public expenditure is an excellent case in point. Based on informal interviews with serving and former senior civil servants and ministers (whom they term collectively 'political administrators') supplemented by observation of meetings, the authors managed to penetrate into parts of the political system about which little is known at first hand other than from the suspect sources of ministerial memoirs.

> Probably less is known about the characteristic behaviour of civil servants and their political masters than about fertility cults of ancient tribes. We certainly know less about the customs and mores of finance officers and Treasury principals than about witch doctors and faith healers, though each shares a bit of the other's function. (Heclo and Wildavsky, 1974, p. lxix)

The analysis seeks to understand the way in which the Treasury deals with spending departments and controls their desire to increase expenditure on departmental programmes. They bring out how delicate is the process by which both sides bargain with each other. The Treasury does not like to give a flat 'no' to proposals from departments, because that would refer matters upwards to ministers and clog up the Cabinet's business. Instead, constant haggling goes on between the Treasury, holding the purse strings, and departments. Proposals from departments are scrutinized very closely, and the tightly knit Whitehall network ensures that information circulates freely so that departments find it inadvisable to withhold information from the Treasury. Many departments find it advantageous to submit their case to the Treasury in the form of arguments for and against, coming down in the end in favour. This is to pre-empt the Treasury discovering a contrary argument itself, and coming to see this as outweighing the positive arguments. A great deal rests on a relationship of trust between principals and assistant secretaries in the Treasury and departmental finance officers with whom they deal. This is strengthened by circulation of civil servants between the Treasury and spending departments, so that both sides have had experience on the other side of the table. The Treasury is only rarely 'bounced' into making a commitment which in the end turns out to be far more costly than predicted. The building of Concorde is an example; in the end it cost five or six times what had originally been predicted. But departments rarely try on such manoeuvres, because they know that next time they will be found out, and future proposals scrutinized even more rigorously. The relationship of trust will be scarred.

The price which Heclo and Wildavsky paid for access to those they talked to and observed was not to say much about the *content* of policies affecting particular departments. So the account has a slightly bloodless air to it, since no specific policies are examined.

They nevertheless provide a very perceptive account of the *form* of policy-making so far as control of public expenditure is concerned. It demonstrates what can be achieved by case-study methods applied to the policy process itself, and the insights which it can yield.

Earlier reference was made to the social scientist as adviser and consultant, and it is now time to return to this. What role the adviser or consultant plays depends on the model of the policy process which is being used. Reverting for a moment to the earlier discussion in Chapter 1, it may be less useful to think of policy as a series of discrete events than as an evolutionary process in which it is difficult to identify a clear-cut group of decision-makers or clear and unambiguous goals being consistently pursued. Research is but one among a number of often competing and contradictory sources contributing to this process of diffuse decision-making. What Carol Weiss calls 'knowledge creep' and 'decision accretion' (1980) means that the influence of social science is likely to be more indirect than direct, gradually permeating into the outlooks and discussions of decision-makers, providing new ways of conceptualizing the world as much as providing cut-and-dried findings to be applied immediately to a particular 'decision'.

To this process, qualitative research can play a particularly valuable role in giving the policy-maker a 'feel' for what is happening 'out there'.

> The political arena in which policy is formulated is one where the key actors are not researchers. They are politicians or generalists, individuals who, of necessity, must 'stay in touch', 'cover their bases', 'stay close to the folks back home', and any number of other such stock phrases. As a group, politicians function as arbitrators, mediators, reconcilers and referees over the allocation of our collective resources. Qualitative research can speak to them with an authenticity, with a sense of 'how things really are' that can allow them to utilise information relevant to their policy-making roles. (Rist, 1984, pp. 165–6)

'The prince ought always to take counsel, but only when he wishes, not when others wish' (Machiavelli, 1952, p. 127). Politicians are busy people with little time for reading or reflection when in government office. Their permanent officials, too, though they read closely the daily and weekly press, are primarily concerned with running the machine. Advisers and consultants can therefore play a particularly important role in interpreting the results of social science research in an accessible way. There are a variety of different types of role which the adviser may play (cf. Benveniste, 1973, pp. 7–17) but their common characteristic is that they offer advice aside from and to some extent independent of the official government machinery.

One form of advice is that filtered via Congressional or parliamentary committees (cf. Atkinson, 1984; Weiss, 1987) or government or parliamentary commissions (cf. Wolanin, 1975; Bulmer, 1983a), all of which use advisers or experts. A particularly interesting case is the one-man or one-woman commission, which investigates a problem for the government. Recent examples in Britain include Professor Jim Gower's review of investor protection and Lord Rothschild's review of the SSRC. But this advice is offered at arm's length, through a body constitutionally separate from the executive. The focus here is on advisers within the executive.

Five types of more personal advice to ministers may be distinguished. The first is that provided by central policy planning units, such as the Central Policy Review Staff described in Chapter 1. CPRS included several social scientists who deployed their knowledge, and drew on the work of others, in producing reports for ministers and the Cabinet (cf. Heclo and Wildavsky, 1974, pp. 304–39; Plowden, 1981). The second is that provided by professional groups within government. In British central government, the group most likely to offer advice on economic and social policies is that of the economic advisers, who perform a dual role as professional economic analysts performing a research function, and advisers commenting on the economic implications of particular courses of action. The third is provided by independent consultants brought in to advise on particular areas of policy. The Overseas Development Ministry employs a social scientist in that capacity. Other examples come from the use of industrial sociologists in private industry. The fourth is the use of political special advisers by government ministers and Cabinet members. In Britain, members of both Labour and Conservative administrations have appointed a small number of such special advisers to their private offices, but on the civil service payroll (Heclo and Wildavsky, 1981, xlvi–xlix). Several have been academic experts on their subject, such as Professors Brian Abel-Smith and Maurice Peston (cf. Abel-Smith, 1980, and Peston, 1980); others political figures or young aspirants acting as a dogsbody.

Fifthly, members of administrations in both London and Washington rely on members of 'think-tanks' and informal groups to try out ideas and develop lines of policy. Sometimes this occurs in opposition, to be put into practice when in office, a phenomenon which has led to Brookings being termed the alternative government. Often it occurs through more partisan bodies like the Fabian Society (centre-left Labour) or the Centre for Policy Studies (market-oriented Conservative). Some members of such groups may become special advisers to ministers, but others – like the role of Richard Titmuss discussed by Banting (1979) – may advise in an informal capacity. Anthony Crosland's relationship with Dr Michael Young seems to have been rather similar (Bulmer, 1985). Advisers feed ideas to ministers and act as a sounding board for their own policy ideas.

Different types of adviser display different degrees of political partisanship, from none to a high degree. All of them, however, if from a social science background, deploy their social science knowledge in an essentially qualitative way. It is true that groups like CPRS and professional economists as advisers make extensive use of quantitative knowledge. But in presenting findings and ideas to ministers they have to achieve their own qualitative synthesis.

Consider the case of economic advisers. Sir Alec Cairncross, for many years chief economic adviser to the British government, has emphasized (1981, p. 16) how much advice is offered verbally. Even economic advisers, let alone ministers, do not have time to plough through the literature, and personal contact is the medium of most exchanges of ideas. Lord Croham, Permanent Secretary to the Treasury from 1968 to 1974, thought the job of giving economic advice to a politician was an art rather than an exercise based on science.

> The academics who came into Whitehall and made a successful contribution were those who were able to synthesise the thinking going on around them, and the contributions of their colleagues, and to translate that into practical terms which would allow a government to formulate policy, and to explain what it was doing. (Quoted in Cairncross, 1981, p. 29)

Very few mastered that art.

A different example is provided by Lisl Klein's illuminating account of her experiences of five years as social sciences adviser to Esso (Klein, 1976). In describing the achievements and ultimate frustrations of performing that role, she places considerable emphasis on the importance of face-to-face contact within the organization, both to overcome the limitations of being confined within a small box on the organization chart and to be able to explain in person the potential contribution of social science to managers quite ignorant of what it had to offer. In actual projects she carried out, her work involved analysing and understanding situations and interpreting the social situation to managers or other professional advisers. In the redesign of airport refuelling at London Airport, for example, which also involved ergonomists and psychologists, she was able to explain to the staff what was going on, stick up for them in relation to her scientific colleagues whose scientific enthusiasm she had to restrain, and ensure that the form of the redesign took account of the human needs of the workforce (Klein, 1976, pp. 81–95). This was essentially a qualitative role, depending upon observation of and involvement in the work setting and its redesign.

Advisers to government and private industry are not primarily researchers, but they do use qualitative methods of analysis and presentation. It is therefore justified to discuss them in this chapter even though their role is orthogonal to that of the conventional researcher. The chapter as a whole has aimed to clarify the ways in which qualitative methods may be used in policy research, and to an extent justify their use in the face of dismissive criticism. Their growing value is increasingly recognized both in the output of policy researchers and in several recent works (cf. Cook and Reichardt, 1979; Agar, 1980; Walker, 1985; Finch, 1986). As a cautionary note, however, one should end by reminding the reader of the limits of qualitative methods, relating particularly to external validity.

There are three problems facing the qualitative researcher who seeks to convince the policy-maker. First, how representative is the case studied of all cases with which the policy-maker will deal? To what extent can one generalize from one street corner in Washington DC (Liebow, 1967) to all young black American men? Despite the value of comparative case-studies, this remains a major weakness of the case-study approach. Secondly, analytically, how successful is the case-study in defining and studying its problem? This has been controversial, for example, in studies of community power. How far do local community power studies omit the question of 'non-decisions' (cf. Bachrach and Baratz, 1963), who does *not* get what, when and how (Heclo, 1973, p. 96)? Such an issue is a special case of the counterfactual in social policy research. Bachrach and Baratz in their study of anti-poverty programmes in Baltimore (1970) show that it is possible to tackle it empirically. The potential limitations of perspective of the case-study need to be borne in mind.

Finally, what is the relationship between the case and some wider universe which the researcher seeks to throw light on? It may be asked, case of what? What warrant is there for treating Coffield *et al.*'s four families, or Marsden's 116 one-parent families, as related to the category of 'deprivation' or 'poverty' with which one is concerned more generally? Some of the clashes between proponents of careful empirical study of social policy and those who espouse broader societal critiques, particularly of a neo-Marxist kind, have been known to founder on this point. Societal critiques have not been brought very successfully within the orbit of case-study analysis. The challenge to integrate theory with empirical research remains, to raise niggling questions about the adequacy of the framework within which a particular case-study is carried out. A number of the case-studies discussed in this chapter – by Marsden, by Coffield *et al.*, by Heclo and Wildavsky – explicitly address broader theoretical issues and the significance of findings for explanation. It is a connection that all qualitative researchers need to be aware of.

III

Problems of Analysis and Inference

10

The Role of Theory in Applied Social Science Research

Applied social science research is sometimes seen by its practitioners as both an empirical and an empiricist undertaking, empirical in concerning itself with what is happening in society and empiricist in holding that in some sense the facts speak for themselves. An inquiry such as the General Household Survey, for example, presents factual data about social conditions in British society, and could be seen as an undertaking not requiring any input from social science. In fact such a crude view of the scope of applied social science is untenable. Even if the data are not collected or analysed in order to test specific theoretical hypotheses, the formulation of topics for investigation, the conceptualizations used and the design of the study embody theoretical assumptions which may need to be spelled out. These theoretical elements in even the most mundane empirical study are often unrecognized, yet are an integral part of applied social scientific research (cf. Bulmer, 1982).

Consider the example of the General Household Survey discussed in Chapter 5, which is a prime source for the study of morbidity. Such a focus in the survey has involved some prior judgement that morbidity was a significant social problem and that it could be investigated by survey methods eliciting statements about people's subjective state (rather than, say, by medical examination). The GHS is thought to be suitable because it enables morbidity data to be related to significant social variables such as social class, education, employment, housing and so on. This, however, entails theoretical assumptions about the likely causes of morbidity, and the social forces which produce differential morbidity experience. The measurement of social variables involves conceptualizing the nature of those variables. The best example is social class, but it applies to a lesser degree to employment or education. What are the rules according to which respondents are assigned to particular categories, and how are those rules arrived at (cf. Bateson, 1984)? The formulation of such rules requires theoretical ideas to be brought into play in order to justify the particular categories to be used.

Social scientists, it is true, sometimes push this point too hard, suggesting that the explication of the theoretical complexities is itself a sufficient activity, and looking down upon mere empirical investigation. This is to carry the argument about the theory-ladenness of observation too far, and to miss the most significant connection between theory and empirical inquiry, namely their mutual interdependence. This has been a commonplace of general methodological discourse in sociology going back at least to T. H. Marshall's plea for 'stepping stones into the middle distance' (1963) and Robert Merton's discussion of 'theories of the middle range' (1957). Those conducting applied policy research need to be aware also of the theoretical dimensions of their inquiries.

What do social scientists mean by 'theory' when they invoke it as an element in social inquiry? At least four different dimensions may be distinguished: (1) the conception of the problem; (2) the general orienting framework used; (3) the analysis of concepts; (4) the understanding and explanation of social processes. These will be discussed in turn. The conception of the problem refers to the way in which the whole problem being dealt with is conceived of. This may not be apparent from some of the examples discussed in earlier chapters, because they are all drawn from within a broadly environmentalist and social-determinist framework. The problem is clearer when one looks at the social causation of disease (discussed by Blume in Chapter 12), where one is concerned with the interaction between physiological influences upon the individual and broader social factors which impact upon the individual's state of health.

Criminology provides a very clear example of the importance of how the problem is conceived, and of how such conceptions may change over time. Take, for example, the work of the Home Office Research Unit, which in its early years, far from being empiricist, was influenced by contemporary criminological theory and was far from proceeding in a theoretical vacuum. Its guiding conception was the then prevalent 'medico-psychological' model of deviant behaviour, reflected in a definition of the aim of crime-reduction in terms of providing more effective treatment for offenders: 'many criminologists located the major determinants of delinquent behaviour firmly within the individual, and, in particular, identified emotional disturbance resulting from unsatisfactory human relationships (especially those within the family) as a major source of motivation' (Clarke and Cornish, 1983, p. 13). Such a theoretical view had dominated English criminological thinking for more than fifty years. It influenced pressures for better facilities for physical, mental and psychological investigation which were associated with the child guidance movement and the call to establish 'observation centres' for delinquents by such reform bodies as the Howard League. The view underlay some of the officially sponsored research in the prewar period, and influenced those like the Gluecks and H. Mannheim whose backgrounds were sociological or legal rather than psychiatric.

One of the first major attacks on this approach was that in 1959 by Barbara Wootton in *Social Science and Social Pathology*. The developing work of the Home Office Research Unit, with its emphasis on the possibility of administrative decision affecting the future behaviour of those convicted of criminal acts, also did a good deal to undermine the medico-psychological model. It was shown to provide too static and too simple a view of offending and one that expected too much from treatment. Unrealistic expectations about treatment were built up which put too much weight on background experiences and dispositional factors. Research evidence on reconviction rates showed that pre-treatment factors explained only a small proportion of the variance. Age, history of offending and the situational environment of the penal institution were shown to have a considerable influence upon outcome. In particular, the delinquent's current environment seemed to be much more important than the medico-psychological model would imply.

Like the large-scale social experiments discussed in Chapter 8, the work of the unit was tending to show small effects from particular alternative penal treatments, in other words treatments were relatively ineffective. An alternative model was developed by members of the unit which was framed in terms of environmental influences and learning theory. This emphasized the determining role of current environment over emotional inheritance and upbringing. Example and opportunity were key factors in the committing of deviant acts, and once committed the act becomes part of the individual's behavioural repertoire. Since delinquent acts are learned in particular environments, they will only be repeated under closely similar conditions. Consistency in behaviour therefore depends upon consistency in environment. Delinquent behaviour, as seen by the model, is sustained by situational variables specific to the individual. Hence the need to focus upon situation and environment in seeking to account for delinquent acts (Clarke and Cornish, 1983, pp. 36–8). This alternative model goes some way to explaining the fortuitous nature of much delinquency and the conditions under which it becomes more persistent. It can also show why compliant behaviour while in custody may not persist on release in a different environment which again provides opportunities to commit delinquent acts. The theory also has its critics, for example critical criminologists who adopt a much more thoroughgoing critique of the norms and institutions of crime control in industrial society (cf. Taylor, Walton and Young, 1973; 1975).

The point which this contrast of approaches demonstrates is that different conceptions of a common problem – how to explain the committing of delinquent acts – entailed different approaches to the study and explanation of that problem. These differences involved the empirical testing of alternative theories and their acceptance and rejection, but they also entailed a prior choice about the type of explanation to pursue. Policy research which takes 'obvious' social problems as its subject-matter, whether concerned with the aetiology of conditions or with the effectiveness of intervention to tackle the problem, must make some theoretical assumptions about the most general features of the problem and how it is to be explained.

The second dimension through which theory enters into policy research consists of general orientations to problems. 'Such orientations involve broad postulates which indicate *types* of variable to be taken into account rather than specifying determinate relationships between particular variables' (Merton, 1957, pp. 87–8). The two chapters which follow address in different ways the significance of this consideration. The discussion of ecological analysis in the next chapter brings out the importance of *levels* of analysis in policy research, and the differing implications which can be brought out of analysis at various levels. Studies at the *area* level, though particularly congruent with the interests of policy-makers, may lead to mistaken inferences about the association between geographical space and the distribution of social problems. Problems may be conceptualized as the properties of areas, instead of the attributes of individuals. Areas are therefore targeted as suitable for policy intervention by virtue of the concentration within them of particular social conditions. Resources are diverted to areas rather than to individuals, thus not necessarily reaching those for whom they were originally intended but others living in that area who were not socially disadvantaged. The so-called 'ecological fallacy' carries through into policy-making.

The differences in orientation discussed in Chapter 12 are rather different. These concern the approaches adopted by different disciplines. Though writing of the attempt by academics to explain health inequalities, these carry through into practice, since particular forms of intervention are based upon particular orientations. The epidemiological approach, closely allied as it is to medical practice, is particularly influential. Thus, for example, particular patient groups may be identified from epidemiological evidence as in need of special attention, and the patients who present certain social characteristics may be singled out for special attention. As Blume brings out, social administration and sociology adopt rather different orientations to the explanation of health inequalities, one concentrating on variables subject to direct policy manipulation through administrative change, the other to more fundamental causative factors which may not be so susceptible to policy manipulation.

The third dimension in terms of which theory may be defined is the analysis of concepts. Conceptual language fixes our perceptions, and hence influences thought and behaviour. One function of conceptual clarification is to make explicit the character of data subsumed under a concept. Merton gives the example (1957, pp. 90–1) of Sutherland's studies of white-collar crime. At the time he carried out his study, when ecological explanations still flourished, there was a much higher rate of crime in the lower than in the higher social classes. Crime tended therefore to be viewed as 'caused' by poverty, poor housing, feeble-mindedness and other conditions associated with membership of the lower classes. Sutherland insisted upon a definition of 'crime' in terms of violation of the criminal law (congruent with his focus upon white-collar crime) and extended it to include white-collar criminality in the professions and business (not reflected in official statistics of crime). When he did so, the supposed high association between crime and social class diminished. Similar analyses have been conducted in relation to certain types of offence – so-called 'crimes without victims' in particular – to show that the concept used entails definition of particular acts in a particular way. For example, if the law proscribes homosexual acts between consenting adults, it may be argued that the definition of such behaviour as a 'crime' throws more light on the nature of the criminal law than it does upon such behaviour in society. This line of argument has been pushed furthest by so-called 'labelling' theorists, who emphasize that certain definitions of crime and delinquency are socially constructed and socially imposed.

'Crime' definition may pose particular difficulties because of its normative dimension, but similar problems arise with more straight-forward concepts. The pitfalls in the definition and measurement of physical disability have been discussed elsewhere (Bulmer, 1982, pp. 68–79) but are no less serious. Even such apparently straightforward conditions are susceptible to measurement in various ways, starting from different definitions. These definitions, in turn, embody particular theoretical positions. Concepts, however, do not constitute a theory. A good deal of social science remains at the stage of developing and clarifying concepts and classifications. One despairing applied research manager and foundation official remarked some years ago apropos British sociologists of the day: 'give a sociologist a grant and he will spend seven years sharpening his tools'. Only when concepts are interrelated in the form of a scheme can one speak of a proper theory beginning to emerge.

The fourth dimension of theory, then, which some term 'theory-proper', is the understanding and explanation of social processes. Such accounts are typically, but not exclusively, aetiological and causal in nature. The extreme difficulty of producing compelling social explanations, which has already been alluded to, should at this point be underlined. Producing satisfactory causal explanations is far from easy, and the logical problems of causal inference are considerable. A wide variety of different analytic methods are used. These include the elaboration of cross-tabular analysis, path analysis, regression analysis, log-linear analysis and so on, which are treated in standard methods texts. Different analytic routes may be sought to the same goal, but even if these suggest different ways of understanding the determinants of social behaviour, there is a shared underlying concern for pattern and structure. Frequently, particularly where survey data are being analysed, empirical generalizations are the product of analysis of the data. These are isolated propositions summarizing observed uniformities of relationships between two or more variables. For example, in Table 4.3 above an association was demonstrated in GHS data between smoking and social class. Whereas 36 per cent of all men aged 16 and over were smokers in 1984, there was evident a steady class gradient: 49 per cent of unskilled manual, 45 per cent of semi-skilled manual, 40 per cent of skilled manual workers, 30 per cent of intermediate and junior non-manual workers, 29 per cent of employers and managers and 17 per cent of professional men were current cigarette smokers. This suggests a proposition to the effect that there is an inverse relationship between social class and propensity to smoke. The higher the social class, the less likely a person is to smoke. The lower the social class, the more likely a person is to smoke. This is an empirical generalization based on General Household Survey data.

Such empirical generalizations are common in epidemiology (see

Chapter 12). They only take one so far, however. Such propositions are essential, but a series of such generalizations only provides the raw materials for analysis and theoretical understanding.

> The theoretic task, and the orientation of empirical research toward theory, first begins when the bearing of such uniformities on a set of interrelated propositions is tentatively established. The notion of directed research implies that, in part, empirical inquiry is so organised that if and when empirical uniformities are discovered, they have direct consequences for a theoretic system. (Merton, 1957, pp. 95–6)

Theory in social science consists of a set of interrelated propositions, or hypotheses, which are set out in advance of the inquiry being conducted and are tested by means of empirical research. In principle, social scientists strive to formulate social laws, but in practice such laws (comparable to laws shown to exist in the natural sciences) have been very difficult if not impossible to establish, other than in a trivial sense. By theory, then, is meant a set of interrelated propositions which account for the phenomenon which is the object of study. These propositions make reference to more general and abstract properties of society as part of the explanation which is offered.

Thus, epidemiologists make extensive use of the concept of social class. Blume quotes Susser, who points out that the focus is usually upon the importance of individual behaviour in accounting for the health problem which is the dependent variable. An instance of the attempt to achieve a fuller epidemiological explanation is to be found in studies of the connection between social class and mental illness, referred to briefly in Chapter 11 on ecological analysis. The link between persons diagnosed as schizophrenic and low social class has been well established as an empirical generalization, both in the United States and Britain. Can one proceed beyond that to a theory of its causation? What does the relationship mean? Faris and Dunham's study in Chicago (1939) suggested an ecological explanation: that social pathology was concentrated in the deteriorating inner city areas of the zone of transition.

Their research set off a controversy which continues, and for the solution of which alternative theoretical explanations have been tested. 'Is it that the multiple deprivations of the social environment which they described *breed* an excess incidence of schizophrenia? Or . . . is it merely that the victims of schizophrenia, perhaps in the early stages of the illness or precursor disturbance, *drift* into these areas of the city?' (Morris, 1957, p. 220). The association between the two variables at one point in time does not show which hypothesis is more plausible. Is it that there is some genetic predisposition to the condition which leads to higher concentration in lower social classes? Or is there a high prevalence due to social selection and segregation? Do those in lower social classes drift there from higher social classes because they, like others, are unable to cope and to maintain close emotional relationships?

To test the two alternative epidemiological theories involved establishing how lower-class schizophrenic patients came to be there, and thus tracking their movements over time, Goldberg and Morrison (1963) studied new patients admitted to a metropolitan hospital with a diagnosis of schizophrenia. This setting ensured a uniform diagnosis and assessment of the patients by psychiatrists. Case histories were collected of the patients, including information on occupation before admission, father's occupational career, and careers of grandfathers, uncles and brothers and sisters. The study showed that the distribution by social class of father (or of other relatives) was similar to the general population. What appeared to happen was that either at school or in later adolescence the men were unable to make the grade. They did not start the jobs arranged for them; they retreated into semi- or unskilled work; or they dropped out of the labour market altogether. Thus their social class as measured by occupation declined below that of their families to the point of hospital admission.

This study was complemented by a documentary survey of first admissions to mental hospital in a national sample, which showed the usual surplus of young men diagnosed schizophrenic in social class five. The occupation at admission was then compared with father's occupation shown on the birth certificates of the young men. This showed a distribution by social class of the fathers close to the national average. Both these studies thus provided support for the hypothesis of downward drift into social class 5 rather than some genetic transmission of the condition from one generation to another.

As Blume suggests in Chapter 12, the disentangling of such gross associations, and the testing of alternative epidemiological theories, is but the starting point of analysis. Gross rates in themselves tell one relatively little about the social processes and mechanisms whereby class inequalities are translated into health outcomes. Take a relationship discussed earlier between social class and smoking. Over time, as Table 10.1 shows, smoking in Britain has declined

Table 10.1 Changes in the Prevalence of Cigarette Smoking by Sex and Socio-Economic Group, Great Britain, 1972–1984

Socio-economic group	Percentage smoking cigarettes						
	1972	1974	1976	1978	1980	1982	1984
MEN							
Professional	33	29	25	25	21	20	17
Employers and managers	44	46	38	37	35	29	29
Intermediate and junior non-manual	45	45	40	38	35	30	30
Skilled manual	57	56	51	49	48	42	40
Semi-skilled manual	57	56	53	53	49	47	45
Unskilled manual	64	61	58	60	57	49	49
All aged 16 and over	52	51	46	45	42	38	36
WOMEN							
Professional	33	25	28	23	21	21	15
Employers and managers	38	38	35	33	33	29	29
Intermediate and junior non-manual	38	38	36	33	34	30	28
Skilled manual	47	46	42	42	43	39	37
Semi-skilled manual	42	43	41	41	39	36	37
Unskilled manual	42	43	38	41	41	41	36
All aged 16 and over	42	41	38	37	37	33	32

Source: General Household Survey, Cigarette smoking: 1972 to 1984, OPCS Monitor Series, GHS 85/2 (OPCS, 1985).

differentially by social class. Among both men and women, the proportion smoking cigarettes declined between 1972 and 1984 by approximately half among professional people, compared to by less than a quarter among semi- and unskilled manual workers. What accounts for this difference? A variety of possible explanations might be proposed. One is that those in higher social classes are more aware of scientific evidence about the harmful effects of smoking and more receptive to messages from health education sources. Another is that in so far as smoking is a response to and means of relief of stress, those in lower social classes lead more stressful lives and therefore find it more difficult to abandon the habit. A third is that smoking is a habit, and that those in lower social classes are socialized into more habitual and traditional forms of action – for example, the work that they do is typically monotonous and repetitive. They may therefore find it more difficult to change their habits than those in higher social classes whose work requires them to be more flexible and adaptive (cf. Hart, 1985, pp. 21–2). These explanations are speculative, but they illustrate an important point, that there are mediating factors in any pattern of relationships, and that these factors typically refer both to the social circumstances of those studied, specific events which happen to them, and the subjective meanings which they attach to action.

The complexity of disentangling the various causal influences at work may be illustrated from work discussed in Chapter 12. These are the studies of the social causes of depression among working-class women by George Brown and his associates (1975, 1978). The starting point of this work is the observation that in general surveys of the population, which include an assessment of the mental state of the respondent, the incidence of symptoms of depression is much higher among working-class than among middle-class women. How is this finding to be explained? It is yet another broad association between a background social variable and a dependent variable which is a health state. Brown goes beyond merely decomposing social class to argue that one must show *how* social factors impinge upon the individual (why some become sick and others do not in similar circumstances), and what other factors mediate between society and the individual response.

In analysing depression among working-class women, they distinguish two types of intermediate factor: structural–environmental factors and 'host' or vulnerability factors. The former refers to the influence of external social circumstances, the latter to those characteristics of the individual which singly or in interaction affect his or her susceptibility to disease. The former include family and work, housing, nutrition, air pollution, availability of medical care and so on. The latter include age, sex and genetic factors; previous medical history and the outcome of previous disease; and social and psychological factors such as attitudes to treatment, feelings of well-being and security, smoking, drinking and so on.

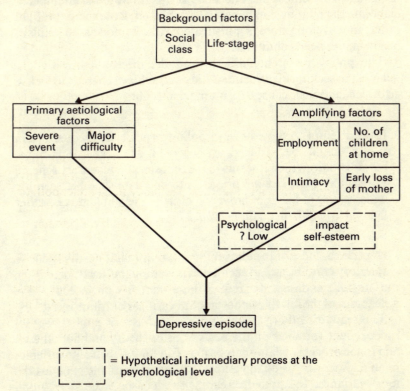

Figure 10.1 *A simplified causal model of the relationship between social class and the onset of depressive illness.*
Source: Brown, NiBhrolchain and Harris, 1975, p. 246.

Figure 10.1 shows a simplified causal model of the variables thought to influence outcome. Compressing the discussion without much elaboration, four types of factors are distinguished, which combine structural, environmental and vulnerability factors. Background factors are primarily structural. Primary aetiological factors are precipitating conditions, principally a severe event or major difficulty experienced by the person who becomes depressed prior to the onset of depression. Amplifying factors include one structural factor, employment, but primarily relate to vulnerability from early loss of mother, lack of an intimate relationship and demands from children at home. An additional consideration is introduced in the dotted box, psychological state of mind, with the suggestion that a further vulnerability factor, low self-esteem, increases the likelihood of the onset of depression. The study shows the value of attempts to elaborate the relationship between variables (cf. Rosenberg, 1968) in order to develop more sophisticated causal models to explain problematic social conditions.

The policy researcher differs from the discipline-based social scientist in seeking to influence policy and achieve changes as well as to understand basic causes. As Blume points out,

> If the attempt to show how, in policy terms, class inequalities in health might be reduced is accepted as a goal for social administration, then it seems to me that some explanatory scheme is essential. How else are priorities to be established between the wide variety of forms of provision clearly relevant (amongst other factors) to health inequalities? (pp. 270–1)

For instance, most of the class differential in infant deaths is due to respiratory conditions and accidents (including traffic accidents). To initiate policies designed to reduce these gradients, one needs to have a clear idea of the relative importance of various contributory factors.

This leads directly to another point. The basic researcher chooses independent variables on the basis of prior theory and hypotheses, and in the process of data analysis may fish for independent variables in an ad hoc way, using the criterion of which variable explains the most variance. In applied research, the focus is necessarily upon those independent variables which are most susceptible to influence by the policy-maker. These will not necessarily explain a very large amount of the variance, but can be affected by policy action. Rossi, Wright and Wright (1978) give the example of crime victimization studies, which show that city size and density of population explain a good deal of the variance observed. These are not susceptible to policy manipulation, whereas police patrolling practices, which explain only a small amount of the variance, are susceptible to influence and therefore are more salient to policy-makers. Of course, in many types of study variables do not conveniently fall into black and white categories like that. In the study of health, for example, variables such as accidents may be identified which are of equal interest to basic and applied research.

The Black Report recommends various measures to try to reduce the mortality rate from accidents to young children in working-class families (Townsend and Davidson, 1982, pp. 189–90). These include regulations to improve safety in the home, further measures to segregate pedestrians from motorists, and improved public awareness campaigns. These are simple or relatively simple policy measures which could be introduced at moderate cost. The report's own analysis of the causation of childhood accidents points, however, to the underlying causes of accidents in the material and cultural situation of the working-class child. 'Households in occupational classes IV and V simply lack the means to provide their children with as high a level of protection as that which is found in the average middle-class home. This can mean both material and non-material resources' (ibid., p. 128). Brown and Harris suggest that one reason for the higher accident rate among working-class children is the higher incidence of stressful life events among mothers (1978, p. 283–4). Variables such as these are less susceptible to direct manipulation, and explain in part why the effects of policy measures, where these have been studied by rigorous methods, appear frequently to be rather slight.

One reason is the complexity of social causation. Many different factors contribute to a given outcome. In the typical research problem, the investigation is dealing with a complicated network of linkages between a relatively large number of causal variables and the explanandum. Nor are these variables all of equal importance. The social scientist is often struggling with such large numbers of variables that it is difficult to estimate accurately those influences which are important for policy (Lieberson, 1985, pp. 185–6).

Indeed, the indeterminacy, from a policy-maker's point of view, in the causal analyses produced over the years by social scientists is one good reason why they have shifted their attention to evaluation studies and social experiments such as those discussed in Chapter 8. The indeterminacy of causal analysis in criminology has been a source of dissatisfaction, and it was explicitly argued that more progress might be made if causal analysis was avoided. Walter Reckless (1940, p. 2) was one of the first to express scepticism about the fruitfulness of causal analysis. He was echoed in 1955 by Mannheim and Wilkins (the latter on the staff of the Home Office) who argued that 'in criminology, research with the emphasis on decisions rather than finding out things (particularly 'causes') is certainly likely to take us much further much faster' (1955, p. 216). Barbara Wootton four years later maintained that there was a growing consensus that 'questions which begin with "why" are exceptionally difficult, and generally so far beyond our capacity that they are best left alone' (1959, p. 198).

Similar sentiments were expressed by Patrick Moynihan, social scientist, politician and participant as a Washington bureaucrat in the American 'War on Poverty', in his reflections on that attempt at community mobilization:

> social science is at its weakest, at its worst, when it offers theories of individual or collective behavior which raise the possibility, by controlling certain inputs, of bringing about mass behavioral change. No such knowledge now exists. Evidence is fragmented, contradictory, incomplete . . . Causal insights of the kind that can lead to the prediction of events are interesting, absorbing but they are hardly necessary to the management of a large open political system . . . The role of social science lies not in the formulation of social policy, but in the measurement of its results. The great questions of government have to do not with what *will* work but with what *does* work . . . public policies emerging for legislative–executive collaboration will constantly move in one direction, then another, following such whim, fashion or pressure that seems uppermost at the moment. What government and the public most needs to know in the aftermath of this process is whether there was anything to show for the effort and if so what. (1969, pp. 191, 193–4)

Moynihan then follows this analysis by arguing for evaluation research, quoting evidence he gave to a Congressional committee in 1966 making the case for an evaluation research capability within the General Accounting Office. Two decades later the GAO contained, at Congressional behest, a large evaluation research institute fulfilling requirements written into federal legislation that the outcomes of enactments should be systematically studied. Moynihan's disparagement of causal analysis is somewhat over-drawn, perhaps reflecting the savaging which he himself received when he ventured an applied social science analysis of the problems of the black family earlier in the decade (see Rainwater and Yancey, 1967). The basic difficulty is not the irrelevance of causal analysis but the multiplicity and complexity of influences and the difficulty of drawing clear conclusions for purposes of policy analysis (see

Lieberson, 1985). The critique is illuminating, however, in pointing to the considerations which have led to a shift in attention to the evaluation of outcomes of policy intervention.

There is no need to recapitulate here the substance of Chapter 8 on evaluation research and social experimentation. The account there brought out that such research designs focus upon the results of specific policy interventions rather than on the underlying causes of social behaviour. In that sense the studies are more narrowly conceived than attempts to build causal theories. In the case of social experiments, the design attempts to be considerably more rigorous than most survey designs through its ability to introduce the experimental variable and to assign subjects randomly to experimental and control groups. One of the striking results of such studies has been the relatively small effects shown for experimental innovations. There are a number of possible reasons for this, including the relatively short time-scale over which most experiments have run, and the capacity of human beings to resist change and innovation and follow traditional patterns of behaviour. This does not discredit that type of study, but suggests caution about the more exaggerated claims which are made on its behalf as a panacea for policy research.

From the standpoint of an effective applied social science theory, the most important future task is to develop workable interdisciplinary approaches to the study of particular social issues. Blume at the end of Chapter 12 suggests how this might be done for health inequalities. It is unlikely in the extreme that any of the social sciences will develop analytic theory as rigorous and generally utilized as micro- or macro-economics. The analytic potential of theory in social sciences other than economics lies in theories of the middle range, applying to a particular substantive area such as crime, or health or poverty. Within those areas, effective policy research requires more integrated theories than exist at present. Often there are quite powerful and well-developed theories in sociology, or in economics or in psychology, but poor efforts are made to try to integrate them. Efforts to clarify the foundations for successful interdisciplinary co-operation are few and far between. In practice in research the outcome too often is dominance by one particular discipline among several (e.g. economics) or reduction to a lowest common denominator of shared methodology (see Glennerster and Hoyle, 1972). Academic social policy needs to think through much more systematically what interdisciplinary work entails. There are some encouraging signs (e.g. Culyer, 1981). Moreover, social science is but one input into the policy-making process. If its theoretical voice is uncertain or discordant, then its already debatable influence will be reduced still further. More efforts need still to be made to explore the potential for interdisciplinary theory-building on particular subjects.

It would be misleading to finish this chapter conveying the implication that social science theory is wholly determinist. As Clarke and Cornish point out in their discussion of criminology (1983), the social scientist must be prepared for the unpredictability of behaviour. The element of indeterminacy and uncertainty of human affairs remains as an ever-present challenge to social science, both to increase the power of explanations which are produced and to build an action-frame of reference into its theories. A vivid case of the relevance of this consideration is the policy-making process itself. As suggested in Chapter 1, this cannot be boiled down into a single model or formula, but must allow for the messiness and the open-endedness of the real world. Perhaps in the realm of theory, the applied social scientist would do best to follow A. N. Whitehead's dictum: 'Seek simplicity, and distrust it.'

11

The Ecological Fallacy: Its Implications for Social Policy Analysis

The methods of analysis which social scientists use have major implications for the conclusions that they reach. By 'methods of analysis' here is meant not social surveys or observation, rigorous evaluation or field experiment, but the analytical framework or general orientation that is brought to bear on the problem studied, and the assumptions embodied in that framework. A classic example is provided by Durkheim's analysis of the causation of suicide. In *Le Suicide* ([1897] 1951), he systematically eliminated the possibility that there were psychological causes and suggested instead that the causes of suicidal behaviour and differential rates had to be sought at the level of society. He then distinguished three types of suicide: egoistic, altruistic and anomic. This analytic framework set the bounds for the explanation which followed.

The analytic framework considered in this chapter is that defined in terms of geographical space. Social phenomena are spatially distributed, and both analyses of social conditions and policies framed to deal with inequity and inequality are often couched in spatial terms. For example, British social policy has been concerned for some years with the economic and social policies directed to inner city areas, and the urban deprivation associated with them. The urban racial disturbances in Britain in London and Toxteth in Liverpool in 1981 and in Birmingham and London in 1985 were merely the most dramatic manifestation of the problems created by industrial decline, low incomes, poor housing, disadvantage in education and inferior life chances of those resident in the inner city (see Berthoud, 1976; Gittus, 1976). For research, there are two challenges. One is to determine the spatial distribution of social problems, the incidence geographically of different conditions such as poor housing or high mortality rates. The other is 'the more difficult, and politically more significant question of whether the fact of spatial concentration itself constitutes at least some kind of partial explanation of the overall incidence of deprivation' (Norris, 1979, pp. 19–20). Does space have any explanatory relevance?

There are powerful pragmatic reasons encouraging people to think that it has. Services are provided by local authorities and health authorities in terms of local administrative boundaries, for a particular area or subdivision of an area. The area is the unit of service provision, those administering the service will tend to see the area as a whole and perhaps possessing a particular character, and data about the activities of the local or health authority will often be available only in aggregate form for the area. When one moves to a higher level, some services (such as social security) are provided to individuals (through local offices) as individuals, not by virtue of living in a particular area. But for many types of service – education is an example – such individual delivery is not appropriate or feasible. Central government expenditure is therefore channelled to the local level through existing administrative units. Moreover, as the extent of urban deprivation has been identified, discrimination has been possible between different areas. Both the arcane procedures of the Rate Support Grant (see Foster, Jackman and Perlman, 1980), channelling central government finance to local authorities, and the application of the RAWP formula to DHSS allocations to health regions (see Chapter 4) have been a means of redistributing resources. The limited geographical area covered by the units of English local administration has permitted central government to discriminate between authorities in resource allocation and in acknowledging different needs of different areas (Lawless, 1979). In research terms, the most extensive and representative data source, the population census, is only available in aggregate form. Since 1961 data have been available down to the level of enumeration districts containing about 200 households. Those who use such data do not have information about individual characteristics and work instead with data relating to small geographical areas. Those who have used such data extensively have necessarily been constrained to look at the distribution of social and economic characteristics spatially.

Thus presumptions about the relevance of space are built into both administrative practice and some types of social science analysis, frequently without recognizing that formal administrative units may not be meaningful social units (Etzioni and Lehman, 1967, p. 12). Existing administrative boundaries are convenient demarcations, but they do not necessarily provide the most useful cross-section of the population for analytic purposes. Indeed, it is with the potential

mismatch between inferences made between sets of aggregate data at
various levels, and between data about individuals, that the so-called
'ecological fallacy' is concerned. Its implications for policy research
are considerable.

As early as 1895, one finds the English statistician G. Udny Yule
publishing an article in the *Economic Journal* entitled 'On the
correlation of total pauperism with the proportion of out-relief'. He
was examining a claim made by Booth in his book *The Aged Poor in
England and Wales* (1894, p. 63) that the proportion of out-relief
given in poor law unions bore no relation to the total percentage of
pauperism. Booth's conclusion was based on an ecological analysis:
he had listed twenty groups of unions according to industrial
character with the highest in pauperism at the top, and against each
was listed the percentage ratio of the cost of out-relief to total relief,
the percentage of crowding, the type of administration, and persons
per acre. Yule disputed this, and drew a scatter plot of the rate of
pauperism (proportion of population in receipt of relief) to the ratio
of out-relief to in-relief (number of out-paupers to one in-pauper),
which showed a marked, if skewed, correlation.

This is an early example of an ecological correlation, indeed before
the statistical development of correlation analysis as it is known
today. One characteristic of an aggregate (in this case a poor law
union or group of unions) was related to another characteristic of the
aggregate, to see whether there was any relationship between the two.
The analysis was conducted entirely at the aggregate level; there was
no reference to individuals. Another example may make this clearer.
W. S. Robinson in his classic paper on ecological correlation (1950)
compared the relationship between colour and illiteracy in the
United States measured on different bases. Grouping the census data
into nine regional divisions, he showed the proportion of each
division which was black and the proportion of each division which
was illiterate. The ecological (Pearson) correlation was 0.946, a near-
perfect relationship. When the data were grouped by the forty-eight
states, listing for each state the proportion black and the proportion
illiterate, the ecological (Pearson) correlation was 0.773. However,
when the *individual* (Pearson) correlation was calculated for the four
cells in Table 11.1, considering each variable as properties of
individuals rather than of geographic areas, the result was 0.203, very
much lower than the ecological correlations.

This result identifies the ecological fallacy, the falsity of making
inferences from ecological correlations about the properties of
statistical aggregates, to individual correlations about the properties

of individuals within those aggregates. While it is theoretically possible for an ecological and individual correlation to be equal, in reality this is very rarely the case. The only reasonable assumption is that an ecological correlation is almost certainly not equal to its corresponding individual correlation.

Table 11.1   *The Individual Correlation between Colour and Illiteracy for the United States, 1930 (for the Population 10 Years Old and Over, thousands)*

	Black	White	Total
Illiterate	1,512	2,406	3,918
Literate	7,780	85,574	93,354
Total	9,292	87,980	97,272

Source: US Census, 1930, presented in Robinson, 1950, p. 353.

Statistically, this can be demonstrated with reference to Table 11.1. An ecological correlation measures the relationship between the *marginal* frequencies of the table, while the individual correlation depends upon the *internal* frequencies of the four cells in the body of the table. The marginal frequencies in a fourfold table do not determine the internal frequencies. There are a large number of sets of internal frequencies which are compatible with the same marginal frequencies. Two hypothetical examples are given in Tables 11.2 and 11.3, the first to show an individual correlation of zero, the second to show a very high individual correlation. Yet both have the same marginal frequencies as Table 11.1.

Table 11.2   *Hypothetical Adaptation of Table 11.1 to Show an Individual Correlation of Zero between Colour and Illiteracy, Leaving Marginal Frequencies Unchanged*

	Black	White	Total
Illiterate	374	3,544	3,918
Literate	8,918	84,436	93,354
Total	9,292	87,980	97,272

Table 11.3   *Hypothetical Adaptation of Table 11.1 to Show a Very High Individual Correlation between Colour and Illiteracy, Leaving Marginal Frequencies Unchanged*

	Black	White	Total
Illiterate	3,718	200	3,918
Literate	5,574	87,780	93,354
Total	9,292	87,980	97,272

In short, the within-areas marginal frequencies which determine the percentages from which the ecological correlation is computed do not fix the internal frequencies which determine the individual correlation. Thus there need be no correspondance between the individual correlation and the ecological correlation. (Robinson, 1950, p. 354)

The ecological correlation between colour and illiteracy at regional or state level thus says nothing about what the individual relationship is likely to be. The ecological correlation itself is not without significance, and it is possible that similar historical circumstances and economic circumstances caused certain American states to import and retain a large black population, and to neglect their school systems, leading to higher illiteracy. But this is not the same as the relationship in the ecological correlation, that those who are illiterate are also black. As the individual correlation reveals, this is a fallacious inference.

Yet inferences about relationships between summary statistics concerning aggregates such as regions, local government units, constituencies, wards, enumeration districts, institutions and organizations continue to be widely used in social science research and in policy research. Duncan, Cuzzort and Duncan (1961) have pointed out that the problem is not simply one of making misleading inferences about individual relationships from aggregate data. It is also found between geographical areas at different levels. In the example given earlier, the ecological correlation between colour and illiteracy was higher at the regional level than at the state level. There may very well be differences in inferences made about results between regions, sub-regions, local authorities, wards and enumeration districts when ecological correlations are calculated. Conclusions derived from studies made at one scale should not be expected to apply to problems whose data are expressed in terms of other scales.

The relationship between ecological and individual inferences is not wholly arbitrary or unpredictable. Duncan and Davis (1953), for example, showed that in making ecological inferences about relationships at an area level, the marginal frequencies of tables set limits which are absolute maxima and minima for the values of possible individual correlations. Examining 1940 census tract data for Chicago about the percentage of blacks engaged in domestic service, they show that for the sum of the 935 tracts of the city, their estimate of the individual (Pearson) correlation from the marginals of tables is between 0.126 and 0.355, that is, that between 25 and 40 per cent of occupied female blacks must be engaged in domestic service. In Tables 11.1 to 11.3, the proportion of whites and blacks who are illiterate is set by the marginal row total of 3,918. Thus a maximum of no more than 4.5 per cent of whites and 42.2 per cent of blacks *could* be illiterate if the values in the four cells were unknown. (In practice, if the value of one cell and the marginal totals are known, the other cell totals can be computed.)

Goodman (1959) suggested that ecological regression was more satisfactory as a method of inference than ecological correlation, and that the method could be used to estimate individual correlations making certain assumptions. The algebraic derivation of the method is set out in the article, but its numerical application may be illustrated here. Applied to Robinson's literacy data, the bounds for individual correlation following Duncan and Davis's (1953) method are between −0.7 and +0.60, while the estimated individual correlation from the marginal frequencies (assuming the cell frequencies are not known) is 0.38. This is not very close to the true value (0.203) but closer than the ecological correlation (0.95) or the maximum and minimum bounds. Applying his method to Duncan and Davis's data on the relationship between black women and domestic service in Chicago, Goodman estimates that the individual correlation must lie between 0.13 and 0.35, and it is estimated at 0.25, which is close to the known true value from individual cell data of 0.29. A further point is that the approximation to the individual correlation is greater the finer the geographical breakdown of the aggregate data. Thus census tract or enumeration district data are preferable to community area or local authority level data in computing the least possible maximum and the greatest minimum for an (unknown) individual correlation.

Rather than pursue what rapidly becomes a very technical discussion (cf. Goodman, 1959; Duncan, Cuzzort and Duncan, 1961; Boudon, 1963; Shiveley, 1969), it is more useful to consider some related problems in inferring relationships between different levels of data. Howard Alker (1969) has proposed a typology of ecological fallacies, distinguishing three different types:

(1) fallacies of decomposition or disaggregation, from higher to lower levels of aggregation, of which Robinson's fallacy is the archetype;
(2) fallacies of aggregation, making mistaken inferences from lower to higher levels of aggregation;

(3) fallacies of aggregation from one subpopulation to another at the same level of analysis.

The individualistic fallacy is an example of the second type, confusing relationships among individuals with those governing aggregates. For example, it does not follow that because labourers tend to be socially radical there will be an equally high tendency to express radical opinions in economically advanced states with high proportions of labourers in their populations. Marxist theory has not infrequently come unstuck on this point, and indeed globally revolution occurred in societies like Russia and China to which classical Marxism least applied.

A different type of fallacy, related to its ecological and individualistic cousins, is that of cross-level fallacies. These can occur, for example, in the use of functional or systems theory in sociology or political science, attributing to collectivities (such as society or the political system) attributes of the behaviour and attitudes of individuals. This fallacy of the wrong level often consists

> not in making *inferences* from one level of analysis to another, but in making *direct translation of properties or relations* from one level to another, i.e. making too simple inferences. The fallacy can be committed working downwards, by projecting from groups or categories to individuals, or by working upwards, by projecting from individuals to higher units. (Galtung, 1967, p. 45)

The tendency to shift between macro- and micro-analysis common to several social science disciplines also exemplifies the fallacy. There is a particular problem in economics where both micro and macro theory are well developed and the potential problems in shifting between different levels more apparent (see Theil, 1954; Peston, 1959/60). In sociology, functionalist theories of religion posit societal forces which lead people to hold religious beliefs, and endow society with pseudo-psychological properties, diverting attention from individuals and their beliefs and actions. The implications for the handling of empirical data are considerable. No assumption should be made about the homogeneity of influences between different levels. Indeed it can be argued that 'When the relationship is different on two levels, that is exactly when we should be most interested; for societal processes are not simply a function of the summation of subunits but have an organic entity themselves' (Lieberson, 1985, p. 109).

Alker also points to the existence of contextual effects and contextual fallacies. Returning to Robinson's example, if in addition to calculating the individual correlation one standardizes for level of industrialization and urbanization, the correlation is reduced still further to about 0.05. Thus it appears that the relationship between race and illiteracy is a largely spurious one, explicable in terms of industrial opportunity and the depressing effect of traditional ruralism upon black educational aspirations and opportunities. The need to examine context points to developing multi-variate analysis to examine relationships between independent and dependent variables (cf. Simon, 1957; Blalock, 1964; Rosenberg, 1968).

The key issues that emerge from this discussion for research on social policy are the following. (1) Ecological correlations in themselves are unreliable and probably misleading as a guide to relationships between attributes of individuals. (2) This is because aggregation is often inappropriate to the analyst's interest, though it may be the only level at which data are available. (3) Aggregated data are unsatisfactory in part because they contain no aggregation of *relations* between different characteristics of individuals (Hope, 1978, p. 354). (4) In shifting from one unit of analysis to another, one is very likely to affect the manner in which outside (and possibly disturbing) influences are operating on the dependent and independent variables being studied (Blalock, 1964, p. 98). It is therefore particularly necessary to pay attention to confounding variables in a relationship. A number of examples of this will be given later in the chapter.

The implications of the ecological fallacy are common to a number of social science disciplines. The widespread nature of the analytical problem will be briefly reviewed before focusing specifically on social policy. Problems of ecological inference have been perhaps most apparent in political science, particularly in the study of voting behaviour. Many studies of the determinants of voting have depended upon aggregated data for small geographical areas, since the polling preferences of individuals are confidential and inviolable. For most of the twentieth century, political scientists have been trying to make inferences about voting patterns from such aggregated data. Whether the reasons for Catholic Al Smith's defeat in the American presidential election of 1928 (Ogburn and Talbot, 1929; Lichtman, 1974; 1979, pp. 27–34, 40, 94), the sources of support for the National Socialists in German elections up to 1933 (Pollock, 1944; Loomis and Beagle, 1946; O'Lessker, 1968; Hamilton, 1982) or the politics of the American south (Key, 1949), ecological data have been the sole source. Electoral returns from subdivisions of the electoral unit being studied are tabulated and analysed so as to identify recurring patterns of voter turnout and preference varying in space and time. These voting patterns are then related to a wide variety of political, social and economic data about the areas and their populations, and finally the observed patterns of electoral behaviour are explained in terms of the most significant correlations between the socio-economic environment and party support (Ranney, 1962, pp. 93–4).

Such studies have also been used with historical voting data, for example linking precinct or ward voting to ethnic, religious, economic or other variables revealed in nineteenth-century census data (Stone, 1981, p. 25). Lichtman has warned historians of the dangers of making inferences from this type of data, and cautioned about excessive reliance upon Goodman's solution in terms of ecological regression (1974). Ranney (1962) contrasts ecological data with sample survey data about behaviour of individual electors, and suggests that the ecological data should be used to study the behaviour of electorates, without trying to make strained and possibly fallacious inferences about individual voting. Electorates, in his view, are not merely arithmetic sums of individuals but units playing special and significant roles in the political process, worthy of analysis in their own right.

Geography might be expected to be the discipline least likely to be receptive to Robinson's critique, since its rationale depends on the analysis of the spatial distribution of phenomena. Traditionally, before Robinson, geographers did not pay much attention to the problem of whether relationships drawn from areal data could be applied to units other than areas.

> For example, if a statistician computes the proportion of a population which is of foreign birth in each census tract of a city and correlates it with the census tract proportion of home owners, finding a positive relationship, can he conclude that the foreign born are more likely than the natives to own their own homes? Much early work . . . appeared to assume that such inferences are justified, although no mathematical rationale for them was available. (Duncan, Cuzzort and Duncan, 1961, p. 9)

Geographers have been notoriously hazy about how they define the 'geographical individual' (Harvey, 1969, p. 278) and this contributed to the failure until recently to grasp the implications of the ecological fallacy. Most use of correlation procedures by geographers makes use of areal data, yet is often used to draw inferences about individuals. Yet, as Harvey has noted, 'confusion about these issues underlies a good deal of confusion over inferential procedures in geography. Inferences made about one population cannot, without assumptions, be extended to other populations' (ibid., p. 279).

Social geographers in particular, however, have not only been open to influences from other social sciences, modifying a pure spatial determinism (cf. Jackson and Smith, 1984), but have shown awareness of the problems posed by the ecological fallacy. There is an increasingly fruitful debate in social geography and urban sociology about the extent to which spatial distribution may actually explain social behaviour and social problems. Sociological critics such as Pahl (1966), Castells (1968), Stacey (1969), Abrams (1978) and Saunders (1979, 1981) have asked what is specifically 'urban' or 'rural' about the social phenomena found in areas labelled in those terms. Geographers such as Herbert and Johnston (1976, p. 1) specifically distinguish social problems *in* the city from social problems *of* the city which are created by patterns of population concentration. They give poverty as an example of the former, residential segregation and its social consequences as an example of the latter. For example, certain types of housing may be highly correlated with crime and delinquency. The case of crime and its distribution is discussed further below, but it is relevant that Herbert and Johnston make a distinction between the areal causation and areal exacerbation of problems. It may be that the latter is the more important effect. Geographers of course naturally tend to favour spatial factors.

> In their efforts to derive some kind of spatial causation from the spatial correlation, frequently by virtue of the specifically *spatial* focus of such studies, such 'explanations' are perpetuated at the expense of more fundamental social explanations which, though sometimes recognised, are ignored or set aside. (Hamnett, 1979, pp. 246–7)

Injudicious inferences may push the author into committing the ecological fallacy. In a study of the distribution of schizophrenics in and around Nottingham city centre, Giggs (1973, 1975) identified a correlation between mental state and a whole set of unfavourable life circumstances. These were heavily concentrated in the inner city, slum areas of Nottingham. 'Here, as in other large cities, there are pathogenic areas which seem to destroy mental health ... Some social and urban environmental settings *may* create schizophrenia' (Giggs, 1973, p. 71). He went on to suggest that the identification of highly localized pathogenic areas could be used as a basis for preventative policies, possibly by means of urban renewal. Here is the ecological fallacy given flesh, and used to draw inappropriate conclusions. Though Giggs has subsequently modified his position (1975, 1979), the example illustrates the pitfalls of injudicious reasoning to which aggregate data analysis can lead.

In social policy, there has been increasing awareness of the extent and importance of local geographical variation in the distribution of social characteristics and the need for and provision of services. Berthoud (1976, ch. 6) has paid special attention to geographical variation in income, while the RAWP exercise in health, referred to in Chapter 4, was concerned with variations in the need for health care. Davies (1968) has documented local variation in the personal social services, and Byrne, Williamson and Fletcher (1975) have done the same for education. Davies has formulated the concept of 'territorial justice' to indicate the lack of fit between unequal geographical spread of services and resources, and their optimal allocation in relation to population. The geographical maldistribution of income, wealth, health and a range of other objective social conditions is now well documented (Bulmer, 1982, pp. 59–63).

The discussion will now examine in more detail the geographical distribution of three types of social problem – juvenile crime, educational disadvantage and ill health – in order to explore the uses and limitations of ecological analysis more fully. Juvenile crime is the first. The observation that the incidence of crime is geographically concentrated is an old one. Henry Mayhew, for example, made systematic studies of intra-urban variations in crime in mid-nineteenth-century London. Using statistics for each of the seven police districts of the city, he was able to show that two of these districts, what he termed 'low neighbourhoods', contained two-thirds of the criminals (1862). In the early twentieth century, Burt (1925) mapped juvenile offender rates in London and showed that they were highest adjacent to the central commercial district in what Charles Booth (1891) had identified as poverty areas. A whole range of studies have since been carried out (Herbert, 1982, p. 35), from which one may cite Morris's (1957) study in Croydon, Castle and Gittus (1957) in Liverpool, and Baldwin and Bottoms (1976) in Sheffield (see also Brantingham and Brantingham, 1984).

The *locus classicus* of studies of the geographical distribution of juvenile delinquency, however, remain those of the Chicago school of sociology, particularly of Clifford Shaw and Henry McKay. For these studies not only mapped the distribution of crime and other social problems (cf. Bulmer, 1984, p. 162) but adumbrated an ecological theory to account for the distribution. Shaw and McKay were influenced by the leaders of the school, Robert Park and Ernest Burgess, who laid out a plan for the study of urban phenomena, and directed their students into following it (Park and Burgess, 1925; Burgess and Bogue, 1964; Bulmer, 1984). Shaw and McKay, based at the Institute of Juvenile Research, mapped the homes of juvenile offenders brought before the Cook County court at various periods, using dot maps to show distributions and rate maps (relating offenders to populations at risk) to show areal variation. Analyses were conducted for square-mile grids, seventy-five community areas, and the concentric zones of Burgess's model of city structure. Data were analysed for juvenile delinquency and truancy, and also for adult crime and recidivism. All four were shown to be closely related.

The results of the study showed that truancy and delinquency were highly concentrated in areas adjacent to Chicago's central business district, and that there was a gradient through Burgess's concentric zones from high rates near the centre to low rates in the suburbs (Shaw *et al.*, 1929). Burgess (1925) had hypothesized that urban land use tended to form concentric zones around the central business district. A city would grow outwards from this, and create concentric zones of different character, through processes of invasion and succession. There were five zones: (1) the central business district; (2) the zone in transition: mixed industrial and poor housing; (3) the zone of working-class homes; (4) the residential zone; (5) the commuters' zone. Shaw and McKay applied the model to their data and found that it fitted. They later extended the analysis to nineteen other American cities, and found that it fitted (with two exceptions, Baltimore and Omaha) (1942, 1969).

Shaw and McKay's findings were worked into a theoretical analysis. First, the gradient of delinquency was uniform from city centre to suburb, varying inversely with distance from the centre and regardless of the way in which it was measured. Secondly, despite high population turnover, so that its composition might change completely over a generation, high delinquency rates persisted in the areas near the centres of cities over time. Moreover they were correlated with other social characteristics: poor housing, poverty, a high proportion of the population foreign-born, and the incidence of a range of other social problems. These traits also persisted over time.

These areas of high delinquency Shaw and McKay termed 'delinquency areas'. Thirdly, their explanation of these concentrations was couched in terms of cultural transmission from one generation to another of criminal traits, and the theory of social disorganization, whereby the family and neighbourhood were ineffective in instilling the dominant values of the society. The collapse of neighbourhood social institutions together with a local criminal tradition constituted the cause of high delinquency rates.

It is debatable to what extent this was a truly ecological theory. Shaw and McKay did not concern themselves with symbiosis, competition and the substructure which Park had set out (Alihan, 1938, p. 83). The concentric zone model was used to organize descriptive data, while delinquency was explained largely in social, economic and cultural terms. It is probably more correct to describe the theory as 'areal' rather than 'ecological' (Baldwin, 1979, p. 34). Nevertheless, the theory of delinquency areas tends to have been interpreted within an ecological framework, and has led to ecological inferences being made which perpetrate the ecological fallacy. It is therefore reasonable to treat it here as an example.

As an explanation of the incidence of juvenile delinquency, this theory is particularly prone to the ecological fallacy. Properties may be imputed to areas which may or may not be true of individuals within them. (This error has been even more true of some more recent studies using methods of social area analysis, popular for a time in the 1950s (Baldwin, pp. 43–4).) The hypothesis of Shaw and McKay that slums produce delinquents is also open to argument. To what extent do families living in run-down inner city areas drift there due to social disadvantage, rather than disadvantage being transmitted directly from one generation to another? The results of the British Transmitted Deprivation research programme suggests that the answer is far from clear-cut (Brown and Madge, 1982). Social disorganization theory has come under critical attack, and ecological theories of crime have tended to fade into the background.

The idea of the geographical determination of delinquency areas does, however, persist. Mays, for example, in his studies of such areas on Merseyside, maintained that 'the area as a whole is delinquency producing' (1963, p. 219), despite recognizing that not all persons in such areas were delinquent. The question remains: 'How do delinquency areas arise and take on their characteristics? Does *area* in itself – as a surrogate for a social group sharing a common space –have some kind of independent effect which influences individual behaviour?' (Herbert, 1982, p. 42).

One of the policy implications of Shaw and McKay's work was that extensive urban renewal would mitigate the effects of geographical concentration. Postwar studies in Britain have shown that concentric zones are less significant than the extent and distribution of public housing (Baldwin, 1979, pp. 38–9). This has directed attention away from environmental determinism towards the social processes producing council housing estates with high delinquency. Baldwin and Bottoms (1976) showed marked variation between different estates in Sheffield with similar social composition, and suggested an explanation in terms of public housing allocation, the desire of residents to move from other estates, and the way that adverse reputations of some estates were created and maintained over time. More emphasis has been placed upon the social construction of 'problem' housing estates than on their environmental determination, which includes law enforcement and housing management policies as well as self-fulfilling prophecies fuelled by reputation.

Area policies for dealing with juvenile delinquency have to contend with the reality that 'delinquency areas' contain many non-delinquents, in many cases even a majority of the age group. Many delinquents lived outside such areas. Edwards (1973) in Newcastle on Tyne calculated that the highest ward rate for offences committed by a cohort of boys was 55 per cent. Other studies have produced rates of between 20 and 30 per cent for proportions involved in court cases or with police contacts. 'Place of residence is but one frame of reference for adolescent behaviour. There are others such as family, school and teacher, workplace and interest group which may modify its effects' (Herbert, 1982, p. 41). The concept of 'delinquency area' is one of relative difference between different areas of a city. It is open to the ecological fallacy if it is interpreted to mean that space, location and territory are of independent importance, apart from social and economic factors, and the weight of sociological research into delinquency (not reviewed here) suggests that the latter must be given greater significance. At best delinquency areas identify local circumstances which may promote high offender rates and to which resources to bring about improvement may be directed.

From the point of view of social intervention, policies directed at areas *per se* are not likely to be successful, since they rest upon the ecological fallacy. The more deep-rooted causes of social inequality and disadvantage lie in the society at large exercising its influence upon the life chances of families and individuals. Perhaps the most promising line for area-based policies to pursue are those which tackle social problems indirectly by encouraging local self-help and neighbourhood control. The 'local control' movement in the United States has been one manifestation of this. The local decentralization of British local authority services is another (Bulmer, 1986). Such policies, however, are secondary to the national policies which are required if the rate of juvenile delinquency is to be reduced.

The second example to be discussed at some length is that of educational disadvantage. Social inequality in educational performance has been the subject of extensive research in both the United States and Britain. During the 1960s social science analyses of the problems of combating the effects of poor schooling led to compensatory education programmes of various kinds (Halsey, 1978). These aimed to direct extra resources to assist the learning needs of the most disadvantaged children. One of the influential British documents was the report of the Plowden Committee on Primary Education (1967). Among their recommendations was the application of the principle of 'positive discrimination' to improve the life chances of disadvantaged children. This policy would be achieved by the identification of Educational Priority Areas (EPAs), areas where social and educational disadvantage were concentrated. Additional resources would be directed to schools in these areas.

We ask for 'positive discrimination' in favour of such schools and the children in them, going well beyond an attempt to equalise resources. Schools in deprived areas should be given priority in many respects. The first step must be to raise the schools with low standards to the national average; the second, quite deliberately to make them better. The justification is that the homes and neighbourhoods from which many of their children come provide little support and stimulus for learning. The schools must supply a compensating environment. (Plowden Report, 1967, p. 57)

The schools in deprived areas would be identified by a variety of social indicators relating to their catchment areas and to the schools themselves, including social class composition, income levels, quality of housing, attendance record, proportion of free school meals and proportion of children whose first language was not English. This in itself was not an easy task, involving certain simplifying assumptions (see Little and Mabey, 1972), but in the end, local education authorities were able to identify their EPA schools. The Inner London Education Authority, for instance, developed an Index of Relative School Deprivation which ranked their schools for resource allocation purposes and achieved a high level of agreement between the research results and the judgements of practitioners (Little and Mabey, 1972; Barnes and Lucas, 1975, pp. 241–2). Such rankings were used for a period to allocate special funds for school-building and to provide an extra salary increment for teachers working in such schools.

The point of introducing this example here is to show that the EPA policy adopted on Plowden's recommendation was based on the ecological fallacy. Focusing on schools was administratively and bureaucratically convenient, but it did not necessarily result in directing resources to all the children who most needed them. It did not take account of the diversity of circumstances both within such schools and among children outside such schools. There were good practical reasons for the advocacy and implementation of such a policy via schools, but it did not achieve the objectives it set out to achieve.

Why and how this is so can be shown from research in inner London. This research used the ILEA Index of Relative Deprivation to rank schools. Pupils were ranked on an index composed of eight items. Children scored one point each if (1) the father was in semi- or unskilled manual work, or unemployed, or occupation was not known; (2) the family size was six or more; (3) the child received free school meals; (4) the child was in the lowest quartile on the secondary school transfer profile; (5) the child's country of origin was outside the British Isles; (6) he had been taught by more than one class teacher over the past year; (7) the child had attended more than two schools to date; (8) the child was absent for more than one-third of possible occasions. Children who scored 5 or more out of 8 were deemed 'at risk'; those with scores of 0 or 1 'not at risk'. Both the school index and the child index are rather rudimentary and may be criticized for lacking precision. The child index refers to potential rather than actual disadvantage. Nevertheless, the indexes give a good indication in broad terms of the distribution of disadvantage both between schools and as affecting individuals.

Some of the results of the subsequent analysis are shown in Tables 11.4 and 11.5. From Table 11.4 it can be calculated that one child in twelve (2,500) was multiply disadvantaged in having a score of 5 or more. These children formed a significantly higher proportion of EPA schools than all schools: 16.8 compared to 8.1 per cent. Even so, even in the EPA schools, for every three children in those schools who were 'at risk' of being disadvantaged, four were not. Moreover, 21 per cent of children in EPA schools were identified clearly as not being at risk. On the other hand, nearly 7 per cent of

Table 11.4 *Individual Children at Risk of Disadvantage in ILEA, by Type of School*

Level of risk*	Least privileged (EPA) schools (%)	All other schools (%)	Total (%)
5+	16.8	6.7	8.1
4	17.9	10.6	11.6
3	21.8	18.0	18.5
2	22.1	24.7	24.3
1	15.4	25.5	24.1
0	6.0	14.5	13.3
(Base = 100%)	(4,158)	(26,338)	(30,496)

*Level of risk as defined in the index described in the text.
Source: Barnes and Lucas, 1975, p. 247.

children in all other schools were in the 'high risk' category, and numerically these were greater than the number of children in EPA schools. In fact, only one-third of the multiply disadvantaged children were in EPA schools.

Another way of looking at the question would be to ask what proportion of schools it would be necessary to include to reach what proportion of multiply disadvantaged 'at risk' children? This is shown in Table 11.5. If the programme was extended to include half the schools in the study (the first two columns of Table 9.5b), three-quarters of disadvantaged children would be covered. By expanding to three-quarters of schools (78 per cent of all children), 90 per cent of high-risk children would be reached, but so also would nearly two-thirds of the non-disadvantaged group. Nine per cent of most disadvantaged children are in the most privileged quartile of schools, where they comprise three per cent of those schools' population. Thus, 'for every two disadvantaged children who are in EPA schools, five are outside them. And in EPA schools themselves, disadvantaged children are outnumbered by children who are not disadvantaged' (Barnes and Lucas, 1975, p. 272). To direct resources to EPA schools to help disadvantaged children thus not only commits the ecological fallacy, but is an inefficient and ineffective means of achieving the stated aims of the policy.

The third detailed example of an area of social policy in which ecological analyses have had some influence is health. Geographical studies of the distribution of ill health and disease have been of some importance, but again are liable to lead the unwary into analytical pitfalls. Etzioni and Lehman (1967, pp. 12–13), for instance, cite three studies purporting to show a causal relationship between lower social class and chronic heart disease in the United States, which are

Table 11.5   *Individual Children at Risk of Disadvantage in ILEA, Grouped into Approximate EPA Quartiles by School Group and Level of Risk*

Level of risk	Least privileged quartile	Second quartile	Third quartile	Most privileged quartile	
(a) by school group					
5+	14.3	9.0	5.5	3.3	
4	16.8	12.4	10.1	6.6	
3	21.6	20.3	18.0	13.5	
2	23.0	24.5	25.4	24.0	
1	17.5	22.3	26.9	30.4	
0	6.7	11.4	14.0	22.2	
(Base = 100%)	(7,029)	(9,122)	(7,670)	(6,675)	
(b) by level of risk					Total %
5+	40.5	33.3	17.1	9.0	100
4	33.6	32.0	21.9	12.6	100
3	26.8	32.8	24.5	15.9	100
2	21.9	30.2	26.3	21.6	100
1	16.8	27.6	28.0	27.6	100
0	11.6	25.6	26.4	36.4	100
Total	23.0	29.9	25.2	21.9	100

Source: Barnes and Lucas, 1975, p. 247.

each based upon ecological correlations. In one study, eighty-three health areas in Manhattan were ranked on median income and death rates from arteriosclerotic heart disease, and then inferences made about the relationship between the two variables (Kent *et al.*, 1958). The flaw lies in assuming that in areas of a particular social class, those who died of heart disease are necessarily of that social class. They could be of a different class. There is no necessary relationship between the ecological correlation and the characteristics of the individuals who died of heart disease.

In discussing delinquency areas, reference was made to the concentration of other social problems in such areas, and these problems include the incidence of mental illness and suicide. This has given rise to a range of studies about the distribution of these phenomena and their explanation. In this case the sociological argument is rather more sophisticated, since social isolation is invoked as an intervening variable. R. E. L. Faris and W. Dunham, in another analysis of data for Chicago, suggested in 1939 that there was a high concentration of schizophrenics in run-down inner city areas which were the most disorganized, and that these areas were also the areas with the highest proportion of people living alone. Faris had previously hypothesized (1934) that any form of isolation which cut a person off from intimate social relations for an extended period of time would be likely to lead to the onset of schizophrenia. In the zone of transition, residents in hotels and rooming houses are constantly on the move, so contacts with neighbours are minimized. In other areas, members of minority ethnic groups can become isolated. The harsh competitive character of life in such areas is conducive to social isolation, particularly for a person who is already sensitive or timid. And in such areas the less assertive child whose personality does not match his peer group may be dropped from a gang or never achieve admission (Clausen and Kohn, 1954, pp. 144–5).

Sainsbury's analysis of suicide in London (1955) shows a relationship between various measures of isolation and suicide rates at the borough level (that is, an ecological correlation). He found coefficients of correlation between suicide and the percentage of persons living alone of 0.56, percentage of persons in lodgings and hotels 0.50. He concluded that

a lonely mode of life is an important adverse factor accounting for differential rates of suicide in the boroughs and their subdistricts . . . Certain districts seemed to impose upon residents a solitary, impersonal mode of life . . . The relationship between suicide and solitary mode of life is probably one of cause and effect. (Sainsbury, 1955, pp. 91, 76)

Both types of explanation posit ecological factors as accounting for the distribution of social pathology found. Characteristics of the area are conducive to the appearance of mental illness or the act of suicide. There are two problems with this type of explanation. One is the point already noted about the possible lack of coincidence between ecological and individual characteristics. The second arises even if the first is shown not to be the case. If there *is* a relationship at the individual level between mental illness or suicide and loneliness, how does one explain it? Is it that these areas produce social pathology, or is it explicable in terms of gravitation or drift of those who are mentally ill or suicidal into such areas?

The evidence on this issue is inconclusive, but certainly does not support an ecological explanation unequivocally. British studies such as Goldberg and Morrison (1963) and Parkin, Kenning and Wilder (1971) tend to support a drift hypothesis, while Giggs (1973,

1975) in Nottingham and Gove and Hughes (1980) using aggregate American data support an ecological explanation and reject a 'drift' hypothesis. The problem is a classic one in causal inference: in which direction does the path of causation lie? From social isolation to social pathology, or from a pre-existing condition or mental state which led the individual to move into an inner city area and increase their social isolation? Once again the discussion points to the need to produce precise and detailed evidence relating to the processes by which people arrive at certain outcomes, and to interpret this carefully to determine how a particular social condition arose. In the case of isolation and mental illness, the problem is particularly intractable because one is dealing with interaction between the ill person and significant others throughout their lifetime. Relatively few ecological studies provide adequate evidence of how area characteristics impinge upon the individuals whose behaviour is the dependent variable in the study. Plausible accounts are given of how the characteristics of the area may lead to social isolation, but the connections to individuals are not made adequately.

A final brief illustration of the ecological fallacy at work in the health field is provided by referring back to the RAWP exercise discussed in Chapter 4. This, it will be recalled, was a statistical exercise designed to alter the distribution of health resources between NHS regions so as to give additional resources to regions in greater need. The implementation of the policy led to greater financial stringency in certain wealthier regions, particularly the four metropolitan regions. Faced with static budgets and the need to make economies, these regions resorted to contentious and politically explosive decisions about hospital closures and rationalization. By and large, the hospitals selected for closure were not those serving the more prosperous sections of society, the teaching hospitals with which London is over-provided, but the older local district hospitals in predominantly working-class and lower-income areas. So the effect of RAWP *within* regions was not necessarily to achieve the match between resources and need which the national policy sought to achieve. The explanation for this discrepancy is fairly straight-forward. Within the health service there is a distinction between teaching hospitals and non-teaching hospitals. The teaching hospitals are more generously supported, carry out more high technology medicine, draw patients from wider catchment areas, and have a higher social class profile among their patients. The most powerful consultants teach at such hospitals, and in the RAWP exercise and subsequent cuts, they have been better able to protect their interests than non-teaching hospitals. The subregional distribution of resources is thus conditioned by the realities of status and power. It is the same with ecological correlations in other areas. While area differences may be of some explanatory importance, more basic inequalities of life chances, income, access to housing or education often underlie these geographical differences. It is with such differences between households, families and individuals that the policy-maker is properly concerned.

The discussion in this chapter has been concerned primarily with scientific findings and analyses, and only secondarily with the policy implications of particular conclusions. For example, it was mentioned that Shaw and McKay favoured urban renewal policies as a means of dealing with delinquency areas. Studies of public council housing in Britain suggest that there is no necessary relationship between age and condition of buildings and the incidence of delinquency. Indeed Newman (1972) has suggested that there may be built-in opportunities for crime and vandalism in new estates and flats which were not present in older areas. So they were probably over-optimistic.

What are the direct policy implications of the discussion in this chapter? Just as scientific conclusions drawn from aggregate data may be invalid, so too may policy measures taken be ineffective, because they are based on a false diagnosis. There is undoubtedly some intuitive appeal in the idea that social problems cluster together in particular areas. Townsend (1976) suggests that the exaggeration arises from notions of association and contamination, congregation, inheritance and environmental influences. Destitute, poor, mentally ill and criminal people are believed to seek refuge in certain areas because they feel easy in each other's company and more secure. Poverty, criminality and a range of other social problems are believed to be strongly rooted in certain geographical areas. There is a further belief that these characteristics are self-generating. Whether the theoretical explanation is in terms of the 'culture of poverty' (Lewis, 1966; Banfield, 1970) or the 'cycle of deprivation' (Coffield, Robinson and Sarsby, 1980, pp. 1–3, 157–70), there is a tendency to place the blame both on the area and on the victim, rather than on features of the economic and social structure. Each theory has been criticized as providing too facile an explanation for the persistence of deprivation and disadvantage. To the extent that they provide tacit support for an area-based policy, they are doubly unsatisfactory. The ecological fallacy can become a policy fallacy. Area-based policies for resource allocation, as Townsend points out, have severe weaknesses. First, however socially or economically deprived areas are defined, unless half the areas in the country are included there will be more disadvantaged people living outside such areas than inside them. Yet, clearly, to include as many as half the areas in the country does not facilitate direction of resources to a few areas. The EPA and CDP schemes were small demonstration projects; a national policy for resource allocation at the local level would require clearer guidance than this. Secondly, within all or nearly all areas defined as deprived there will be more persons who are *not* deprived than are deprived. Thus a policy of directing resources to deprived areas would not necessarily reach deprived people. For example, putting extra resources into EPA schools could, theoretically, not benefit any of the children for whom they were intended but provide benefits exclusively for children not from deprived backgrounds. This would be unlikely in practice, but the point is that area-based resource allocation does not necessarily ensure that resources reach those for whom they are intended.

David Donnison, in a critique of policies for priority areas (1974), pointed out the weakness of inferring that social problems were spatially located, and suggested that three questions needed to be answered. First, how concentrated geographically is poverty? Berthoud's work on Greater London (1976, pp. 164–5) is based on analysis of household incomes for small areas (wards) and showed that in 1971–2 the variation among households *within* each ward was almost as great as variation across the whole of the capital. The GLC would have had to cover 38 per cent of all wards (containing in that 38% 1 million households), in order to reach half (300,000) of the households with gross incomes below £1,000 in 1971–2. Even so, according to that analysis, *inner* London did not include such a high proportion of these households. From an aggregate analysis it seemed that an inner ring of London accounted for over 94 per cent of the capital's relatively poor *wards* compared to 40 per cent of its population. This ecological distribution suggested there was a concentration of poverty, yet when poor households and individuals were pinpointed geographically, they were shown to be more widely dispersed and the ecological inference fallacious.

Secondly, where poverty is heavily concentrated (often on council estates as a result of local authority allocation policy), what penalties do such *areas* inflict upon people over and above their social class and position in the income cycle? The discussion of crime earlier suggests that these effects are not so much ecological as socially constructed, in the sense that areas can attract reputations. This affects people's willingness to live there or to move, and may also influence housing management and policing practice. The case of ill health suggests that there may be a process of drift or social selection at work (though this is uncertain) rather than the causation of individuals' problems by the area as such.

Thirdly, what are the best strategies for helping families and individuals living in such areas? Policy-makers are likely to continue to see problems of urban deprivation in spatial terms, because local authority planning, housing and social services, the health services and the police are all organized in this way. Moreover, there are built-in features of the environment and the political process which point to the need for some such areal redistribution of resources. One factor is the gradual loss of population and industry from Britain's largest and from America's older cities to more attractive and prosperous suburban areas, and to the south and south-west of both countries. Policies to deal with its consequences are required. Associated with this is a shift in Britain into owner-occupation, a moratorium on new council house building, and the recognition that the council house stock will be occupied for the next generation predominantly by the more disadvantaged and poorer sections of the working class. This will intensify the problems of some areas, and may call for policies pitched at an area level.

Politically, strong positive support is needed for policies to direct resources to social minorities of whatever kind. The biggest needs are often concentrated in authorities whose revenue-raising capacity is low, so central government support is required. Local authorities themselves do not always go out of their way to provide for the poor and deprived, and need prodding to do so. And central government has little direct responsibility for the provision of social services, and needs to become more involved in this process. Recognition of the multiple character of forms of deprivation points to the need for improved co-ordination, both between central and local government, and between different departments at each level. Lack of effective co-ordination between central government departments has been a particular source of policy confusion and ineffectiveness in framing policies to deal with urban disadvantage. The promotion of local self-help activities, decentralized services and neighbourhood action is growing and being pursued by a number of local authorities. Such fostering of devolution and diversity necessarily has to be done at a (small) area level, since it involves formal organization and co-ordination of some sort.

The same is not true, however, of financial payments and benefits directed from government to individuals. Conventional services need modification to help the most deprived, but as a general strategy area policies are not the best way to do it. 'How can we help the most deprived people who now so often fail to get even those rights and services which were intended for them? That problem cannot be solved in priority areas alone because most of the deprived do not live in such areas and most of the people who live in them are not specially deprived' (Donnison, 1974, p. 135). If that lesson can be learnt, then the ecological fallacy may be at least partially laid to rest.

12

*Explanation and Social Policy:
'The' Problem of Social Inequalities
in Health* *

STUART S. BLUME**

Interest in the socio-economic and environmental causes of inequalities in life expectancy and health within British society has a long history. By the middle of the nineteenth century many within the medical profession had come to recognize that overcrowding and lack of ventilation were involved in the propagation of disease. Poverty was coming to be seen as in some way associated with a particular susceptibility to disease, as well as an all too frequent consequence of chronic sickness. Chadwick's great sanitary report of 1842 (Chadwick, 1965) was largely concerned to demonstrate a relationship between insanitation, defective drainage, inadequate water supply and overcrowded housing on the one hand and disease, high mortality and low life expectancy on the other. Examining data on the proportions of those of different classes having been found fit for military service he came to the conclusion that the working class was actually deteriorating in strength and stature (compared to previous generations) because of the bad conditions in the cities (Chadwick, 1965, p. 250). Chadwick's report was quoted a few years later by Engels, in his study of the condition of the British working class (Engels, 1968). Engels cited similar evidence to that of Chadwick, and he pointed out, as had Farr and some other doctors (Hodgkinson, 1967), the complete lack of medical assistance available to the majority of the working class. Unlike the many reformers who attributed the association between sickness and social

* ©1982 Cambridge University Press. Reprinted with the permission of the Press from the *Journal of Social Policy*, vol. 11, part 1, January 1982, pp. 7–31.
** Professor of Science Dynamics (Wetenschapsdynamica), University of Amsterdam.

conditions to the state of the cities Engels, of course, saw in it the workings of the exploitative economic system.

While it is not possible within the confines of this chapter adequately to explore the developing conceptualizations of the problem in detail, it is worth drawing brief attention to the somewhat later writing of Sir John Simon. In his *Public Health Reports* of the 1860s and 1870s one may see the branching out of various lines of analysis. The rapid development of scientific medicine at that time is reflected in attempts increasingly to show the aetiological importance of *specific* aspects of the living conditions of the poor for the specific diseases then being identified (Simon, 1887). Scientific medicine was increasingly concerned to identify the aetiological agents which intervene between, for example, inadequate lavatory drainage on the one hand and prevalence of 'enteric fever' (typhoid) on the other. Nevertheless, Simon's analysis frequently harks back also to the social conditions themselves, seeing in them source both of disease and of immorality.

In subsequent years the question to which, in their differing ways, Chadwick, Engels and Simon addressed themselves, has not lost its saliency. But the fact is that as a consequence of the disciplinary differentiation which has taken place (Abrams, 1968) the relations between 'health' and the dimensions of social stratification are today treated within what in Britain have since become three more or less distinctive intellectual traditions.

The three traditions to which I refer are the academic fields of social administration, epidemiology and sociology. In this chapter I shall attempt to show, for each in turn, how 'the problem' is conceptualized and indicate what seem to be the strengths and weaknesses of each, as approaches to explanation. In seeking thus to characterize central disciplinary traditions I am not implying that all work in a field is thereby described. In social administration, for example, not only are a variety of social scientific approaches brought to bear, but there is increasing conceptual diversity. The very different work of Bleddyn Davies, of Gough, of Pinker, does not fit neatly into the tradition I shall seek to characterize. Some would go further and argue that social administration is not a 'discipline' at all, but a field of application in which many disciplines converge (Culyer, 1981). I do not intend to analyse this view here: to do so would certainly require recourse to the distinction between the 'social' and 'cognitive' structures of the field. It is possible to make statements about the institutionalization of what we call social administration. Bulmer, for example, writes: 'The academic study of Social

Administration as a distinct subject originated with the growth of the welfare state' (Bulmer, 1981). Despite the fruitful clashes of ideas which now characterize the field, it is nevertheless meaningful to talk of a central tradition: a set of inherited values, norms, objectives, and a common culture. The same may be said, and with similar caveats, of the field of epidemiology.

The purpose of the analysis which this chapter presents is to seek to show, in the final section, that it is possible to characterize a more fully adequate explanation than any one of these approaches individually can provide.

The Social Administration Approach

According to one excellent introductory textbook, the academic study of social administration is concerned 'first . . . with social problems and second . . . with the ways in which society responds to those problems' (Brown, 1977, p. 13). The author goes on to give an indication of just what social problems are. They are, she writes,

> problems which affect not just the individual but the society in which he lives. They arise from individual human needs which are common to all members of society . . . When the needs are not met (by personal or family action) they give rise to problems which society as a whole increasingly tries to tackle. Society does not, of course, always recognise or accept that individual needs give rise to *social* problems . . . (ibid., pp. 13–14)

Sickness is one widely admitted social problem and it figures, together with an account of provision for the alleviation of sickness, in almost all social administration texts. Serious effects of (especially chronic) sickness on family structure, and standard of living, are a matter of major concern, not least for social administration.

It is pertinent to the traditional focus of the field, and a common matter of inquiry, that social problems rarely impact equally upon all segments of society. This is as true of their prevalance as of their implications, and as true of sickness as of homelessness, unemployment, and the whole range of social welfare concerns. Characterization of the problem of social inequalities in health typically proceeds from a presentation of the extensive evidence which exists. First, there is evidence on mortality, provided by the registrar-general. In decennial supplements on mortality, death rates (standardized for age distribution) are derived from comparison of census counts of numbers in occupations grouped into so-called classes, with numbers dying and recorded at death as belonging to each of these groupings of occupations (OPCS, 1978). In the case of children (and married women) it is the occupation of the father (husband) which determines the class to which an individual is ascribed. The most recent data of this kind (for 1970-2), like those for earlier years, show clear class gradients in infant, child and adult mortality.

Secondly, there is some evidence on differential morbidity, or ill health. The best-known and only regular, source of this kind of information is the annual General Household Survey (GHS). This national survey of some 16,000 households presents not the results of clinical investigation but respondents' own recollections of episodes of ill health, distinguishing between acute and chronic (or long-standing) sickness. Broadly speaking the GHS shows clear class gradients in chronic sickness: those in manual occupations, and their families, are much more likely than those in non-manual and professional occupations, and their families, to report the presence of long-standing sickness or disability. Differences in regard to episodes of acute sickness are less clear. It is now frequently pointed out that the likelihood of an individual choosing to define a given symptom of which he or she is aware as 'ill health' (with the implication that normal activities, including work, should be suspended) is likely itself to be class related. That is, the class-related costs of being sick render the working-class respondent less likely to have defined his or her symptom as ill heatlh and so lead to an underestimate of the true class gradient in the GHS.

The third type of evidence relates to the provision and utilization of health services as well as the quality of the services typically available to the different social groups. Titmuss (1976, p. 196) wrote that, despite the establishment of the National Health Service, inequalities in care remained, that 'higher income groups know how to make better use of the service; they tend to receive more specialized attention; occupy more of the beds in better equipped and staffed hospitals'. A good deal of research has since been devoted to determining the extent to which, and the ways in which, this is the case. So far as the preventive health services are concerned, evidence for relative under-utilization by working-class families is clear cut. It covers, *inter alia*, antenatal care (where working-class women are more likely to attend first late in their pregnancy) (Brotherston, 1976), cervical screening (Sansom, Wakefield and Yule, 1972) and immunization (Davie, Butler and Goldstein, 1972).

Analysis of health service expenditure by area has shown that more affluent middle-class areas typically spend more on provision of health services for their populations than do less affluent working-class areas (Tudor Hart, 1971; Noyce, Snaith and Trickey, 1974; Townsend, 1974). The GHS collects information on GP consultation and hospital usage (in-patient and out-patient) and analyses GP consultation (but not hospital usage) by class. Survey data in fact show that at most ages, and for both men and women, unskilled manual workers and their families consult GPs more frequently than do professional and managerial workers and their families, and make more extensive use of hospital out-patient facilities. It has, however, been argued that the proper basis for comparison is not 'rate of consultation' alone, but 'rate of consultation in relation to need'. Brotherston (1976) and Forster (1976) re-analysed GHS data so as to relate the rate of consultation for each socio-economic group to the rate of (self-reported) morbidity for the same group. On this basis (dividing one rate by the other) Brotherston derived what he called 'use–need ratios'. These ratios prove to vary between the socio-economic groups, indicating higher use of GP services in relation to morbidity by the higher groups and a clear class gradient. It is widely accepted, then, that not only are working-class areas less well provided with medical services (particularly so in the case of the inner cities, as the Royal Commission on the National Health Service, 1979, p. 88, showed), but also working-class people make less use of the services which are available, at least in relation to their needs.

Other work, utilizing sociological insights and methods (see below) within a social administration framework, has focused upon aspects of the organization of care. The work of Cartwright and her collaborators has suggested that general practitioners typically give better care to their middle-class patients than to their working-class patients (Cartwright, 1964; Cartwright and O'Brien, 1976). Cartwright and O'Brien showed, for example, that middle-class patients tended to have longer consultations, in which more problems were discussed; and that middle-class patients were able to make better use of their consultations. If I have done no injustice to the social administration approach to exemplification of the problem of social inequality in health, it remains to consider the nature of the *explanation* of the problem which this tradition yields.

Social class, so clearly associated with mortality and at least chronic sickness and disability, is also highly correlated with bad housing (overcrowding, lack of amenities) and with unemployment, as well as (though data are not good) with low (lifetime) income

(Townsend, 1979) and with certain aspects of diet (e.g. vitamin C intake). Inequalities in utilization of the health services – notably the preventive health services – play a double role both as one cause of inequalities in health, and as a problem in themselves which requires explanation. It is not difficult to conclude that inequalities in health in the population can be explained in terms of unequal social provision: that the root of the problem lies in society's failure to ensure that all of its citizens are adequately housed, fed, educated, treated; in its failure to ensure that everyone works in healthy salubrious conditions; and in its failure to eliminate financial poverty, and in particular the financial strains associated with child-rearing. The implication is that if all these problems were to be tackled seriously then the problem of inequalities in health would largely vanish. Clearly the variables which figure in this approach to explanation are those with which social administration (and, at the level of practice, social policy) is concerned, and which constitute its particular focus. Various kinds of evidence can be adduced in support of this view, including the evidence of international comparisons of mortality rates. Anderson, for example, in the course of a comparison of England, Sweden and the USA attributes much of Sweden's health advantage over the USA to its 'high minimum standard of living for everyone and a cultural homogeneity ... Health services are, of course, also a factor in the low mortality rates, but the elimination of poverty in the United States in the sense true for Sweden would be more likely to bring mortality rates closer to Sweden than a policy limited to health services only' (Anderson, 1972, p. 158).

In practice, most research within the social administration tradition has had a rather more specific focus. Some have examined *effects* of sickness or disability upon the individual or upon the family. How do people cope with the financial strains, with unemployment, with the need for care, with the psychological strains, and how serious are these problems for families of different social status or possessing different financial resources (Martin and Morgan, 1975)? Commonly, the problem of health *becomes* the problem of the health services. The problem of inequalities in health becomes the problem of inequalities in provision (and the structure and discriminatory functioning) of services – notably the health services. In dealing with inequalities in availability and use of the health services, with modes of operating which discriminate against use by some social groups, with the failure to match use to social needs, social administration as a discipline feels itself on safe and uncontested ground. This of course is hardly surprising for a field which in a very central sense is concerned with social justice (Titmuss, 1974). In treating the provision of health services, and the equation of use with need, as ends in themselves, notions of social justice properly come to the fore. But how adequate is this approach in providing an explanation of inequalities in health? The adequacy of an explanation is in some respects to be judged by its consistency with the available evidence, and by the amount of such evidence which it seeks to explain. Amongst such evidence statistical data on current inequalities in mortality and morbidity rates are certainly significant. But equally to be addressed by any *adequate* explanation are on the one hand data showing historic changes in such rates, and on the other analyses of health inequalities in other industrial countries.

British experience in reducing the difference in mortality rates between social groups has not been encouraging. Social progress, while reflected in a pronounced (and of course much to be welcomed) overall decline in the various rates of mortality, has not given rise to any significant improvement of the health experience of the manual classes relative to the professional and managerial classes.

For example, Morris and Heady (1955) found that, despite overall progress, in relation to post-neonatal mortality the gap between the social classes was as wide in 1950 as it had been in 1911. This was despite the real progress in levelling standards of living. These authors comment:

This finding was unexpected. At any rate something different was hoped for in the 1930s. Infant mortality . . . is highly sensitive to social conditions. Different sections of the population have been very differently affected by recent social changes; and in the last twenty years, anyhow, full employment, higher real wages, and expanding social services have led to relatively greater improvement in the situation of the building and dock labourers of social class V and the miners in social class III, for example, than of clerks or professional people. As indicated, however, this different experience is not reflected at all in the infant mortality rates . . . (ibid., p. 556)

Much the same has been true of the more recent period. Between 1961 and 1971 the mortality rates of adults in classes IV and V relative to classes I and II actually worsened (Black Report, 1980).

Similar difficulties arise in trying to explain trend data for the USA. The Great Society programmes of the 1960s led to rising income and increased availability of medical care to the poor and there was indeed a decline in overall mortality rate. But the data characterizing social inequalities are complex. In the USA it is ethnic and income differentials, rather than occupational ones, which provide the principal focus of attention in most examinations of inequality, including health inequalities. Over the 1960s, then, the health gap between 'whites' and 'non-whites' narrowed.

> This pattern was in contrast to that in the 1950s when the difference between the racial groups increased. In 1960 infant mortality rates for the two major groups differed by 20.3 per 1,000 live births. By 1972 the difference between them was 11.3 per 1,000; the narrowing of the gap since 1960 was greater after the first four weeks of life . . . when socio-economic factors predominate than in the neonatal period. (Chase, 1977, p. 680)

But other attempts at examining changing inequalities produce a less happy picture. For example, a study which examined mortality rates within the ten richest and ten poorest states for 'whites' and 'non-whites' separately found that although the relative position of blacks and whites within each group of states did not change greatly, the gap between the rich states and the poor states actually widened (Lerner and Stutz, 1977). Health Interview Survey data showed that while the gap between rich and poor in access to a physician (expressed as the percentage who had not visited a physician in the previous two years) had diminished between 1964 and 1973, there was no change in the differential reporting of morbidity. These conclusions held for whites and non-whites separately (Wilson and White, 1977). The point is that indicators of differential health experience may not run parallel, making understanding in terms of gradually more equal distributions of income, service provision and so on, highly ambiguous.

While differential access to health services plays a part in sustaining health inequalities, it cannot provide a total explanation. Backett and associates, for example, sought to relate a wide variety of health indicators to socio-demographic and medical care characteristics at the level of the (pre-reorganization) Regional Hospital Boards (Martini et al., 1977). After a complex statistical analysis, their conclusion was that 'indices constructed from the traditional outcome measures are more sensitive to variations in the socio-demographic circumstances of the population than to the amount and type of medical care provided and/or available' (ibid., p. 306).

Moreover, if availability of health services will not do, it seems that income will not either, since the relationship between income and standardized mortality rate is largely accounted for by social class (OPCS, 1978, p. 151). While it is true that weekly income is a far from adequate measure of the material resources available to a family, nevertheless OPCS data, taken in conjunction with other results available, are indicative of the complexity of the issue. It is worth noting, for example, that the lowest-paid occupations do not always have the highest mortality rates, and the range for a given occupation or occupational group between regions is far greater than can be accounted for by differences in financial circumstances (for example, 'transport and communication workers' ranges between 134 in Wales and 97 in East Anglia).

The next point I want to make is that many studies conducted within the epidemiological framework which I discuss below demonstrate relationships, and implicate factors, which are either vastly more subtle than or outside the scope of the present paradigm. The following examples are illustrative.

A study by Colley and Reid (1970) of the prevalence of respiratory symptoms in (over 11,000) children aged 6–10 was concerned to explore the interplay of social and environmental factors. Respiratory disease provides one of the clearest class gradients in both morbidity and mortality, and among all ages in Britain. In this study, superimposed upon the usual class gradient, was an interesting effect of air pollution. The study was carried out in a number of areas which were grouped into 'high', 'medium' and 'low' (in air pollution). It was found that for class IV/V children, but *not* for class I/II or III, morbidity rose with increasing air pollution: in other words only for children born into classes IV or V was environmental pollution an exacerbating factor. These authors did not consider that the explanation could derive from differences in domestic circumstances (e.g. overcrowding levels, which were not great). Additionally, for all classes morbidity was distinctly higher in Wales, even in rural Wales where pollution was lower. This was felt to require explanation in terms of genetic factors or of selective emigration. Genetic factors were also felt to play a part by Lawrence, Carter and David (1968) in explaining the excessive incidence of congenital abnormalities in Wales, and by Speizer, Rosner and Tager (1976) in explaining the aggregation of respiratory disorder in households found in the US National Health Survey.

The Epidemiological Approach

Epidemiology may be broadly defined as 'the study of the distributions and states of health in human populations'. In recognition of what they take to be its status as the basic science underpinning community health, many epidemiologists would add some such notion as 'for the purpose of surveillance, control, and prevention of health disorders'. Of central interest has always been the effects of environmental conditions upon health: a concern which, within medicine, may be traced back as far as Hippocrates.

Chadwick's sanitary report made extensive use of administrative returns and of epidemiological reasoning: seeking to show the effects of certain environmental factors (notably, of course, sanitary conditions) upon the health of populations as expressed in terms of area mortality rates. Today the epidemiological approach is typically through a variety of refined survey methods, deployed to examine socio-environmental correlates of various diseases or causes of death. Investigation of 'health' in its more positive sense has been more limited, not least because of the problems of operationalizing such a concept (the notable exception being study of the physical and psychological development of children, for which norms have been developed).

On the one hand, therefore, epidemiology can justly claim a long and unbroken tradition of effective application in public health practice. Such effectiveness has frequently had little to do with the theoretical principles upon which a particular recommendation has been based: Chadwick, for example, continued to subscribe to the 'miasma' theory of contagion long after it had been falsified to the satisfaction of most medical scientists. On the other hand, it can also be argued that the field was in fact transformed by the studies of, say, Koch and Pasteur in the latter half of the nineteenth century which postulated, and then isolated, living organisms demonstrably responsible for specific diseases. In so doing these scientists not only produced a redefinition and reclassification of disease(s), but established the concept of causation of disease at the heart of medical science. As a result, an argument might plausibly run, epidemiology acquired a new purpose and hence a new cognitive structure. Today, and as a result, epidemiologists see their field as serving to complement the insights gained from clinical and laboratory study in the understanding of disease aetiologies. According to Morris, the unique importance of epidemiological studies lies in the fact that while clinical cases (and hence the observation which they permit) are almost by definition restricted to the advanced stages of diseases, epidemiology (through, for example, its population survey methods) can assess the prevalence and explore the antecedents and consequences of pre-symptomatic stages. The understanding thereby yielded has transformed the medical picture of many diseases: for example, diptheria, poliomyelitis, hypertension, diabetes (Morris, 1975, p. 126).

The importance of epidemiological methods and findings for medicine has probably increased as a consequence of the decline of infectious diseases and the growing importance (as causes of death and of incapacity) of chronic diseases of complex and *multi*-causal aetiology: ischaemic heart disease, bronchitis, cancers. Epidemiologists here are concerned to assess the prevalence of such conditions within populations distinguished on the basis of specific criteria, and to seek to understand the interaction of environmental and social statuses and conditions with characteristics of the individual ('host' factors). Thus research on hypertension, for example, has focused *inter alia* upon sex, age, ethnic and occupational group differences, on the apparent effects of water hardness and diet (including salt intake), and upon the effects of such physiological characteristics as obesity. But always important for the epidemiologist, in understanding the importance of what appears to be a causal factor, is 'how does it work'.

The correlations yielded by surveys, though they may be a guide to individual or collective preventive action, still require explanation. 'Surveys confirm clinical experience of the importance of family history' (in the aetiology of coronary heart disease) '*which is partly explained* in resemblance of blood pressure levels, blood lipids, and glucose' (Morris, 1975, p. 159, my emphasis). Similarly, the demonstrable associations between cigarette smoking, exercise patterns and obesity and death from coronary heart disease require the postulation of causal *mechanisms* to satisfy the epidemiologist intellectually – even though he may be more than ready to propose policies for reduction in smoking, promotion of outdoor exercise and so on. Such causal mechanisms are likely to require confirmation from – or at least must be plausible in the light of – clinical and/or laboratory studies and biomedical theories.

This symbiotic relationship between epidemiology and clinical medicine, which exists despite the current rift among these branches of medical science in Britain, has another implication. As Susser has observed, 'despite the epidemiologist's insistence on studying populations, his ultimate concern is with health, disease, and death as it occurs in individuals' (Susser, 1973, p. 59). An important consequence is the typical emphasis upon the importance of *individual* behaviour: smoking, drinking, failing to exercise or avail oneself of health care provision.

What then is the place of 'social class' in epidemiology? Susser writes:

> one may say that the circumstances of social class are a direct cause of the variation of mortality rates between social classes. This conclusion could be reached by showing that mortality rates vary consistently with social class, even when such other known factors as age and sex, which influence mortality rates, are controlled.
>
> But we do not find it comfortable to say that the circumstances of social class are a direct cause of the death of an individual or even of numbers of discrete individuals not treated as a social collectivity . . . To try to attribute the death of an individual to his social class position is at once to become aware that additional factors must intervene between social positions and causes of death. The analyst is nudged, as it were, into stating hypotheses to explain the links between social class and the causes of individual deaths. (ibid., p. 51)

This quotation gives some indication of the place of 'social class' within epidemiological explanation. The argument of this chapter is that it is with the second paragraph of the quotation that the real purpose of epidemiology is more or less identified, and hence it follows that social class functions as a variable of indicative – but not explanatory – significance. The same sort of point is made by Suchman:

> Rates analysed in relation to such categories as sex, age, race, marital status, occupation and geographical region are an essential part of the social book-keeping of modern society. In and of themselves, however, these rates offer little by way of explanation. If one's purpose is to explain the relation between demographic factors and coronary heart disease, one cannot help but get lost in a morass of inconclusive correlations . . . Where does the fault lie? The answer is probably to be found in the essential meaningless-ness of gross demographic population categories when viewed as 'causal' variables . . . [they] cannot except in a very limited superficial sense, represent the kind of social phenomena that may cause disease or anything else. (Suchman, 1967a, p. 110)

My argument is that the kind of linkages which epidemiologists seek are those which are plausible from, legitimated by, a clinical medical perspective. The uncertain concept of 'stress' has proved of great utility here.

The epidemiological approach has many strengths. In common with the social administration approach it is action-oriented, and through its links with medicine (clinical and social) there is implicit the notion that the problems to which it addressed itself have solutions (however hard to find). Such solutions may be of a collective kind, and epidemiological research may lead to an emphasis upon increased provision of, for example, such preventive health measures as screening for neural tube defects or a more vigorous programme of whooping cough or polio vaccination. To this extent the common origins of epidemiological work and social administration are in evidence. But epidemiology is nowadays much concerned with what are sometimes known as 'diseases of affluence': ischaemic heart disease, stroke, mental illness and so on. Action here frequently implies the attempt to educate/exhort people to change their behaviour: to stop smoking, exercise more, improve their diet and so on. This preference for behaviour modification, the emphasis upon individual responsibility, reflects the dependence of epidemiology upon individualistic medicine.

The strength of the epidemiological tradition lies also in its explanatory value: as a method it has played an important part in improved understanding of the aetiology of many diseases. Its symbiotic relationship with medicine provides it in return not only with a theoretical unity (rooted in the laboratory sciences which together provide a coherent account of the working of the human body) but also, and as a consequence, with a guide to the selection of variables to be tried out in explanatory hypotheses. It is precisely by virtue of this link with one source of theory that epidemiology is most importantly differentiated from social administration. Similarly, the variables which can be adduced in attempted explanations are not constrained by the subject-matter of social policy (i.e. collective provision and distribution of goods and services). Epidemiologists can, and do, include in their hypotheses such variables as air pollution, climate, water hardness and the secondary effects of previous illness. Thus epidemiologists can make sense of Colley and Reid's work: genetic factors are admissible within an epidemiological approach, and may be invoked as at least a 'residual' factor in explanation. For the same sorts of reasons epidemiology can deal with more complex findings than can social administration. For example, it is clearly important for the epidemiologist whether the link between inadequate maternal nutrition and low birth weight or incidence of congenital abnormalities in offspring is direct and immediate (so that dietary supplementation will alleviate the effects of the neonate) or whether it is rather longer term in its effects so that, as some authors have suggested, the effects are manifest with a lag of one generation, via reduction in the reproductive capacity of female infants (Janerich, 1972; Baird, 1974).

However, though epidemiology is sensitive to the complexity of data of these kinds, yet it has important weaknesses. First, this approach is limited by its inherently individualistic nature. It can provide no explanation of, for example, systematically late presentation for antenatal care by working-class women (leading to higher risks of complications of pregnancy and of perinatal mortality) other than ignorance/inadequacy. It cannot deal with the notion that there may be structural features of society which limit provision of health services in poor areas, or which limit the leisure activities of the poor, or which direct certain people into inherently unhealthy jobs.

Secondly, it seems to me that this tradition as a means of explanation (rather than as a methodology) is unable to provide any account of differential rates of disablement or death due to causes lacking any medically plausible intervening factor. Perhaps the best example is that of accidents to children, on the road, in the home, and at school, which account for fully one-third of all child deaths and show a sharp class gradient. Explanation here has surely to be in terms of structural factors (including account of the resources of time, space and money available to social classes) which themselves directly place the working-class child at greater risk of accident.

Thirdly, it seems to me unable to deal adequately with the *consequences* of sickness or disability, other than for subsequent (ill) health. There is significant evidence, for example, that the economic, occupational and social effects of long-term chronic illness differ substantially between social classes (see Martin and Morgan, 1975; Blaxter, 1976). In understanding class differences in ill health (including disability) the effects of such conditions have to be considered as an aspect of the explanandum.

Sociological Approaches

In contrast to the social administration and epidemiological traditions outlined above sociology offers a variety of conceptual frameworks from which inequalities in health can be, and have been, examined. This variety reflects the 'multi-paradigmatic' character of the discipline.

Many sociologists have explicitly rejected a concern with the social distribution of ill health within the community as their field of inquiry. It has been held that such an approach necessarily embodies a problem definition 'given' by the medical profession, rather than formulated from within sociology itself. According to Freidson, for example, sociology should concern itself rather with the medical profession: its practices, institutions, social relations and power. For this author the 'organization of medical care is considered to be the central issue for a sociological analysis of medicine' (Freidson, 1970, p. 57). In contrast to the social administration approach no (implicit) assumption is made as to the importance of medical care for health: the emphasis which Freidson and others give to the organization of medical care derives from, and is legitimated by, their perception of the nature of their discipline, and by this alone. Freidson grounds his analysis in examination of the professional status and authority enjoyed by medical practitioners, which, he argues, gives Western systems of medical care their basic and characteristic structure. Differences between class or status groups in access to care, and in the nature of the care received, provide one such characteristic in need of explanation. Thus it is suggested not only that (at least within the American health care system) the poor have less choice of physician, but that

> once in consultation, patients markedly lower in status than their physician can be so intimidated as to be reluctant to engage in the exchanges necessary for adequate diagnosis and prescription, and, by virtue of the restraints imposed by the necessity of deference, may subsequently evade contact with the professional (ibid., p. 114)

Similarly, the extent to which individuals suffer 'depersonalization' in health care institutions is said to depend upon the extent to which choice is available, itself shown to depend upon the patient's resources ('financial or sociopolitical'). This analysis leads to certain proposals for change, essentially within professional organization (including a reduction in the extent to which the medical profession itself determines and sanctions standards of care) in the interests of universal access to high-quality care.

Other sociological (or sociologically informed) analyses of systems of medical care are rooted in rather broader critiques of society than is

Freidson's. Navarro (1978), for example, explicitly rejects the view that the structure of medical services or (inequalities in) the consumption of health services can be explained in terms of forces *within* the medical sector. Navarro seeks to show how it is class relations, the class nature of British capitalistic society, which determine all significant aspects of health policy and the structure of health care in Britain. This includes, for him, the structure of the health professions themselves, the resources made available for medical care, the distribution of resources both between the various forms of health care (e.g. hospital care and community health services) and between the health regions. He is able to quote, for example, Noyce, Snaith and Trickey's (1974) study showing how expenditure on health care by regions is proportional to the share of the middle class within their populations. The emphasis on individual responsibility to be found in government's approach to preventive health, exemplified, for example, in *Prevention and Health* (DHSS, 1976), is similarly explicable:

> Reflecting the bourgois bias of the medical research establishment, for example, much priority is given to the supposedly individual causation of disease. One instance, among others, is that most research on heart disease – one of the main killers in society – has focused on diet, exercise, and genetic inheritance . . . However, in a fifteen-year study of ageing, quoted in . . . *Work in America* . . . it was found that the most important predictor of longevity was work satisfaction . . . But very few studies have been done either in the UK or in the US to investigate these socio-political factors. (Navarro, 1978, p. 119)

Like the social administration approach, Navarro draws attention to limitations on the funds made available for health care as well as to inequities in the distribution of such resources, favouring the affluent (capital-owning) social groups and areas. The two approaches differ in that Navarro goes on to offer an explanation of this state of affairs in terms of a Marxian analysis of society.

Rather differently, rejecting their own earlier castigations of the (American) medical care system ('always more for what it did *not* do than for what it did'), Ehrenreich and Ehrenreich (1978) argue that capitalist systems of medical care have to be seen as agencies of social control: as means of maintaining and reinforcing capitalist social relations. From this perspective social inequalities in the receipt of care are an inevitable result of the social function of medical institutions:

because of the visible barriers to entry or because of public knowledge of the treatment experienced by those who do enter . . . [certain services] exert what we will call disciplinary social control in that they *encourage* people to maintain work or family responsibilities – no matter what subjective discomfort they may be experiencing. (ibid., p. 48)

But this function of discouraging the population (and particularly the poor) from abandoning their family and work responsibilities for a 'sick role' (really the idea of 'less eligibility' once more) is only part of the critique. Ehrenreich and Ehrenreich refer also to the growing dependency of society upon the medical profession (brought about through a gradual medicalization of social problems) which amounts (in the US context) to a reinforcement of the power of whites, males and the middle class who make up that profession, and of the acquiescence of dependent groups in the class system. Moreover, it is conceivable, when differences in the therapies which social groups seem sometimes to receive, are considered,

that the actual technical medical treatment of the poor may be a factor in strengthening the feelings of 'low self-worth' which many sociologists claim to detect in the poor – i.e. that the medical system reinforces the sense of class inferiority in those of lower class position when they use its services. (ibid., p. 64)

The analyses outlined above all attempt, in one way or another, to explain the structure of health care (and whether explicitly or implicitly social inequalities in the receipt of care) in terms of fundamental variables of sociological analysis: authority, class relations and so on. A few sociologists try to go further and explain social inequalities in health itself in similar terms. Such a task is facilitated, and moreover accords with sociology's general concern to free itself from medical hegemony in this area, by calling into question the concept (health) which is to be explained. I shall have more to say on this below: suffice it for the moment to point out that notions of health as 'the absence of (medically recognized) disease' on the one hand and as 'well-being' (physical, mental and social, in the well-known WHO phraseology) on the other have confronted each other since the time of the ancient Greeks. Health-as-well-being, divorced from medical nosologies and legitimation, has greater utility for sociology. On such a view, 'well-being' is simply *illustrated* by available data on mortality rates, sickness, child development and so on. It is not difficult to envisage the thesis that inequalities in health (paralleling those in income, in resources of money and time, in control over life, and conditions of work) reflect and reinforce basic inequalities deriving from capitalistic modes of production. Such a view finds empirical support in research suggesting that the very process of capitalistic production is the major source of risk to health in Western society (Eyer, 1977).

Almost as useful in legitimating a distinctively sociological approach to the study of health is Cassel's (1974) attempt to show that so far as the health effects of psycho-social factors are concerned (unlike the effects of micro-organisms), the focus should not be upon specific diseases, but on disease itself. Cassel argues that changing social conditions leading to stress thereby raise susceptibility to disease *in general*. Empirical evidence for such a view is available: Cassel cites the results of a study showing that widowers have a death rate three to five times higher than married men of the same age for every cause of death. Clearly a focus upon 'disease in general' is almost as adequate as a focus upon 'well-being' in liberating sociology from medically determined categories.

An alternative perspective to the Marxian one on links between health and mortality on the one hand and social structure on the other may be traced back to Durkheim. In his famous study of suicide Durkheim tried to show how differences in suicide rates could be explained in terms of the bonds holding societies together: weakening social bonds led to increasing suicide rates. There have been other studies in this tradition, showing, for example, how the social disintegration of a community or village (as exemplified in crime and delinquency rates, frequency of broken homes, weakened communication structures, economic inadequacy and so on) is related to the rate of psychiatric disorder (e.g Leighton *et al.*, *The Character of Danger* (1963), a study of a Canadian maritime population cited by Brown and Harris, 1978).

The sociological approaches, despite their profound differences, have in common the attempt to explain those aspects of health care upon which they have focused in terms of a limited number of theoretically grounded concepts of established validity and utility. The strength of the sociological tradition is particularly apparent when attention is restricted to the working of the health care system, and an explanation of inequalities in the receipt of care is sought. Whether explanation is rooted in the workings of this system itself (as in structural functional sociology), or whether it is argued that explanation can only be in terms of broader social structural variables (e.g. class relationships), the advantages of theoretical coherence, potentiality for explanation of all relevant data (including international data), as well as an historic (diachronic) dimension are present.

But beyond this there are difficulties with traditional sociological forms of explanation which were most valuably articulated by Suchman (1967a). More recently Brown and Harris (1978) have argued that an explanation of ill health in terms of social factors requires some understanding of *how* these factors impinge upon the individual (who does, or does not, become sick). Other concepts are required which provide a link between society and the individual response.

As I argued above, much of the applicability of sociological reasoning seems to rest upon the substitution of 'well-being' or 'disease' for medical disease categories as dependent variable. Brown and Harris argue against this substitution and in favour of specific diagnostic categories. They do so, disagreeing with Cassel, on a number of grounds.

First . . . we will show for instance that *different* kinds of life event influence the onset of schizophrenia and depressive disorders . . . this could not have been demonstrated if 'depression' and 'schizophrenia' had been lumped together in some general category of 'psychiatric disorder'. Much the same may well occur for physical disorders . . . (Brown and Harris, 1978, p. 18)

Secondly, 'There must be a danger that only the broadest and vaguest social measures are likely to show associations across a wide range of disorder' (ibid., p. 18). Thirdly, while there are undoubted problems with diagnostic categories, in the field of psychiatric disorder in particular the problem is not one of diagnosis as such. Classification is always important for understanding: 'And once this is accepted, it would be foolish, in setting up a diagnostic system, to neglect the impressively detailed descriptive work by psychiatrists over the last century' (ibid., pp. 18–19).

Comparison Between the Three Approaches

I have tried to show how three distinctive intellectual traditions with an interest in the problems of class inequalities in health go about the task of explanation. I want now to try to deal with the related questions of how and why their approaches to explanations are actually quite different.

These differences come about in part through the subtle process by which in each case 'the' problem is defined. The distinction between 'disease' (a medically identifiable pathology of the body), 'illness' (the subjective response) and 'sickness' (the social consequence) is well known. So too is that between ill health, health conceived as the absence of disease, and health conceived as a state of general 'well-being'. To attempt to deal with class inequalities here is thus necessarily to make some choice as to precisely what is to be explained. The choice may be expanded to include provision and use of those services (principally but not exclusively medical services) generally accepted as of preventive or curative value. The fact is that each of the three traditions conceptualizes the problem in such a way as to maximize the applicability of its own distinct explanatory variables and theories. (Such a process, in which alternative paradigms 'compete' for the 'right' to define a problem is characteristic not only of approaches to social problems (which are always open to alternative conceptualizations), but of pure science too (Blume, 1977).) Thus it is that social administration focuses in particular upon unequal provision of services, and upon factors leading to lower utilization by the working classes in relation to their needs. Its interest in disease(s) is on the whole limited by the extent to which demonstrable relationships with the results of collective provision and material circumstances are to be found. Epidemiology is concerned to explore the aetiology of specific diseases, implicating specific social conditions and aspects of the physical environment, especially in so far as medically plausible intervening factors can be postulated. Sociology, like social administration, is on safest ground in dealing with the structure of health services. Unlike social administration, however, its explanation of these structures (including those aspects leading to under-utilization by low-status or working-class groups) is in terms of theoretically grounded variables generally employed within sociology for explaining social structures and processes. Liberation of concepts of health/disease from medical diagnostic categories – health as well-being – broadens the field within which sociology seems applicable.

Thus, not only is 'the' problem somewhat differently defined from one tradition to another, but the kinds of variable adduced in explanation also necessarily differ. Some might argue that there is no more to be said: that these are simply three distinct and incommensurable, or reductively related, or complementary forms of explanation. We thus either make an arbitrary choice, or we accept simply that they explain different aspects of the problem in quite different sorts of terms. But is it possible to go no further? I should like to suggest that it is, first in comparison of the three approaches, and subsequently in moving towards a view of what a more complete explanation than each individually provides might look like.

First, it is clear that the three traditions differ in two important respects: their *action orientation* and their *theory orientation*. Action orientation significantly influences the decision 'at what point to stop explaining'. Research upon the social distribution of respiratory disorder in children may suggest that much of the class association is to be explained, for example, in terms of overcrowding in the home. The epidemiologist may accept such a finding on the ground that plausible intervening factors may be identifiable (e.g. enhanced risk of cross-infection). For him, and for the social administrator, overcrowding is sufficiently implicated for recommendations to be made as to the importance, on health grounds, of alleviating overcrowding among large families with children. Housing conditions are a perfectly valid explanatory variable: of demonstrable importance, and implying (and permitting) ameliorative action. Many sociologists, however, would not rest content at this point. For them, this can only be a step towards explanation in terms of variables of sociological significance (e.g. class), even though the (immediate) policy relevance is thereby attenuated or eliminated.

The three traditions differ also in their relationship with theory. For sociology, the health care system, the processes of production of sickness and health, provide an arena in which theoretical ideas about society can be tested. The nature of the 'dominance' exercised by the medical profession can be compared with that of other professions; the process of 'negotiating' the meaning of the symptoms described by a patient to his or her physician can be compared with other instances of negotiating over meaning; the way in which the class structure determines access to and treatment by the health system can be compared with the education system or the system of work. Though sociologies differ profoundly, explanations of aspects of health inequalities derive in each case from a theoretical corpus which research should serve further to articulate. Epidemiology too has a theoretical basis, although a very different one. Its essential orientation is to the working not of society, but of the human body. Its theory is provided by the basic sciences (genetics, physiology, biochemistry etc.) which provide an account of the workings of the human body. For the epidemiologist this human body is located within a population, within a community, which exerts influences with which he is professionally concerned. It is this concern which differentiates him from other medical specialists seeking to understand the aetiology of disease, and which leads some epidemiologists and practitioners of social medicine to criticize the notion of 'the body as a machine' upon which much of medicine is said to be based (McKeown, 1976b). Yet epidemiology is at root no less individualistic than are the basic biomedical sciences with which it is linked in a common endeavour, and it draws upon and contributes to the same theory. It is this theory which permits some sorting of possible explanatory variables.

By contrast, the British social administration tradition does not rest upon an identifiable discrete body of theory. Explanatory variables here are determined by practical social policy: financial support, and the goods and services which collectively are, or should be provided – that is, by the scope of collective provision. It is quite enough that there should be a correlation between, say, overcrowding, or per capita expenditure on preventive health services, and infant mortality. This is so weak a notion of explanation that it can be argued that social administration makes no claim to provide an explanation at all: that social administration is concerned with social inequalities in health not in order to provide an explanation of them, but rather to demonstrate that the generation of health inequalities is one consequence of the injustice of policies being pursued. Whatever the importance of attempting to understand processes of distributive justice in society (and I happen to think it very important), this is a very different intellectual task. It provides little guide to explanation here. Thus problems arise when moral desiderata appear to conflict, as in Syme's findings that people who are highly socially/occupationally mobile through their lifetimes are more likely than those who are not to suffer from coronary heart disease (Syme, Hyman and Enterling, 1964; Syme, Borhani and Buechley, 1965).

Towards a More Adequate Explanation

Let us assume first that the traditional field of interest of social administration – in the extent to which collective provision for social welfare embodies particular conceptions of social justice – be set aside. It seems to me that this is a very different kind of activity from that with which we are here concerned. The importance of such analysis for the political process, for example in seeking to improve the health service, does not depend upon assumptions made as to the importance of health services for health. For present purposes, however, the importance of the health services for health *is* relevant. It seems clear on the basis of evidence presented that an exclusive focus upon health care provision is not sufficient; this is only one aspect of the explanation.

Secondly, it has to be decided whether explanation should focus upon some aggregated notion of health, disease or mortality, or upon specific diagnostic categories given by medical science. Here, it seems to me that the arguments of Brown and Harris in favour of utilization of a classification of diseases are more convincing than those of Cassel. 'Diseases' provide a more satisfactory focus for explanation than 'disease'. Nevertheless we cannot rest content with this since, at least in so far as our search for understanding is intended to have some practical purpose, that purpose must ultimately extend to the promotion of health itself (in its most positive and 'utopian' sense). At present it is difficult to attach much empirical meaning to this notion, despite its sociological utility: it is theoretically and practically difficult to establish 'health norms' for whole populations. Only in the case of child development have norms of physical and mental progress been established, systematic deviations from which certainly merit and require explanation. It therefore seems to me necessary that 'health' as the principal focus of explanation be set aside until significant progress in giving it empirical content has been made. For the moment we are thrown back on to 'diseases', while bearing in mind that the model of explanation to be developed may not prove adequate to the future task of explaining class differences in health itself.

When we turn to consider the formal outlines of a model of explanation, it seems to me that the one proposed in the work of Brown and Harris for explanation of depressive illness in women meets most of our requirements. Broadly speaking, the model is closely akin to that implicit in much epidemiological work. That is, it posits two essential but quite distinct kinds of variables in interaction: first what might be called the 'structural-environmental' factors, and secondly, 'host' factors, or what Brown and Harris term 'vulnerability' factors. The first includes all aspects of the social structure, of the social and physical environment with potential implications for health and disease. It will thus include family and work relations, housing, the availability of different kinds of food-stuffs, air pollution, climate, the availability and structure of health care and so on. The second set of factors includes all those character-istics of the individual which might singly or in interaction affect his or her susceptibility to disease. They would thus include age, sex and genetic factors; they would include previous medical history and the outcomes of previous disease episodes or the effects of chronic conditions; and they would include social, behavioural and psychological factors (such as smoking, dependency relationships, family structure, and perhaps including financial resources, social mobility, attitudes to treatment, feelings of security and so on). A model based upon the interaction of two sets of factors such as these – according to a process or mechanism to be spelled out – has a number of advantages. In the first place it permits the introduction of the whole range of kinds of factors implicated by one or another research tradition, without the need to make dubious assumptions as to causality (e.g. no relationship between class and genetic make-up is assumed). In the second place it allows due attention to the crucial variable of *time* in its two important senses. Thus 'historical time' is reflected in changes in the first set of factors: in the occupational structure, in provision of housing, in changes in the health services and so on. 'Personal time' is reflected in changes in the second set of factors over the individual life cycle. Thirdly, there is a place for sociological research and theory in providing a more basic theoretical grounding, for at least some of the structural-environmental factors, as well as an account of the relations between these. Fourthly, biomedical theory, suggested as basic to epidemiology, has a place in identification of at least some of the vulnerability factors, in establishing relations between these, and in establishing what should count as plausible mechanisms of interaction in the case of specific disease. Clearly the precise content of the model – the factors to be introduced into any specific analysis – will depend upon both medical knowledge of the condition in question and upon a rather different understanding of the socio-environmental factors thought to be of causal significance. Without, therefore, attempting to spell out in more detail the content of any such model, it appears to me that through a multidisciplinary approach of this kind the strengths of each research tradition can be mobilized in the articulation of more adequate forms of explanation of social inequalities in health.

The final issue which I want to raise is that of the implications of this model of explanation for the study of social administration. If the attempt to show how, in policy terms, class inequalities in health might be reduced is accepted as a goal for social administration, then it seems to me that some explanatory scheme is essential. How else are priorities to be established between the wide variety of forms of provision clearly relevant (amongst other factors) to health inequalities? We know for example that most of the class differential in infant deaths is due to respiratory conditions and to accidents (including as a significant element traffic accidents). To establish priorities directed to the reduction of these gradients is necessarily to formulate a clear idea of the relative importance of the factors implicated in these causes of death and, so far as possible, of their casual interrelationships. The particular contribution of social administration must then be to explore the relationships between government policies and the genesis, eradication, exacerbation and distribution of the social-environmental factors implicated in disease. By this is then inevitably implied a concern with the effects of policies conceived far more broadly than has traditionally been the case. I would include, for example, examination of the effects of policies upon family and community structures, upon the urban environment, upon the changing nature (as well as rewards) of work, and upon levels of environmental pollution.

It seems clearly to follow that the agenda for the discipline of social administration is considerably broadened. For its traditional concern with justice in the allocation of resources for health and other services and forms of social provision is as essential as ever. Indeed, it is more essential than ever, at a time when a Secretary of State for Social Services can immediately dismiss (ostensibly on grounds of cost) the report of a working party invited by his predecessor to look into precisely the problem of health inequalities (Jenkin, 1980), while at the same time trying to keep the issue off the political agenda. The integrated research approach which this article proposes must draw strength and example from the nineteenth-century pioneers with which it began.

IV

Policy Implementation

13

The Use and Abuse of
Social Science

This final chapter seeks to draw some of the threads from preceding chapters together and to raise general questions for further consideration. It cannot in the nature of the case be a definitive resolution of the manifold problems in applying social science research to policy. However, it can provide some pointers to important unresolved issues and suggest questions that would repay further attention. Four broad issues will be examined: the obstacles to a fruitful relationship between social science and policy; the relevance of different models of the relationship; the audience and means of diffusion of applied social science knowledge; and a re-consideration of the actual process of policy-making and how social science research fits into that process.

It is appropriate to begin, however, by recapitulating a major implicit theme of the preceding chapters. Whatever else it may be, social science research and analysis applied to policy-making is a *scientific* process, in two senses. The first is that methods of inquiry are used which are replicable and which yield representative, reliable and valid knowledge (or if they do not, then the qualifications to be attached are carefully stated). The second is that the theoretical implications of inquiry are made explicit, if not in the form of explicit theory, then through careful attention to the assumptions underlying inquiry, to concepts and to the rational basis upon which policy recommendations rest. To be sure, as earlier chapters have suggested, there are many reasons for scepticism about the extent to which applied social science research can provide cut and dried answers to problems facing policy-makers. The kind of certainty, or sureness of recommendation, characteristic of at least certain types of natural science research with policy application is usually lacking. Recommendations are more tentative, because the social world is more uncertain and unpredictable and cannot be reduced to law-like statements (or if it can, these are couched at such a high level of generality as to be of little use to the policy-maker). Then there are many problems between analysis being written and policy being implemented, both because of the character of social science knowledge and because of the nature of the policy-making process. Granted all these qualifications, a necessary condition for effective policy research is that the knowledge generated should be produced according to social scientific methods and under the influence of social science theory. This is a *sine qua non* of good policy research, though it is unlikely to be a sufficient condition in itself. Insistence upon good professional research standards – and the adequate training of professional social researchers (cf. Bulmer and Burgess, 1981; Social Research Association, 1985) – is an essential part of ensuring sound research for policy-makers.

A good deal of the recent literature on the social impact of social science research has emphasized the obstacles which exist to its effective utilization. Perhaps the most explicit work of this kind was Robert Scott and Arnold Shore's *Why Sociology Does Not Apply* (1979), but it has not been alone. While such scepticism about the social usefulness of social science is salutary in puncturing the more exaggerated claims of an engineering model of application, criticism should not be taken to the point of suggesting that social science research cannot be applied. For throughout the twentieth century, in the attempts to apply knowledge from the social sciences to policy, there has been a continuing struggle to establish their relevance. Doubt about the value of what the social sciences offers is nothing new.

An early example is provided by the introduction of intelligence tests in the US Army during the First World War by applied psychologists such as Robert M. Yerkes, Walter V. Bingham and Walter Dill Scott. Working in the Office of the Army Surgeon General and the Office of the Adjutant General in 1917 and 1918, they designed and administered the class Alpha and Beta tests, which were used to assess recruits and to make decisions about their posting and promotability. This testing programme set a precedent for the wider use of intelligence tests after the First World War, particularly in US private industry and civil service selection (Lyons, 1969, p. 28). Yet at the time, those introducing the tests had an uphill battle against entrenched opposition within the army. It was primarily the support of the Surgeon General of the day which ensured that they were used as widely as they were. Many regular military officers regarded Yerkes and his staff as 'mental meddlers', 'pests', scientists using the army as a laboratory for their own purposes. Test results not infrequently ran counter to traditional methods of judgement of men, and most serving officers preferred experience to expertise. The

Commander of Fort Dix stated that he needed psychologists as much as he needed 'a board of art critics to advise me which of my men were the most handsome, or a board of prelates to designate the true Christians' (quoted in Kelves, 1968, p. 575). When the war ended, the psychological testing programme was brought to an end, basically because of the army's fundamental objections to the programme. Though its longer-term influence was considerable – it was later shown that the tests were an effective means of selecting officers, the number of whom grew from 9,000 to about 200,000 between the beginning and end of the war – in the short term this major innovation in applied social science fell on stony ground. In Britain, the earliest impetus to mental testing came in the educational field, through its use in picking out able children for selective secondary schooling from the early twentieth century onwards (see Sutherland, 1984).

This British use of applied social science was slight and patchy at first. The United States was the pioneer. Moving on to the New Deal, the election of Franklin D. Roosevelt in 1933 seemed to usher in a new era in the potential for applying the social sciences to the formation of national policy. The years between 1933 and 1940 were both exciting and frustrating and divisive for social scientists in Washington. The New Deal made a permanent place for social scientists in American government at the federal level. Many social scientists, for example, served as policy advisers and political appointees, roles traditionally filled by lawyers and businessmen. 'But a place for social scientists and a place for social science research were – and are – two quite different matters' (Lyons, 1969, p. 52). As policy advisers, social scientists brought their own knowledge to bear on national policy and were aware of the contribution which research might make. They knew it was important to maintain intellectual links with the academic community.

> But their intentions with regard to research – when they had any – could not always be realised. They had joined a government that was shaped for action, led by a President who was highly pragmatic, who moved quickly from problem to problem – sometimes brilliantly, sometimes erratically, sometimes indecisively – and who had little patience with, or capacity for abstract thinking. He prized social scientists who brought important qualities of mind and manner to the process of government as he prized others of similar character and ability. But there is little evidence that he prized social science research for its own sake. (ibid., p. 52)

The travails of social scientists close to government are nothing new.

Social scientists being asked to perform other roles is one way in which their influence may be reduced. Another is what may be termed 'dilution', the creation of 'think-tanks' and other sources of advice to government in which social scientists rub shoulders with others who do not have specialist knowledge but have other knowledge claims, perhaps as practitioners. The British study group Political and Economic Planning (PEP), founded in 1931, provides an interesting case in point. Created to try to show that sensible planning could help to overcome the crisis of the Great Depression and improve Britain's social and economic position, it produced a stream of pamphlets and studies aiming to provide a dispassionate, non-partisan analysis of current policy problems. Until recently, the social science input to its work was not predominant. It drew rather upon

> a broad base of research staff and collaborators drawn not only from the so-called social sciences but also from the natural sciences, technology, industrial and commercial management, politics and law and public administration, and indeed from practical men and women in the informed community generally. (Isserlis, 1981, p. 168)

This group of friends and colleagues which shaped PEP's output sought to provide an impetus to policy change, but were themselves often members, or younger potential members, of the Establishment (a curious British term referring to the inner circle of political, economic and cultural elites: cf. Thomas, 1959). Isserlis concludes that PEP had its widest influence when operating in this broadly based way, shaping its analysis by general collaboration and politically aware discussion rather than simply relying on a technical social science output.

In part, such dilution may be explained by the slow development of the social sciences in Britain and the lack of social scientists available. But it is also generally characteristic of a certain amateur British way of doing things, giving no special credence to technical knowledge, but great weight to what William James called 'acquaintance with', that is first-hand practical experience. 'He who does knows.' It is represented par excellence by the British generalist administrator in the higher reaches of the civil service, well-educated, intelligent, superbly *au fait* with the working of the Westminster and Whitehall political system, adviser to ministers and policy-formulator, who moves fairly rapidly from one subject to another and so does not develop particularly great expertise on any subject, nor possesses technical knowledge such as the social sciences offer. (For a further discussion of these characteristics and their consequences see Bulmer, 1987.)

Another form of dilution occurs on governmental commissions to which social scientists are not infrequently appointed, but almost always in a minority alongside other professionals, generalists, political figures and lay persons, to whom they have to try to convey their special knowledge. The social scientist as a minority, trying to keep his or her end up against a generally sceptical audience, is not as unusual as some critics (such as Lindblom and Cohen, 1979) seem to believe.

More recently, the debates within both American and British government about the place of the social sciences in national science policy indicate considerable uncertainty about their scientific status and their potential contribution. In the United States in 1946 the social sciences were explicitly excluded by Congress from the scope of the newly established National Science Foundation, and it was not until 1968 that they finally became incorporated into NSF's mainstream (Miller, 1982, p. 205). In Britain, government support for the social sciences proceeded slowly, only becoming a major commitment after the report of the Heyworth Committee in 1965 resulted in the establishment of the Social Science Research Council (somewhat analogous to the Division of Social and Economic Sciences of NSF with additional responsibilities to support graduate study). Even then, the SSRC budget has remained miniscule compared to the support for its fellow research councils covering science and engineering, medicine, agriculture and the natural environment.

Then in the early 1980s, the advent of conservative administrations in both Washington and London, committed to cutting the scale of government expenditure and sceptical about the value of the contribution made by the social sciences, challenged social scientists to look anew at the case for their support. In the USA, effective lobbying by the social sciences collectively, and support from natural scientists, enabled the harsher effects of the cuts initially proposed by the Reagan administration budget to be curtailed (Miller, 1987). In Britain, the main argument centred around the future of the Social Science Research Council. The Secretary of State for Education, Sir Keith Joseph, would clearly like to have abolished the Council, but Lord Rothschild, whom he appointed to carry out an independent review, strongly recommended that it remain in existence

(Rothschild, 1982). The main change effected, apart from a further budget reduction and an alteration of the system of support for graduate students, was a symbolic change of name from Social Science Research Council to Economic and Social Research Council, the term 'science' being deemed otiose (Flather, 1987). Government antagonism and the Rothschild review did, however, sharply increase the level, if not the quality, of debate about usefulness and social worth. It was widely recognized that there were lacunae and difficulties in applying social science knowledge, and the case made at the time by social scientists in their own defence did not exaggerate social usefulness of the knowledge which they provided.

The strain of negativity in recent writing on applied social research has almost certainly been overdone. The most extreme example is provided by Charles Lindblom and David Cohen's essay *Usable Knowledge* (1979). They maintain that social science and social research are only weakly understood by their own practitioners and that their practice is crippled by that misunderstanding. In particular, some social scientists appear to believe that social problem-solving is a scientific activity. They consider that the ways in which society, collectively through the political process, deals with problems which it faces are amenable to influence by scientific analysis and rational recommendation. Hence in the real world professional social inquiry is the best method of approaching social problems, and so far superior to all others to warrant disregard for them. This view, according to Lindblom and Cohen, is quite mistaken. Knowledge from applied social science is almost never conclusive; for that and other reasons almost never independently authoritative. At best, the knowledge produced by professional social inquiry is an increment to other knowledge, including that of practitioners. Only when social science findings are linked to other sources of knowledge, which independently support each other, do they become authoritative.

Written in a highly idiosyncratic style, *Usable Knowledge* is a hatchet job upon the supposed pretensions of applied social science. The difficulty with the argument, reasonable though some of the points are, is that the main object of attack is a straw man. Few social scientists today would make the claims to authoritativeness which Lindblom and Cohen attribute to them. It is quite true, as Lindblom has shown, that the process of policy-making is a complex, disjointed and incremental one in which many types of knowledge have a role to play. But a majority of applied social scientists are well aware of these characteristics of the policy-making process, if only by bitter experience, and it is unhelpful to erect as an object of attack a stereotypical view which few hold. Lindblom and Cohen do not provide a convincing overall view.

Another critical account which does less than justice to the realities of applying social science is Scott and Shore's *Why Sociology Does Not Apply* (1979). Starting from the view that a dominant theme of American sociology has been the view that knowledge can transform society in obvious, self-evident and desirable ways, they hold that many sociologists have a mistaken conception of the influence of research on policy.

> Procedures presently used in our field imply that these relation-ships are straightforward, if at times complicated. They assume that the most direct way to develop a genuinely policy-relevant social science is through the continued conduct of basic research into questions that reflect disciplinary concerns, and that the conduct of applied social science differs in no significant way from the conduct of any other kind of research in our field. (ibid., p. 222)

They foresee a schism developing between social scientists doing routine disciplinary research, and policy researchers doing work on policy questions. As an example, drawn from their own experiences with the New Jersey negative income tax experiment, they contrast academic research on the social nature and consequences of poverty with policy analysts more concerned with the state of poverty legislation at the present time.

Some of their criticisms of the disciplinary proclivities of social scientists are well taken. They are right to insist upon social scientists paying more attention to the policy process to identify the issues and questions of greatest relevance to the work of those engaged in social policy-making. Policy researchers need to concentrate upon those variables which are susceptible to manipulation by the policy-maker, a point made in the previous section of this book. Yet Scott and Shore draw too sharp a distinction between the disciplinary proclivities of social scientists and the very specific applied focus required of the policy researcher. It is as if they are contrasting basic research on the one hand and tactical research on the other (Bulmer, 1978, pp. 8–9), without allowing that there may be an intermediary strategic kind which draws upon social science concepts and themes but is also directed to a policy domain and the workings of social processes within it. They draw too sharp a line between basic and applied research and imply that there are no bridges to be built across the gap between the two. The ambiguity is caught more aptly in terms like 'the uneasy partnership' (Lyons, 1969) or 'the uncertain connection' (Lynn, 1978) rather than in firm statements that in principle the chasm is unbridgeable.

One of the reasons for the negative view of the potential applicability of social science derives from the over-optimism of some social scientists when recruited as advisers and consultants to government. L. J. Sharpe (1978) has well pinpointed some of their failings, including lack of appreciation of how the policy process operates, their status as guests, and the other inputs which go into determining what the final policy outcome will be. The perils of this path have been pithily summarized by James Q. Wilson of Harvard: 'Getting good social science research is different from consulting good social scientists. The latter, unless watched carefully, will offer guesses, personal opinions, and political ideology under the guise of "expert advice" ' (1978, p. 91). The perennial danger of experts being drawn into policy-making and believing that they have unique insight, on the basis of the specialist knowledge, into the problems to be dealt with derives more from their personal position close to the centre of authority than it does from their credentials as social scientists.

A different source of scepticism lies in the perception that policy research is imbued with values, and that the social scientist has to make value choices. In an extreme version, all differences of view are seen as a matter of taste and no standards are admitted for judging the rightness or wrongness of particular analyses. Most statements of the problem of objectivity are less extreme, but discussion of these issues is particularly likely to slide into a non-judgemental cynicism. Raising such issues often seems to have the effect of instilling a disbelief in the possibility of objective scientific inquiry and leading quickly to various forms of shallow relativism. An example of the dangers of this path is provided by Vic George and Paul Wilding's book, *Ideology and Social Welfare* (1976), which argues that it is impossible to understand adequately the views of those who write about social welfare policy without taking account also of their social values and their social and political ideas. They then contrast four groups of thinkers: anti-collectivist, reluctant collectivist, Fabian socialist and Marxist theorists of social policy. Our concern here is not so much with their substantive discussion of social welfare policy as with the juxtaposition of four contrasting schools of thought as though the validity of each depended upon the value standpoint which they take up. There is no attempt, for example, to test the theories against empirical evidence which might support or refute them.

This is not to say that many of the choices faced in policy-making and policy research are not ultimately of a moral kind. Martin Rein is right to say that

> There is no central, abiding, over-arching principle that can fill the gaps in understanding, resolve the quandaries of action, order the conflicts of human purposes or resolve the conflicting interpretations of action that competing frameworks pose ... I am inclined to take the view that these dilemmas are desirable, because they pose moral choices and hence permit a debate about moral purposes. If there were no dilemmas in social action, then there would be no opportunity for meaningful moral discourse on human affairs. (Rein, 1976, p. 259)

But it is doubtful whether a value-critical stance in itself is a sufficient basis for an effective form of policy research. As argued in the previous section, policy research requires explicit attention to theory. It also requires soundly based empirical evidence. The two need to be brought together and tested against each other. Too great an emphasis upon the ineluctability of value-impregnation weakens that impulse and gives reign to a critical scepticism which presents an exaggerated and one-sided picture of what the social sciences can offer policy-makers.

Negative criticism of the potential of social science can thus be taken too far and induce an ingrained scepticism about the possibilities of knowledge application which is not warranted. A more reasonable starting point for a summing up is a critical consideration of the various models of the research–policy relationship which have been put forward. Lindblom and Cohen may, for example, be interpreted as attacking an extreme form of the 'engineering' model of utilization. Since, however, this has been widely criticized (see Weiss, 1977, pp. 4–18; Bulmer, 1982, pp. 42–9), it cannot be held to be representative of current thinking of how researchers and policy-makers interact.

The relative merits of the 'enlightenment' and 'engineering' models have been discussed in an earlier book (Bulmer, 1982, pp. 151–67) and will not be repeated here. Finding the 'enlightenment' model in general more persuasive is, however, only the starting point for discussion, since its outlines are hazy, and the precise types of knowledge which exert influence, means by which they do so and time-scale within which they operate are left vague. The earlier discussion suggested three different ways in which influence was exercised: by encouraging policy-makers to conceptualize the issues they were faced with, by giving political ammunition to different actors in the policy-making process, or by providing an input to an interactive setting that produces policy outcomes.

A recent discussion by Patricia Thomas (1985) contrasts three different patterns of influence. She puts more emphasis upon the roles played by the researcher, but in a more specific sense than that mentioned earlier, since she characterizes their mode of operation. Her first type, the 'limestone' model, portrays the influence of social science research on policy as analogous to 'the action of water through limestone. You may know where the water falls on the limestone, but there is no means of knowing what route it will take down the various levels, or where it will emerge through unexpected fissures' (Robin Guthrie, quoted in Thomas, 1985, p. 99). This is the purest type of enlightenment, but leaves the social scientist rather far removed from the policy arena and uncertain what influence social science research may have.

Thomas's two other types involve the researcher in seeking a more direct or immediate effect by influencing government in a purposeful way. The second, the Gadfly model, involves the researcher both in conducting research and in communicating its results in a way that challenges the status quo, teasing and provoking the system while still remaining on good terms with those who work within it. The Gadfly is usually radical in his or her thinking, not constrained by the political feasibility of the recommendations though sufficiently aware of political realities not to range too widely from lines of feasible policy. But the Gadfly is in touch with officials and perhaps politicians at several levels, and maintains a relationship with them over time. The third model is the Insider model. The Gadfly remains aloof from the day-to-day business of government, the Insider makes it his or her business to burrow into the corridors of power, knowing the government machine, and being prepared in some circumstances to reach an accommodation with government by avoiding conclusions that are not politically feasible, or adapting research objectives to cover matters of current government concern. Often the Insider may be funded in his or her research directly by the government department, though this may curtail freedom to publish. Both the Gadfly and the Insider feed their research results into the policy debates of government and those on its periphery like pressure groups, but do not control the outcome. Their influence is thus exercised through personal networks, but the effect may be one of 'enlightenment' through better conceptualization by policy-makers of interaction, rather than direct use of the results to determine policy. Indeed, Thomas begins her discussion of the three models by observing that 'government policy-making only occasionally takes conscious account of social research. It is one of many influences that may shape policy' (1985, p. 97).

The Gadfly and Insider models are useful, but there is a limitation in conceiving of impact primarily in terms of the roles played by individual social scientists. An overall view must take account of the knowledge-base and the means by which knowledge is diffused for use. One of the limitations of many discussions of social science impact is to treat the social sciences on a par with the natural sciences, and to base theories upon highly rationalistic assumptions about human behaviour and a calculus of action. Economic theories of 'rational expectations', which assume that people act as if they are actually conversant with economic theory, are a case in point. Amitai Etzioni (1985) has suggested that a model of application for social science analogous to that of medicine may be a fruitful line to pursue.

Medical knowledge is made up of three components: findings from a variety of basic sciences such as physiology, biochemistry, physics and so on; medical knowledge not derived from or directly reducible to other sciences; and rules of conduct to cope with circumstances of high uncertainty. These three components are not unique to medicine but are typical of any field which deals with complex but only partially known systems. Policy-makers deal routinely with such systems, and therefore the model of medical knowledge can be applied to policy-making. Policy-makers do draw upon a number of different contributory disciplines in reaching decisions. They also possess knowledge of the policy and governmental process not reducible to any particular discipline, for example the knowledge of the working of the governmental machine so highly prized by senior civil servants. And they operate in situations of great uncertainty where the outcome of their actions and of policies is highly uncertain.

There are of course major differences. The goal of medicine is relatively clear and straightforward, whereas government policy-makers are often pursuing multiple, conflicting or obscure goals. And the structure of decision-making is unitary in medicine whereas in policy-making it is pluralistic and contested. This does not, however, render the comparison useless.

We can learn from the way medical facts, theories and methods relate to one another, and are used, even if goal-setting and decision-making structures are quite different. Or, to put it differently, once policymakers set their goals through whatever system they use to reach their decisions, they will still face knowledge issues similar to those faced in the practice of medicine. (Etzioni, 1985, p. 385)

Etzioni then develops a critique of the narrowness of economic policy-making, comparing it to the medical model, and arguing for a broader 'socio-economic' approach, incorporating variables such as political, social, cultural and environmental factors. The interest of the medical analogy here, however, is rather in illuminating the knowledge-base of much contemporary social policy-making. Policy-makers frequently complain that discipline-based research is too narrow for their purposes. They need to look at a problem from several points of view, not partially through the eyes of one perspective. Yet at the same time, policy-makers operate under conditions of great uncertainty, and here again the medical model is illuminating as a way of conceptualizing the choices faced. The analogy pins down more precisely the knowledge-base than do mistaken analogies with engineering or loose comparisons with subjects like history which do not pretend to be scientific as that term is usually understood. Medicine does claim to be scientific, but it is applied science with a strong element of practical knowledge as an integral part, and an irremediable indeterminacy in the outcomes of its treatments with which it has constantly to deal.

A clearer view of the knowledge-base is helpful, but it only goes so far. The analogy with medicine breaks down when one turns to the means by which knowledge is diffused for use. Medicine is highly centralized and access controlled to those professionally trained in university medical schools whose teachers are the repository of the more advanced contemporary knowledge of the subject. The policy domain is by comparison wide open and lacking in authoritative lines of action. There is no agreed training for either policy-making or policy research, and no professional body to which those involved can belong. In the United States a considerable proportion may hold a Ph.D., but elsewhere in the industrial world such high academic qualifications are unusual. The realm of policy-making is one in which many more competing pressures operate.

Various types of diffusion may usefully be classified in terms of the differing aims of the researcher and the methodological character- istics of the research. Five clusters can be distinguished: intelligence and monitoring; consumer perspectives; 'hard' evidence of impact and effectiveness; social consultancy; and social reform. The results of intelligence and monitoring are fed direct to policy-making civil servants and their political masters, but also diffuse more widely through the political system. Inquiries like the General Household Survey and Family Expenditure Survey are excellent examples of research which diffuse in this way. The main results are fairly straightforward descriptive distributions, although the surveys can also form the basis of more analytical secondary analyses. The data collected is confined to objective, measurable characteristics. Though the results of such inquiries may occasionally feed directly into a policy decision, a much more important use is as background information providing a sense of the directions in which society is moving, and perhaps occasionally of the effectiveness of policy (for example, in reducing smoking; see p. 215).

Research providing 'consumer perspectives' is a second type, covered in Chapter 6 on opinion polling. As indicated there, there are several logical objections to basing policies directly upon the results of such research, but its findings percolate to varying degrees into the consciousness of social scientists and policy-makers, influencing the ways in which they perceive issues. For example, recent research upon attitudes of the public toward the welfare state (such as Taylor-Gooby, 1982, 1985) has shown marked ambivalence on the part of working-class respondents to the benefits derived from state services. These are valued, but on the other hand there is reluctance to pay higher taxes to provide improved benefits. This has been interpreted by academics as a possible consequence of changes in working-class consumption patterns and a possible cause of changes in voting. The effects of such knowledge upon the formation of policy are indirect, provided of course the knowledge is well founded, which requires careful scrutiny.

'Hard' evidence of impact and effectiveness of potential policy changes, such as may in principle be yielded by large-scale social experiments, can in theory impact rather directly upon policy. Usually conducted at the behest of officials or politicians with direct interests in the outcome of possible intervention, results may be fed back into the government machine and acted upon. However, since the effects demonstrated by such experiments are frequently so small, they tend to provide negative rather than positive evidence. Though their results become known in due course to the social science community, their immediate effects are felt most directly within government circles. Their impact on a wider public is slight.

Social science research is also diffused and interpreted to policy-makers by social scientists acting as consultants. Here Patricia

Thomas's stress on the importance of following through research to ensure that findings are communicated to those in a position to influence policy is critical. She argues for it as a strategy for making research more effective. Social scientists playing the Insider role are in a good position to diffuse the results of research in this way. But it can happen in other ways; for example, through social scientists involved in bodies like the Central Policy Review Staff, or as special political advisers to ministers, or as professional advisers within a ministry or department (the best example of this in Britain is the role of members of the Government Economic Service). This is again an instance of research tending to perform an 'enlightenment' function, but much depends upon the particular channels of influence and the presence of a consultant at the right time in the right place.

Research may also, as Keith Banting makes clear in Chapter 3, be used to promote social reform. Research and action are integrated in order to produce pressure for change in a predetermined direction. Research diffusion of this type may or may not be party-political, and the advocacy may or may not be undertaken by the researcher. Thomas distinguishes as a variant of both Gadfly and Insider models what she calls the 'pressure group' model, where the results of research are taken up by an interest group, which presses for action based upon the findings with the encouragement or tacit agreement of the researcher. This tradition has a long and distinguished history in Britain, but its limitations as well as its strengths should be borne in mind. Over-strong political identification may lead to the closing off of other avenues for the diffusion of research, for example, to permanent civil servants who maintain a stance of political neutrality.

Cross-cutting these five types of research is the specificity of the knowledge which is produced by social science research and which it is proposed to apply. Economics has been most successful in developing both global theories to account for and predict the behaviour of the economy as a whole (though alternative approaches to macro-economic modelling and management remain firmly entrenched) and in producing micro-economic theories and empirical studies of economic behaviour which can be used in more specific applications. In other social sciences, it is the more specific types of knowledge which have more likelihood of being applied, whether the results of operational research in wartime, the refinement of random sampling, or the techniques of testing capacity and skill in educational and industrial psychology. More general theories of social behaviour have not been notably successful in direct application, though they may often indirectly inform policies through influencing the premises upon which they are based. For example, sociological studies of stratification had a powerful effect on the development of ideas about equality of educational opportunity and in documenting its absence – that is, the existence of inequality of opportunity.

Typologies of routes of diffusion of this kind have only a certain usefulness, for they do not permit one to identify, for particular pieces of research, in which direction its influence has been felt. The problem of tracing influence has been compared to Rabindranath Tagore's story of the holy man who wandered the roads, searching for the touchstone of truth. At first he examined every pebble with care, then in a more perfunctory way, and as the years passed he would pick up a pebble, touch it to his waist chain, and discard it without a glance. One day in gazing at his chain, he was amazed to see that it had finally turned to gold. So at some point he had held the touchstone in his hand, but when and where he knew not. For most pieces of policy-oriented social research, one is in this situation. One can, however, say something about the audience to which research is aimed, the means of diffusion and the specificity of the product.

The audience for applied social science research may clearly vary. It includes senior ministers, legislators, civil servants, other professionals with an interest in the field, journalists, members of pressure groups, clients (if a service is at issue) and members of the lay public. In fact, a good deal of research is addressed to none of these but to fellow social science researchers. One of the problems of researchers based in academic institutions is that their reference group is others like themselves who will make peer group judgements of them. Hence there is a built-in tendency to address one's work to one's peers. This tendency can be counteracted in several ways. If research is conducted for a client, the client will expect a report setting out the principal findings which result. If the research has relevance to practitioners it can be communicated to them through magazines aimed at that audience (for example, in the social services field, *Social Work Today, Community Care* and *Health and Social Services Journal*). If aimed at high-level policy-makers in government, a personal presentation may be the ideal solution if it can be arranged. In the case of child poverty discussed in Chapter 1, Abel-Smith and Townsend's academic research re-analysing FES data was presented at a press conference just before Christmas to achieve maximum media exposure, and the momentum gained was used to launch the Child Poverty Action Group.

These examples suggest that the question of audience is inseparable from the medium used to disseminate the results of research. The British quality daily press is read carefully by politicians and civil servants, as are the *New York Times* and *Washington Post* in the USA. They can thus be a particularly important medium for the presentation of research results in popular form. Weekly magazines are also an important medium of communication, particularly ones focusing on social science and social affairs like *New Society* and *The Economist*. A Director of Social Services, for example, describes reading avidly each week the reviews in *New Society*, circulating relevant extracts to key people in his department, and ordering books for the library (Hamson, 1983, p. 11). Magazines aimed at a professional audience (for example, the *Times Educational Supplement* to teachers) are often an important channel of communication. Each of these forms of publication may be supplemented by writing in person to senior civil servants and ministers to draw the results of research to their attention, and by speaking to conferences of various kinds, at which senior policymakers and professionals will be present.

The conventional output of academics appears in learned journals and in books. These may be the means by which some types of applied research are communicated. The growing number of specialist journals in particular fields with an applied emphasis means that there is some prospect of reaching other specialists (for example, in social services research through the *British Journal of Social Work* or *Policy and Politics*), though how far practitioners and policy-makers read them is open to doubt. For thoughtful professionals abstracting services can perform something of the same function as scientific journals like *Nature* or *The Lancet* perform in science and medicine respectively, but they are unevenly available in the policy fields with which social scientists are concerned. Books are a favoured means of reporting the results of social science research, ranging from the specialized monograph published by a university press to the popular essay put out by a paperback house. Book publication is particularly attractive to academics, much less so to those working in independent institutes or directly for government. There may be some relation between the quality of mimeographed reports which academics deliver to their contractors and the subsequent greater efforts which go into writing for book publication. In general, the prestige of book publication among an academic researcher's peers is inversely proportional to its readership. Certainly popularization and simplification of research results is frowned upon, even though it may be essential for wider dissemination. Many practitioners, of course, do not have the time or inclination to read books, which is why some of the other media are such important channels of publication.

Many policy researchers do not work in the academic world, but for government or independent research bodies. Here the standard form of research report is the mimeographed document for internal use (sometimes, depending on its outside availability, termed a 'semi-publication' or 'grey literature' (Chillag, 1983)). Such works are not ignored. A Director of Social Services writes: 'I find it is the *internal* publications that are well read, because my social workers are interested to know what is happening in their Division compared to different parts of the country' (Hamson, 1983, p. 12). But their reception may be very variable, depending on their readability, relevance and interest to the policy-maker who receives them. Occasionally, a government attempts to bury such a report, usually unsuccessfully. This happened to the Coleman Report (1966) on equality of educational opportunity in America and to the Black Report in 1980 on inequalities of health in Britain (Townsend and Davidson, 1982). Both became best-sellers and key works of social science and policy reference.

Effectiveness of communication also depends – particularly in the case of 'grey literature' which does not have the benefit of professional editing – upon the quality of the English and the clarity of communication. Often both verbally and numerically, the ability of social scientists to communicate to lay people or other professionals is poor. Commenting on reports from academics to the department, a head of social science research management at the DHSS in the early 1980s observed that 'the reports themselves are inevitably late; they are over-indulgent; too long; often not properly thought out and rarely summarised. They represent a ground-clearing operation before the real job of writing for publication – nearly always publication for an academic audience – gets under way' (Barnes, 1983, p. 21). But the limitations of some of the products of social science go beyond this. Not always, but too frequently, prose is verbose, jargon-laden and even obscure, and quantitative informa-tion is not presented simply enough for the non-numerate to comprehend. Such lapses are inexcusable, given the guides to good writing (Gowers, 1975; Strunk and White, 1973) and numerical presentation (Zeisl, 1968; Tufte, 1983) which are available. Poor writing is one of the chief causes of the social sciences having a bad press.

Some commentators, particularly on the American scene, have discerned the emergence of what may be called research brokers, mediating between the producer of research on the one hand and the consumer or client on the other.

> Brokerage implies not line authority but second-order authority to bring together those who take executive action or engage in scientific activity ... [It helps] build up some of the lateral relationships that are always too weak when complicated relationships are required between ... different modes of action such as the political and the intellectual. (Kogan and Henkel, 1983, p. 173)

Brokers may fill a variety of formal positions. They range on one side from academic advisers and research entrepreneurs – sometimes playing the role of 'Gadfly' or 'Insider' – to officials and staff to politicians with a particular interest in the results of research. They may also include ex-academics who have gone to work in government. The brokerage role is most effectively developed in economics. In Britain, for example, members of the Government Economic Service, headed by a distinguished economist at a grading just below the top of the civil service hierarchy, are involved in economic management in the Treasury and in economic advice-giving in other departments (see Cairncross, 1981). They maintain close connections with economic research institutes (especially those involved in macro-economic modelling) and with the wider community of professional economists. There is some movement in both directions with the academic world. In other social sciences, the position is much more cloudy, reflecting the uncertain status of the 'softer' social sciences in the eyes of many policy-makers, and the lack in Britain of formal positions outside research itself on the one hand, and special advisers or assistants to politicians on the other, for those who would play the broker role. Even in the United States, where the social sciences are much more integrated into government (cf. Sharpe, 1975; Bulmer, 1987), the brokering role is under-developed; many people look on it as a resting place rather than a goal, and do not stay in it long enough to develop major expertise (Sundquist, 1978, p. 144). It is possible that the growth in US universities of schools of public policy will lead to greater professionalization, but this depends upon the receptivity and adaptiveness of the government machine as well as upon the availability of suitable personnel. It also depends upon the receptivity of the government machine to inputs from the social sciences, to which we now turn to draw the book to a close.

The process of policy-making was discussed in general terms in Chapter 1. How social science research is seen to feed into it depends in part on the model of policy-making which one espouses. It depends also, however, upon the arrangements which the formal system of government provides for a social science research contribution to be fed in. In both British and American central government, the last quarter of a century has seen the development of elaborate structures both for commissioning social science research from external academic sources, market research firms and profit-making and non-profit research institutions, and for creating in-house research capability. In the United States, the principal agencies of the former are the social science branches of the National Science Foundation, the National Institutes of Health, and the research budgets of the main federal departments, but there are a very wide variety of other sources including the private foundations (of which Ford and Rockefeller are only the best known), private industry, the media and other operating arms of government and public enterprises. In Britain, the main sources of support are central government directly, the (government-supported) Economic and Social Research Council, private foundations, commercial organizations, and local government and public enterprises (Bulmer, 1982, p. 135). Pluralism is not just a feature of the policy process; it is also a characteristic of the sources of social science advice which are available to policy-makers. The American scene with its much larger scale, three tiers of government, and a much more achievement-oriented academic ethos exemplifies this par excellence.

The organization of British social policy research is dominated to a greater degree by central government (in the main indirectly through the ESRC and the University Grants Committee), but even there pluralism is evident to a degree. The British preference for indirect forms of funding means that resources for basic facilities and research in social science are distributed through intermediary organizations run by peers from the academic community. Within central government the commissioning and management of research is not unitary, and arrangements are more varied than is generally appreciated (see Blume, 1982). British central government departments enjoy a considerable degree of autonomy, and research provision for government is not centralized, except in so far as the Office of Population Censuses and Surveys (OPCS) provides a single census-taking and social survey capability. Each department controls its own programme and budget, contracting out fieldwork to OPCS as appropriate. The policies which departments pursue can vary considerably. They may, like the Home Office, carry out most of their research 'in-house', or like the DHSS have a small in-house unit but a large external programme. Research programmes vary in their time-frame. Bodies like the Manpower Services Commission use research to establish relevant characteristics of client groups (such as the long-term unemployed or unqualified school leavers) or to evaluate current policy initiatives in terms of coverage or impact. Departments like the Department of Employment and the Home Office use research in part as an aid to medium-term planning, for example in charting changes in labour markets, or trends in homeworking, or the effects of custodial treatment of offenders. Part of the DHSS research budget is devoted to the objective of understanding complex problems such as mental illness, or violence in marriage, or the sources of social care. An unusually large proportion of the department's budget is used to fund rolling programmes in university-based (but DHSS-supported) research units covering the health and personal social services.

There are differing degrees of fit, too, between academic fields and disciplines and particular departments. The relationship is close in the case of the Home Office (with criminology) and the Department of Education and Science. The DHSS deals with heterogeneous topics like health that draw on a range of disciplines, not all of which fit easily together. The MSC deals with an area – training – which lacks adequate academic recognition, hence a good deal of their work has been commissioned from market research sources.

The departments' own systems for managing research also vary, and are subject to change over time. In some departments, in-house researchers are posted to administrative divisions, and do not work centrally. The Department of the Environment follows this pattern, as a result of reducing its commitment to social science research after the Conservatives came to power in 1979. Some departments maintain a central research unit in which much of the department's research activity is concentrated. The Home Office Research and Planning Unit (formerly the Home Office Research Unit) is the best example (see Cornish and Clarke, 1987). This unit is also responsible for managing the smaller amount of externally funded Home Office research. In the DHSS, the research management of external research is handled by the Chief Scientist's Office. The Office also has a small in-house group for social security research, but its main function is the supervision of the £11 million programme (in 1984) of external research. In some cases, departments prefer research to be conducted at arm's length in quangos or independent research institutes. One example has been Home Office treatment of race relations research, which for a long time it tended to regard as too sensitive. It was content to leave inquiries in this field to the Community Relations Commission and its successor, the Commission for Racial Equality (Home Office, 1975, pp. 2–7).

A detailed study over several years of the DHSS research management system by Kogan and Henkel reinforces this picture of pluralism and complexity. Their general conclusions are worth quoting.

> Policies can only be implemented successfully and practice improved in the areas of social welfare if those who seek to analyse issues and suggest solutions are interactive and reflexive. Government must be authoritative as it determines its policy priorities and allocates money to researchers. But the concepts to which it can better apply its energies are interaction rather than steerage; impact, implementation, policy communities and domains of concern, rather than rationalistic or imperative planning ... Research and government are not single entities. Different levels of institutions and different groups in the whole research-government complex have their own knowledge systems, their own reference groups, their own values and their own interests to pursue. They pursue them with different styles and with different intensities ... The 'results' of this research–policy encounter are therefore exceedingly complicated and varied because so many groups and other variables come into it, and the kind of result, if any, is also strongly related to movements in the polity and society at the time. (Kogan and Henkel, 1983, pp. 170, 171)

Even if the comfortable simplicities of the rational model of policy-making are firmly laid to rest – as they have been in the course of the journey through this book – it does not mean that social science has a slight or non-existent influence upon policy. Rather it has to be recognized that this influence is exercised in interaction with other contributions to the policy process, and that the precise manner of that influence is difficult to pin down and is even elusive. It is not easy to find examples of instrumental use of social research by public officials to frame particular policies, nor of cases where particular research studies have changed the policy which was implemented. Even in the successful case of child poverty research discussed in Chapter 1, academic research identified the problem and helped to bring pressure to bear on government to act. It did not influence the precise form of the measures which government took to tackle the problem.

The influence of social science upon social policy is, in the main, a diffuse rather than a specific one. It is true that certain types of descriptive inquiry by government perhaps have a certain immediate impact of a relatively minor sort. But there are relatively few pieces of simple descriptive data which has an instant effect. Moves in the Retail Prices Index or the unemployment rate apart, most social data requires interpretation and setting in context before it can be applied to policy. And that process is immediately one to which factors other than knowledge play a part. The actors in the policy-making world, however, have absorbed a good deal of social science indirectly.

> Social science, by helping to structure people's perception of social reality, seems to have pervasive effects. It provides an underlying set of ideas, models of the interaction of people, conditions and events, which enter into our images of how the world works. (Weiss, 1980, p. 397)

There is no cause for social scientists to be fainthearted. Even when faced with attacks on their *raison d'être* from philistine politicians and sceptical bureaucrats, they can be confident that their work does, in myriad indirect and ramified ways, impinge upon the main actors in the policy-making process and thereby influence policy. Sometimes its influence is more direct, though not necessarily more effective as a result. The last half century has seen the rise of applied social science from almost nothing to a very substantial presence on the public stage. Social problems such as health inequality, educational disadvantage, family poverty or race conflict are viewed very differently today from what they were fifty years ago, in no small measure due to the impact of social science research. This is not to say that there is agreement among applied social scientists in their diagnoses of causes or of possible intervention strategies. In part, this is what gives the social sciences their verve and intellectual excitement. Nor is society noticeably nearer achieving a solution to these problems. Social policy-making remains intractable, complex and uncertain. Though the social sciences can rightly claim to be useful, they offer no panacea.

Bibliography

Aaron, H. (1978), *Politics and the Professors* (Washington DC: Brookings Institution).

Abel-Smith, B. (1966), *Labour's Social Plans* (London: Fabian Society Tract 369).

Abel-Smith, B. (1978), *National Health Service: The First 30 Years* (London: HMSO).

Abel-Smith, B. (1980), ' "Don't have a go at romantic fiction if you know nothing about sex" ', *Times Higher Education Supplement*, 27 June, p. 10.

Abel-Smith, B., and Townsend, P. (1965), *The Poor and the Poorest* (London: Bell).

Abrams, P. (1968), *The Origins of British Sociology 1834–1914* (Chicago: University of Chicago Press).

Abrams, P. (1978), 'Towns and economic growth: some theories and problems', in P. Abrams and E. A. Wrigley (eds), *Towns in Societies* (Cambridge: Cambridge University Press), pp. 9–33.

Acland, H. (1979), 'Are randomized experiments the Cadillacs of design?', *Policy Analysis*, vol. 5, no. 2, pp. 223–41.

Agar, M. H. (1980), *The Professional Stranger: An Informal Introduction to Ethnography* (New York: Academic).

Alihan, M. A. (1938), *Social Ecology: A Critical Analysis* (New York: Columbia University Press).

Alker, H. R. Jr. (1969), 'A typology of ecological fallacies', in M. Dogan and S. Rokkan (eds), *Quantitative Ecological Analysis in the Social Sciences* (Cambridge, Mass.: MIT Press), pp. 69–86.

Allardt, E. (1977), 'On the relationship between objective and subjective predicaments', Research Report 16, University of Helsinki Research Group for Comparative Sociology.

Anderson, O. W. (1972), *Health Care: Can There Be Equity?* (New York: Wiley).

Andrews, F. M. and Withey, S. B. (1976), *Social Indicators of Well-Being* (New York: Plenum).

Askham, J. (1975), *Fertility and Deprivation: A Study of Differential Fertility amongst Working-Class Families in Aberdeen* (Cambridge: Cambridge University Press).

Atkinson, A. B. (1984), 'Taxation and social security reform: reflections on advising a House of Commons select committee', *Policy and Politics*, vol. 12, no. 2, pp. 107–18.

Bachrach, P., and Baratz, M. S. (1962), 'The two faces of power', *American Political Science Review*, vol. 56, pp. 947–52.

Bachrach, P., and Baratz, M. S. (1963), 'Decisions and nondecisions: an analytic framework', *American Political Science Review*, vol. 57, pp. 641–51.

Bachrach, P., and Baratz, M. (1970), *Power and Poverty: Theory and Practice* (New York: Oxford University Press).

Baird, D. (1974), 'Epidemiology of low birth weight: changes in incidence in Aberdeen 1948–1972', *Journal of Biosocial Science*, vol. 6, p. 323.

Baldwin, J. (1979), 'Ecological and areal studies in Great Britain and the United States', in N. Morris and M. Tonry (eds), *Crime and Justice: An Annual Review of Research*, Vol. 1 (Chicago: University of Chicago Press), pp. 29–66.

Baldwin, J., and Bottoms, A. E. (1976), *The Urban Criminal* (London: Tavistock).

Banfield, E. C. (1970), *The Unheavenly City: The Nature and Future of an Urban Crisis* (Boston, Mass.: Little, Brown).

Banting, K. G. (1979), *Poverty, Politics and Policy* (London: Macmillan).

Barnes, H. E. (1948), *An Introduction to the History of Sociology* (Chicago: University of Chicago Press).

Barnes, J. H. (1983), 'Social research and a government department', in *The Dissemination of Research Findings in Social Work* (Bristol: University of Bristol Dartington Social Research Unit), pp. 20–2.

Barnes, J. H., and Lucas, H. (1975), 'Positive discrimination in education: individuals, groups and institutions', in J. Barnes (ed.), *Educational Priority*, Vol. 3: *Curriculum Innovation in London EPAs* (London: HMSO), pp. 237–89.

Barnes, R., and Birch, F. (1975), *The Census as an Aid in Estimating the Characteristics of Non-Response in the General Household Survey*, New Methodology Series NM1 (London: OPCS Social Survey Division).

Barnett, H. (1953), *Innovation: The Basis of Cultural Change* (New York: McGraw Hill).

Bateson, N. (1984), *Data Construction in Social Surveys* (London: Allen & Unwin).

Bayley, M. (1973), *Mental Handicap and Community Care* (London: Routledge & Kegan Paul).

Bebbington, A. C. (1984), 'The General Household Survey: a research resource for the elderly', *GHS Newsletter* (of the ESRC Data Archive), no. 1, September, pp. 22–8.

Bebbington, A. C., and Davies, B. (1980), 'Territorial need indicators: a new approach, Part I', *Journal of Social Policy*, vol. 9, pp. 145–68.

Bebbington, A. C., and Davies, B. P. (1983), 'Equity and efficiency in the allocation of the personal social services', *Journal of Social Policy*, vol. 12, pp. 309–30.

Bentley, A. F. ([1908] 1967), *The Process of Government*, ed. P. Odegard (Cambridge, Mass.: The Belknap Press of Harvard University).

Benveniste, G. (1973), *The Politics of Expertise* (Berkeley, Calif.: Glendessary Press).

Berk, R., and Rossi, P. (1976), 'Doing good or worse: evaluation research politically re-examined', *Social Problems*, vol. 23, no. 3, pp. 337–49.

Berthoud, R. (1976), *The Disadvantages of Inequality: A Study of Social Deprivation* (London: Macdonald & Jarvis).

Black Report (1980), *Report of the Working Group on Inequalities in Health (Chairman Sir Douglas Black)* (London: Department of Health and Social Security), mimeo (see also Townsend and Davidson, 1982).

Blalock, H. M. Jr. (1964), *Causal Inference in Non-Experimental Research* (Chapel Hill, NC: University of North Carolina Press).

Blau, P. M. (1963), *The Dynamics of Bureaucracy: A Study of Interpersonal Relationships in Two Government Agencies*, revised edn (Chicago: University of Chicago Press).

Blaxter, M. (1976), *The Meaning of Disability* (London: Heinemann).

Blume, S. S. (1977), 'Policy as theory', *Acta Sociologica*, vol. 20, no. 3, p. 247.

Blume, S. S. (1982), *The Commissioning of Research by Central Government: A Report Commissioned by the Research Careers Executive Panel* (London: Social Science Research Council).

Booth, C. (1891), *Life and Labour of the People*, Vol. II: *London (Continued)* (London: Williams & Norgate).

Booth, C. (1894), *The Aged Poor in England and Wales* (London: Macmillan).

Booth, C. (1897), *Life and Labour of the People of London*, 9 vols. (London: Macmillan).

Boothroyd, P., and Rees, W. (1984), 'Impact assessment from pseudo-Science to planning process: an educational response' in *Impact Assessment Bulletin*, vol. 3.

Boruch, R. F. (1987), 'Comparative aspects of randomized experiments for planning and evaluation', in Bulmer (ed.) (1987).

Boruch, R. F., and Cecil, J. S. (1979), *Assuring the Confidentiality of Social Research Data* (Philadelphia, Penn.: University of Pennsylvania Press).

Boruch, R. F., McSweeny, J., and Soderstrom, E. J. (1978), 'Randomized field experiments for program planning, development and evaluation: an illustrative bibliography', *Evaluation Quarterly*, vol. 2, no. 4, pp. 655–95.

Boudon, R. (1963), 'Propriétés individuelles et propriétés collectives: un problème d'analyse ecologique', *Revue Française de Sociologie*, vol. 4, pp. 275–99.

Brantingham, P., and Brantingham, P. (1984), *Patterns of Crime* (New York: Macmillan).

Brotherston, J. (1976), 'Inequality: is it inevitable?', in C. O. Carter and J. Peel (eds), *Equalities and Inequalities in Health* (London: Academic), pp. 73–104.

Brown, A., and Kiernan, K. (1981), 'Cohabitation in Great Britain: evidence from the General Household Survey', *Population Trends*, vol. 25, pp. 4–10.

Brown, G. W., and Harris, T. (1978), *The Social Origins of Depression: A Study of Psychiatric Depression in Women* (London: Tavistock).

Brown, G. W., NiBhrolchain, M., and Harris, T. O. (1975), 'Social class and psychiatric disturbance among women in an urban population', *Sociology*, vol. 9, pp. 225–54.

Brown, M. (1977), *Introduction to Social Administration in Britain*, 4th edn (London: Hutchinson).

Brown, M., and Madge, N. (1982), *Despite the Welfare State: A Report on the SSRC/DHSS Programme of Research into Transmitted Deprivation* (London: Heinemann).

Bryman, A. (1984), 'The debate about quantitative and qualitative research', *British Journal of Sociology*, vol. 35, pp. 75–92.

Bulmer, M. (ed.) (1978), *Social Policy Research* (London: Macmillan).

Bulmer, M. (1979), 'Concepts in the analysis of qualitative data', *Sociological Review*, vol. 27, pp. 653–77.

Bulmer, M. (ed.) (1980a), *Social Research and Royal Commissions* (London: Allen & Unwin).

Bulmer, M. (1980b), 'Why don't sociologists make more use of official statistics?', *Sociology*, vol. 14, no. 4, pp. 505–23.

Bulmer, M. (1981), 'The British tradition of social administration: moral concerns at the expense of scientific rigour', *Hastings Center Report*, vol. 11, no. 2, pp. 35–42.

Bulmer, M. (1982), *The Uses of Social Research: Social Investigation in Public Policy-Making* (London: Allen & Unwin).

Bulmer, M. (ed.) (1983a), 'Social science and policy-making: the use of research by governmental commissions', special issue of *American Behavioral Scientist*, vol. 26, no. 5, pp. 553–680.

Bulmer, M. (1983b), 'The social sciences', in J. W. Chapman (ed.), *The Western University on Trial* (Berkeley: University of California Press), pp. 100–17.

Bulmer, M. (1984), *The Chicago School of Sociology: Institutionalisation, Diversity and the Rise of Sociological Research* (Chicago: University of Chicago Press).

Bulmer, M. (1985), 'A scholar outside the university', *Minerva*, vol. 23, no. 1, pp. 166–72.

Bulmer, M. (1986), *Neighbours: The Work of Philip Abrams* (Cambridge: Cambridge University Press).

Bulmer, M. (ed.) (1987), *Social Science Research and Government: Comparative Essays on Britain and America* (Cambridge: Cambridge University Press).

Bulmer, M., and Burgess, R. (eds) (1981), 'The teaching of research methodology', special issue of *Sociology*, vol. 15, no. 4, pp. 477–602.

Bulmer, M., and Warwick, D. P. (eds) (1983), *Social Research in Developing Countries: Surveys and Censuses in the Third World* (Chichester, Sussex: Wiley).

Burgess, E. W. (1925), 'The growth of the city', in Park and Burgess, op. cit., pp. 47–62.

Burgess, E. W., and Bogue, D. (eds) (1964), *Contributions to Urban Sociology* (Chicago: University of Chicago Press).

Burgess, R. (ed.) (1982), *Field Research: A Sourcebook and Field Manual* (London: Allen & Unwin).

Burt, C. (1925), *The Young Delinquent* (London: University of London Press).

Bustelo, E. S. (1983), 'Social impact assessment: basic needs and income distribution', *International Sociological Association Research Committee on Sociotechnics Newsletter*, no. 8, pp. 9–17.

Butler, D., and Kitzinger, U. (1976), *The 1975 Referendum* (London: Macmillan).

Butterfield, H. (1931), *The Whig Interpretation of History* (London: Bell).

Byrne, D., Williamson, W., and Fletcher, B. (1975), *The Poverty of Education* (London: Martin Robertson).

Cairncross, A. (1981), 'Academics and policy makers' in F. Cairncross (ed.), *Changing Perceptions of Economic Policy* (London: Methuen), pp. 5–32.

Calder, A. (1985), 'Mass-observation 1937–1949', in M. Bulmer (ed.), *Essays on the History of British Sociological Research* (Cambridge: Cambridge University Press), pp. 121–36.

Campbell, A., Converse, P. E., and Rogers, W. L. (1976), *The Quality of*

American Life: Perceptions, Evaluations and Satisfactions (New York: Russell Sage).

Campbell, D. T. (1969), 'Reforms as experiments', *American Psychologist*, vol. 24, pp. 409–29.

Campbell, D. T. (1979), ' "Degrees of freedom" and the case study', in Cook and Reichardt, op. cit., pp. 49–67.

Campbell, D. T., and Stanley, J. C. (1963), *Experimental and Quasi-Experimental Designs for Research* (Chicago: Rand McNally).

Cantril, H. (1965), *The Pattern of Human Concerns* (New Brunswick, NJ: Rutgers University Press).

Caplan, N., Morrison, A., and Stambaugh, R. (1975), *The Use of Social Science Knowledge in Policy Decisions at the National Level* (Ann Arbor, Mich.: Institute for Social Research).

Carley, M. J. (1980), *Rational Techniques in Policy Analysis* (London: Heinemann).

Carley, M. J. (1981), *Social Measurement and Social Indicators: Issues of Policy and Theory* (London: Allen & Unwin).

Carley, M. J., and Bustelo, E. S. (1984), *Social Impact Assessment and Monitoring: A Guide to the Literature* (Boulder, Colo.: Westview Press).

Carlisle, E. (1972), 'The conceptual structure of social indicators', in A. Shonfield and S. Shaw (eds), *Social Indicators and Social Policy* (London: Heinemann), pp. 23–32.

Cartwright, A. (1964), *Human Relations and Hospital Care* (London: Routledge & Kegan Paul).

Cartwright, A., and O'Brien, M. (1976), 'Social class variations in health care', in M. Stacey (ed.), *The Sociology of the NHS*, Keele University Sociological Review Monograph No. 22, pp. 77–99.

Cassel, J. (1974), 'Psychological processes and "stress": theoretical formulations', *International Journal of Health Services*, vol. 4, p. 471.

Castells, M. (1968), 'Y-a-t' il une sociologie urbaine?' *Sociology du Travail*, vol. 1, pp. 72–90 (translated as 'Is there an urban sociology?' in C. G. Pickvance (ed.), *Urban Sociology: Critical Essays* (London: Tavistock, 1976), pp. 33–50).

Castle, I. M., and Gittus, E. (1957), 'The distribution of social defects in Liverpool', *Sociological Review*, vol. 5, pp. 43–64.

Central Policy Review Staff (CPRS) (1975), *A Joint Framework for Social Policy* (London: HMSO).

Central Policy Review Staff (CPRS) (1977), *Review of Overseas Representation* (London: HMSO).

Chadwick, E. (1965), *Report of the Sanitary Condition of the Labouring Population of Great Britain*, ed. with an introduction by M. W. Flynn (Edinburgh: Edinburgh University Press).

Challis, D. J., and Davies, B. P. (1980), 'A new approach to community care for the elderly', *British Journal of Social Work*, vol. 10, pp. 1–18.

Chapman, R. A. (ed.) (1973), *The Role of Commissions in Policy-Making* (London: Allen & Unwin).

Chase, H. C. (1977), 'Infant mortality and its concomitants 1960–72', *Medical Care*, vol. 15, no. 8, p. 662.

Chen, H., and Rossi, P. (1980), 'The multi-goal, theory-driven, approach to evaluation: a model linking basic and applied social science', *Social Forces*, vol. 59, pp. 106–22.

Childs, H. L. (1965), *Public Opinion: Nature, Formation and Role* (New York: van Nostrand).

Chillag, J. P. (1983), 'Grey literature: an underused resource', *Research, Policy and Planning*, vol. 1, no. 2, pp. 10–13.

Clark, T. N. (1974), 'Can you cut a budget pie?', *Policy and Politics*, vol. 3, pp. 3–31.

Clarke, R. V. G., and Cornish, D. B. (1983), 'Editorial introduction' to R. Clarke and D. Cornish (eds), *Crime Control in Britain: A Review of Policy Research* (Albany, NY: State University of New York Press), pp. 3–54.

Clausen, J. A., and Kohn, M. L. (1954), 'The ecological approach to social psychiatry', *American Journal of Sociology*, vol. 15, pp. 140–51.

Coates, K., and Silburn, R. (1970), *Poverty, The Forgotten Englishmen* (Harmondsworth: Penguin).

Coffield, F., Robinson, P., and Sarsby, J. (1980), *A Cycle of Deprivation? A Case Study of Four Families* (London: Heinemann).

Cohen, D. K., and Garet, M. (1975), 'Reforming educational policy with applied social research', *Harvard Educational Review*, vol. 45, pp. 17–43.

Cohen, D. K., and Weiss, J. A. (1977), 'Social science and social policy: schools and race', in C. H. Weiss (ed.), *Using Social Research in Public Policy Making* (Lexington, Mass.: Lexington/D. C. Heath), pp. 67–83.

Cole, S., and Lucas, H. (1981), *Models, Planning and Basic Needs* (Oxford: Pergamon).

Coleman Report (1966), *Equality of Educational Opportunity* by J. S. Coleman, E. Q. Campbell, C. J. Hobson, J. McPartland, A. Mood, F. D. Wingfield and R. L. York (Washington DC: Office of Education, US Department of Health, Education and Welfare).

Colley, J. R. T., and Reid, D. D. (1970), 'Urban and social class origins of childhood bronchitis in England and Wales', *British Medical Journal*, vol. 2, p. 213.

Comar, C. (1978), 'Bad science and social penalties', *Science*, vol. 200, 16 June, p. 1225.

Comroe, J. H. Jr., and Dripps, R. D. (1976), 'Scientific basis for the support of biomedical science', *Science*, 9 April, pp. 105–11.

Cook, T. D., and Campbell, D. T. (1979), *Quasi-Experimentation: Design and Analysis Issues in Field Settings* (Chicago: Rand McNally).

Cook, T. D., and Reichardt, C. (eds) (1979), *Qualitative and Quantitative Methods in Evaluation Research* (Beverly Hills, Calif.: Sage).

Cornia, G. A. (1982), 'Development strategies for the 1980s: old myths and new ideas', in *UNCTAD Discussion Paper No. 4* (Geneva: UNCTAD).

Cornish, D. B., and Clarke, R. V. G. (1987), 'Social science in government: the case of the Home Office Research and Planning Unit', in Bulmer (ed.) (1987).

Cottrell, K. (1985), 'An acute indicator for an acute problem', *Health and Social Services Journal*, 26 Sept., pp. 1196–7.

Cragg, A., and Dawson, T. (1981), *Qualitative Research Among Homeworkers*, Department of Employment Research Paper No. 21 (London: DoE).

Crawford, E. T., and Biderman, A. D. (1969), 'The functions of policy-oriented social science' in E. Crawford and A. Biderman (eds), *Social Scientists and International Affairs* (New York: Wiley), pp. 233–43.

Cullen, I. G. (1978), 'Measuring the impact of urban social policies', paper presented to the Ninth World Congress of Sociology, University College, London, Bartlett School of Architecture and Planning, mimeo.

Culyer, A. J. (1981), 'Economics, social policy and social administration: the interplay between topic and discipline', *Journal of Social Policy*, vol. 10, no. 3, pp. 311–29.

Culyer, A. J. (ed.) (1983), *Health Indicators* (Oxford: Martin Robertson).

Dalton, M. (1959), *Men Who Manage* (New York: Wiley).

Daniel, W. W. (1968), *Racial Discrimination in England* (Harmondsworth: Penguin).

Davie, R., Butler, N., and Goldstein, H. (1972), *From Birth to Seven* (London: Longman).

Davies, B. P. (1968), *Social Needs and Resources in Local Services* (London: Michael Joseph).

Davies, B. P. (1981), 'Strategic goals and piecemeal innovations: adjusting to the new balance of needs and resources', in E. M. Goldberg and S. Hatch (eds), *A New Look at the Personal Social Services* (London: Policy Studies Institute), pp. 46–67.

Davies, B. P., and Challis, D. (1981), 'A production relations evaluation of the meeting of needs in community care projects', in E. M. Goldberg and N. Connelly (eds), *Evaluative Research in Social Care* (London: Heinemann), pp. 177–98.

Davison, W. P. (1968), 'Public opinion: introduction', in D. L. Sills (ed.), *International Encyclopaedia of the Social Sciences* (New York: Macmillan and Free Press), Vol. 13, pp. 188–97.

Deakin, N. (1970), *Colour, Citizenship and Britsh Society* (London: Panther).

De'Ath, C. (1982), 'Social impact assessment: a central tool in land-development planning', *International Social Science Journal*, vol. 34, pp. 441–50.

Dell, S. (1979), 'Basic needs or comprehensive development: should the UNDP have a development strategy?', *World Development*, vol. 7, pp. 291–308.

De Neufville, J. I. (1975), *Social Indicators and Public Policy* (Amsterdam: Elsevier).

De Neufville, J. I. (1981), *Social Indicators of Basic Needs: Quantitative Data for Human Rights Policy*, Institute of Urban and Regional Development Working Paper No. 351 (Berkeley: University of California).

Department of Employment (1975), 'The unstatistical reader's guide to the Retail Price Index', *Department of Employment Gazette* (October), pp. 971–8.

Department of Employment (1985), 'Retail Prices Index: annual revisions to the weights', *Employment Gazette*, vol. 93, no. 3, pp. 103–5.

Deutscher, I. (1973), *What We Say/What We Do: Sentiments and Acts* (Brighton, Sussex: Scott Foresman).

DHSS (1976), *Prevention and Health: Everybody's Business* (London: HMSO).

DHSS Statisticians (1972), 'Politics and the statistics of poverty: a rejoinder', *The Political Quarterly*, vol. 43, pp. 232–5.

Dicey, A. V. (1905), *Lectures on the Relation between Law and Public Opinion in Britain during the Nineteenth Century* (London: Macmillan).

Dillman, D. A. (1978), *Mail and Telephone Surveys: The Total Design Method* (New York: Wiley).

Donnison, D. V. (1967), *The Government of Housing* (Harmondsworth: Penguin).

Donnison, D. (1972), 'Research for Policy', *Minerva*, vol. 10, no. 4, pp. 519–36 (reprinted in Bulmer (1978), pp. 44–66).

Donnison, D. V. (1974), 'Policies for priority areas', *Journal of Social Policy*, vol. 3, pp. 127–35.

Donnison, D. (1982), *The Politics of Poverty* (Oxford: Martin Robertson).

Donnison, D. V., and Ungerson, C. (1982), *Housing Policy* (Harmondsworth: Penguin).

Dore, R. P. (1973), *British Factory, Japanese Factory* (London: Allen & Unwin).

Dror, Y. (1964), 'Muddling through – science or inertia?', *Public Administration Review*, vol. 24, pp. 153–7.

Duesenberry, J. S. (1960), 'Comment', in *Demographic and Economic Change in Developed Countries*, Universities-National Bureau Committee for Economic Research (Princeton, NJ: Princeton University Press), pp. 231–4.

Duncan, O. D. (1969), *Toward Social Reporting: Next Steps* (New York: Russell Sage).

Duncan, O. D., Cuzzort, R. P., and Duncan, B. (1961), *Statistical Geography: Problems in Analysing Areal Data* (Glencoe, Ill.: Free Press).

Duncan, O. D., and Davis, B. (1953), 'An alternative to ecological correlation', *American Sociological Review*, vol. 18, pp. 655–6.

Durkheim, E. ([1897] 1951), *Suicide* (London: Routledge & Kegan Paul).

Edwards, A. (1973), 'Sex and area variations in delinquency in an English city', *British Journal of Criminology*, vol. 13, pp. 121–37.

Ehrenreich, B., and Ehrenreich, J. (1978), 'Medicine and social control', in J. Ehrenreich (ed.), *The Cultural Crisis of Modern Medicine* (New York: Monthly Review Press).

Encel, S., Marstrand, P. K., and Page, W. (eds) (1975), *The Art of Anticipation* (London: Martin Robertson).

Engels, F. (1968), *The Condition of the Working Class in Britain in 1844* (London: Allen & Unwin).

Ermich, J., and Overton, E. (1984), *Minimal Household Units: A New Perspective in the Demographic and Economic Analysis of Household Formation*, Policy Studies Institute Research Paper 84/1 (London: PSI).

Ermich, J. *et al.* (1982), 'A study of household formation based on the General Household Survey', in GHS, op. cit., pp. 215–20.

Etzioni, A. (1967), 'Mixed scanning: a "third" approach to decision-making', *Public Administration Review*, vol. 27, pp. 385–92.

Etzioni, A. (1985), 'Making policy for complex systems: a medical model for economics', *Journal of Policy Analysis and Management*, vol. 4, pp. 383–95.

Etzioni, A., and Lehman, E. W. (1967), 'Some dangers in "valid" social measurement', *Annals of the American Academy of Political and Social Science*, vol. 373 (September), pp. 1–15.

Eversley, D. (1978), 'A question of numbers', in Bulmer, op. cit., pp. 271–301.

Eyer, J. (1977), 'Prosperity as a cause of death', *International Journal of Health Services*, vol. 7, no. 1, p. 125.

Faris, R. E. L. (1934), 'Cultural isolation and schizophrenic personality', *American Journal of Sociology*, vol. 39, pp. 155–69.

Faris, R. E. L., and Dunham, H. W. (1939), *Mental Disorders in Urban Areas* (Chicago: University of Chicago Press).

Ferber, R., and Hirsch, W. Z. (1982), *Social Experimentation and Economic Policy* (Cambridge: Cambridge University Press).

Fieghan, G. C., Lansley, P. S., and Smith, A. D. (1977), *Poverty and Progress in Britain 1953–1973* (Cambridge: Cambridge University Press).

Finch, J. (1986), *Research and Policy: The Uses of Qualitative Methods in Social and Educational Policy* (Brighton: Falmer Press).

Finer Committee (1974), *Report of the Committee on One-Parent Families* (chairman Sir Morris Finer), Cmnd 5629 (London: HMSO).

Fitzsimmons, S. J., and Lavey, W. G. (1976), 'Social Economic Accounts System (SEAS): toward comprehensive community-level assessment procedures', *Social Indicators Research*, vol. 2, pp. 389–452.

Fitzsimmons, S. J., and Lavey, W. G. (1977), 'Community: towards an integration of research, theory, evaluation and public policy', *Social Indicators Research*, vol. 4, pp. 25–66.

Flather, P. (1987), 'Pulling through: conspiracies, counterplots and how the SSRC escaped the axe in 1982', in Bulmer (ed.), (1987).

Flowerdew, A. D. J. (1980), 'A commission and a cost-benefit study', in Bulmer, 1980a, pp. 85–109.

Forster, D. P. (1976), 'Social class differences in sickness and general practice consultations', *Health Trends*, vol. 8, p. 29.

Foster, C., Jackman, R., and Perlman, M. (1980), *Local Government Finance in a Unitary State* (London: Allen & Unwin).

Freidson, E. (1970), *Professional Dominance* (New York: Atherton).

Frey, J. H. (1983), *Survey Research by Telephone* (Beverly Hills, Calif.: Sage).

Friedman, M. (1962), *Capitalism and Freedom* (Chicago: University of Chicago Press).

Galtung, J. (1967), *Theories and Methods of Social Research* (London: Allen & Unwin).

Gardner, M. J., Crawford, M. D., and Morris, J. N. (1969), 'Patterns of mortality in middle and early old age in the county boroughs of England and Wales', *British Journal of Preventive and Social Medicine*, vol. 23, p. 133.

Gauhar, A. (1982), 'What is wrong with basic needs?', *Third World Quarterly*, vol. 4, p. 204.

Gehrmann, F. (1978), 'Valid empirical measurement of quality of life?', *Social Indicators Research*, vol. 5, pp. 73–110.

General Household Survey (GHS) (1981), *General Household Survey 1979* (London: HMSO for OPCS Social Survey Division).

General Household Survey (GHS) (1982), *General Household Survey 1980* (London: HMSO for OPCS Social Survey Division).

General Household Survey (GHS) (1985), *General Household Survey 1983* (London: HMSO for OPCS Social Survey Division).

George, V., and Wilding, P. (1976), *Ideology and Social Welfare* (London: Routledge & Kegan Paul).

Ghai, D. *et al.* (1979), *Planning for Basic Needs in Kenya* (Geneva: ILO).

Giggs, J. A. (1973), 'The distribution of schizophrenics in Nottingham', *Transactions of the Institute of British Geographers*, vol. 59, pp. 55–76.

Giggs, J. A. (1975), 'The distribution of schizophrenics in Nottingham: a reply', *Transactions of the Institute of British Geographers*, vol. 64 (March), pp. 150–6.

Giggs, J. A. (1979), 'Human health problems in urban areas', in D. T. Herbert and D. M. Smith (eds), *Social Problems and the City: Geographical Perspectives* (Oxford: Oxford University Press), pp. 84–116.

Gilbert, G. N., Arber, S., Dale, A., and Rajan, L. (1985), *The General Household Survey Series (i) Class (ii) Gender (iii) Poverty*, three tapes (York: Longman Micro Software).

Gittus, E. (1976), 'Deprived areas and social planning', in D. T. Herbert and R. J. Johnston (eds), *Spatial Perspectives on Problems and Policies*, Vol. 2 (New York: Wiley), pp. 209–33.

Glennerster, H., and Hoyle, E. (1972), 'Educational research and educational policy', *Journal of Social Policy*, vol, 1, pp. 193–212.

Goffman, E. (1961), *Asylums* (Harmondsworth: Penguin).

Goldberg, E. M. and Morrison, S. L. (1963), 'Schizophrenia and social class', *British Journal of Psychiatry*, vol. 109, pp. 785–802.

Golding, P. and Middleton, S. (1982), *Images of Welfare* (Oxford: Martin Robertson).

Goodman, L. (1959), 'Some alternatives to ecological correlation', *American Sociological Review*, vol. 64, pp. 610–25.

Gordon, I., Lewis, J., and Young, K. (1977), 'Perspectives on policy analysis', *Public Administration Bulletin*, vol. 25, pp. 26–35.

Gouldner, A. W. (1954), *Patterns of Industrial Bureaucracy* (New York: Free Press).

Gove, W. R. and Hughes, M. (1980), 'Reexamining the ecological fallacy', *Social Forces*, vol. 58, pp. 1157–77.

Gowers, E. (1975), *The Complete Plain Words* (Harmondsworth: Penguin).

Grant, S. D. (1978), *Disparity Reduction Rates in Social Indicators: A Proposal for Measuring and Targeting Progress in Meeting Basic Needs*, New York: Overseas Development Council Monograph No. 11.

Grossman, M. (1972), *The Demand for Health: A Theoretical and Empirical Investigation* (New York: National Bureau of Economic Research).

Groves, R. M., and Kahn, R. L. (1979), *Surveys by Telephone* (New York: Academic).

Hakim, C. (1980), 'Homeworking: some new evidence', *Department of Employment Gazette*, vol. 88, no. 10, pp. 1105–10.

Hakim, C. (1982), *Secondary Analysis in Social Research* (London: Allen & Unwin).

Hakim, C., and Dennis, R. (1982), *Homeworking in Wage Council Industries*, Department of Employment Research Paper No. 37 (London: DoE).

Hall, J. (1976), 'Subjective measures of quality of life in Britain: 1971–1975', *Social Trends*, vol. 7 (London: HMSO), pp. 47–60.

Hall, J., and Perry, N. (1975), *Aspects of Leisure in Two Industrial Cities* (London: SSRC Survey Unit).

Halsey, A. H. (1978), 'Government against poverty in school and community' in M. Bulmer (ed.), *Social Policy Research* (London: Macmillan), pp. 139–59.

Hamilton, R. F. (1982), *Who Voted For Hitler?* (Princeton, NJ: Princeton University Press).

Hammersley, M., and Atkinson, P. (1983), *Ethnography: Principles in Practice* (London: Tavistock).

Hamnett, C. (1979), 'Area-based explanations: a critical appraisal', in D. T. Herbert and D. M. Smith (eds), *Social Problems and the City: Geographical Perspectives* (Oxford: Oxford University Press), pp. 244–60.

Hamson, J. (1983), 'The view of a Director of Social Services', in *The Dissemination of Research Findings in Social Work* (Bristol: University of Bristol Dartington Social Research Unit), pp. 10–12.

Hart, N. (1985), 'Inequalities in health: the sociological approach', paper delivered to joint Royal Statistical Society and Society for Social Medicine meeting, 25 June, Colchester, University of Essex, mimeo.

Hartmann, P. G., and Husband, C. H. (1974), *Racism and the Mass Media: A Study of the Role of the Mass Media in the Formation of White Beliefs and Attitudes in Britain* (London: Davis Poynter).

Harvey, D. (1969), *Explanation in Geography* (London: Arnold).

Hatry, H. P. *et al.* (1977), *How Effective Are Your Community Services? Procedures for Monitoring the Effectiveness of Municipal Services* (Washington DC: Urban Institute).

Havelock, R. G. (1969), *Planning for Innovation through Dissemination and Utilization of Knowledge* (Ann Arbor, Mich.: Institute for Social Research).

Headey, B. (1977), 'Governing parties as agenda setters', paper presented at the American Political Science Association annual meeting.

Heclo, H. (1973), 'Review article: policy analysis', *British Journal of Political Science*, vol. 2, pp. 83–108.

Heclo, H. (1974), *Modern Social Politics in Britain and Sweden* (New Haven, Conn.: Yale University Press).

Heclo, H. (1977), *A Government of Strangers: Executive Politics in Washington* (Washington, DC: Brookings Institute).

Heclo, H., and Rein, M. (1980), 'Social science and negative income taxation', in *The Utilisation of the Social Sciences in Policy-Making in the United States: Case Studies* (Paris: Organization for Economic Co-operation and Development), pp. 29–66.

Heclo, H., and Wildavsky, A. (1974) (1981), *The Private Government of Public Money* (London: Macmillan) (2nd edn 1981).

Herbert, A. P. (1961), 'Anything but action? A study of the uses and abuses of committees of inquiry', in R. Harris (ed.), *Radical Reaction* (London: Hutchinson for the Institute of Economic Affairs), pp. 251–302.

Herbert, D. T. (1982), *The Geography of Urban Crime* (London: Longman).

Herbert, D. T., and Johnston, R. J. (eds) (1976), *Spatial Perspectives on Problems and Policies*, Vol. 1 (New York: Wiley).

Hill, M. (1976), *The State, Administration and the Individual* (London: Fontana).

Hirschi, T., and Selvin, H. (1973), *Principles of Survey Analysis* (New York: Free Press).

Hodgkinson, R. (1967), *The Origins of the National Health Service: The Medical Services of the New Poor Law* (London: Wellcome Historical Medical Library).

Hogwood, B. W., and Gunn, L. A. (1984), *Policy Analysis for the Real World* (Oxford: Oxford University Press).

Hoinville, G., and Courtenay, G. (1979), 'Measuring consumer priorities', in T. O'Riordan *et al.* (eds), *Progress in Resource Management and Environmental Planning*, Vol. 1 (New York: Wiley).

Hoinville, G., and Smith, T. M. F. (1982), 'The Rayner review of government statistical services', *Journal of the Royal Statistical Society*, series A, vol. 145, no. 2, pp. 195–207.

Home Office (1975), *Race Relations Research: A Report to the Home Secretary by the Advisory Committee on Race Relations Research* (London: HMSO).

Hope, K. (1978), 'Indicators of the state of society', in Bulmer, op. cit., pp. 244–67 and 354–61.

Hough, M., and Mayhew, P. (1983), *The British Crime Survey: First Report*, Home Office Research Study No. 76 (London: HMSO).

Hough, M., and Mayhew, P. (1985), *Taking Account of Crime: Key Findings from the 1984 British Crime Survey*, Home Office Research Study No. 85 (London: HMSO).

Husen, T. and Kogan, M. (eds) (1984), *Educational Research and Policy: How Do They Relate?* (Oxford: Pergamon).

Hyman, E. L. (1983), 'Pitfalls in environmental impact assessment', *Impact Assessment Bulletin*, vol. 2, pp. 196–205.

IBGE (1979a), *Indicadores Sociais-Relatorio 1979 – Brasil* (Rio de Janeiro: IBGE (DEISO)).

IBGE (1979b), *Indicadores Sociais – Tabelas Selecionadas* (Rio de Janeiro: IBGE (DEISO)).

IBGE/UNICEF (1981a), *Perfil Estatistico de Cirancas e Maes no Brasil – Caracteristicas Socio-Demograpficas* (Rio de Janeiro: IBGE).

IBGE/UNICEF (1981b), *Perfil Estatistico de Cirancas e Maes no Brasil – Aspectos Nutricionais* (Rio de Janeiro: IBGE).

Ignatieff, M. (1981), 'State, civil society and total institutions: a critique of recent social histories of punishment', in M. Tonry and N. Morris (eds), *Crime and Justice: An Annual Review of Research*, Vol. 3 (Chicago: University of Chicago Press), pp. 153–92.

ILO (1977), *The Basic Needs Approach to Development* (Geneva: International Labour Organization).

ILO (1981), *First Things First: Meeting the Basic Needs of the People of Nigeria* (Addis Ababa: International Labour Organization).

Isserlis, S. (1981), 'Plus ça change . . .', in J. Pinder (ed.), *Fifty Years of Political and Economic Planning: Looking Forward 1931–1981* (London: Heinemann), pp. 162–70.

Jackson, P., and Smith, S. J. (1984), *Exploring Social Geography* (London: Allen & Unwin).

Jackson, W. V. (1984), 'Assessing performance in local government', *Long Range Planning*, vol. 17, no. 3, pp. 24–31.

Janerich, D. T. (1972), 'Maternal age and spina bifida: longitudinal v. cross-sectional analysis', *American Journal of Epidemiology*, vol. 95, p. 389.

Janowitz, M. (1970), 'Sociological models and social policy', in M. Janowitz, *Political Conflict: Essays in Political Sociology* (Chicago: Quadrangle Books), pp. 243–59.

Janowitz, M. (1972), 'Professionalization of sociology', *American Journal of Sociology*, vol. 78, pp. 105–35.

Jarman, B. (1983), 'Identification of underprivileged areas', *British Medical Journal*, vol. 286, pp. 1705–9.

Jarman, B. (1984), 'Underprivileged areas: validation and distribution of scores', *British Medical Journal*, vol. 289, pp. 1587–92.

Jenkin, P. (1980), 'Foreword' to Black Report, op. cit.

Joseph, K., and Sumption, J. (1979), *Equality* (London: Murray).

Jowell, R., and Airey, C. (eds) (1984), *British Social Attitudes: The 1984 Report* (Aldershot: Gower).

Jowell, R., and Hoinville, G. (1969), 'Opinion polls tested', *New Society*, 7 August.

Jowell, R., and Witherspoon, S. (eds) (1985), *British Social Attitudes: The 1985 Report* (Aldershot: Gower).

Kallen, D. B. P. *et al.* (eds) (1982), *Social Science Research and Public Policy-Making* (Windsor, Berks. NFER–Nelson).

Kanter, E. R. (1977), *Men and Women of the Corporation* (New York: Basic Books).

Kazdin, A. E. (1982), *Single-Case Research Designs: Methods for Clinical and Applied Settings* (New York: Oxford University Press).

Kelves, D. J. (1968), 'Testing the Army's intelligence: psychologists and the military in World War I', *Journal of American History*, vol. 55, no. 3, pp. 565–81.

Kemsley, W. F. F., Redpath, R. U., and Holmes, M. (1980), *Family Expenditure Survey Handbook* (London: HMSO).

Kennedy, L. W., Northcott, H. C., and Kensel, C. (1978), 'Subjective evaluation of well-being: problems and prospects', *Social Indicators Research*, vol. 5, pp. 457–74.

Kent, A. P. *et al.* (1958), 'A comparison of coronary artery disease in health areas of Manhattan', *American Journal of Public Health*, vol. 48, pp. 200–7.

Kerner Report (1968), *Report of the National Advisory Commission on Civil Disorders* (Washington DC: US Government Printing Office).

Kershaw, D. T. (1972), 'A negative income-tax experiment', *Scientific American*, vol. 227, no. 4, pp. 19–25.

Key, V. O. Jr. (1949), *Southern Politics in State and Nation* (New York: Vintage).

Klein, L. (1976), *A Social Scientist in Industry* (Aldershot: Gower).

Knox, P. L. (1976a), *Social Priorities for Social Indicators* (Dundee: University of Dundee Department of Geography Occasional Paper No. 4).

Knox, P. L. (1976b), 'Social well-being and North Sea oil: an application of subjective social indicators', *Regional Studies*, vol. 10, pp. 423–32.

Knox, P. L. (1978), 'Territorial social indicators and area profiles', *Town Planning Review*, vol. 49, pp. 75–83.

Kogan, M., and Henkel, M. (1983), *Government and Research: The Rothschild Experiment in a Government Department* (London: Heinemann).

Komarovsky, M. (ed.) (1975), *Sociology and Public Policy: The Case of Presidential Commissions* (New York: Elsevier).

Kuz, T. J. (1978), 'Quality of life and objective and subjective variable analysis', *Regional Studies*, vol. 12, pp. 409–17.

Land, K. C. (1983), 'Social indicators', in R. H. Turner and J. F. Short, Jr. (eds), *Annual Review of Sociology*, Vol. 9 (Palo Alto, Calif.: Annual Reviews Inc.), pp. 1–26.

Lang, R., and Armour, A. (1981), *The Assessment and Review of Social Impacts* (Ottowa: Federal Environmental Assessment and Review Office).

Larson, D. A., and Wilford, W. T. (1979), 'The physical quality of life index: a useful social indicator?', *World Development*, vol. 7, pp. 581–4.

Lawless, P. (1979), *Urban Deprivation and Government Initiative* (London: Faber).

Lawrence, K. M., Carter, C. O., and David, P. A. (1968), 'Major CNS malformations in South Wales II', *British Journal of Preventive and Social Medicine*, vol. 22, p. 212.

Layard, R., Piachaud, D., and Stewart, M. (1978), *The Causes of Poverty*, Royal Commission on the Distribution of Income and Wealth, Background Paper No. 5 (London: HMSO).

Leacock, E. B. (ed.) (1971), *The Culture of Poverty: A Critique* (New York: Simon & Schuster).

Le Grand, J. (1982), *The Strategy of Equality* (London: Allen & Unwin).

Le Grand, J. (1985), 'Inequalities in health: the human capital approach', paper delivered to joint Royal Statistical Society and Society for Social Medicine meeting, 25 June, London School of Economics (mimeo).

Leipziger, D. M., and Lewis, M. A. (1980), 'Social indicators, growth and distribution', *World Development*, vol. 8, pp. 299–302.

Lerner, M., and Stutz, R. N. (1977), 'Have we narrowed the gap between the poor and the non-poor?' *Medical Care*, vol. 15, p. 8.

Letwin, W. (ed.) (1983), *Against Equality* (London: Macmillan).

Lewis, J. (1980), *The Politics of Motherhood: Child and Maternal Welfare in England, 1900–1939* (London: Croom Helm).

Lewis, O. (1966), *La Vida: A Puerto Rican Family in the Culture of Poverty in San Juan and New York* (New York: Random House).

Lichtman, A. J. (1974), 'Correlation, regression and the ecological fallacy: a critique', *Journal of Interdisciplinary History*, vol. 4, pp. 417–33.

Lichtman, A. J. (1979), *Prejudice and Old Politics: The Presidential Election of 1928* (Chapel Hill, NC: University of North Carolina Press).

Lieberson, S. (1985), *Making It Count: The Improvement of Social Theory and Research* (Berkeley, Calif.: University of California Press).

Liebow, E. (1967), *Tally's Corner: A Study of Street Corner Men* (Boston: Little, Brown).

Lindblom, C. (1979), 'Still muddling, not yet through', *Public Administration Review*, vol. 39, pp. 517–26.

Lindblom, C. (1980), *The Policy-Making Process*, 2nd edn (Englewood Cliffs, NJ: Prentice Hall).

Lindblom, C., and Cohen, D. K. (1979), *Usable Knowledge* (New Haven, Conn.: Yale University Press).

Lipsky, M. (1980), *Street Level Bureaucracy: Dilemmas of the Individual in Public Services* (New York: Russell Sage).

Lipsky, M., and Olson, D. J. (1977), *Commission Politics: The Processing of Racial Crisis in America* (Rutgers, NJ: Transaction Books).

Little, A. N., and Mabey, C. (1972), 'An index for designation of Educational Priority Areas', in A. Shonfield and S. Shaw (eds), *Social Indicators and Social Policy* (London: Heinemann), pp. 67–93.

Littrell, W. B., Sjoberg, G., and Zurcher, L. A. (1983), *Bureaucracy as a Social Problem* (Greenwich, Conn.: JAI Press).

Loney, M. (1983), *Community Against Government: The British Community Development Project, 1968–1978 – A Study of Government Incompetence* (London: Heinemann).

Loomis, C., and Beagle, J. A. (1946), 'The spread of German Nazism in rural areas', *American Sociological Review*, vol. 11, pp. 724–35.

Lukes, S. (1974), *Power: A Radical View* (London: Macmillan).

Lynn, L. Jr. (ed.) (1978), *Knowledge and Policy: The Uncertain Connection* (Washington DC: National Academy of Sciences).

Lyons, G. M. (1969), *The Uneasy Partnership: Social Science and the Federal Government in the Twentieth Century* (New York: Russell Sage).

McConville, S. (1981), *A History of English Prison Administration*, Vol. 1: *1750–1877* (London: Routledge & Kegan Paul).

McCrossan, L. (1984), *A Handbook for Interviewers: A Manual of Social Survey Practice and Procedures on Structured Interviewing* (London: HMSO, for OPCS Social Survey Division).

Machiavelli, N. ([1513] 1952), *The Prince* (New York: Menta).

McKennell, A. C., Bynner, J., and Bulmer, M. (1987), 'The links between policy, survey research and academic social science: America and Britain compared', in Bulmer (ed.) (1987).

McKeown, T. (1976a), *The Modern Rise of Population* (London: Arnold).

McKeown, T. (1976b), *The Role of Medicine: Dream, Mirage or Nemesis?* (London: Nuffield Provincial Hospitals Trust).

MacRae, D. (1985), *Policy Indicators: Links between Social Science and Public Debate* (Chapel Hill, NC: University of North Carolina Press).

Mannheim, H., and Wilkins, L. T. (1955), *Prediction Methods in Relation to Borstal Training*, Home Office Studies in the Causes of Delinquency and the Treatment of Offenders No. 1 (London: HMSO).

Marris, P., and Rein, M. (1972), *Dilemmas of Social Reform: Poverty and Community Action in the United States* (London: Routledge & Kegan Paul).

Marsden, D. (1973), *Mothers Alone* (Harmondsworth: Penguin).

Marsh, C. (1979), 'Opinion polls – social science or political manoeuvre?', in J. Irvine, I. Miles and J. Evans (eds), *Demistifying Social Statistics* (London: Pluto), pp. 268–88.

Marsh, C. (1982), *The Survey Method* (London: Allen & Unwin).

Marsh, C. (1984), 'Back on the bandwagon: the effect of opinion polls on public opinion', *British Journal of Political Science*, vol. 15, no. 1, pp. 51–74.

Marshall, T. F., Fairhead, S. M., Murray, D. J. I., and Iles, S. C. (1978), 'Evaluation for democracy', in *Social Research in the Public Sector*, Proceedings of a conference of the European Society for Opinion and Marketing Research (mimeo), pp. 41–61.

Marshall, T. H. (1963), *Sociology at the Crossroads* (London: Heinemann).

Martin, J., and Morgan, M. (1975), *Prolonged Sickness and the Return to Work* (London: HMSO).

Martini, C. J. M. *et al.* (1977), 'Health indexes sensitive to medical care variation', *International Journal of Health Services*, vol. 7, p. 293.

Maslow, A. (1970), *Motivation and Personality* (New York: Harper & Row).

Mayer, J., and Timms, N. (1970), *The Client Speaks* (London: Routledge & Kegan Paul).

Mayhew, H. (1862), *London Labour and the London Poor* (London: Griffin-Bohn).

Maynard, A., and Ludbrook, A. (1982), 'Inequality, the National Health Service and health policy', *Journal of Public Policy*, vol. 2, no. 2, pp. 97–116.

Mays, J. B. (1963), 'Delinquency areas: a re-assessment', *British Journal of Criminology*, vol. 3, pp. 216–30.

Meadows, D. *et al.* (1972), *The Limits to Growth: The First Report of the Club of Rome* (New York: Universe Books).

Meidinger, E., and Schnaiberg, A. (1981), 'Social impact assessment as evaluation research', in H. E. Freeman and M. A. Solomon (eds), *Evaluation Studies Review Annual*, Vol. 6 (Beverly Hills: Sage), pp. 93–121.

Merton, R. K. (1957), *Social Theory and Social Structure*, 2nd edn (Glencoe, Ill.: Free Press).

Miles, I. (1985), *Social Indicators for Human Development* (London: Frances Pinter).

Miller, R. B. (1982), 'The social sciences and the politics of science: the 1940s', *The American Sociologist*, vol. 17, pp. 205–9.

Miller, R. B. (1987), 'Social science under seige: the political response, 1981–1984', in Bulmer, 1987.

Ministry of Labour (1964), *Method of Construction and Calculation of the Index of Retail Prices*, Studies in Official Statistics No. 6 (London: HMSO).

Morgenstern, O. (1960), *On the Accuracy of Economic Observations* (Princeton, NJ: Princeton University Press).

Morris, M. D. (1979), *Measuring the Condition of the World's Poor: The Physical Quality of Life Index* (Oxford: Pergamon).

Morris, J. N. (1975), *Uses of Epidemiology*, 3rd edn (Edinburgh: Churchill Livingstone).

Morris, J. N., and Heady, J. A. (1955), 'Social and biological factors in infant mortality: mortality in relation to father's occupation in 1911–1950', *The Lancet*, vol. 1, p. 554.

Morris, T. P. (1957), *The Criminal Area: A Study in Social Ecology* (London: Routledge & Kegan Paul).

Moser, C. A. and Kalton, G. (1971), *Survey Methods in Social Investigation* (London: Heinemann).

Moss, L., and Goldstein, H. (eds) (1979), *The Recall Method in Social Surveys*, Studies in Education (n.s.) No. 9 (London: University of London Institute of Education).

Moynihan, D. P. (1969), *Maximum Feasible Misunderstanding: Community Action in the War on Poverty* (New York: Free Press).

Muir, W. K. Jr. (1977), *Police – Street Corner Politicians* (Chicago: University of Chicago Press).

Murphy, M. J. (1983), 'The life course of individuals in the family: describing static and dynamic aspects of the contemporary family', in *The Family: British Society for Population Studies Conference 1983*, OPCS Occasional Paper No. 31 (London: Office of Population Censuses and Surveys), pp. 50–70.

Murphy, M. J. (1984a), 'Fertility, birth timing and marital breakdown: a reinterpretation of the evidence', *Journal of Biosocial Science*, vol. 16, pp. 487–500.

Murphy, M. (1984b), 'The use of the GHS for studying the family', ESRC Data Archive, *GHS Newsoetter* (of the ESRC Data Archive), no. 1, September, pp. 17–18.

Murphy, M. J., and Sullivan, O. (1983), *Housing Tenure and Fertility in Post-War Britain*, CPS Research Paper No. 83-2 (London: Centre for Population Studies, London School of Hygiene and Tropical Medicine).

Murthy, M. N., and Roy, A. S. (1983), 'The development of the sample design of the Indian National Sample Survey during its first 25 rounds', in Bulmer and Warwick (eds) (1983), pp. 109–24.

Navarro, V. (1978), *Class Struggle, The State and Medicine* (London: Martin Robertson).

Newman, O. (1972), *Defensible Space* (New York: Macmillan).

New Society (1976), 'Killing a commitment: the Cabinet v. the children', *New Society*, 17 June.

Nicholson, W., and Wright, S. R. (1977), 'Participants' understanding of the treatment in policy experimentation', *Evaluation Quarterly*, vol. 1 (May), pp. 245–68.

Nieburg, H. L. (1984), *Public Opinion: Tracking and Targeting* (New York: Praeger).

Noelle-Neumann, E. (1984), *The Spiral of Silence: Public Opinion – Our Social Skin* (Chicago: Univesity of Chicago Press).

Norris, G. (1979), 'Defining urban deprivation', in C. Jones (ed.), *Urban Deprivation and the Inner City* (London: Croom Helm), pp. 17–31.

Noyce, J., Snaith, A. M., and Trickey, J. (1974), 'Regional variations in the allocation of financial resources to the community health services', *The Lancet*, vol. 1, p. 554.

Office of Population Censuses and Surveys (OPCS) (1978), *Occupational Mortality: Registrar-General's Decennial Supplement for England and Wales 1970–72* (London: HMSO).

Office of Population Censuses and Surveys (OPCS) (1980), *Classification of Occupations* (London: HMSO).

Ogburn, W. F., and Talbot, N. S. (1929), 'A measurement of the factors in the Presidential Election of 1928', *Social Forces*, vol. 8, pp. 175–83.

O'Lessker, K. (1968), 'Who voted for Hitler: a new look at the class basis of Nazism', *American Journal of Sociology*, vol. 74, pp. 63–9.

Oppenheim, A. N. (1966), *Questionnaire Design and Attitude Measurement* (London: Heinemann).

Pahl, R. E. (1966), 'The rural–urban continuum', *Sociologica Ruralis*, vol. 6, pp. 3–4.

Palmer, P. A. (1936), 'The concept of public opinion in political theory', in *Essays in History and Political Theory in Honour of Charles Howard McIlwain* (Cambridge, Mass.: Harvard University Press), pp. 230–57.

Park, R. E., and Burgess, E. W. (1925), *The City* (Chicago: University of Chicago Press).

Parkin, D., Kenning, P., and Wilder, J. (1971), *Mental Illness in a Northern City* (London: Psychiatric Rehabilitation Association).

Parlett, M., and Hamilton, D. (1976), 'Evaluation as illumination: a new approach to the study of innovatory programs', in G. V. Glass (ed.), *Evaluation Studies Review Annual*, Vol. 1 (Beverly Hills: Sage), pp. 140–57.

Patrick, J. (1973), *A Glasgow Gang Observed* (London: Eyre Methuen).

Payne, S. L. (1951), *The Act of Asking Questions* (Princeton, NJ: Princeton University Press).

Pelto, P. J., and Pelto, G. H. (1978), *Anthropological Research: The Structure of Inquiry* (Cambridge: Cambridge University Press).

Peston, M. (1959/60), 'A view of the aggregation problem', *Review of Economic Studies*, vol. 27, pp. 58–64.

Peston, M. (1980), 'A professional on a political tightrope', *Times Higher Education Supplement*, 11 July, pp. 10–11.

Pigou, A. C. (1924), *The Economics of Welfare* (London: Macmillan).

Pinker, R. (1971), *Social Theory and Social Policy* (London: Heinemann).

Platt, J. (1972), 'Survey data and social policy', *British Journal of Sociology*, vol. 23, pp. 77–92 (reprinted in Bulmer, 1978, pp. 104–20).

Plowden Report (1967), *Children and Their Primary Schools*, Report of the Central Advisory Council for Education (England) (London: HMSO).

Plowden, W. (1971), *The Motor Car and Politics in Britain 1896–1970* (London: Bodley Head).

Plowden, W. (1977), 'Developing a joint approach to social policy', in K. Jones (ed.), *The Yearbook of Social Policy 1976* (London: Routledge & Kegan Paul), pp. 35–43.

Plowden, W. (1981), 'The British Central Policy Review Staff', in P. R. Baehr and B. Wittrock (eds), *Policy Analysis and Policy Innovation: Patterns, Problems and Potentials* (London: Sage), pp. 61–91.

Plummer, K. (1983), *Documents of Life* (London: Allen & Unwin).

Pollock, J. K. (1944), 'An areal study of the German electorate, 1930–1933', *American Political Science Review*, vol. 38, pp. 89–95.

Popper, K. (1972), *Objective Knowledge* (Oxford: Clarendon Press).

Poquet, G. (1980), 'The limits to global modelling', *International Social Sciences Journal*, vol. 32, pp. 284–99.

Premfors, R. (1983), 'Governmental commissions in Sweden', *American Behavioral Scientist*, vol. 26, no. 5, pp. 623–42.

Prottas, J. M. (1979), *People-Processing: The Street-Level Bureaucrat in Public Service Bureaucracies* (Lexington, Mass.: Heath).

Punnett, R. M. (1973), *Front-Bench Opposition* (London: Heinemann).

Qureshi, H. (1985), 'Exchange theory and helpers on the Kent Community Care scheme', *Research, Policy and Planning*, vol. 3, no. 1, pp. 1–9.

Rainwater, L. (1970), *Behind Ghetto Walls* (Harmondsworth: Penguin).

Rainwater, L., and Yancey, W. L. (eds) (1967), *The Moynihan Report and the Politics of Controversy* (Cambridge, Mass.: MIT Press).

Ranney, A. (1962), 'The utility and limitations of aggregate data in the study of electoral behavior', in A. Ranney (ed.), *Essays on the Behavioral Study of Politics* (Urbana, Ill.: University of Illinois Press), pp. 91–102.

RAWP (1976), *Sharing Resources for Health in England: Report of the Resource Allocation Working Party* (London: HMSO).

Reckless, W. (1940), *Criminal Behavior* (New York: McGraw Hill).

Reichardt, C., and Cook, T. D. (1979), 'Beyond qualitative *versus* quantitative methods', in Cook and Reichardt, op. cit., pp. 7–32.

Rein, M. (1976), *Social Science and Social Policy* (Harmondsworth: Penguin).

Reiss, A. J. (1968), 'Stuff and nonsense about social surveys and observation', in H. S. Becker *et al.* (eds), *Institutions and the Person* (Chicago: Aldine), pp. 351–67.

Reiss, A. J. (1971), *The Police and the Public* (New Haven, Conn.: Yale University Press).

Richardson, H. M. Jr., and Forgette, E. (1979), 'The Satisfaction of Basic Needs Index (SBNI): a progress report', paper presented to the Fifth IIASA Symposium on Global Modelling, Laxenburg.

Richardson, J. J., and Jordan, A. G. (1979), *Governing Under Pressure: The Policy Process in a Post-Parliamentary Democracy* (Oxford: Blackwell).

Rist, R. (1984), 'On the application of qualitative research to the policy process: an emergent linkage', in L. Barton and S. Walker (eds), *Social Crisis and Educational Research* (London: Croom Helm), pp. 153–70.

Rist, R. (1987), 'Social science analysis and congressional uses: the case of the United States General Accounting Office, in Bulmer (ed.) (1987).

Rivlin, A. M., and Timpane, P. M. (eds) (1975), *Ethical and Legal Issues in Social Experimentation* (Washington, DC: Brookings Institution).

Robbins Report (1963), *Higher Education. Report of the Committee Appointed by the Prime Minister under the Chairmanship of Lord Robbins 1961–1963* Cmnd 2154 (London: HMSO).

Roberts, R. (1971), *The Classic Slum* (Manchester: Manchester University Press).

Robinson, W. S. (1950), 'Ecological correlation and the behavior of individuals', *American Sociological Review*, vol. 15, pp. 351–7.

Rose, R. (1972), 'The market for policy indicators', in A. Shonfield and S. Shaw (eds), *Social Indicators and Public Policy* (London: Heinemann), pp. 119–41.

Rose, R. (1974), *Politics in England*, 2nd edn (Boston: Little, Brown).

Rosenberg, M. (1968), *The Logic of Survey Analysis* (New York: Basic Books).

Rosenhan, D. L. (1982), 'On being sane in insane places', in M. Bulmer (ed.), *Social Research Ethics* (London: Macmillan), pp. 15–37 (first published in *Science*, vol. 179, 19 January 1973, pp. 250–8).

Rossi, P., and Berk, R. (1983), 'The scope of evaluation activities in the United States', in S. E. Spiro and E. Yuchtman-Yaar (eds), *Evaluating the Welfare State: Social and Political Perspectives* (New York: Academic), pp. 179–203.

Rossi, P., Wright, J. D., and Wright, S. (1978), 'The theory and practice of applied social research', *Evaluation Quarterly*, vol. 2, no. 2, pp. 171–91.

Rossi, R. J., and Gilmartin, K. J. (1979), *Handbook of Social Indicators* (New York: Garland).

Rothschild, Lord (1971), 'The organisation and management of government research and development', in *A Framework for Government Research and Development*, Cmnd 4814 (London: HMSO).

Rothschild, Lord (1982), *An Enquiry into the Social Science Research Council*, Cmnd 8554 (London: HMSO).

Royal Commission on the NHS (1979), *Report of the Royal Commission on the National Health Service*, Cmnd 7615 (London: HMSO).

Rubinstein, J. (1973), *City Police* (New York: Farrar, Straus & Giroux).

Rutter, M. *et al.* (1979), *Fifteen Thousand Hours: Secondary Schools and Their Effects on Children* (London: Open Books).

Sainsbury, P. (1955), *Suicide in London: An Ecological Study*, Maudsley Monograph No. 1 (London: Chapman & Hall for the' Institute of Psychiatry).

Sandbach, F. (1980), *Environment, Ideology and Policy* (Oxford: Blackwell).

Sansom, G. D., Wakefield, J., and Yule, E. (1972), 'Cervical cytology in the Manchester area: changing patterns of response', in J. Wakefield (ed.), *Seek Wisely to Prevent* (London: HMSO).

Saunders, P. (1979), *Urban Politics: A Sociological Interpretation* (London: Hutchinson).

Saunders, P. (1981), *Social Theory and the Urban Question* (London: Hutchinson).

Schneider, M. (1974), 'The quality of life in large American cities: objective and subjective social indicators', *Social Indicators Research*, vol. 1, pp. 495–509.

Schuman, H., and Presser, S. (1978), 'Attitude measurement and the gun control paradox', *Public Opinion Quarterly*, vol. 41, pp. 427–38.

Science Policy Research Unit (1973), 'The limits to growth controversy', *Futures*, vol. 3, special issue.

Scott, R. A., and Shore, A. R. (1979), *Why Sociology Does Not Apply: A Study of the Use of Sociology in Public Policy* (New York: Elsevier).

Scott, W. (1981), *Concepts and Measurement of Poverty, United Nations Research Institute for Social Development*, Report No. 81-1 (Geneva: UNRISD).

Scriven, M. (1967), 'The methodology of evaluation', in R. W. Tyler, R. M. Gagne and M. Scuven (eds), *Perspectives of Curriculum Evaluation* (Chicago: Rand McNally), pp. 39–83.

Seers, D. (1977), 'The prevalence of pseudo-planning', in M. Faber and D. Seers (eds), *The Crisis of Planning* (London: Chatto & Windus), pp. 19–38.

Selowsky, M. (1981), 'Income distribution, basic needs and trade-offs with growth', *World Development*, vol. 9, pp. 73–92.

Sharpe, L. J. (1975), 'The social scientist and policy-making', *Policy and Politics*, vol. 4, no. 2, pp. 7–34 (partially reprinted in Bulmer, 1978, pp. 302–12).

Sharpe, L. J. (1978), 'Government as clients for social science research', in Bulmer, op. cit., pp. 67–82.

Shaw, C. (ed.) (1966), *The Jack Roller: A Delinquent Boy's Own Story* (Chicago: University of Chicago Press).

Shaw, C., and McKay, H. (1942), *Juvenile Delinquency and Urban Areas* (Chicago: University of Chicago Press).

Shaw, C. and McKay, H. (1969), *Juvenile Delinquency and Urban Areas*, revised edition with an introduction by James F. Short Jr. (Chicago: University of Chicago Press).

Shaw, C., Zorbaugh, F. M., McKay, H. D., and Cottrell, L. S. (1929),

Delinquency Areas: A Study of the Geographic Distribution of School Truants, Juvenile Delinquents and Adult Offenders in Chicago (Chicago: University of Chicago Press).

Shaw, I. (1976), 'Consumer opinion and social policy', *Journal of Social Policy*, vol. 5, pp. 19–32.

Sherwin, C. W., and Isenson, R. S. (1967), 'Project Hindsight', *Science*, vol. 156, 23 June.

Sherwin, C. W. *et al.* (1966), *First Interim Report on Project Hindsight*, summary (Washington DC: Defense Documentation Center), June.

Shiveley, W. P. (1969), ' "Ecological" inference: the use of aggregate data to study individuals', *American Political Science Review*, vol. 63, pp. 1183–96.

Sieber, S. D. (1973), 'The integration of fieldwork and survey methods', *American Journal of Sociology*, vol. 78, no. 6, pp. 1335–59.

Simon, H. (1957), *Models of Man* (New York: Wiley).

Simon, J. (1887), *Public Health Reports*, edited for the Sanitary Institute of Great Britain by E. Seaton (London: Sanitary Institute).

Sinclair, I., and Clarke, R. V. G. (1981), 'Cross-institutional designs', in E. M. Goldberg and N. Connelly (eds), *Evaluative Research in Social Care* (London: Heinemann), pp. 101–13.

Social Research Association (1985), *The State of Training in Social Research* (London: Social Research Association).

Speizer, F. E., Rosner, B., and Tager, I. (1976), 'Familial aggregation of chronic respiratory disease', *International Journal of Epidemiology*, vol. 5, p. 167.

Stacey, M. (1969), 'The myth of community studies', *British Journal of Sociology*, vol. 20, pp. 134–47.

Stack, C. (1974), *All Our Kin: Strategies for Survival in a Black Community* (New York: Harper & Row).

Stanley, N. S. (1981), 'The extra dimension: a study and assessment of the methods employed by Mass-Observation in its first period 1937–1940', thesis submitted for the degree of D.Phil. (CNAA), Birmingham Polytechnic.

Starr, P. (1982), *The Social Transformation of American Medicine* (New York: Basic Books).

Steinbruner, J. (1974), *The Cybernetic Theory of Decision-Making* (Princeton, NJ: Princeton University Press).

Stigler, G. (1946), 'The economics of minimum wage legislation', *American Economic Review*, vol. 36, pp. 358–65.

Stohr, W. B., and Taylor, D. R. F. (1981), *Development from Above or Below?* (Chichester: Wiley).

Stone, L. (1981), *The Past and the Present* (London: Routledge & Kegan Paul).

Stouffer, S. A. (1950), 'Some observations on study design', *American Journal of Sociology*, vol. 55, pp. 355–61.

Streeten, P. *et al.* (1981), *First Things First: Meeting Basic Needs in Developing Countries* (New York: Oxford University Press).

Strunk, W. Jr., and White, E. B. (1973), *The Elements of Style*, 2nd edn (New York: Macmillan).

Suchman, E. (1967a), 'Appraisal and implications for theoretical development', in S. L. Syme and L. G. Reeder (eds), *Social Stress and Cardio-vascular Disease, Milbank Memorial Fund Quarterly*, vol. 45, no. 2 (April), Part 2, pp. 109–13.

Suchman, E. A. (1967b), 'Principles and practice of evaluative research', in J. T. Doby (ed.), *An Introduction to Social Research*, 2nd edn (New York: Appleton-Century-Crofts), pp. 327–51.

Sundquist, J. L. (1978), 'Research brokerage: the weak link', in Lynn, op. cit., pp. 126–44.

Sundquist, J., and Schelling, C. (eds) (1969), *On Fighting Poverty* (New York: Basic Books).

Susser, M. (1973), *Causal Thinking in the Health Sciences* (New York: Oxford University Press).

Sutherland, G. (1984), *Ability, Merit and Measurement: Mental Testing and English Education 1880–1940* (Oxford: Clarendon Press).

Syme, S. L., Borhani, N. O., and Buechley, R. W. (1965), 'Cultural mobility and coronary heart disease in an urban area', *American Journal of Epidemiology*, vol. 823, p. 334.

Syme, S. L., Hyman, M. M., and Enterling, P. E. (1964), 'Some social and cultural factors associated with the occurrence of coronary heart disease', *Journal of Chronic Diseases*, vol. 17, p. 227.

Tawney, R. H. (1931), *Equality* (London: Allen & Unwin).

Taylor, I., Walton, P., and Young, J. (1973), *The New Criminology: For a Social Theory of Deviance* (London: Routledge & Kegan Paul).

Taylor, I., Walton, P. and Young, J. (1975), *Critical Criminology* (London: Routledge & Kegan Paul).

Taylor-Gooby, P. (1982), 'Two cheers for the welfare state: public opinion and private welfare', *Journal of Public Policy*, vol. 2, no. 4, pp. 319–46.

Taylor-Gooby, P. (1985), *Public Opinion, Ideology and State Welfare* (London: Routledge & Kegan Paul).

Teer, F., and Spence, J. D. (1973), *Political Opinion Polls* (London: Hutchinson).

Tester, F. (1981), 'SIA: Approaching the Fourth World', in F. Tester and B. Mykes (eds), *Social Impact Assessment: Theory, Method and Practice* (Calgary: Detselig).

Theil, H. (1954), *Linear Aggregation of Economic Relations* (Amsterdam: North-Holland).

Thomas, H. (ed.) (1959), *The Establishment* (London: Blond).

Thomas, P. (1985), *The Aims and Outcomes of Social Policy Research* (London: Croom Helm).

Titmuss, R. M. (1974), *Social Policy* (London: Allen & Unwin).

Titmuss, R. M. (1976), *Commitment to Welfare*, 2nd edn (London: Allen & Unwin).

Tizard, B. 'Varieties of residential nursery experience' in J. Tizard, I. Sinclair and R. V. G. Clarke (eds), *Varieties of Residential Experience* (London: Routledge & Kegan Paul).

Torgerson, D. (1980), *Industrialisation and Assessment: Social Impact as a Social Phenomena* (Toronto: York University Publications in Northern Studies).

Townsend, P. (1972), 'Politics and the statistics of poverty', *Political Quarterly*, vol. 43, pp. 103–12.

Townsend, P. (1974), 'Inequality in the NHS', *The Lancet*, vol. 1, p. 1179.

Townsend, P. (1976), 'The difficulties of policies based on the concept of area deprivation', Barnett Shine Foundation Lecture, Department of Economics, Queen Mary College, London.

Townsend, P. (1979), *Poverty in the United Kingdom* (Harmondsworth: Penguin).

Townsend, P., and Davidson, N. (1982), *Inequalities in Health: The Black Report* (Harmondsworth: Penguin) (see also Black Report, 1980).

Triseliotis, J. (1973), *In Search of Origins* (London: Routledge & Kegan Paul).

Trow, M. (1957), 'Comment on "Participant observation and interviewing: a comparison" ', *Human Organisation*, vol. 16, no. 3, pp. 33–5.

Tudor Hart, J. (1971), 'The inverse care law', *The Lancet*, vol. 1, p. 405.

Tufte, E. R. (1983), *The Visual Display of Quantitative Information* (Cheshire, Conn.: Graphics Press).

UNESCO (1976a), 'The use of socio-economic indicators in development planning' in *Meeting of Experts on Indicators of Social and Economic Change*, Final Report SHC-76/CONF. 607/1 (Paris: UNESCO).

UNESCO (1976b), *Meeting of Experts on Indicators of Quality and Quality of Life*, SS/CH/38 (Paris: UNESCO).

UNESCO (1978), *Indicators of Environmental Quality and Quality of Life*, SS/CH/38 (Paris: UNESCO).

UNESCO (1981a), *Socio-Economic Indicators for Planning* (Paris: UNESCO).

UNESCO (1981b), *Women and Development: Indicators of Their Changing Role* (Paris: UNESCO).

United Nations Environment Programme (1980), *Guidelines for Industrial Environmental Impact Assessment and Environmental Criteria for the Siting of Industry* (Paris: UNEP, distributed by New York: UNIPUB).

Van Maanen, J. (ed.) (1983), *Qualitative Methodology* (Beverly Hills, Calif.: Sage).

Walker, R. (ed.) (1985), *Applied Qualitative Research* (Aldershot: Gower).

Watson, J. D. (1968), *The Double Helix* (London: Weidenfeld & Nicolson).

Watts, H. W., and Rees, A. (1976–7), *The New Jersey Income Maintenance Experiment*, 3 vols. (New York: Academic).

Weber, Max (1949), *The Methodology of the Social Sciences*, translated by E. A. Shils and H. A. Finch (Glencoe, Ill.: The Free Press).

Weiss, C. H. (1972), *Evaluation Research: Methods for Assessing Program Effectiveness* (Englewood Cliffs, NJ: Prentice Hall).

Weiss, C. H. (1973), 'Where politics and evaluation research meet', *Evaluation*, vol. 1, no. 3, pp. 37–45.

Weiss, C. H. (1977), 'Introduction', in C. H. Weiss (ed.), *Using Social Research in Public Policy Making* (Lexington, Mass.: D. C. Heath), pp. 1–22.

Weiss, C. H. (1980), 'Knowledge creep and decision accretion', *Knowledge: Creation, Diffusion, Utilization*, vol. 1, no. 3, pp. 381–404.

Weiss, C. H. (1987), 'Congressional committee staffs (do, do not) use analysis, in Bulmer (ed.) (1987).

Weiss, C. H., and Bucuvalas, M. (1980), *Social Science Research and Decision-Making* (New York: Columbia University Press).

Weiss, J. A. (1976), 'Using social science for social policy', *Policy Studies Journal*, vol. 4, no. 3, p. 236.

Weiss, R. S., and Rein, M. (1972), 'The evaluation of broad-aim programs: difficulties in experimental design and an alternative', in C. H. Weiss (ed.), *Evaluating Action Programs* (Boston: Allyn & Bacon), pp. 236–49.

White, P. (1983), 'Design of the Labour Force Survey in Britain from 1984', in *Labour Force Surveys of Britain and Canada* (Edinburgh: University of Edinburgh Survey Methodology Group Seminar Report, 15 December), pp. 5–8.

Williams, B. (1962), 'The idea of equality', in P. Laslett and W. G. Runciman (eds), *Philosophy, Politics and Society*, second series (Oxford: Blackwell), pp. 110–31.

Wilson, J. Q. (1978), 'Social science and public policy: a personal note', in Lynn, op. cit., pp. 82–92.

Wilson, R. W., and White, E. W. (1977), 'Changes in morbidity, disability and consultation differentials between the poor and the non-poor. Data from the Health Interview Survey 1964 and 1973', *Medical Care*, vol. 15, no. 8, p. 636.

Wing, J. (1981), 'Monitoring in the field of psychiatry', in E. M. Goldberg and N. Connelly (eds), *Evaluative Research in Social Care* (London: Heinemann), pp. 259–74.

Winter, J. M. (1977), 'The impact of the First World War on civilian health in Britain', *Economic History Review*, vol. 30, pp. 487–507.

Wolanin, T. R. (1975), *Presidential Advisory Commissions* (Madison, Wis.: University of Wisconsin Press).

Wootton, B. (1959), *Social Science and Social Pathology* (London: Allen & Unwin).

Yule, G. U. (1895), 'On the correlation of total pauperism with the proportion of out-relief', *Economic Journal*, vol. 5, pp. 603–11.

Zeisl, H. (1968), *Say It With Figures* (New York: Harper).

Index